Tenth Edition

BEHAVIOR MANAGEMENT
A PRACTICAL APPROACH FOR EDUCATORS

Thomas M. Shea
Southern Illinois University—Edwardsville, Emeritus

Anne M. Bauer
University of Cincinnati

Boston   Columbus   Indianapolis   New York   San Francisco   Upper Saddle River
Amsterdam   Cape Town   Dubai   London   Madrid   Milan   Munich   Paris   Montreal   Toronto
Delhi   Mexico City   São Paulo   Sydney   Hong Kong   Seoul   Singapore   Taipei   Tokyo

Vice President and Editorial Director: Jeffery W. Johnston
Executive Editor: Ann Castel Davis
Editorial Assistant: Penny Burleson
Marketing Manager: Joanna Sabella
Senior Managing Editor: Pamela D. Bennett
Production Editor: Sheryl Glicker Langner
Production Manager: Meghan DeMaio
Creative Director: Jayne Conte
Cover Image: Campbell Laird/images.com/Corbis
Cover Designer: Suzanne Behnke
Photo Coordinator: Carol Sykes
Photo Researcher: Lori Whitley
Full-Service Project Management/Composition Service: Anita Singh/Aptara®, Inc.
Printer/Binder/Cover Printer: R.R. Donnelley & Sons
Text Font: 10/12 Palatino

Every effort has been made to provide accurate and current Internet information in this book. However, the Internet and information posted on it are constantly changing, so it is inevitable that some of the Internet addresses listed in this textbook will change.

Photo Credits: Hugo Felix/Shutterstock, p. 2; © Monkey Business Images/Shutterstock, pp. 28, 44, 122; Alexander Raths/Shutterstock, p. 64; Lisa F. Young/Fotolia, p. 76; © goodluz/Fotolia, p. 92; © Kirill Kedrinski/Fotolia, p. 152; Annie Pickert/Pearson, p. 174; Corbis RF, p. 198; racorn/Shutterstock, p. 232; © ZUMA Press, Inc./Alamy, p. 250.

Library of Congress Cataloging-in-Publication Data

Shea, Thomas M., 1934–
    Behavior management : a practical approach for educators / Thomas M. Shea,
Anne M. Bauer. — 10th ed.
      p. cm.
    Previous eds. entered under : Walker, James Edwin, 1941–
    Includes bibliographical references and index.
    ISBN-13: 978-0-13-708504-0 (alk. paper)
    ISBN-10: 0-13-708504-4 (alk. paper)
    1. Teaching.   2. Individualized instruction.   3. Problem children—Education—United States.
 I. Bauer, Anne M. II. Walker, James Edwin, 1941– Behavior management. III. Title.
    LB1027.W29 2012
    371.102'4—dc22

2011008020

10 9 8 7 6 5 4

www.pearsonhighered.com

ISBN 10:   0-13-708504-4
ISBN 13: 978-0-13-708504-0

To all those students, colleagues, family members, reviewers, and editors who have made this text a reality—thank you most sincerely.

PREFACE

This tenth edition of *Behavior Management: A Practical Approach for Educators* addresses ethical, research-based strategies to support the development of positive behaviors in children, youth, and adults. This edition contains further revisions based on both the continuing evolution of behavior management and comments and information from students, professionals, and reviewers. This has required that the text be reorganized with the addition of a new chapter (Chapter 4: Response to Intervention) and several new sections.

Education and behavior management have changed considerably since the first edition of this book. We no longer refer to "behavior modification" and recognize the role of the individual in managing his or her behavior. The ways we view behavior has morphed from distinct frameworks to an integration of evidence on development and the construction of knowledge, the impact of biology on behavior, behavioral learning theory, and the ecological foundations of growth and development. It is written in a practical way for inservice and preservice teachers, families, and paraprofessionals for applying behavior management techniques in both general and special education settings, as well as in the home and community.

The text opens with a definition of behavior management and a discussion of the ethical application of behavior management interventions, including the principles of normalization, fairness, and respect; federal laws governing services for persons with disabilities, especially children; and techniques for the individualization of instruction and related services (Chapter 1). In Chapter 2, models for understanding human behavior, including the constructivist/developmental, environmental, biobehavioral, and behavioral, are explored. The chapter includes an integrative perspective applied to coordinate the four models into a manageable assessment-intervention model of human behavior. The chapter ends with a discussion of comprehensive interventions and keystone behaviors.

Chapter 3 focuses on the principles of behavior management, the consequences of behavior, and the schedules of reinforcement. Each of the five essential principles is discussed and exemplified. The consequences of behavior include positive reinforcement, extinction, negative reinforcement, and punishment. The chapter concludes with a discussion of fixed and variable ratio and interval schedules of reinforcement.

In this edition we have added a chapter on response to intervention (Chapter 4). The role of the student, parent, teacher, and school community in providing support so that all students can succeed is the basis of this chapter. This discussion leads into the discussion of functional behavioral assessment (Chapter 5). The chapter defines functional behavior assessment and its role in intervention design, describes how to conduct functional behavior assessment and the steps in that process, and discusses setting events and positive behavioral support. The chapter concludes with a discussion of how to evaluate the intervention plan.

Chapter 6 discusses the design of behavior improvement plans. It reviews selecting behaviors to be changed, collecting and recording pre-intervention or baseline data, identifying reinforcers, implementing interventions, collecting and recording intervention data, and evaluating the effects of the behavior change process. The chapter includes methods for selecting potentially effective reinforcers, including child, parent, and teacher interviews and direct observation.

Chapters 7 and 8 describe behavior management methods and strategies. Chapter 7 presents, in detail, methods for increasing behavior: positive reinforcement, shaping, contingency contracting, self-management, token economy, and modeling. Chapter 8 provides an extensive discussion of methods for reducing behavior, including differential reinforcement, extinction, reprimands, loss of privileges, time-out, and desensitization. The discussion of time-out is couched in concerns for the child's rights, the teacher's responsibilities, and legal considerations.

Chapter 9 has been significantly revised while maintaining the emphasis on interpersonal and intrapersonal behavior change. This chapter now focuses on prosocial classroom design and management, with an emphasis on meeting all students' needs through Universal Design for Learning (UDL). The chapter retains information on structures such as Responsive Classroom, Quality Schools, the Circle of Courage, and expressive media. The use of behavior influence techniques are also included.

In Chapter 10, attention is focused on environmental and biobehavioral interventions. The discussion begins with an overview of naturalistic and environmental interventions. We review group composition, group process, and class meetings, including open meetings, problem-solving meetings, and decision-making meetings. The antecedents of effective management are presented in some detail, including space, materials, and equipment; walls, ceilings, and bulletin boards; floor space; storage space; procedures; cuing; transitions; and schedules. Biobehavioral interventions discussed in the chapter are diet and medication. The chapter concludes with a section on the educator's role in biobehavioral interventions, including referral, collaborating with medical professionals, modifying classroom structures and curriculum, obtaining permission to administer medication, and administering and safeguarding medication in the classroom and school.

Chapter 11 focuses on working with parents. The integrative perspective is reviewed as it applies to working with parents in home and school and the benefits of parent involvement for the children and adolescents, parents, and teachers. Strategies for assessing parents' readiness and need for parent participation are presented. The chapter concludes with suggestions for implementing parent and family collaboration.

We end the text with discussions of issues that influence the application of behavior management strategies in contemporary society (Chapter 12). The perennial issue of homework is described. In addition, legal factors related to the use of seclusion and restraints in schools are discussed. The recognition of the pervasive nature of bullying and cyberbullying has led us to include a discussion of the nature and interventions for these situations. The role of culture in designing appropriate interventions concludes the chapter.

To support the students' learning, chapter objectives and key terms are presented at the beginning of each chapter, and skill-building performance activities are found at the end of each chapter. In addition, Web resources are provided. The text includes a glossary and name and subject indexes. An instructor's manual with a test bank of true-false, multiple-choice, and short-answer questions supports the information in the text. Sample worksheets and forms that can be used to assess, monitor, and replace undesirable behaviors are also found here.

Perhaps the greatest strengths of the text are the many examples and vignettes taken from classrooms, homes, and the authors' experiences. As in past editions, every effort has been made to write in readable, nontechnical language for a broad audience of students, parents, professionals, and paraprofessionals concerned with the education and management of children and adolescents.

ACKNOWLEDGMENTS

Co-authors Thomas M. Shea and Anne M. Bauer wish to express their appreciation to the late Dr. James E. Walker, who has been co-author for the previous editions of this text. In 1974 Dr. Walker suggested the writing of a simple text in behavior modification. It was published in 1976 and has since evolved into the present comprehensive text.

We wish to thank the reviewers of this and previous editions for their time and constructive suggestions. The reviewers for this tenth edition were Cassandra F. Barnes, D'Youville College; Shirley Fortney, West Virginia Wesleyan College; Joseph Gagnon, University of Florida; Cindi Nixon, Francis Marion University; and Charles P. Resavy, Wilkes University.

We also wish to acknowledge the assistance and support of our many colleagues, friends, and students who have been exposed to and have responded to the materials in the text in its various editions. We have profited greatly from their comments and suggestions. Several students have been closely engaged in this edition, editing, tracking down wayward references, and reading for clarity. Thank you Ally, Jean, Micky, Renny, and Sarah for your help.

And thank you again to Kevin, Jane, Riley, and our grandchildren Owen, Emma, and Dylan, who would love to see their names in print in a book and who keep us young

BRIEF CONTENTS

CONTENTS

After completing this chapter you will be able to do the following:

Define behavior management and explain its purposes.

Discuss ethical issues regarding the use of behavior management interventions.

Describe various perspectives of the ethics of behavior management.

Discuss ethical and professional guidelines for the application of behavior management interventions.

Explain the principles of normalization, fairness, and respect.

Explain selected laws governing education and services for persons with disabilities.

Describe procedures for the individualization of education for learners with disabilities.

CHAPTER OBJECTIVES

After completing this chapter, you will be able to do the following:

1. Define behavior management and explain its purposes.
2. Discuss ethical issues regarding the use of behavior management interventions.
3. Describe various perspectives of the ethics of behavior management.
4. Discuss ethical and professional guidelines for the application of behavior management interventions.
5. Explain the principles of normalization, fairness, and respect.
6. Explain selected laws governing education and services for persons with disabilities.
7. Describe procedures for the individualization of education for learners with disabilities.

An Introduction to Behavior Management

CHAPTER 1

KEY TERMS

Aversives

Behavior management interventions

Ethics

Formalism

Individualized Education Program (IEP)

Individualized Transition Plan (ITP)

Individuals with Disabilities Education
  Improvement Act of 2004

Principle of fairness

Principle of normalization

Principle of respect

Public Law 103–382

Public Law 107–110

Section 504

Self-discipline

Transition services

Utilitarianism

Ms. Romero watches as Suzanne, wiping her eyes on her sleeve, slowly leaves the fourth-grade classroom. It has been a long, trying day for both teacher and student.

Ms. Romero feels exhausted. At this moment, she dislikes teaching. She is uncomfortable reprimanding and scolding children, especially Suzanne, who tries so very hard to sit still and pay attention yet whose mind seems to wander constantly and who never remembers the correct materials. It seems as if she has had the same conversation with Suzanne and some of the other students a dozen or more times since school began last month.

The students are too active to settle down to enjoy language arts. Ms. Romero tries to find interesting books. She has tried writing names on the board. She has tried calling parents. She has taken away free time. The students never change. The state proficiency tests are in March, with teacher and principal evaluations linked to student performance on the test. How is she going to make them learn?

Ms. Romero knows that her current efforts are not only ineffective; they also don't match what she wants for her students. She wants them to love to read. She wants them to feel valued in her classroom. Yet she feels as if she is just putting in time. She is exhausted and can't even remember driving home after school. She is grouchy and short tempered with her husband and children.

What are the research-based practices that Ms. Romero can use to engage her students in learning?

Larry sits in the gym bleachers, anxiously waiting for Mr. Veritas to finish organizing the volleyball game. The whole class, except Larry, is choosing sides and preparing to begin the game. Larry wishes he could be part of the activity, but he can't. He's afraid to let the others know that he's a poor player. He doesn't know exactly why he's a poor player, but every time a group game is organized, he must refuse to participate. He says, "No, I won't," "I can't," "I don't feel good," or "That's a dumb game."

Larry knows Mr. Veritas is unhappy with him but also very concerned about him. But Larry just can't play those games. He thinks it's really too bad that Mr. Veritas doesn't like him because Mr. Veritas is a nice guy and would be an interesting friend.

Mr. Veritas quickly organizes the teams, and the volleyball game begins. He believes that he must hurry and talk to Larry.

"Poor kid," Mr. Veritas thinks, "he's really OK, but he just won't play team games. Perhaps he refuses because he's heavier than the other students. No, others in the class aren't in good physical condition, and they play team sports. Perhaps Larry is afraid he's not a good enough player. I'll talk to him again and see what I can do to help."

What are effective strategies for helping Larry increase his participation in team activities?

Ms. Komfort hums a little tune to herself as she cruises along Interstate 55 out of Memphis. What a marvelous day! What a great year it has been at John F. Kennedy Elementary School with her 25 first-graders! For the first time in her teaching career, Ms. Komfort has interested, responsive, and enthusiastic children in her class. If the next 4 months of the school year are as good as the past 5 months, she will remain in teaching forever.

"Sure hope it continues," she thinks.

How can Ms. Komfort maintain her children's enthusiasm for learning throughout the year?

Teachers wish to teach; it is what they are prepared to do and the reason they are employed and assigned to a school, a classroom, and a group of children for approximately 180 days each school year. Teachers may become frustrated when behavioral problems limit their instructional time and strategies.

As a result of the theoretical, experimental, and pragmatic efforts of many scholars and practitioners, teachers have been made increasingly aware of a number of variables that must be considered to establish effective and efficient transactions between teachers and children. Teachers have become keenly aware of the following:

- Every child is a unique individual, *similar* to all other children in many respects yet *different* from all other children.
- No single set of strategies or remedial procedures is effective under *all conditions* with *all children*. We must remain open minded and give thoughtful consideration to many theoretical and methodological points of view if we are to effectively aid children.

Educators have also become aware that the child's cognitive, affective, sensory, and psychomotor learning domains are inextricably interwoven. We understand that the child acts and reacts as a whole being. We recognize that an intervention in one domain may have an impact on another. A cognitive strategy may influence how the student feels about school. A sensory intervention may have an impact on the student's activity level. These linkages emphasize the need to base our decisions on data and research.

■ *Examples*

Todd, a 6-year-old first-grader, was diagnosed by a psychiatrist as having "attention deficit disorder/impulsive type." According to his teacher, Todd was distractible in the classroom, constantly running about, touching children, and damaging materials.

Todd's psychiatrist prescribed medication to increase levels of certain chemicals in his brain. The medication has been effective in modifying Todd's behavior. He has begun to read more fluently, and his behavior has improved in the classroom, especially during group activities. Todd has been heard to say, "See how good I am" and "I'm a big boy now."

Changes in Todd's behavior have influenced his cognitive skills (reading) and his affective behavior (in group activities). In addition, his self-concept appears to have improved.

Scott, an 11-year-old fifth-grader identified as having a learning disability, had experienced difficulty in throwing and catching a ball and in running bases. He is "rough" on materials, breaking the point on his pencils and erasing holes in his paper throughout the day.

Scott is now enrolled in a program that includes occupational therapy and adapted physical education. As a result of these interventions, he has developed skills in throwing, catching, and running.

Scott's teacher has noted that as Scott is increasing his competency in the psychomotor area, he is also improving cognitively (in such activities as reading and writing) and socially (his group behavior and peer relationships have improved).

Again, it is evident that changes in one learning domain influence the individual's competency in the other areas of learning.

Maryellen, a 13-year-old ninth-grader, was identified by a school psychologist as processing information more slowly than her peers. Maryellen had experienced difficulty in academic subjects throughout her school years. Although she could learn and did learn the basic skills, she required more time and instruction than her classmates. As a consequence of her academic difficulties, Maryellen usually received Ds and Fs on report cards. Over the years, she developed an "I don't care" attitude toward schoolwork and school. This attitude caused her to be frequently reprimanded and punished by her teachers.

On entering high school, Maryellen was placed in a remedial program. In this program, academic work was designed to be responsive to Maryellen's rate and level of learning. Evaluations were based on individual performance.

Her teacher reports Maryellen is happier and more motivated. Maryellen's change in academic program has influenced her affective behavior.

This text is written from the point of positive behavioral support and the ecological perspective. We recognize that these perspectives are two of several conceptual frameworks available to the practitioner for use in efforts to understand and change behavior. Using an ecological perspective allows the practitioner to consider strategies from various perspectives.

The present chapter is devoted to a definition of behavior management, guidelines for the ethical application of behavior management interventions, selected public laws affecting services for persons with disabilities, and procedures for the individualization of the education of learners with disabilities.

DEFINITION OF BEHAVIOR MANAGEMENT

The majority of school staff meeting and discussion time and many hours of parents' home time are devoted to considerations of behavior management. The same few—but important—questions are asked repeatedly:

- How can this child's behavior be changed? Should I change it?
- Should I punish this behavior? Is it right to punish students?
- Should I discuss this behavior with the individual? Should I ignore it? Does he or she even know it is a problem?
- Will this intervention work? Is it ethical? What if there are side effects?

In this text, **behavior management interventions** are defined as all those actions (and conscious inactions) teachers and parents engage in to enhance the probability that children, individually and in groups, will develop effective behaviors that are personally fulfilling, productive, and socially acceptable (Shea & Bauer, 1987).

Behavior management is a teacher function that must be studied, planned, and objectively used and evaluated, with equal emphasis given to all relevant variables: the individual or group whose behavior is being studied, the behavior under consideration, the setting in which the behavior occurs, the individual applying the intervention, and the purpose of the intervention. An effective intervention for one specific behavior of one specific child in a particular setting may be ineffective under another set of circumstances when applied by a different individual to change a different behavior. More specifically, behavior management must be individualized.

According to Garbarino (2008), we live and function in an increasingly complex society and, as teachers, we are confronted with increasing amounts of disruptive student behavior. School personnel must demonstrate leadership, creativity, and patience as they develop more effective methods for preventing and responding to inappropriate student behaviors. School personnel will be more effective when responding to disruptive behavior if "discipline" or "student management" is seen as an opportunity to teach students alternative ways to meet their needs within the school setting (Skiba & Peterson, 2003).

With the passage of the No Child Left Behind Act of 2001, many federal school programs have required educational practitioners to use interventions with rigorous, scientific evidence. Whitehurst (2003) contends that the interventions should be evaluated by these steps:

1. Identify strong evidence of effectiveness, such as the use of control groups, collection of outcome data, and the size of the effect of the intervention.
2. If there isn't strong evidence, is it supported by evidence, such as comparison groups and prospective measurement of outcomes?

The hope is that by using interventions for which there is rigorous evidence, advances in education may occur that are equivalent to those that have occurred with the application of rigor to the field of medicine.

The goal of school and classroom discipline should be to increase behavior conducive to learning and replace undesirable behavior (Rokeach & Denver, 2006). Rokeach and Denver contend that discipline must be a learning experience that helps student improve their behavior, keeps them in school, and communicates that we want them in school and care about them. Current discipline systems tend to impose negative strategies that emphasize consequences rather than learning. They contend that effective discipline does include consequences, but it does so in a context of respect for students and their families and a commitment to their educational success.

Self-discipline, the goal of all behavior management, is the process of attaining control over one's personal behavior in a variety of circumstances in association with many individuals and groups. Cartledge, Tillman, and Johnson (2001) suggest that discipline is something a person should possess rather than something imposed on the person or something done to the person. Self-discipline is discussed in detail in Chapter 2.

ETHICS OF BEHAVIOR MANAGEMENT

The Question of Ethics

Qualitative and quantitative research has led to the description of principles of learning and their resultant interventions for the management of human behavior. The evidence is rigorous: controlled research studies have demonstrated that these principles are accurate.

However, practitioners cannot sweep aside the ethical issues created by the application of these principles to the processes of human learning. The principles of learning have caused confusion, concern, and in some cases anxiety among those individuals holding more traditional views of human behavior. In the application of behavior management interventions, the following questions are considered:

- Who shall decide who will be the manager of behavior? Whose behavior is to be managed?
- Who will control those who strive to control behavior?
- What type of interventions shall be applied? Why will they be applied? Who determines that they are legitimate? Why have they been determined to be legitimate?

These questions have vast implications for our future (as individuals and as members of the human species) and for the future of society. The behavior management practitioner must consider and respond to these questions.

When such questions are applied to the education of children, they have profound implications for educational practice. Teachers do indeed change students' behavior. The queries are rephrased here to emphasize these implications, which are not only philosophical issues but also pragmatic issues of immediate importance to educators:

- What is a child?
- Is a child free to make choices? Should a child be free to make choices?
- Can an educator modify a child's behavior? Can another child? A parent?

- Who shall determine whose and which behaviors are to be changed?
- Which interventions shall be applied in the classroom and school to change children's behavior?

The central issue is the contributions of nature and environment on behavior. The behaviorist emphasizes the external environment and maintains that the influence of the environment is systematic, constant, and the prime determinant of behavior. This systematic, constant influence is observable and measurable. As a result, actions can be explained by means of the principles of changing behavior and supporting learning. The principles are derived by applying the scientific methods of discovery to the modification of human behavior.

In addition to the issues of whether and how human beings can be controlled, professionals in psychology, the social sciences, and education have focused attention on the issue of the means of control. Many professionals suggest that the overt controls applied to human behavior by means of behavior modification interventions are unacceptable and can lead to unethical practices. These individuals fail to recognize or acknowledge that all interaction exerts some influence over behavior. For example, traditional nondirective and directive psychotherapeutic interventions, such as client-centered counseling, individual and group psychotherapy, and psychoanalysis, have as their objective to change the child's behavior or to encourage the child to change his or her behavior with the therapist's assistance. The nondirective therapist and the permissive teacher influence the child's behavior, and this influence limits the child's freedom of choice. Such limiting (or controlling), rather than being denied, should be recognized, evaluated, and monitored for the child's benefit.

Ethical Perspective

The **ethics** of behavior management can be approached from several points of view: political, legal, professional, and scientific. An extensive discussion of each is not feasible in this text; thus, the reader is urged to continue the study of the ethics of behavior management using the chapter references.

From a political perspective, the current quest for excellence in the schools has become standardized, with each state required to develop standards and to assess student proficiency. In this effort, children and youth whose behavior continues to challenge the system are rarely treasured. They do not enhance the school's "pass rate" on proficiency tests. There is tension between the individual rights of students with and without disabilities and the common good when resolving discipline issues (McCarthy & Soodak, 2007). It is at this point in development of education that educators find themselves discussing the ethics of behavior management. Students with behavioral problems, unequally valued alongside their compliant and achieving peers, bring teachers who are accountable for student achievement to the point of using behavior management methods and strategies that would not be applied with the more highly valued students and during less stressful and competitive times (Cartledge et al., 2001). Noguera (2003) found that school personnel most frequently punish the student with the greatest needs, including academic, economic, social, and behavioral/emotional needs. In addition, this group of punished students includes an overrepresentation of African American and Latino students as well as students from diverse cultural, ethnic, and linguistic groups. These students are more likely to be suspended, expelled, or re-moved from the classroom by either in-school suspension or an alternative placement. The implementation of zero-tolerance policies in schools has dramatically increased the incidence of suspension and expulsion.

Legally, proactive decisions are rare. The nature of the courts and the legislatures is to react to the misuse or potential misuse of various interventions rather than to ac-tively set standards. It also appears that decisions and laws are concerned primarily with students without identified disabilities and confined to corporal punishment, sus-pension, and expulsion. Few decisions and laws focus on the use of specific methods of behavior management or aversives in general.

Summarizing and defining the implications of research in behavior management must be approached with great caution. In general, however, definitive empirical re-search is scant; much of the published research concerns students with more severe dis-abilities. Aversive procedures usually generate only short-term gains, with little long-term improvement. There has been considerable activity among professional, parent, and citizen organizations with regard to the use of aversive and other behavior man-agement interventions. Few position statements discuss the use of any and all behavior management procedures regardless of the theories from which they are derived. Most statements are concerned with the use of behavioral strategies.

From an ethical perspective, it is generally agreed that the principles underly-ing behavior management interventions can provide practitioners with the means to an end, but the principles cannot decide the end of intervention: That decision depends on the practitioner's values (Poussaint, 2005). Behavioral ethics are the individual's behavior that is judged according to accepted norms or occurring in the context of larger social prescriptions (Trevino, Weaver, & Reynolds, 2006). Individuals function from an individual ethical decision framework. **Formalism** suggests that all individ-uals are born with rights and needs that are superordinate to the interests of society. Formalism influences an individual's ethical awareness by rule- or principle-based rationales. From this point of view, behavior management interventions that intrude on an individual's rights are unethical. **Utilitarianism** suggests that the interests of society precede the interests of the individual. From this perspective, the use of aver-sive management is deemed acceptable if it facilitates the movement of the individ-ual from the position of "burden on society" to "contributing member." Yet in U.S. society, the formalist perspective of ethics is the most acceptable for governing our actions.

Scheuermann and Evans (1997) discuss the use of controversial interventions and ethical practice in the education of learners with emotional and behavioral disorders. They are concerned that unproven interventions lacking a research base are being applied with learners by practitioners in the effort to improve learner performance. The authors reinforce the position of Hippocrates that the practitioner's first and most im-portant concern in the education and treatment of learners is to "do no harm." Simpson (1995) describes controversial interventions as those lacking research findings to support their effectiveness yet promising extraordinary success. Simpson suggests that "any treatment, program, strategy, or technique that is unsupported by objective data produced through systematic manipulation of variables and repeated inquiries by inde-pendent evaluators" (p. 20) is controversial.

Nickel (2008) presents several characteristics of controversial interventions. Controversial treatments:

- are based on one simplistic scientific theory. For example, a child must crawl before he or she walks, so practicing crawling will enhance development.
- offer drastic improvement or cures.
- provide little or no specific objectives, contending that the student is "better."
- are effective for a wide range of disabilities—for example, megavitamins help Down syndrome as well as attention deficit disorder.
- rely on anecdotal information to document effectiveness.
- are so effective that there is no need to do controlled studies.

Green (1996) offers suggestions for avoiding the selection of unproven interventions for application with learners with behavior problems:

1. Be skeptical: If it sounds too good to be true, it usually is.
2. Question the promoters of the intervention about how it works and how they know that it works.
3. Ask to see the research results or other evidence of its effectiveness.
4. Obtain and read the research and, if concerned, ask an expert to interpret the research.
5. Proceed with care. Go slowly. Question why the application must be applied exclusively and do not eliminate presently effective interventions.
6. Ask if the intervention is "reasonable."

The Council for Exceptional Children (2010) contends that, ethically, special educators must work with other professionals and with parents in an interdisciplinary effort as they manage behavior. Ethical practice includes:

- applying only those disciplinary methods and behavioral procedures for which you have received instruction on their use and which maintain the dignity of the individual or the basic human rights of persons with exceptionalities;
- clearly specifying goals and objectives for behavior management practices in individualized education program;
- following policies, statutes, and rules established by legal and local agencies regarding disciplinary methods and behavioral procedures; and
- preventing and intervening when a colleague's behavior is detrimental to exceptional students.

The Council for Exceptional Children, though, has continued to allow the use of aversive techniques, maintaining that they are ethical when repeated trials of other methods have failed and only after consultation with parents and appropriate agency officials. This text, however, does not condone the use of aversive techniques in any setting.

The Rights of Children

In his seminal work, Allen (1969) proposed three principles to guide individuals in the helping professions in their actions toward clients (children and adults) with disabilities. These principles serve as the foundation of all behavior management decisions made by teachers of both general and special education students. They are (a) the principle of normalization, (b) the principle of fairness, and (c) the principle of respect for the dignity and worth of the individual.

PRINCIPLE OF NORMALIZATION.   The **principle of normalization** is to let the person with a disability or who varies from his or her peers obtain an existence as close to the "norm" as is possible (Farrell, 1995). Winance (2007), argues that practitioners must avoid interpreting normalization as bringing individuals with disabilities into line with some sort of "able-bodied" norm. Rather, normalization should involving working with individuals with disabilities to provide supports in the environment to reduce the impact that the disability may have on typical interactions with others and the environment.

Before implementing an intervention, the practitioner must respond to the following question: Will the implementation of this specific intervention reduce the impact of the disability on the child's interactions with others and the environment or simply eliminate the child (and the behavior) as an inconvenience or annoyance to others in the environment, such as the child's teacher, peers, administrator, and parents?

Many children attend programs for learners with disabilities simply because they are different; that is, they are African American, Hispanic, Asian American, or Native American or perceived to be "slow learners," "nonreaders," "poor achievers," or "low achievers." These children may be segregated primarily because they are an annoyance or inconvenience to others; they challenge the system (Shea & Bauer, 1994). In this "special placement," their opportunity to succeed is inhibited or restricted, if not totally frustrated.

Wehmeyer and Palmer (2003) conducted a survey study of self-determination with regard to the adult outcomes for students with cognitive disabilities (mental retardation or learning disabilities). The students were surveyed 1 and 3 years after leaving school to determine what they were doing in major life areas (employment, independent living, or community integration). Self-determination was said to have two meanings: personal and political (Wehmeyer & Schalock, 2001).

At the personal level, one is self-determined if there are causal agents in their lives. Jones (2006) contends that in order to learn self-determination, individuals with disabilities must be aware of their strengths and weaknesses. They should understand their special education services and monitor their own behavior. Perhaps most important, self-determination must be taught, with increased student participation and decision making. This shift from teacher control may be uncomfortable for some professionals.

■ *Example*

Mr. Cortez, a special educator, consistently praised his students regardless of their performance. Every paper received a star, and he often remarked to the students, "You are too, too smart." When Elizabeth was included in second-grade social studies, she burst into tears when she had errors corrected on her paper. Mr. Cortez disregarded the need for Elizabeth to have honest evaluation of her efforts and accommodations that mitigated the image of her disability on her performance. Rather, he prevented her from making the same errors that all second-graders make, emphasizing her "special" placement.

PRINCIPLE OF FAIRNESS.   The **principle of fairness** is fundamental fairness—due process of law—which requires that in decision making affecting one's life, liberty, or vital interests, the elements of due process will be observed, including the right to notice, to a fair hearing, to representation by counsel, to present evidence, and to appeal an adverse decision (Allen, 1969).

Although this principle is phrased in legal terminology, it can be simply stated: Is the intervention selected to change this child's behavior fair to the child as an individual? Is the impact of the consequence equitable in terms of the impact of the behavior?

At times interventions are arbitrarily applied on the whim of a practitioner without concrete evidence that the child is, in fact, exhibiting the target behavior. Frequently, interventions are applied that only serve to prohibit the child from finding any success in school. For example, a child who has difficulty learning French grammar is prohibited from going to recess, playing on the school athletic teams, and so on. This child may be capable of meeting success only in these prohibited activities. As do all humans, the child has a need for success. Interventions such as these are unfair.

Unfairness also occurs when a practitioner refuses to apply an intervention that is obviously needed if the child is to function in school. For example, we are confronted with practitioners who will not use tangible rewards simply because they do not "believe in them." Yet the child whom they are attempting to help is found to respond only to tangible rewards.

Other examples of unfairness might include the following:

- refusal to try to modify a child's behavior systematically;
- arbitrary placement of a child in a special therapy or instructional program without first attempting classroom interventions; or
- unwillingness of teachers to provide needed services or request consultation because they believe that seeking help is a sign of incompetence.

If the principle of fairness is to be implemented, we must begin all decisions from the point of view of the child's welfare: What does this child need?

■ *Example*

Ms. McMicken does not believe in medication for students identified with attention deficit hyperactivity disorder. Rather, she believes that if the students try hard enough, they can learn to manage their behavior. She believes that the parents of these children don't have them play outside enough, allow them to watch too much TV, and "let them get by" with being unruly. Though Micah is supposed to leave her room at 11:30 to go to the office to receive his medicine daily, she frequently forgets or doesn't interrupt Micah to get the medication. Micah is typically attentive until noon or so, then he has more and more problems being attentive. Ms. Micken unfairly blames Micah for not retaining control over his behavior, remarking that he is fine in the morning.

Mr. Lance, the art teacher, indicated that he would be unable to schedule the students in Ms. Carter's class for students with emotional/behavioral disorders because they would be unsafe with the many materials he used. Ms. Carter met with Mr. Lance and the principal, arguing that her students had as much a right to art class as the others. Mr. Bell, the principal, indicated to Mr. Lance that he needed to find time for the students in Ms. Carter's class and that it would be unfair to eliminate art from their schedule because of their identification as having emotional/behavioral disorders.

PRINCIPLE OF RESPECT.   The **principle of respect** is one's right to be treated as a human being and not as an animal or a statistic (Allen, 1969).

In actions toward children, are practitioners demonstrating respect for them as human beings? All interventions must be judged against this question. When the intervention is evaluated from this point of view, many common "therapeutic" practices are found to violate the principle of respect. The following are examples:

- physical punishment (spankings, slaps, and paddling);
- psychological punishment (sarcasm, embarrassment, and name-calling);
- deprivation (prohibiting a child normal opportunities for success, food, water, or typical school activities);
- segregation (arbitrary special class placement);
- isolation (inconsistent, long-term use of time-out);
- medication (capricious use of symptom-control medications or failing to consistently and appropriately administer mediation); and
- extrahuman punishment (use of aversives, restraints, and electric shock).

All these interventions have been used and remain in use today. Generally, they are applied by individuals who justify the use of any means to attain their end. All these interventions have been justified by some as the "only way" to accomplish an objective. These techniques are used (and justified) frequently simply because they are convenient, efficient, and seemingly effective.

A beaten child will comply, an electric prod will get a child to pay attention, and segregation and isolation will reduce conflict. However, practitioners must establish limits on the interventions that can be applied with children (Turnbull, Wilcox, Turnbull, Sailor, & Wickham, 2001). They must judge these interventions in the light of this third principle. Could or do the interventions inflict damage on the individual child or relegate the child to a less-than-human classification?

All behavior management practitioners *must* develop an ethical system that incorporates the principles of normalization, fairness, and respect for the dignity and the worth of the child. This value system must avoid the pitfall of justifying any means to attain a desired end.

Any intervention can be misused and abused if the person using it lacks an ethical system of personal and professional values. Practitioners must never forget that knowledge is power and that with power comes the responsibility to apply that power for the benefit of all persons.

■ *Example*

Alva used a series of accommodations and technologies to assist her with her visual impairment. She used recorded books. Ms. Lugano, the seventh-grade language arts teacher, was known for her sarcasm and what she referred to as her "dry sense of humor," something she used with little regard for her students' feelings. On the first day of class Alva turned in her handwritten essay, for which Ms. Lugano had forgotten to give her ridged paper. Ms. Lugano looked at the paper and said, "This is a mess. How blind are you anyway? Maybe we should just have someone write for you."

Melanie was identified as having learning disabilities in terms of processing language. Her teacher, Mr. Nguyen, talked with her and her special education supplementary teacher about increasing her participation in class. Mr. Nguyen indicated that he understood that she needed a chance to generate her response before he called on her. He respected her language needs and agreed to stand in front of her for a moment before he asked her a question. That way Melanie could focus on the language Mr. Nguyen used and formulate an answer. Mr. Nguyen also indicated that his questions would be at the appropriate knowledge level to ensure that Melanie could respond in a reasonable time.

PUBLIC LAW AND PERSONS WITH DISABILITIES

This section discusses federal legislation that has and will continue to have a significant impact on the lives of persons with disabilities.

Current federal legislation related to special education can be traced to the 1975 Education for All Handicapped Children's Act. With its initial mandate for all students ages 5 through 21, this legislation promoted concepts such as the "least restrictive environment" and "free, appropriate, public education." As the legislation evolved with its amendments, the age of students to be served became ages 3 to 21, and additional considerations, including a name change from "handicapped children" to "individuals with disabilities" were put in place.

Public Law and Behavior Management

THE INDIVIDUALS WITH DISABILITIES EDUCATION IMPROVEMENT ACT OF 2004.   The **Individuals with Disabilities Education Improvement Act of 2004** reauthorized the Individuals with Disabilities Education Act (IDEA) and aligned accountability systems for students with disabilities with those described in the No Child Left Behind Act (see p. xx). Provisions related to the **Individualized Education Program (IEP)**, due process, discipline, and federal grants and activities became effective on July 1, 2005; the aspects related to highly qualified teachers became effective immediately upon enactment in December 2004. The final regulations were published on August 14, 2006 (United States Department of Education 2007).

THE IEP PROCESS AND THE INDIVIDUALS WITH DISABILITIES EDUCATION IMPROVEMENT ACT.   The Individuals with Disabilities Education Improvement Act requires benchmarks and short-term objectives for students who do not take districtwide or statewide assessments. The 1% of students with disabilities who have alternative goals and assessments must have short-term objectives. However, if parents still want objectives on the IEP, the team needs to identify them (U.S. Department of Education, 2007).

Plans for the transition to work and living in the community must be a part of the IEP no later than the first IEP when the child is 16 years old. In addition, the new law requires measurable postsecondary goals in education, employment, or independent living skills. Other agencies may also be invited to send a representative, and the child must be invited to the IEP. If students transfer to a new school district, the services comparable to the existing IEP must be in effect until a new IEP is developed.

IEPs are only written for children as soon as they turn 3 years old. For students with disabilities younger than 3 years old, an Individualized Family Services Plan (IFSP) is written. If the child turns 3 years old during the school year, the IFSP becomes the IEP. The IFSP contains a statement of specific early intervention services based on peer-reviewed research, to the extent practicable; a statement of the measurable results or outcomes that are developmentally appropriate for the child; and a description of the appropriate transition services.

DUE PROCESS AND DISCIPLINE AND THE INDIVIDUALS WITH DISABILITIES EDUCATION IMPROVEMENT ACT.   Changes in the provisions related to discipline, for the most part, make it easier for schools to remove students with disabilities. Students with disabilities have the right to remain in their educational placements during an appeal on a school code violation that can result in removal for more than 10 days. IDEA allowed students to "stay put" unless the violations involved drugs, weapons, or dangerous behavior. In addition, the burden of proving that a student's behavior is related to a disability has shifted from the school district to the parent.

IDEA falls short of requiring functional behavioral assessments and behavior intervention plans. Rather, the language related to behavior plans is limited, suggesting that positive behavioral interventions and supports be used and that consultation related to these strategies should be provided. The use of functional behavioral assessment is not required but is, rather, urged to be used as appropriate (Zirkel, 2009a).

The new law also strives to provide for less adversarial ways for resolving disagreements between parents and school districts. A due process complaint notice must be submitted by whomever is initiating the impartial due process hearing, and both schools and parents have the opportunity to have several IEP work sessions to address the disagreements. The impartial hearing decisions must be based on issues affecting the student's education rather than procedural issues. In addition, attorney fee reimbursement to the state or school district may be ordered for complaints that are determined to be frivolous, unreasonable, or without basis. The qualifications for hearing officers have also been made more specific.

SECTION 504 OF THE REHABILITATION ACT OF 1973.   Students do not need to meet the criteria of IDEA to receive accommodations and services. If a student has a mental or physical impairment that has a significant impact on a major life activity—such as learning—he or she may receive accommodations and services (Zirkel, 2009b). The Amendments to the Americans with Disabilities Act, effective January 1, 2009, expanded the eligibility for individual student Section 504 Plans and overlapped the regulations of 504 plans with IEPs. One challenge, however, is that 504 plans may emerge as "consolation prizes" (Zirkel, 2009, p. 69) for parents concerns about their students who do not qualify for services under IDEA. Accommodations such as extended time in districtwide or statewide testing, for example, may be provided to students with mental or physical impairments as described by Section 504 even if they do not have an IEP. Concentration and attention are major life activities that may be affected by the "mental or physical impairment."

PUBLIC LAW 103–382.   With the passage of **Public Law 103–382** by Congress in 1994 (referred to as the Gun-Free Schools Act), student discipline and control entered a new era (Pipho, 1998). The law mandated that the states to receive funds under the Elementary and Secondary Education Act (ESEA) have "zero tolerance" for weapons in the schools. In the law, "weapon" is defined as guns, bombs, grenades, rockets, and missiles. It does not include knives and common fireworks.

Within 2 years of the passage of Public Law 103–382, all states came into compliance. The law required the states to mandate a 1-year expulsion policy, which allows the chief administrative officer in each school district to modify on a case-by-case basis. The law requires that students expelled for weapons violations be referred to either the criminal or juvenile court system.

According to Pipho (1998), since the passage of Public Law 103–382, the states have generally mandated legislation to broaden the definition of weapon and increase the discretion the local administrators have in the law's implementation. Some states have enacted legislation or regulations to govern "accidental situations" and broaden the definition of "weapon" to include drugs, alcohol, and other items. Accidental situations are those situations in which a student accidentally brings a banned item to school. Other considerations that appear to be a consequence of the Gun-Free Schools and zero-tolerance mandates include procedures for the transfer of students with disciplinary records from school to school.

The Council for Exceptional Children (2008) affirms the need for a safe school climate but also argues that a positive climate is needed. It has published a policy to ensure that discrimination, harassment, and bullying are not tolerated. The policy argues that clear policies should be in place that support a school climate conducive to respect and dignity for all individuals. Reporting bullying and harassment should be mandatory for all educators, and a range of resources should be available to support all students.

Etscheidt (2006) suggests that the need for school safety must be balanced with the need to provide programs for students with disabilities. To remove a student with a disability, the school district must show that maintaining the student in his or her placement may result in injury to the child or others. Etscheidt urges preventive measures to decrease violence in the schools, including a climate in which the school and teachers are viewed as members of a community. This sense of community, combined with conflict resolution programs and parent partnerships, may reduce the tension related to having students with emotional/behavioral disorders in the school. Administrators are well aware of the tension between individual rights and the common good and rely heavily on negotiating skills to mitigate school crises (McCarthy & Soodak, 2007).

PUBLIC LAW 107–110: NO CHILD LEFT BEHIND. On January 8, 2002, **Public Law 107–110** was signed into law by President George W. Bush as the reauthorization of the Elementary and Secondary Education Act of 1965. Public Law 107–110 is known as the No Child Left Behind Act. This legislation is designed to hold schools accountable for the academic achievement of their students. Though concerned with all students, the legislation has specific implications for learners with disabilities, special educators, and special education policy and practice, as well as students from various other racial, ethnic, and linguistic cultures. No Child Left Behind focuses on a broad range of issues with regard to the academic achievement of students (Council for Exceptional Children, 2004; Schrag, 2003).

One of the key components of No Child Left Behind is accountability. This includes annual testing of students in Grades 3 through 8 on state-selected tests in reading, math, and science. Schools must demonstrate adequate yearly progress (AYP) toward meeting 100% proficiency in reading, math, and science for all students within 12 years, and states must demonstrate incremental improvement over the 12-year period. Parents of students in schools that fail to demonstrate adequate yearly progress for

2 consecutive years may transfer their child to another public school if the state permits public school choice. Districts must pay the cost of transporting the child.

Demonstration projects are also funded by No Child Left Behind. One hundred fifty school districts have entered into performance agreements with the U.S. Department of Education to combine funds from specified non–Title I grant programs to improve educational achievement. Additional flexibility has been provided to seven states in the use of federal funds for state administration and activities with local demonstration projects.

Low-performing schools receive both support and sanctions. Financial and technical assistance is provided to districts to facilitate improvement of student achievement in low-performing schools. Supplemental instructional services, such as tutoring, after-school classes, and summer classes must be provided if a school fails to demonstrate adequate yearly progress for students who are disadvantaged or low achieving for 3 consecutive years. Corrective actions are linked to the number of years that schools do not meet their annual yearly progress goals, specific to the number of years of lack of progress.

The majority of the No Child Left Behind legislation impacts either directly or indirectly on the education of learners with disabilities simply because they are members of the school community. The two areas of greatest concern to those responsible for the education of learners with disabilities are school accountability and personnel certification and licensure (Council for Exceptional Children, 2004). Of particular significance to those responsible for the education of learners with disabilities are adequate yearly progress and the graduated accountability measures. If a child with disabilities (in Grades 3 through 8) attends a school that fails to make adequate yearly progress toward meeting the 100% proficiency goals in reading and math by 2014, potentially the school will face a series of remedial actions intended to improve performance of students failing to make adequate yearly progress (Council for Exceptional Children). Additional pressure is placed on students with disabilities to attain the standards of the general education curriculum. Yell, Katsiyannas, and Shiner (2006) urge teachers and school districts to develop relevant assessments that lead to meaningful programming for students with disabilities.

An additional challenge pertains to districtwide and statewide testing. Ninety-five percent of students with disabilities must participate in statewide tests. The accommodations provided to each student must be described in his or her IEP.

Table 1.1 provides a summary of the public laws that significantly impact classroom behavior management.

INDIVIDUALIZED PROGRAMS

The 2007 Regulations of Individuals with Disabilities Education Improvement Act describe three parts of an IEP. First, a written statement includes a description of the student's present level of academic achievement and functional performance. This statement should include descriptions of how the disability affects the school-age student's involvement and progress in the general education curriculum or, in the case of preschool children, how the disability affects the preschool-age child's participation in appropriate activities. The second aspect is a statement of measurable annual goals—including both academic and functional goals—that support the child in making

TABLE 1.1   Legislation with an impact on behavior management

Legislation	Date	Impact on Behavior Management
Section 504	1973	If a student has a disability as defined in the Rehabilitation Act of 1973, behavioral interventions may be required to be in place.
Gun-Free Schools Act	1994	Zero tolerance for weapons (guns, bombs, grenades, rockets, missiles) in schools.
No Child Left Behind	2002	Students must demonstrate adequate yearly progress; corrective actions for low-performing schools and their students.
Individuals with Disabilities Education Improvement Act	2004; 2006	A student with disabilities can be removed for a school code violation for up to 10 days.
		The parent must provide documentation that a student's behavior is related to his or her disability in order to avoid suspension/expulsion.
		IEPs for students with behavioral issues must include positive behavioral supports.

progress in the general curriculum or to meet other educational needs that result from the disabilities. For students who do not participate in districtwide or statewide assessments and who take alternative assessments based on alternative achievement standards, benchmarks or short-term objectives are required. This is a significant simplification from past regulations that required that each annual goal be broken into 3- to 5-month benchmarks for all students. The third aspect includes how the student's progress toward those goals will be measured and reported.

The IEP is developed by a team of individuals, including:

- the parents of the student with a disability;
- at least one of the student's general education teachers;
- at least one of the student's special education teachers;
- a representative of the school district who is qualified to provide or supervise the unique needs of students with disabilities, is knowledgeable about general education, and is knowledgeable about the district's resources;
- a professional who can interpret the instructional implications of the evaluation results;
- an individual who, at the discretion of the parent or district, has knowledge or special expertise regarding the child or services; and
- the student with a disability, when appropriate.

Though the Individuals with Disabilities Education Improvement Act of 2004 describes these individuals as members of the team, it also allows that, if the parent or district agrees, one of the members described need not attend the meeting. In addition, a particular expert may be excused from the meeting with the agreement of the parent and district and if the professional submits written input into the IEP. Both of these exceptions require written consent from the parent. In general, the IEP is in effect at the beginning of the school year. In addition, for children who are moving from early intervention services, the individual family service plan (IFSP) should be considered. If students are transferring school districts, the services described in the student's IEP are to be implemented until a new IEP is developed. Records are to be sent to the new school district promptly.

A sample IEP based on the U.S. Department of Education Model IEP format is presented in Figure 1.1.

Cosmopolitan School District

INDIVIDUALIZED EDUCATION PROGRAM

Name: Julie Lively

School: Terrace School

Address: 108 Terrace Ave., West Lyndon, CT

Date of Birth: 7/24/98

Date of IEP Conference: 8/27/11

Date of Initial Placement: 9/15/11

The Individualized Education Program (IEP) is a written document that is developed for each eligible child with a disability. The Part B regulations specify, at 34 CFR §§300.320-300.328, the procedures that school districts must follow to develop, review, and revise the IEP for each child. The following document sets out the IEP content that those regulations require.

A statement of the child's present levels of academic achievement and functional performance including:

- how the child's disability affects the child's involvement and progress in the general education curriculum (i.e., the same curriculum as for nondisabled children) or for preschool children, as appropriate, how the disability affects the child's participation in appropriate activities. [34 CFR §300.320(a)(1)]

Julie has strong skills in reading, spelling, mathematics, language arts, and content areas. In large and small group activities, Julie responds impulsively, shouting out responses or reporting that other students are "looking at her" or "bothering" her. She is distractible, often leaving the group to look out the window or check on the classroom gerbil. On the program, she responds physically when bumped during typical play and wanders from game to game.

- A statement of measurable annual goals, including academic and functional goals designed to:
- meet the child's needs that result from the child's disability to enable the child to be involved in and make progress in the general education curriculum. [34 CFR §300.320(a)(2)(i)(A)]
- meet each of the child's other educational needs that result from the child's disability. [34 CFR §300.320(a)(2)(i)(B)]

Julie will interact appropriately with others in class and on the playground in both large and small group activities.

- for children with disabilities who take alternate assessments aligned to alternate achievement standards (in addition to the annual goals), a description of benchmarks or short-term objectives. [34 CFR §300.320(a)(2)(ii)]

Continued

FIGURE 1.1 Sample Individualized Education Program

Julie does not take alternative assessments.

- A description of:
  - how the child's progress toward meeting the annual goals will be measured. [34 CFR §300.320(a)(3)(i)]
  - When periodic reports on the progress the child is making toward meeting the annual goals will be provided, such as through the use of quarterly or other periodic reports, concurrent with the issuance of report cards. [34 CFR §300.320(a)(3)(ii)]

1. Julie will interact appropriately in social studies class through the implementation of a behavior contract. Behavior will be charted and graphed, a home-school notebook will be provided, and a weekly conference call with parents will take place.
2. Julie will interact appropriately during "opening activities" through the implementation of a behavior contract. Behavior will be charted and graphed, a home-school notebook will be provided, and a weekly conference call with parents will take place.
3. Julie will interact cooperatively during morning recess, with observational time-out imposed when she is physically aggressive with another student. Behavior will be charted and graphed, a home-school notebook will be provided, and a weekly conference call with parents will take place.

- A statement of the special education and related services and supplementary aids and services, based on peer-reviewed research to the extent practicable, to be provided to the child, or on behalf of the child, and a statement of the program modifications or supports for school personnel that will be provided to enable the child:
  - to advance appropriately toward attaining the annual goals. [34 CFR §300.320(a)(4)(i)]
  - to be involved in and make progress in the general education curriculum and to participate in extracurricular and other nonacademic activities. [34 CFR §300.320(a)(4)(ii)]
  - to be educated and participate with other children with disabilities and nondisabled children in extracurricular and other nonacademic activities. [34 CFR §300.320(a)(4)(iii)]

An inclusion support teacher will meet with Julie and her teacher each week to review progress. In addition, the inclusion support teacher will call Julie's parents weekly for an update and make comments in the home-school daily report card.

- An explanation of the extent, if any, to which the child will not participate with nondisabled children in the regular classroom and in extracurricular and other nonacademic activities. [34 CFR §300.320(a)(5)]

Julie will fully participate in the general education curriculum and in extracurricular and other nonacademic activities.

- A statement of any individual appropriate accommodations that are necessary to measure the academic achievement and functional performance of the child on State and districtwide assessments. [34 CFR §300.320(a)(6)(i)]

Due to her distractibility Julie will be tested in a small group and will have the option of extended time to complete the test.

- If the IEP Team determines that the child must take an alternate assessment instead of a particular regular statewide or districtwide assessment of student achievement, a statement of why:
  - the child cannot participate in the regular assessment. [34 CFR §300.320(a)(6)(ii)(A)]
  - the particular alternate assessment selected is appropriate for the child. [34 CFR §300.320(a)(6)(ii)(B)]

Continued

Julie participates in the districtwide assessment.

- The projected date for the beginning of the services and modifications and the anticipated frequency, location, and duration of <u>special education and related services</u> and <u>supplementary aids and services</u> and <u>modifications and supports.</u> [34 CFR §300.320(a)(7)]

Service, Aid, or Modification	Frequency	Location	Beginning Date	Duration
Behavioral Contract	Daily	Social Studies, Morning Work	9/15/11	1 year
Buddy system on playground	Daily	Playground	9/15/11	Reevaluate after 3 months
Home-school daily report; weekly phone call	Daily/weekly	Classroom	9/15/11	Reevaluate after 3 months

Public Law 101–476 mandated that a plan for **transition services** be included in the IEP for learners with disabilities who are 14 years of age. A sample **Individualized Transition Plan (ITP)** is presented in Figure 1.2.

Cosmopolitan School District
INDIVIDUALIZED EDUCATION PROGRAM

Name: Carmine Marquez   Date of Birth: 2/27/93

School: Life Design Center   Initiation Date: 1/16/11

Review Date: 3/16/11

Beginning not later than the first IEP to be in effect <u>when the child turns 16, or younger if determined appropriate by the IEP Team</u>, and updated annually thereafter, the IEP must include:

- Appropriate measurable postsecondary goals based upon age-appropriate transition assessments related to training, education, employment, and, where appropriate, independent living skills. [34 CFR §300.320(b)(1)]

Carmine will ride the public bus to his busboy job.
Carmine will complete training for the position of busboy.
Carmine will purchase uniforms for his job at the mall.

- The transition services (including courses of study) needed to assist the child in reaching those goals. [34 CFR §300.320(b)(2)]

Transition Services (Including Courses of Study)
Busboy training program will be conducted by Metro Transport Services.
Job shadowing will be provided by the Ohio Bureau of Vocational Rehabilitation.

RIGHTS THAT TRANSFER AT AGE OF MAJORITY

- Beginning not later than 1 year before the child reaches the age of majority under state law, the IEP must include a statement that the child has been informed of the child's rights under Part B of the IDEA, if any, that will, consistent with 34 CFR §300.520, transfer to the child on reaching the age of majority.

FIGURE 1.2 Sample Individualized Transition Plan

Finally, Public Law 99–457 mandated that an IFSP be developed for all children who are under its protection. The IFSP is similar to the IEP but emphasizes the importance of the family to the child's education and related-services program. A sample IFSP is presented in Figure 1.3.

Cosmopolitan School District
INDIVIDUAL FAMILY SERVICE PLAN

Date Completed 5/12/11   Date Evaluated   4/15/11

Dates Reviewed _____

Name Tran, Quang   DOB   6/12/09   Sex   F

Home Address   97853 Manchester

Telephone (Home)   555-4341   (Work)   555-7616 (Ext. 17) Mother

Parent(s)/Guardian(s)   Bill and Lahn Tran

Individual Family Service Plan Team

Name	Role/Function	Signature
Bill Tran	Parent/Guardian	
Lahn Tran	Parent/Guardian	
Charlotte Haine	Case Manager	
Janie Race	MSW	
Debra Schwatz	Sp/Lang	

Services (Frequency, Intensity, and Duration)

Immediate, daily, 3 hrs, preschool

_____

_____

_____

_____

Signatures of Parent(s) or Guardian(s)

I/we have participated in the development of this Individual Family Service Plan for our child and our family. I/we understand this IFSP, give our permission for its implementation, and will cooperate in its implementation.

_____ (signature) _____5/12/11_____ (date)

_____ (signature) ___May 12, 2011___ (date)

FIGURE 1.3 Sample Individualized Family Services Plan

Individual Family Service Plan (continued)

Assessment Instruments and Procedures

Observation in preschool/home

Sample language with Vietnamese interpreter

Health and Medical Information

Moderate hearing impairment

Developmental Levels

Motor skills—OK - Eye contact—OK

Can localize sound with aids

Does not sign – parents concerned about signing in "English"– they often speak Vietnamese to child

Child's Strengths

Very social, curious and interested, explores freely. Makes great effort to communicate, tries approximations

of both Vietnamese and English words

Child's Needs

Speech training, signing as needed, more socialization; consistent use of English at school; support with parents

re: signing

Family's Strengths

Strong and willing family

Family's Needs

Training in signing and speech

Help in obtaining information and planning future

Address issues of language

OUTCOMES

Objectives	Strategies	Duration	Responsible Person(s)
Verbal communication skills	Discussion play	3 months	Teacher/Sp/Lang
Socialization	Community preschool	3 months	Case Manager
Signing	Formal training and	3 months	Case Manager, teacher,
	generalizations into preschool		parent, sp/Lang.
	and home		

FIGURE 1.3 Continued

A correlation can be made between the IEP process and the steps in the behavior change process (described in detail in Chapter 4). Briefly, the behavior change process requires the following steps:

(a) Collect baseline data (IEP assessment).

(b) Select objectives for the behavior change program (IEP short-term instructional objectives).

(c) Design and implement a specific behavior change intervention or strategy (IEP instructional or educational program).

(d) Collect intervention data to evaluate the effectiveness of the behavior change intervention (IEP evaluation).

Summary Points

- Each child is a unique individual, similar to other children yet different from other children. Due to this uniqueness, no single strategy or procedure is effective under all conditions for all children.
- Behavior management interventions are all those actions (and conscious inactions) teachers and parents engage in to enhance the probability that children and youth will develop effective behaviors.
- A specific strategy or technique that is effective under one set of circumstances for one child may be ineffective in another situation for another child.
- Aversive contingencies typically result in short-term effects and little long-term gain. In addition, they may increase avoidance and have a negative impact on relationships.
- The Council for Exceptional Children presents a code of ethics which indicates that professionals apply only methods and procedures that do not undermine the dignity or human rights of an individual. In addition, goals and objectives should be identified in the IEP.
- The principles of normalization, fairness, and respect are the foundation of behavior management.
- Public law (refer back to Table 1.1) has a significant impact on behavior management in the classroom.

- The Individuals with Disabilities Education Improvement Act requires each student with disabilities to have an IEP, collaboratively developed by parents, general educators, and special educators, that responds to the student's individual needs.
- The IEP must contain present levels of a student's performance, including a statement of how the disability affects the student's progress in general education, measurable goals and benchmarks, all needed services and supports, extent of nonparticipation with learners without identified disabilities, progress reporting, modifications for participation in mandated assessments, and transition needs for learners age 14 and older.
- Section 504 of the Rehabilitation Act of 1973 states that individuals with disabilities who are not enrolled in special education may receive accommodations and adaptations.
- The No Child Left Behind Act holds schools accountable for the academic achievement of their students. Annual testing is required, and specific corrective actions are designed for schools that fail to demonstrate adequate yearly progress.

Projects

1. Relate the principles of normalization, fairness, and respect to the standards of the Council for Exceptional Children for the ethical application of behavior management interventions.
2. The No Child Left Behind Act requires each school and district to publish a "report card" on their yearly progress. Request the No Child Left Behind Report Card for three local school districts and compare them. Describe the setting and population of each school and the yearly progress of the students involved.
3. Request the discipline guidelines of several schools. How is "zero tolerance" described? What provisions are made for students with disabilities within the discipline guidelines?

Web Resources

For the U.S. Office for Special Education Program's responses to questions about discipline and behavior management for students with disabilities, visit this site: *www.wrightslaw.com/advoc/articles/discipline_faqs_osep.htm*

For more information about the Individuals with Disabilities Education Improvement Act of 2004 and discipline, visit this site: *www.nichcy.org/reauth/discipline.doc*

For the full ethics statement of the Council for Exceptional Children, visit this site: *www.cec.sped.org/ps/ps-ethic.html*

References

Allen, R. C. (1969). *Legal rights of the disabled and disadvantaged* (GPO 1969-0-360-797). Washington, DC: U.S. Department of Health, Education, and Welfare and National Citizens Conference on Rehabilitation of the Disabled and Disadvantaged.

Cartledge, G., Tillman, L. C., & Johnson, C. T. (2001). Professional ethics within the context of student discipline and diversity. *Teacher Education and Special Education, 24*(1), 25–37.

Council for Exceptional Children (CEC). (2008). CEC's Policy on Safe and Positive School Climate. Arlington, VA: Council for Exceptional Children 2008 Policy Manual.

Council for Exceptional Children. (2010). *CEC Ethical Principles for Special Education Professionals.* Retrieved December 23, 2010, from www.cec.sped.org/Content/NavigationMenu/ProfessionalDevelopment/ProfessionalStandards/EthicsPracticeStandards/default.htm#code_ethics

Etscheidt, S. (2006). Least restrictive and natural environments for young children with disabilities. *Topics in Early Childhood Special Education, 26*(3), 167–178.

Farrell, P. (1995). The impact of normalization on policy and provision for people with learning difficulties. *Issues in Special Education and Rehabilitation, 10*(1), 47–54.

Garbarino, J. (2008). *Children and the dark human experience.* New York: Springer Science.

Green, G. (1996). Evaluating claims about treatments for autism. In C. Maurice, G. Green, & S. Luce (Eds.), *Behavioral interventions for young children with autism* (pp. 15–28). Austin, TX: Pro-Ed.

Jones, M. (2006). Teaching self-determination. *Teaching Exceptional Children, 29*(1), 12–17.

McCarthy, M. R., & Soodak, L. C. (2007). The politics of discipline: Balancing school safety and rights of students with disabilities. *Exceptional Children, 73*(4), 456–474.

Nickel, R. E. (2008). Controversial therapies for young children with developmental disabilities. In W. Dunn (Ed.), *Bringing evidence into everyday practice* (pp. 335–342). New York: Slack.

Noguera, P. A. (2003). Schools, prisons, and social implications of punishment: Rethinking disciplinary practices. *Theory into Practice, 42*(4), 341–350.

Pipho, C. (1998). Living with zero tolerance. *Phi Delta Kappan, 79*(10), 725–726.

Poussaint, A. (2005). Spanking as a discipline tactic. Retrieved December 23, 2010, from www.familyeducation.com/article/0,1120,62-2014,00.html

Rokeach, M., & Denver, J. (2006). Front-loading due process: A dignity-based approach to school discipline. *Ohio Sate Law Journal, 67,* 277–301.

Scheuermann, B., & Evans, W. (1997). Hippocrates was right: Do no harm: Ethics in the selection of intervention. *Beyond Behavior, 8*(3), 18–22.

Schrag, J. A. (2003). No Child Left Behind and its implications for students with disabilities. *The Special Edge, 16*(2), 1, 10–12.

Shea, T. M., & Bauer, A. M. (1987). *Teaching children and youth with behavior disorders* (2nd ed.). Upper Saddle River, NJ: Merrill/Pearson.

Shea, T. M., & Bauer, A. M. (1994). *Learners with disabilities: A social systems perspective of special education.* Madison, WI: Brown & Benchmark.

Simpson, R. (1995). Children and youth with autism in an age of reform: A perspective on current issues. *Behavioral Disorders, 21*(1), 7–20.

Skiba, R., & Peterson, R. (2003). Teaching the social curriculum: School discipline as instruction. *Preventing School Failure, 47*(2), 66–73.

Trevino, L. K., Weaver, G. R., & Reynolds, S. J. (2006). Behavioral ethics in organizations: A review. *Journal of Management, 32,* 951–975.

Turnbull, III, H. R., Wilcox, B. L., Turnbull, A. P., Sailor, W., & Wickham, D. (2001). IDEA, positive behavioral supports, and school safety. *Journal of Law and Education, 30*(3), 131–144.

U.S. Department of Education, (2007). *IDEA Regulations: Individualized Education Program (IEP) Meetings and Changes to the IEP.* Washington, DC: Office of Special Education Programs.

Wehmeyer, M. L., & Palmer, S. B. (2003). Adult outcomes for students with cognitive disabilities three years after high school: The impact of self-determination. *Education and Training in Developmental Disabilities, 38*(2), 131–144.

Wehmeyer, M. L., & Schalock, R. L. (2001). Self-determination and quality of life: Implications for special education services and supports. *Focus on Exceptional Children, 33*(8), 1–16.

Whitehurst, G. J. (2003, April). *The Institute of Education Sciences: New wine, new bottles.* Paper presented at the annual meeting of the American Educational Research Association, Chicago.

Winance, M. (2007). Being normally different? Changes to normalization processes: From alignment to work on the norm. *Disability and Society, 22*(6), 625–638.

Yell, M. L., Katsiyannas, A., & Shiner, J. G. (2006). The No Child Left Behind Act, adequate yearly progress, and students with disabilities. *Teaching Exceptional Children, 38*(4), 32–29.

Zirkel, P. A. (2009a). What does the law say? *Teaching Exceptional Children, 41*(5), 73–75.

Zirkel, P. A. (2009b). What does the law say? New Section 504 student eligibility standards. *Teaching Exceptional Children, 41*(4), 68–71.

CHAPTER OBJECTIVES

After completing this chapter, you will be able to do the following:

1. Discuss the relationships between ideas, actions, and outcomes (i.e., theories, interventions, and results).

2. Characterize the basic principles and components of four models of human behavior (developmental/constructivist, biobehavioral, environmental, and behavioral).

3. Describe the integrative framework and discuss its implications for analyzing behavior management problems and selecting, implementing, and evaluating interventions.

4. Recognize the value of keystone behaviors and comprehensive interventions.

5. Identify several evidence-based practices related to effective management.

Models of
Human Behavior

CHAPTER 2

KEY TERMS

Behavior

Behavioral psychology

Behavioral model

Biobehavioral model

Comprehensive interventions

Congruence

Development

Developmental and constructivists models

Ecological model

Ecology

Environment

Evidence-based practice

Integrative framework

Keystone behaviors

A group of four college students studying to be teachers and their instructor, Professor Garfunkel, were observing a class of children with behavior problems. The subject of their observation was the behavior of 6-year-old John, who had recently been enrolled in the class.

    The group observed John's behavior for 10 minutes and then closed the blinds of the observation window to discuss and evaluate their observations. After a brief discussion, they reached consensus on the behavior they observed:

- John entered the classroom, slammed the door, took off his coat and hat, and dropped the clothing to the floor.
- John ran to the toy box, picked up a truck, ran it over the top of a desk and a bookcase, then dropped it.
- John picked up a doll that was near the toy box, banged it several times on the floor, and tossed it at the teacher's assistant.
- John ran around the room three times. While running, he bumped into two children.
- John stopped near the sand table and twirled around on his toes, with his hands fully extended above his head, six or seven times before running to the sink.
- John stopped in front of the sink and turned on both faucets. He looked into the sink and remained in this position for the final 4 minutes of the observation period, rocking and flipping his fingers.

After the students reached agreement on the behaviors that John exhibited in the classroom during the 10-minute observation period, Dr. Garfunkel asked each student to discuss what he or she thought to be the reason for John's behavior. The following summaries by James, Charlotte, Melissa, and Richard, respectively, are inferences about John's behavior:

- John behaves as he does because his behaviors are reinforced in the environment. He has been rewarded for similar behavior in the past by the teacher or assistant. The teacher reinforced his behavior during our observation by attending to his behavior in her attempts to stop him.

(James is enrolled in experimental psychology courses this semester.)

- John is hyperactive as a result of traumatic or congenital brain injury. He should be administered appropriate symptom-control medication.

(Charlotte is an ex-premed student who transferred into special education this semester.)

- John behaves the way he does because he has not yet learned other ways to respond. As one of the youngest children in the classroom, he has not constructed the routines and activities that occur in the classroom.

(Melissa is enrolled in child development this semester.)

- John behaves as he does because of the classroom environment. It is noisy, confusing, cluttered, and lacks organization. He is only imitating what he sees others doing in the classroom. John needs an uncluttered, orderly, structured classroom environment with explicit routines and expectations.

(Richard is an ex-sociology major who recently transferred to special education.)

Each student interpreted John's behavior from a perspective that evolved from his or her personal formal and informal learning and experience (Shea & Bauer, 1987). The perspectives articulated by the four students represent only a few of the many perspectives on human behavior available in the literature.

The various theories of psychology—the study of human behavior—applied in the education of children and youth in managing behavior are based in part on the theorist's perspective of the principles underlying human conduct and thought.

There are several perspectives on human behavior. Each of these points of view has an impact on how we interact with students to increase their positive behaviors and performance. Four perspectives are addressed in this chapter: developmental and constructivist, biobehavioral, behavioral, and ecological. The chapter concludes with a discussion of evidence-based practices related to effective classroom and behavior management.

MODELS OF HUMAN BEHAVIOR

What makes us behave as we do toward self, others, and the environment? How can we change our behavior and the behavior of others from unproductive to productive? From unacceptable to acceptable? From destructive to constructive?

Four of the responses theoreticians have made and continue to make to these questions are the developmental and constructivist, biobehavioral, ecological, and behavioral explanations of human behavior. Argyris and Schon (1992) call the perspective from which we analyze and attempt to understand behavior our "theory-of-action," philosophy, or "espoused beliefs." They are those beliefs that guide our actions in our work with children. The vignettes of the four pre-service teachers that introduced this chapter are examples of the influence that one's perspective on the etiology of human behavior may have on the inferences one makes about behavior and how one responds to behavior. In this section, these theoretical models are related to the behavior of children.

Ideas, Actions, and Outcomes

The beliefs of teachers are a primary consideration in the implementation of practices and strategies in the classroom (Vadasy, Jenkins, Antil, Phillips, & Pool, 1997). In an intervention, ideas, actions, and outcomes are tied together and greatly affect each other. Ideas, in and of themselves, are inert unless active energy is added to their influence. Active energy, by itself, is meaningless and chaotic unless it is directed. In an intervention, the conceptual framework or model directs and channels action by providing an analysis of the nature of the problem that dictates the intervention and by suggesting the outcome or result toward which the intervention is directed. According to Fink (1988), it is often presumed that teachers' "espoused beliefs" govern their actual behavior. However, we frequently find that considerable variance exists between behavior and philosophy. Training and experience can decrease this discrepancy.

Educators' perceptions of children and the behavior children exhibit are in large part determinants of the behavior management interventions selected and imposed (Killoran, 2003). For example, the teacher who perceives the child as determined primarily by the environment approaches the problems of behavior management from a radically different point of view from the teacher who perceives a child as controlled primarily by biobehavioral factors. The teacher who perceives the child as controlled by the environment may change the location of the child's seat, develop additional rules for movement and behavior, or reorganize the lesson format or teaching strategy. The teacher who views the child as a product of development may encourage the child to expand his or her construction of the expectations of the classroom. The teacher who sees biobehavioral factors as significant in the child's behavior may provide the child with a highly structured learning environment that includes repeated drill and practice of lessons or may refer the child to the appropriate medical personnel for treatment.

Each of the models of human behavior presented in the following section is an explanation of behavior; each has led to the development of instructional strategies or methodology for application with all children, and sometimes more specifically for those with behavior problems. More specifically, conceptual models are ways of looking at behavior.

Developmental and Constructivist Models

The primary concern of **developmental and constructivist models** of behavior is whether students develop as persons and progress through developmental tasks (Scarlett, Ponte, & Sing, 2009). Rather than quantitative changes in scores or ratings, the developmental and constructivists models emphasize qualitative changes in the way students organize their thinking as they address various tasks. When using developmental and constructivist approaches, students' errors are analyzed in terms of student growth rather than whether a response is correct or incorrect. For example, a 4-year-old child may refer to a person who cooks as a "cooker" rather than a "cook." Even though this is incorrect in terms of vocabulary, the child is demonstrating that he or she understands that by adding "er" to a verb you can transform the verb into a noun representing the person who performs the verb.

■ *Example*

Joey's teacher, Mr. Lotus, was becoming concerned about Joey's behavior. Joey was far more active than his kindergarten peers. Joey was very excited about everything that happened in the classroom. He loved the stories during circle time and scooted closer and closer to the book to the extent that Mr. Lotus had to ask him to move back. He sang the class songs boisterously, and he often sang and talked out loud to himself when working on puzzles or with blocks. When praised he would hug the instructional assistant who was typically with him because of his activity level. In reviewing Joey's records, he remembered having noted that Joey was the youngest student in the classroom. Though it was mid September, he was still 4 years old, with a birthday on September 29, the day before the kindergarten-age cutoff date. Joey was an active, happy, curious 4-year-old in a kindergarten classroom in which some children were already 6 years old. He had not yet developed the self-management skills constructed by his older classmates.

Constructivist approaches are typically employed for both academic and prosocial behaviors. These approaches target process rather than achievement. The goal of developmental approaches is to link what the student is doing in the short term to long-term goals for the student. For example, a teacher would not emphasize accuracy by providing correct answers but would help students develop problem-solving skills. As a consequence, synthesis, application, and "figuring things out" are emphasized over memorizing facts and steps in sequence. Rather than beginning a lesson with a rule, such as "when dividing fractions invert and multiply," the teacher may pose a conceptual problem, such as "Repainting the lines on the basketball court takes three quarters of a gallon of paint. The lines are clear on the southern side of the gym, so only the northern half of the court needs painting. How much paint will be needed?" Such a contextualized problem may be solved in a variety of ways and depicted through diagrams or sketches. The teacher may lead the students to an understanding of how the problem could be represented through the division of fractions.

Constructivism is grounded in developmentally appropriate practice (National Association for the Education of Young Children, 2009). In developmentally appropriate practice, both curriculum and management strategies match the student's levels of understanding and development. It is not as simple, however, as allowing students to explore independently with the teacher hoping that they will happen on the desired learning outcomes. Rather, constructivism contends that persistent support in successfully completing the opportunities provided to the students assists them in developing appropriate self-management and organizational skills.

The three core components of developmentally appropriate practice emphasize the role of responsive adults in the child's education. First, decision making is grounded in the teacher's knowledge about (a) child development and learning in general, (b) the child as an individual, and (c) the child's cultural context. Second, goals must be both challenging and achievable, pushing the child to new learning grounded in what the child knows and is able to do. The third core component of developmentally appropriate practice is that teachers are intentional about everything involving the children, classroom environment, curriculum strategies, assessment, and interaction toward the child's developmental goal. In developmentally appropriate practice, development and learning result from the continuous interaction of maturation and experience.

Recognizing that challenging behaviors in young children are most often a response to events in the environment, gathering information about events associated with the behavior is essential. The developmental/constructivist model contends that the primary reason students may demonstrate an undesired behavior is that they lack the language and/or social skills needed to act differently. The emphasis then, is on teaching appropriate replacement behaviors. The environment is managed to reduce the likelihood of an inappropriate behavior. To ensure that behavior change is durable, interventions should include the family and should be implemented over time and in various environments (Dunlap et al., 2006).

Biobehavioral Model

The **biobehavioral model** of the etiology of learning and behavior problems of children places emphasis on organic origins of human behavior. Recognition of the role of neurological functioning on the behavior and learning of children is gaining greater attention with the growing knowledge about how the brain works.

■ *Example*

Amanda had been medically diagnosed with attention deficit disorder–inattentive type. She would appear to be daydreaming, would make comments that were off the topic, and was disorganized with regard to her assignments and her locker. Amanda's mother met with the teacher, Ms. Lohman, and indicated that the psychiatrist with whom they were working indicated that Amanda's problems were related to inconsistent levels of the neurotransmitters in her brain and that one important aspect of her treatment was using medication. The medication that Amanda would begin taking in the morning before she came to school would stimulate the secretion of neurotransmitters and maintain a higher level in her brain. This would increase the efficiency of the part of her brain that manages attention.

Biobehavioral models of behavior use knowledge of brain functioning to provide insights into the changes seen in individual students' actions. The limbic area in the brain works to process emotion and memory and is mature when the student reaches 10 to 12 years of age. The frontal area comprises rational and executive control, directing problem solving and using cognitive processing to monitor and control the emotions that begin in the limbic area. The frontal lobes mature when the student is 22 to 24 years of age. Sousa (2009) uses this discrepancy in development to explain that emotions drive the actions of preadolescents and adolescents: Emotional attention precedes cognitive recognition. Sousa contends that preadolescent and adolescent students are more likely to respond emotionally than rationally, which may result in poor decisions related to behavior.

Three other structures in the brain are key to understanding behavior in the biobehavioral model (Aron, Behrens, Smith, Frank, & Poldrack, 2007). The orbitofrontal cortex acts as a braking mechanism, postponing decision making for a few milliseconds to allow reflection. This signal goes to the thalamus area, stopping movement. Then, the message goes to the orbitofrontal area to plan a new response or stop an impulsive response.

Biobehaviorists maintain that though behaviors may be caused by neurological functioning, students can learn to manage their behaviors. Various strategies related to this model are described later in this text.

Ecological Model

The impact of the **environment** on human behavior is a dominant theme in contemporary society. Many decisions made by governments, corporate groups, and individuals are made with a conscious awareness of the relationship between people and the environment. Environmental impact studies are standard, accepted components of all proposals to construct highways, airports, dams, lakes, industrial complexes, high-rise buildings, and so on. Professionals as well as laypersons are increasingly concerned with any environmental changes that may affect human behavior, such as those concerning recreation areas, water pollution, waste disposal, and nuclear power. Many are concerned with the effects of environmental changes on issues such as employment, human services, and neighborhood composition.

■ *Example*

Marco, a second-grade student, had been doing quite well. He followed directions, asked for help when he needed it, and initiated interactions with his peers and teacher. After a few months of school, however, Ms. Maroni, his teacher, noticed a pattern emerging. Every other Monday Marco would return to school with what Ms. Maroni's instructional assistant called "a chip on his shoulder." When asked to do things, he would say phrases such as "Make me" and "No way." When he didn't receive requested help immediately, he would whine and make statements such as "You don't want me here." In conversation with Marco's father, Ms. Maroni learned that Marco spent every other weekend with his mother and new stepfather. Two teenage stepbrothers were making it clear that Marco was disturbing their lifestyle. To try to impress them, Marco was trying to emulate their language. By Wednesday of each week, Marco's behavior had moderated.

Ecology is the study of the interrelationships between an organism and its environment. As it applies to education, ecology is the study of the reciprocal relationship between the child or group and others (individuals, groups, and objects) in the environment. McConnell (2002) describes ecological interventions as those that promote learning through manipulating or arranging general aspects of the physical and social environment. These changes may include changing activities or schedules, or changing the nature and composition of the student's peer group.

The chain reactions that occur in ecological interventions are exemplified in Parsons's (1964) seminal concept of the sick role. Four societal expectations encourage individuals labeled "sick" to assume this role (Woolfolk, 2001):

1. Sick persons are relieved of their normal role obligations.
2. Because they are sick, they are not morally responsible for their condition.
3. Sick persons must express their desire to return to normal functioning.
4. Sick persons must seek technically competent help from appropriate caretakers (psychiatrists, psychologists, social workers, and teachers).

The application of the **ecological model** in educational programs for children is characterized by (a) an awareness of the impact of the environment on the group and individual and the monitoring and manipulation of the environment for the benefit of the individual and group and (b) an awareness of the dynamic reciprocal interrelationship that exists between the group and individual and the environment and the monitoring and manipulation of this relationship for the benefit of the individual and group. Ecological interventions may be necessary for other more intense interventions to occur (McConnell, 2002).

Dunlap et al. (2006) provide several evidence-based considerations related to ecological approaches to addressing challenging behaviors. They argue that intervention must be based on assessment of the relationship between the student's behavior and the environment. By changing features of the student's activities and social and physical environment, it is possible to reduce challenging behavior. Most significantly, perhaps, is their conclusion that high quality educational environments and teacher interactions are associated with fewer behavioral problems.

Behavioral Model

Behavioral psychology employs a scientific approach to the examination of behavior—including verbal behavior and private events. The behavioral perspective maintains that all behavior is a function of the interaction between events in the environment and the behavior itself. Applied behavioral analysis, often used by behaviorists, involves studying behavior with significance to participants in the natural setting. Applied behavioral analysis often uses functional behavioral analysis (described in detail in Chapter 5) to identify the antecedents and consequences of a behavior and to use this information in designing interventions to change behavior (Gresham, Watson, & Skinner, 2001).

■ *Example*

One of Todd's educational goals was to persist at a task until completion. As Todd worked on an assignment, his teacher circulated through the room. As she passed Todd, who was concentrating on the task, she quietly said, "You're really sticking to it, Todd," and then she put a tally mark on an index card on his desk. At the end of the day, Todd returned the card to his teacher, and together they charted how many tally marks he had received. After accumulating three cards with at least 10 tally marks, Todd received a pass to read to a small group of first-graders, an activity Todd greatly enjoyed.

The behavior manager is concerned primarily with what behavior an individual exhibits and what intervention can be designed and imposed to change this observable behavior. For the behavior modification practitioner, behavior is defined as all human acts that are observable and measurable, excluding biochemical and physiological processes. The behavioral theorists and practitioners see the causes of human behavior as existing outside the individual in the immediate environment. Thus, the individual's behavior is determined primarily by external forces.

Those adhering to the behavior modification model assume that all human behavior (adaptive and maladaptive) is the consequence of the lawful application of the principles of reinforcement. These rules, described in Chapter 3, are an indication of the behavior manager's belief that human behavior is controlled by the individual's impinging environmental stimuli. The individual's behavior is changed by manipulation of environmental stimuli.

Behavioral model, including behavior modification techniques and their applications to individual and group behavior problems, has its roots in the writings and research of Bandura (1969), Skinner (1971), and Wolpe (1961), among others. Although theorists continue to debate various constructs and interventions within this theoretical model, practitioners have successfully applied its principles to a variety of human problems. Among the problem behaviors that have been modified as a consequence of the application of behavior modification interventions are the symptoms of psychoses, autism, neuroses, marital conflicts, specific learning problems, motivational problems, and speech problems. Researchers and practitioners have successfully modified tantrums, verbal and physical aggression, interpersonal interaction patterns, eating habits, mutism, and so on. Various behavior modification interventions in the school have been successfully implemented with children with disabilities. The goal of behavior modification interventions in the classroom with children with behavioral disorders (and, indeed, with all individuals) is best summarized by Hewett (1968) as "the identification of maladaptive behaviors which interfere with learning and assisting the child in developing more adaptive behavior" (p. 34).

The procedures for applying behavior modification in the educational setting require the teacher to (a) observe and clarify the behavior to be changed, (b) select and present potent reinforcers at the appropriate time, (c) design and impose, with consistency, an intervention technique based on the principles of reinforcement, and (d) monitor and evaluate the effectiveness of the intervention. The steps in the behavior change process are presented in detail in Chapter 6.

INTEGRATIVE FRAMEWORK

As discussed in the previous sections, the behavior of children is a complex, dynamic phenomenon that may be perceived from various points of view. As the following examples show, the perceptions of parents, teachers, and others involved with children with behavior problems can have an enormous effect on assessment and intervention.

■ *Examples*

John was born on December 23, 1997, in Central City Regional Hospital. He was a premature child with Down syndrome. When John was born, Martha, his mother, was alone in the delivery room, with the exception of the nurses and doctor. She was glad that the long, tiring pregnancy was over. Martha was only 16 years old, and the pregnancy had been very difficult. Martha had never heard the phrase "Down syndrome"; she had no idea what the doctor was talking about when she was informed of John's problem. Martha only knew that John was not "right," and because she wanted a perfect baby, this made her unhappy. Her friends all had perfect babies.

Martha had no one to turn to during this crisis except the staff at the community shelter for single and indigent mothers, where she had been living for the past 5 months. John's father was still in high school and could not help with the baby; John's father's parents refused to let their son even talk to Martha. Martha's parents put her out of the house when they discovered that she was pregnant. Her only contact with family was through Aunt Jean, who came to visit her at the shelter. Aunt Jean had troubles of her own and couldn't help Martha very much.

Martha hoped the school would let her return so she could graduate with her friends. The principal said the school board was thinking about opening a nursery in the high school. But now that John was "different," she wondered whether John would be accepted even if a nursery were opened.

The social worker at the shelter said she would help Martha get on welfare, get food stamps, and find a studio apartment in the city. The social worker said low-cost housing was available in some areas of the city for people on welfare. Martha knew she couldn't return to her job at the fast-food restaurant. She wouldn't make enough money to support herself and John.

Paul was born on December 23, 1997, in West Suburban Medical Center. He was a full-term child with Down syndrome. When Paul was born, his father, George, was with his mother, Mary, in the delivery room, as were several nurses and doctors. As a result of tests given during the early stages of pregnancy, the parents were aware that Paul was to be born with Down syndrome.

This was Mary's third pregnancy; it was for the most part unexceptional, and the delivery was routine. Mary was 28 years of age. Her two other children, a boy and girl, were in elementary school and doing well in academics and in co-curricular and community activities. The children enjoyed school, taking after their parents, who were both college graduates and professionals.

Mary and George had read a great deal about Down syndrome during the past few months and hoped that Paul would be born without medical complications. Though they were not overjoyed to be the parents of a child with potentially serious disabilities, they felt prepared and equal to the challenge. Both sets of grandparents were aware of the problems that Paul might present and volunteered to help when Mary and her baby returned home from the hospital. This was important because George, the manager of a department in a computer firm, could not take many days off work. Mary was going to remain home with the baby for 6 weeks before returning to her job as a special education teacher.

The local chapter of the Down Syndrome Association was in telephone contact with the family while mother and baby were in the hospital. The association recommended a visit with the parents of a child with Down syndrome. Mary and George accepted the offer. The medical center made arrangements for Mary and George to be interviewed by a home visitor who specialized in developmental disabilities. This professional arranged to visit the parents in their home and enroll Paul in an infant stimulation program.

John and Paul have been given the same diagnosis, however, their social systems are vastly different. Their ability to achieve their potential depends on the developmental contacts in which they live.

Children's behavior can be perceived from a psychodynamic, biobehavioral, behavioral, or environmental point of view. The very complexity and diversity of the theoretical perspectives and children's behavior preclude simple assessment and intervention. However, through the application of an **integrative framework**, it may be possible to coordinate the extant perspectives into a manageable assessment-intervention model (Shea & Bauer, 1987).

From an ecological perspective, rather than being seen as rooted within the child or in the environment exclusively, behavior is seen as a result of the interaction between the child, the child's idiosyncratic behaviors, and the unique environments in which the child functions (Forness, 1981). Ecological practitioners would suggest that traditional practitioners are missing educationally and socially relevant variables because of their limiting single-model perspective.

Before discussing the integrative framework, it is necessary to become familiar with a few specialized terms:

1. **Ecology** is the interrelationship of humans with the environment and involves reciprocal association (Thomas & Marshall, 1977). According to Scott (1980), ecology is all the surroundings of behavior. From this point of view, it is assumed that the child is an inseparable part of an ecological unit, which is composed of the child, the classroom, the school, the neighborhood, and the community.

2. **Development** is defined as the continual adaptation of the child and the environment to each other. It is seen as progressive accommodation that takes place throughout the life span between growing individuals and their changing environments. It is based on "the person's evolving conception of the ecological environment and his relationship to it, as well as the person's growing capacity to discover, sustain, and alter its properties" (Bronfenbrenner, 1979, p. 9).

3. **Behavior** is the expression of the dynamic relationships between the individual and the environment (Marmor & Pumpian-Mindlin, 1950). Behavior occurs in a setting that includes specific time, place, and object props as well as the individual's previously established pattern of behavior (Scott, 1980). To understand behavior, it is necessary to examine the systems of interaction surrounding the behavior; assessment is not restricted to a single setting. In addition, according to Bronfenbrenner (1977), examination must take into account those aspects of the environment beyond the immediate situation in which the individual is functioning and that impact on the behavior.

4. **Congruence** is the match, or goodness of fit, between the individual and the environment. Thurman (1977) suggests that the individual whom we judge to be normal is functioning in an ecology that is congruent: The individual's behavior is in harmony with the norms of the environment. When congruence is lacking, the individual is viewed as either deviant or incompetent.

The integrated framework presented here includes several interrelated contexts that influence an individual's development. These contexts, which affect the individual's development and behavior, are the *ontogenic system*, the *microsystem*, the *mesosystem*, the *exosystem*, and the *macrosystem* (Belsky, 1980; Bronfenbrenner, 1979). These systems, or contexts, have recently been referred to by Shea and Bauer (1987) as (a) the learner (ontogenic system), (b) interpersonal relationships (microsystem), (c) relationships between settings (mesosystem), (d) group interactions (exosystem), and (e) society (macrosystem). The relationship of the five systems is depicted in Figure 2.1.

The ontogenic system includes the child's personality, skills, abilities, and competencies. Each student exhibits intraindividual factors for working the environment. Among the many factors included in this system are the child's intelligence, coping skills, and academic skills.

The microsystem includes the interrelationships within the immediate setting in which the individual is functioning, such as the teacher-child and child-child relationships in the classroom. It must be remembered that both teacher and child are actors and reactors in the classroom environment.

The mesosystem comprises the interrelationships among the settings in which the child is actually functioning at a particular point in time. It is a system of microsystems. The mesosystem may include relationships among school, home, church, work, and community.

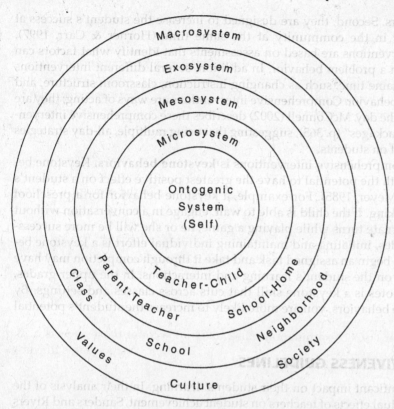

FIGURE 2.1 The five systems of the integrative framework

Source: T. M. Shea & A. M. Bauer. (1987). *Teaching Children and Youth with Behavior Disabilities* (2nd ed.). Upper Saddle River, NJ: Merrill/Pearson.

The exosystem is the larger social system in which the microsystem and mesosystem are embedded. It includes both formal and informal social structures, such as law enforcement, recreational, political, and economic systems. Though a child may not actively participate in these systems or be directly influenced by them, they do influence the child's microsystem and mesosystem and thus, indirectly, the child.

The final system—the macrosystem—includes the overriding cultural beliefs and values as well as the general perceptions of the social institutions common to a particular culture in which the child is functioning. The beliefs, values, and attitudes of the macrosystem directly and indirectly influence the child's behavior. Areas of the macrosystem that may impact the child include society's perceptions of education, teachers, special education, children, children with disabilities, and so on.

From these definitions, the ontogenic system is related most closely with psychodynamic and biobehavioral conceptual frameworks. The microsystem is closely related to the behavioral perspective. Interventions related directly and indirectly to the mesosystem are usually described as environmental interventions.

Comprehensive Interventions and Keystone Behaviors

One recent shift in thinking about students who present challenging behaviors is that of **comprehensive interventions**. Comprehensive interventions take on two goals concurrently. First, they are aimed at producing rapid, lasting, and generalized reduction in challenging behaviors. Second, they are designed to increase the student's success at home, at school, or in the community at the same time (Horner & Carr, 1997). Comprehensive interventions are based on assessments that identify what factors can predict and maintain a problem behavior. In addition, several different interventions may be used at the same time, such as changing instruction, classroom structure, and the consequences of behavior. Comprehensive interventions are ways of acting; they are applied throughout the day. McConnell (2002) describes these comprehensive interventions as "treatment packages" (p. 365), suggesting that using multiple, all-day strategies have the most impact on students.

The focus of comprehensive interventions is **keystone behaviors**. Keystone behaviors are those with the potential to have the greatest positive effect on a student's behavior (Evans & Meyer, 1985). For example, a keystone behavior for a preschool child may be turn taking. If the child is able to wait, engage in a conversation without interrupting, or alternate turns while playing a game, he or she will be more successful. In the early grades, initiating and maintaining individual effort is a keystone behavior. Being able to begin an assigned task and take it through completion may have a significant impact on the student's learning and interactions. In the upper grades, being able to take notes is a keystone skill that cuts across classes and settings. By identifying keystone behaviors, you are more likely to increase the student's potential for success.

TEACHER EFFECTIVENESS GUIDELINES

Teachers have a significant impact on their students' learning. In their analysis of the cumulative and residual effects of teachers on student achievement, Sanders and Rivers (1996) found that the effects of teachers on student achievement are both additive and cumulative with little potential for students to "catch up" with their peers. In addition, when teacher effectiveness increases, the lower achieving students are the first to benefit. Wright, Horn, and Sanders (1997), in their study utilizing the teacher evaluation model in Tennessee, demonstrated that the most significant factor affecting student academic gain is teacher effectiveness. Unfortunately, the residual effects of ineffective teachers were still measurable 2 years later.

When discussing effective teaching of students with behavior problems, it is important to examine both what teachers feel and believe as well as what they do.

Webber, Anderson, and Otey (1991) proposed mindsets to make the teaching-learning process more effective and less stressful for both teacher and students. Webber and associates state that it is essential for teachers to believe that all problems have solutions and that a single problem may have many solutions. Effective teachers are realistic in their perception of the problems they and their students confront. They teach from a realistic perspective and remain optimistic toward self, students, and the tasks that they confront. Teachers perceive students with a sensitivity that allows them to understand student behavior.

According to Webber et al. (1991), teachers of students with behavior problems must recognize that at times they may be psychologically hurt by their students. They must be prepared to suffer some pain in their interactions with students. The discomfort students with behavior problems inflict on others is frequently symptomatic of their personal emotional difficulties rather than a personal attack. Teachers should plan to accommodate such personal discomfort and to prevent it from becoming overwhelming.

Teachers must be careful not to become enmeshed in what Webber et al. (1991) refer to as "junk thoughts." They must think rationally and eliminate irrational thoughts as they work with students.

Finally, life in the classroom is often funny or humorous. Effective teachers understand that a sense of humor is essential to survival in the classroom. McEwan (2001) and the Educational Research Service Bulletin (2001) suggests that effective teachers are:

- dedicated to teaching and facilitating learning and growth;
- caring for students, parents, colleagues, and personal well-being (effective teachers empathize with students, respect them, and treat them fairly);
- leaders to students, parents, and colleagues;
- able to organize and manage a classroom, behavior, and time;
- enthusiastic towards teaching and students;
- able to motivate students;
- learners themselves;
- in tune with the cultures and subcultures within which they, their students, and their students' families live and work; and
- engaged in a rich and varied intellectual life.

Classroom management strategies—what teachers do—have been documented by Oliver and Reschly (2007). A strong aspect of classroom management is strong instruction and classroom organization. Oliver and Reschley describe **evidence-based practices** that enhance classroom organization and behavior management. They describe these practices as:

- a structured environment with a daily, visible schedule and clear traffic patterns that ease movement and minimize distractions;
- active supervision and student engagement, with teachers scanning, making positive comments, providing high rates of opportunities to respond, and multiple ways of engaging students;
- schoolwide positively stated behavioral expectations that are visible, taught, reinforced, and monitored;
- classrooom behavioral rules linked to schoolwide expectations that are also visible, taught, reinforced, and monitored;
- classroom routines that are systematically taught, reinforced, and monitored;
- group-wide efforts to encourage appropriate behavior at both the class-wide and individual levels;
- collecting data on the frequency of appropriate behavior within the classroom environment;
- behavior reduction strategies that are anchored in preventing inappropriate behavior, differentially reinforce competing behaviors, and effective use of consequences; and
- descriptions of how a teacher should feel and be and what the teacher should do in evidence-based practice that emphasize the need to be positive, explicit, and consistent when working with students.

Summary Points

- A teacher's beliefs about behavior—that is, his or her perspective—have an impact on his or her interactions with students and the interventions he or she chooses.
- The developmental/constructivist model emphasizes the need for students to develop as persons and progress through a series of tasks.
- The biobehavioral model suggests that an individual's behavior has an organic or physical cause. Increased emphasis has been placed on brain structures and functions in this model.
- The ecological model suggests that an individual is an inseparable part of a social system, and his or her behavior is a result of a specific setting or environment.

- The behavioral model suggests that an individual's behavior is a result of the events in the environment that maintain it. Through managing the antecedents and consequences of a behavior, the behavior may be changed.
- An integrated perspective suggests that an individual develops within a series of developmental contexts.
- Keystone behaviors are those that have the potential to make the greatest positive effect on an individual's behavior.
- Comprehensive interventions are designed to produce rapid, lasting, and generalized behavior change, and their aim is to increase the student's success at home, school, or in the community.

Projects

1. Identify a behavior such as a problem with homework completion, attending poorly to task, or poor class participation. Describe how the challenging behavior could be described using each of the theoretical perspectives.

2. Using the Internet, search for information on one of the traditional models of the etiology of human behavior. Identify the major proponents of the model and several agencies or schools that are applying the model.

Web Resources

For additional information about teacher effectiveness, visit this site:
www.learningpt.org

For additional information about the systems approach, visit this site:
www.edpsycinteractive.org/materials/sysmdlo.html

References

Argyris, C., & Schon, D. A. (1992). *Theory in practice: Increasing professional effectiveness.* San Francisco: Jossey-Bass.

Aron, A. R., Behrens, T. E., Smith, S., Frank, M. J., & Poldrack, R. A. (2007). Triangulating a cognitive control network using diffusion-weighted magnetic resonance imaging (MRI) and functional MRI. *Journal of Neuroscience, 27,* 3742–3752.

Bandura, A. (1969). *Principles of behavior modification.* New York: Holt, Rinehart & Winston.

Belsky, J. (1980). Child maltreatment: An ecological integration. *American Psychologist, 53,* 320–335.

Bronfenbrenner, U. (1977). Toward an experimental ecology of human development. *American Psychologist, 32,* 513–531.

Bronfenbrenner, U. (1979). *The ecology of human development.* Cambridge, MA: Harvard University Press.

Dunlap, G., Strain, P., Fox, L., Carta, J. J., Conroy, M., Smith, B. L., et al. (2006). Prevention and intervention with young children's challenging behaviors: Perspectives regarding current knowledge. *Behavioral Disorders, 32*(1), 29–45.

Educational Research Service Bulletin. (2001). *Highly Effective Teachers, 29*(4), 1–2.

Evans, I. M., & Meyer, L. H. (1985). *An educative approach to behavior problems: A practical decision model for interventions with severely handicapped learners.* Baltimore: Paul H. Brookes.

Fink, A. H. (1988). The psychoeducational philosophy: Programming implications for students with behavioral disorders. Behavior *in Our Schools, 2*(2), 8–13.

Forness, S. R. (1981). Concepts of learning and behavior disorders: Implications for research and practice. *Exceptional Children, 48,* 56–64.

Gresham, F. M., Watson, T. S., & Skinner, C. H. (2001). Functional behavioral assessment: Principles, procedures, and future directions. *School Psychology Review, 30*(2), 156–172.

Hewett, F. M. (1968). *The emotionally disturbed child in the classroom: A developmental strategy for educating children with maladaptive behavior.* Boston: Allyn & Bacon.

Horner, R. H., & Carr, E. G. (1997). Behavioral support for students with severe disabilities: Functional assessment and comprehensive intervention. *Journal of Special Education, 31,* 84–104.

Killoran, I. (2003). Why is your homework not done? How theories of development affect your approach to the classroom. *Journal of Instructional Psychology, 30*(4), 309–314.

Marmor, J., & Pumpian-Mindlin, E. (1950). Toward an integrative conception of mental disorders. *Journal of Nervous and Mental Disease, 3,* 19–29.

McConnell, S. R. (2002). Interventions to facilitate social interaction for young children with autism: Review of available research and recommendations for educational intervention and future research. *Journal of Autism and Developmental Disorders, 32*(5), 351–372.

McEwan, E. K. (2001). *Ten traits of highly effective teachers: How to hire, coach, and mentor successful teachers.* Thousand Oaks, CA: Corwin.

National Association for the Education of Young Children (NAEYC). (2009). *Developmentally appropriate practice in early childhood education programs serving children from birth through age 8.* Washington, DC: NAEYC.

Oliver, R. M., & Reschly, D. J. (2007). *Effective classroom management: Teacher preparation and professional development.* Washington, DC: National Comprehensive Center for Teacher Quality.

Parsons, T. (1964). *The social system.* New York: Free Press.

Sanders, W. L., & Rivers, J. C. (1996). *Cumulative and residual effects of teachers on future student academic achievement (Research Progress Report).* Knoxville: University of Tennessee Value-Added Research and Assessment Center.

Scarlett, W. G., Ponte, I. C., & Singh, J. P. (2009). *Approaches to behavior and classroom management.* Thousand Oaks, CA: Sage.

Scott, M. (1980). Ecological theory and methods for research in special education. *Journal of Special Education, 4,* 279–294.

Shea, T. M., & Bauer, A. M. (1987). *Teaching children and youth with behavior disorders* (2nd ed.). Upper Saddle River, NJ: Merrill/Pearson.

Skinner, B. F. (1971). *Beyond freedom and dignity.* New York: Knopf.

Sousa, David A. (2009). *How the brain influences behavior.* Thousand Oaks, CA: Corwin Press.

Thomas, E. D., & Marshall, M. J. (1977). Clinical evaluation and coordination of services: An ecological model. *Exceptional Children, 44,* 16–22.

Thurman, S. K. (1977). Congruence of behavioral ecologies: A model for special education programming. *Journal of Special Education, 11,* 329–333.

Vadasy, P. F., Jenkins, J. R., Antil, J. R., Phillips, N., & Pool, K. (1997). The research to practice ball game: Classwide peer tutoring and teacher interest implementation, modification. *Remedial Special Education, 18*(3), 743–745.

Webber, J., Anderson, T., & Otey, L. (1991). Teacher mindsets for surviving in 80 classrooms. *Intervention in School and Clinic, 26*(5), 288–292.

Wolpe, J. (1961). The systematic desensitization treatment of neuroses. *Journal of Nervous and Mental Disease, 132,* 189–203.

Woolfolk, R. (2001). The concept of mental illness: An analysis of four pivotal issues. *The Journal of Mind and Behavior, 22*(2), 161–178.

Wright, S. P., Horn, S. P., & Sanders, W. L. (1997). Teacher and classroom context effects on student achievement: Implications for teacher evaluation. *Journal of Personnel Evaluation in Education, 11*(1), 57–67.

CHAPTER OBJECTIVES

After completing this chapter, you will be able to do the following:

1. Discuss and exemplify the principles of management.

2. Identify and illustrate the consequences of behavior.

3. Understand and characterize the concepts of generalization and discrimination.

4. Describe and give examples of the most common schedules of reinforcement.

Principles of Behavior Management

CHAPTER 3

KEY TERMS

Consequences

Continuous schedule

Differential reinforcement

Discrimination

Extinction

Fading or thinning

Fixed interval schedule

Fixed ratio schedule

Generalization

Maintenance

Negative reinforcement

Positive reinforcement

Principles of management

Punishment

Reinforcers

Schedule of reinforcement

Target behavior

Variable interval schedule

Mr. Rodrigues has completed his first semester as principal of San José Mission High School. It has been a challenging semester for the new principal, but something is not going right among the faculty and staff. The morale of the office staff is low and teachers are not motivated. Students are only physically there, and the community acts as if it doesn't know the school exists. Mr. Rodrigues wonders how he might create a more positive and exciting educational atmosphere. Conversations among staff and teachers suggest that Mr. Rodrigues is an administrator who believes that being paid for a job should be ample reward. At the beginning of the academic year, when teachers came into his office to talk about a specific student, Mr. Rodrigues would reply, "Aren't you a licensed teacher? Is there a reason you can't figure this out?" The former principal allowed teachers who were at the PTO meetings to come in 15 minutes before the students on the following morning. Mr. Rodrigues stopped this policy, stating, "This is a profession, not a factory job. Coming to meetings is part of the deal."

Maybe if Mr. Rodrigues were taught something about the basic principles of reinforcement, his relations with his staff, students, and the community would improve.

Mr. Whiteside, a high school science teacher, is having extreme difficulty maintaining class order and enforcing safety regulations. He is also having difficulty getting students to clean up after their labs. He feels that he is constantly yelling at his students to wear their protective glasses and to sit down or stand quietly and listen to his instructions before beginning a lab project. He seems to be always reprimanding various students for not cleaning their glassware and work areas. He's had it with his job and thinks that next fall he will retire early.

Perhaps if Mr. Whiteside completed a course in behavior management in the classroom, he could increase his control over the students and have neater, cleaner, safer labs.

Most of us go through life unaware of the many factors that influence the way they behave. We may be unaware that as "normal" human beings we tend to be attracted to those experiences that are pleasurable and avoid those that are not pleasurable. We receive pleasure from smiles, positive comments, a pat on the back, an excellent grade in a course, and a bonus in our paychecks. We avoid situations where physical or mental pain is inflicted by persons we don't like to be around.

According to Downing, Moran, Myles, and Ormsbee (1991), "Individual behavior is influenced by what occurs immediately before (antecedent) and after (consequent) the action or response" (p. 86). The consequences and probable consequences of behavior, more than any other factor, determine the behavior that an individual exhibits (Shea & Bauer, 1987). In the field of behavior management, the consequences of behavior are called **reinforcers**.

Reinforcers can be classified in a number of ways. They may be classified as tangible or primary reinforcers (food, drinks, and tokens) and social or secondary reinforcers (praise, smiles, and other signs of approval).

For example, why does a child attend school? What reinforces school-attending behavior? Students go to school because of the following:

1. Their parents send them to school, and attending and doing well pleases the parents.
2. The people at school give students more attention than the people at home.
3. The students plan after-school activities with friends during the morning recess.
4. The students appreciate the hot meal provided each noon by the school.

A student may attend school for both tangible (hot food) and social (attention and friends) reinforcers.

Reinforcers may be positive (rewarding, pleasure giving) or negative (aversive, punishing). Tangible and social reinforcers may be positive reinforcers—that is, desirable consequences for which behavior is exhibited; or they may be negative—that is, undesirable consequences for which behavior is inhibited.

Students who consider school aversive might exhibit inappropriate behavior in an attempt to avoid school. If students were successful in this attempt, the inappropriate behavior would increase; thus, school-attending behavior would decrease. For example, two situations that would result in an increase in school-avoiding behavior are the following:

1. Students are allowed to remain at home during the school day because they complain of being ill.
2. Students are allowed to remain at home because a homework assignment is not completed.

If students were not allowed to avoid school through exhibiting these behaviors, these behaviors would probably decrease.

The consequences of behavior, then, are the determinants of behavior. Human beings tend to repeat behaviors that in their perception are, positive, rewarded, or praised. They tend not to repeat behaviors that in their perception are negative, punished, or ignored.

In the remainder of this chapter, the basic principles of management are presented and exemplified. These principles can be systematically applied by the teacher in the classroom and by the parents in the home.

The effective and efficient application of behavior management techniques involves more than the simple memorization and application of the principles of management. For effective implementation, it is necessary that the teacher, parent, or caregiver be intuitive, creative, and empathetic.

PRINCIPLES OF MANAGEMENT

The **principles of management** are a set of rules to be applied in the behavior change process. Behavior change relies heavily on these principles when planning and implementing a behavior change program.

Principle 1: Reinforcement Is Dependent on the Exhibition of the Target Behavior

If we are attempting, with planned intervention, to change a specific behavior (i.e., a **target behavior**) in an individual, we must reinforce only the behavior we are planning to change and only after that behavior is exhibited. In planning and implementing an intervention, we must *take caution to ensure that nontarget behaviors are not reinforced unwittingly.*

■ *Examples*

Ms. Jones was attempting to increase Bill's in-seat behavior in her classroom. It had been ascertained through systematic observation that Bill received attention from Ms. Jones for his out-of-seat behavior. When Bill was out of his seat, Ms. Jones proceeded to reprimand him, asking him to please return to his seat or stopping class until he returned to his seat. Although Bill was receiving negative attention (in Ms. Jones's perception), his attempts to receive attention—positive or negative—were apparently being met in this situation. Bill's behavior (being out of his seat) kept increasing as Ms. Jones's behavior (scolding) kept increasing.

Ms. Long was faced with a problem similar to that of Ms. Jones—Jerry's in-seat behavior. She was reported to have said that she had to dust Jerry's chair every morning because he never used it. At first she applied Ms. Jones's technique: yelling. Then she planned a behavior management intervention. She would totally ignore Jerry's out-of-seat behavior. She would in no way reinforce this particular inappropriate behavior. However, whenever Jerry's overactive bottom hit his assigned seat, she would immediately reward him. She would praise him in front of the whole class, if necessary, and pat his shoulder.

As a result of this intervention, not only did Jerry learn to sit in his seat, but Ms. Long discovered she liked him.

In the second example, the approach was effective in bringing about the desired behavior. In the first example, however, Ms. Jones is still scolding, and Bill is still enjoying all the attention he is receiving from his teacher and peers. So, if we desire to modify a specific behavior, we must reinforce *only* that behavior and *only* after it is exhibited.

Principle 2: The Target Behavior Is to Be Reinforced Immediately After It Is Exhibited

The importance of presenting the reinforcer immediately after the target behavior is exhibited cannot be overstressed. This principle is especially true during the initial stages of the behavior change process, when we are attempting to establish a new behavior. Inappropriate and nonfunctional behaviors occur from time to time in every individual's behavioral repertoire. If reinforcers are delayed in a planned intervention program, nontarget behaviors (rather than the target behavior) may be accidentally or unwittingly reinforced, thus increasing the probability that a nontarget behavior will be exhibited in the future.

■ *Example*

Mr. Riley was attempting to increase the number of math problems Pat completed during the period. He planned to reward Pat immediately after he completed each assigned group of problems. The number of problems in each group would be increased on a weekly basis if Pat responded to the intervention as predicted.

Mr. Riley was very inconsistent in the presentation of the reinforcer (tokens to be used for a homework-free day). As a result, Pat spent considerable time waiting at his desk and waving his hand frantically to gain his teacher's attention.

After a few weeks, it was found that the intervention program was ineffective in increasing the number of completed problems. However, Pat now sat at his desk for much longer periods of time with a bored expression.

Mr. Riley became aware of Pat's behavior and of his personal inconsistency. He began to reinforce Pat immediately after Pat had completed each group of problems. Within a short time, Pat was completing his problems and had doubled his production and earned a day without homework.

When attempting to establish a new behavior or to increase the frequency of an existing behavior, we must reinforce that behavior as soon as it occurs.

Principle 3: During the Initial Stages of the Behavior Change Process, the Target Behavior Is Reinforced Each Time It Is Exhibited

If newly acquired behavior is to be sustained at the appropriate frequency, the reinforcer must be administered each time the behavior is exhibited. Frequently, beginning behavior managers reinforce new but not yet habituated behaviors with such inconsistency and so infrequently that the child becomes confused and the target behavior does not become an established part of the child's behavioral repertoire.

■ Examples

Ms. Traber worked several months with Matt, gradually shaping his behavior through rewarding approximations of a desired behavior (in this case, a complete sentence). Finally, after 6 months, Matt said a complete sentence: "I want a candy." Matt was immediately rewarded with a candy, and for the next several weeks he consumed many candies; he was given many opportunities to receive the reward. In addition, during this phase of the behavior change process, Matt increased his variety of complete sentences to include "I want a glass of milk," "I want some juice," "I want some soda," "I want a puzzle," and the like.

Russell never requested any materials or assistance in the junior high school classroom without whining, screaming, or both. He would yell, "I want my paper" or "Give me some help." Mr. Hicks had taken about as much of this behavior as he could tolerate. He decided to ignore all whining and screaming from Russell. Russell's initial reaction to being ignored dramatically increased his inappropriate behavior, but Mr. Hicks stuck to the plan.

After 2 weeks of mutual frustration, Russell raised his hand one day during social studies. He politely requested Mr. Hicks's assistance. He immediately received the assistance, verbal praise, and a pat on the back. Mr. Hicks was very pleased with Russell (and himself). A mutual admiration society developed and continued.

Mr. Hicks then focused his attention on the problem of another student in the class. As a result, Mr. Hicks became an inconsistent reinforcer, and Russell began whining and screaming anew.

Mr. Hicks forgot that Russell's inappropriate behavior had been learned over 12 or 13 years and could not be changed overnight or after only a few successes.

A newly acquired, unconditioned, or not fully habituated behavior cannot be sustained if it is not reinforced each time it occurs. Consistent reinforcement during the initial stages of the behavior change process is essential.

Principle 4: When the Target Behavior Reaches a Satisfactory Level, It Is Reinforced Intermittently

Although this principle may appear to be a contradiction of Principle 3, it is not. The behavior manager must be consistent in the application of inconsistent (intermittent) reinforcement *after* the target behavior is established at a satisfactory level. This practice appears to be the way in which a newly acquired behavior can be firmly established and become self-sustaining.

Once a target behavior has been established at a satisfactory level, the presentation of the reinforcer is changed from continuous to intermittent. This change in the reinforcer presentation increases the probability that the behavior will be maintained at a satisfactory level. It appears that if the student whose behavior is being changed does not know exactly when the reinforcer will be given but does know that reinforcement will occur, the target behavior will continue to be exhibited at a satisfactory level. Intermittent reinforcement of behavior is sometimes referred to as **fading or thinning** the reinforcement schedule and is successful in maintaining behaviors (Rasmussen, 2006).

■ *Examples*

Ms. Williams wished to increase Phil's frequency of voluntary responses during current event discussions. In this situation, poker chips were used as a reinforcer. The chips could be saved and cashed in at the end of the discussion period for a specific event (e.g., having lunch with a favorite teaching assistant, being first in the lunch line).

Initially, Ms. Williams reinforced Phil each time he volunteered a response during the discussion. After several weeks, Phil's frequency of responses was at a satisfactory level—that is, it was equal or nearly equal to the average frequency of responses of the other members of the discussion groups. At this point in the behavior management process, Ms. Williams changed from giving continuous reinforcement to giving intermittent reinforcement.

With intermittent reinforcement, Phil's behavior remained at a high level. Phil became aware that he would be rewarded when he responded, although not every time. It also became evident to Ms. Williams that Phil was enjoying his participation in class discussions.

Mr. Jones and Ms. Walker had similar problems in their classroom groups. In Mr. Jones's room, Jared would not participate in class discussions. In Ms. Walker's room, Herman presented the same problem.

Mr. Jones wished to increase the frequency of Jared's responses during group discussions. He introduced an intervention similar to the one used by Ms. Williams in the previous example. However, once Jared had attained an acceptable level of performance, Mr. Jones discontinued all reinforcement. Because of the lack of reinforcement, Jared's newly acquired behavior decreased.

Ms. Walker also initiated an intervention program to increase Herman's level of participation. Ms. Walker kept Herman on the continuous reinforcement schedule until he became bored with the tokens and the tangible rewards he could purchase with them. Like Mr. Jones's program, Ms. Walker's was ineffective. Herman's participation decreased to its original level. He remained an infrequent participant in group discussions.

The reinforcement schedules most commonly applied in formal behavior management intervention are discussed later in this chapter.

Principle 5: If Tangible Reinforcers Are Applied, Social Reinforcers Are Always Applied with Them

All reinforcement, even during the initial phases of the behavior change process, must include the presentation of social and tangible reinforcers simultaneously if a tangible reinforcer is used. The purpose of the behavior change process is to help the student perform the target behavior not for a tangible reward but for the satisfaction of personal achievement. As discussed in Chapter 2, the goal of all behavior management is self-control or self-discipline.

If tangible reinforcers, such as tokens, chips, candy, stars, smiling faces, or checks, are presented, they must always be accompanied by a social reward, such as a smile, a pat on the back, praise, or a wink. In this way, the child associates the social reinforcer with the tangible reinforcer. As the behavior change process progresses, the tangible reinforcer is extinguished (phased out), and the target behavior is maintained by social reinforcers alone. If the change process is effective, behavior is maintained by self-satisfaction, occasional unplanned social reinforcers, and delayed tangible rewards.

■ *Examples*

When Ms. Williams was initially attempting to increase Phil's discussion group participation (see example in previous section), she provided Phil with verbal praise and a token each time he exhibited the desired behavior. However, when Phil was placed on an intermittent schedule, Ms. Williams continued to provide consistent social reinforcement but only occasional token reinforcement. During the final phase of the behavior change process, Phil was provided only intermittent social reinforcement to maintain the desired behavior.

Mr. Whiteface wanted to increase George's hand-raising behavior. A grape was given to George every time he raised his hand. The reward was delivered by a dispenser affixed to George's desk. When George raised his hand, Mr. Whiteface would push a button to activate the dispenser and release a grape.

In this way, Mr. Whiteface rewarded George consistently. In addition, he gave George social reinforcers for the new behavior. He would say "That was very good, George," "I like the way you are raising your hand, George," or "Fine," "Great," "Good."

After 6 months on the program, George functioned with intermittent social reinforcement only. The dispensing of grapes had been terminated, and George's hand-raising behavior remained at a high rate.

Practitioners are cautioned to apply this important principle when using reinforcers: Always *apply tangible and social reinforcers simultaneously if tangible reinforcers are used.*

CONSEQUENCES OF BEHAVIOR

Behavioral **consequences** (results) have a direct influence on the behavior a child exhibits. Behavior can be modified—that is, increased, initiated, or extinguished—by systematic manipulation of its consequences. The possible consequences of human behavior are classified as positive reinforcement, extinction, negative reinforcement, and punishment.

Table 3.1 contains several examples of (a) classification of the consequence, (b) appropriate and inappropriate behavior, (c) the consequence of that behavior (not necessarily a planned intervention), and (d) the probable effect of the consequence on the behavior in the future.

TABLE 3.1   Behavior: Consequence, probable effect, and classification

Classification	Original Behavior Exhibited	Consequence	Probable Effect on the Original Behavior in the Future
Positive reinforcement	Jane cleans her room.	Jane's parents praise her.	Jane will continue to clean her room.
Positive reinforcement	Shirley brushes her teeth after meals.	Shirley receives a nickel each time.	Shirley will continue to brush her teeth after meals.
Extinction	Jim washes his father's car.	Jim's car-washing behavior is ignored.	Jim will stop washing his father's car.
Positive reinforcement	Alton works quietly at his seat.	The teacher praises and rewards Alton.	Alton will continue to work quietly at his seat.
Reprimand	Gwenn sits on the arm of the chair.	Gwenn is reprimanded each time she sits on the arm of the chair.	Gwenn will not sit on the arm of the chair.
Negative reinforcement	Bob complains that older boys consistently beat him up, and he refuses to attend school.	Bob's parents allow him to remain at home because of his complaints.	Bob will continue to miss school.
Punishment	Elmer puts Elsie's pigtails in the paint box.	The teacher takes away Elmer's recess.	Elmer will not put Elsie's pigtails in the paint box.
Extinction	Shirley scolds Joe.	Joe ignores Shirley's scolding.	Shirley will stop scolding Joe.
Negative reinforcement	Jason complains of headaches when it is time to do homework.	Jason is allowed to go to bed without doing his homework.	Jason will have headaches whenever there is homework to do.

Positive Reinforcement

Positive reinforcement is the presentation of a desirable reinforcer after a behavior has been exhibited. The reinforcer, or consequences of behavior, tends to increase or sustain the frequency or duration with which the behavior is exhibited in the future (Alberto & Troutman, 2002). Everyone receives positive reinforcement throughout each day. The process of positive reinforcement involves increasing the probability of a behavior recurring by reinforcing it with something appropriate and meaningful to the individual (Downing et al., 1991). A reinforcer is reinforcing only if it is perceived as reinforcing by the individual.

■ *Examples*

Kevin has received a superior report card and is praised by his parents and brother. As a result of the positive reinforcer (praise), the probability of Kevin's continuing to study hard and receive superior report cards in the future is increased. If Kevin's report card were ignored or severely criticized because of a single poor grade, the probability of his continuing his efforts and receiving superior report cards in the future would be decreased.

Ms. Pompey has identified stars as positive reinforcers with her classroom group. She puts a star on Cynthia's paper because Cynthia has successfully completed her homework assignment. Cynthia enjoys receiving stars. By placing a star on Cynthia's paper, Ms. Pompey knows she is increasing the probability of Cynthia's completing her homework assignments in the future.

Extinction

Extinction is the removal of a reinforcer that is sustaining or increasing a behavior (Alberto & Troutman, 2002). It is an effective method for decreasing undesirable behaviors exhibited by individuals (Downing et al., 1990). Unplanned and unsystematically applied extinction techniques have been applied naturally throughout history. For example, parents tend to ignore many unacceptable behaviors exhibited by children, such as roughhousing, arguing, and showing reluctance to go to bed, in the hope that these behaviors will decrease in frequency. The ineffectiveness of ignoring as an unplanned intervention is frequently a result of the inconsistency of its application rather than its inadequacy as a behavior change technique. For example, we insist that there be no roughhousing or arguing and that the child be in bed at the designated time one day but do not insist on these rules the next day. The inconsistency on our part, as a teacher or parent, tends to confuse children and reinforce the unacceptable behavior.

Extinction involves the removal or withdrawal of the reinforcer responsible for maintaining behavior. In the classroom setting, the target behavior will be extinguished once the reinforcer has been withdrawn for a sufficient period of time.

■ *Examples*

John, a ninth-grader, was always making funny sounds with his mouth in Mrs. Rawlin's class. These activities got him a lot of attention not only from his peers but also from Mrs. Rawlin. She usually stopped the class and told John how immature he was behaving for his age and that he was making a fool of himself. The class responded with laughter. John laughed the loudest. After several meetings with the school counselor about John's classroom behavior, Mrs. Rawlin agreed to implement another approach.

Eight-year-old Robin was constantly tattling on every child who committed the slightest transgression within his purview. Robin's teacher, Ms. Fye, was reinforcing Robin's behavior by responding and attending to him when he tattled on others. Finally, Ms. Fye planned an intervention program employing extinction to decrease Robin's behavior; she would ignore all his tattling.

Each time Robin approached her to tattle on a classmate, Ms. Fye did one of the following:

1. She intervened before Robin had an opportunity to tattle and focused his attention on another topic (picture, book, and so on).
2. She turned her back on Robin and attended to another child who was performing appropriately.
3. She turned her back on Robin and walked away without any sign of recognition.

During the initial phase of the behavior change process, Robin's tattling increased for a brief period. Robin appears to be learning appropriate ways of gaining attention and acceptance.

During the extinction process, two behavior response phases occur. During the initial phase, immediately after the reinforcer sustaining the behavior has been removed,

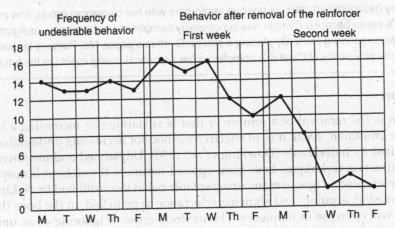

FIGURE 3.1 Frequency of Robin's tattling behavior a week before the removal of the reinforcer and 2 weeks afterward

the target behavior usually increases or decreases dramatically. During the second phase, the target behavior changes systematically (McSweeney & Swindell, 2002).

The response during the initial phase is a natural one that occurs when an individual is suddenly confronted with a situation in which established methods of gaining goals become nonfunctional. It is natural to become confused under such conditions and to continue to try the previously effective method of attaining a goal.

It is during this initial phase that beginning practitioners frequently throw up their hands in frustration and abandon a project. However, if they persist, the behavior will in all probability end.

Robin's rate of tattling before and during the extinction process is presented in Figure 3.1. The reader should note that Robin's tattling behavior increased on the first 3 days of extinction, then decreased dramatically during the next 7 days.

The teacher or parent should be patient and consistent; the behavior will change.

Negative Reinforcement

Negative reinforcement is the removal of an already operating aversive stimulus (negative reinforcer). As a consequence of the removal of the aversive stimulus, the target behavior is strengthened. Several examples of this process are presented in this section and in Tables 3.1 and 3.2. For example, removing the requirement to work separately from the group when the student works steadily for a period of time can increase the student's ability to remain with the group (Gardner, Wacker, & Boelter, 2009).

TABLE 3.2   Effects of consequences

	Positive Reinforcer	Aversive Stimulus
Add	Positive reinforcement (behavior increases)	Punishment (behavior decreases)
Remove	Extinction (behavior decreases)	Negative reinforcement (behavior increases or decreases)

As stated, negative reinforcement is the removal of an aversive stimulus in an effort to change the frequency of a behavior. In contrast, punishment is the addition of an aversive stimulus or the subtraction (taking away) of a pleasurable item or activity in an effort to change the frequency of a behavior.

■ *Example*

A group of students at their desks is working very diligently after the teacher has stated that they will not be required to do homework assignments that weekend if their classroom assignments are completed before the end of the day.

In this example, the homework assignment, which was already given by the teacher, is the aversive stimulus (most students perceive homework as aversive). It is removed, and as a result the students' in-classroom work is increased.

The following example is provided to offer additional clarification of negative reinforcement.

■ *Example*

Mr. and Mrs. Reynolds have a 2-year-old daughter, Alice, who wakes up crying (aversive stimulus) in the middle of the night. She wants to sleep with Mommy and Daddy. In an effort to get their sleep and stop Alice from crying, the parents permit her to sleep with them (thus removing the aversive stimulus of crying). By allowing Alice to sleep in their bed, the parents are increasing both their and Alice's sleeping behavior.

However, the parents' method of stopping Alice's crying (allowing Alice to sleep with them) actually reinforces the frequency of the crying.

Cipani (1995) suggests that some empirical research links inappropriate behaviors during instructional tasks with factors other than teacher attention. Research has found that inappropriate behavior may be maintained because of its effect on the lesson or assignment.

■ *Example*

Mrs. McGinnis has given Marylou a spelling assignment. Marylou has a reading problem. For her, the assignment is very aversive. She hates spelling. She has tried over and over to learn her spelling words, without success. Immediately after being given the assignment, Marylou becomes restless and goes off task. She begins to tap her pencil on the desk, hum loudly, and tap her foot.

Mrs. McGinnis becomes distracted by Marylou's inappropriate behavior and reprimands her. Marylou answers the teacher back and as a consequence is sent to the back of the classroom to sit in the "think about your behavior" chair. She leaves her spelling on her desk.

In this example, spelling is an aversive or a negative reinforcer for Marylou. It is interfering with her appropriate classroom behavior.

Cipani (1995) suggests three questions that teachers should ask to diagnose whether negative reinforcement is a factor in maintaining inappropriate behavior:

- Does the inappropriate behavior serve to stop instruction or the completion of an assignment?
- Does the learner have the skill and ability to complete the assignment task?
- Does the frequency of inappropriate behavior increase when specific instructional conditions are present?

Finally, Cipani (1995) suggests that to remediate behavior problems caused by negative reinforcement, the teacher must either (a) provide the student with a strong incentive to engage in the aversive task or (b) develop the student's level of competency in the task to a point at which the task becomes less aversive.

Punishment

Punishment, a group of behavioral reduction procedures, appears to be the most frequently used of the behavior change techniques. The behavior reduction procedures include (from the least to the most intrusive and restrictive) differential reinforcement, extinction, verbal aversives, response cost, time-out, overcorrection, and physical aversives (Kerr & Nelson, 2002). Each of these procedures is presented in detail in Chapter 6.

Although it is frequently used with children, punishment is perhaps the least effective of the behavior management interventions discussed in this text. Those using punishment have been reinforced by its immediate result; however, it has been determined that the long-term effects of punishment are limited. McDaniel (1980) points out that punishment tends to suppress the undesirable behavior rather than extinguish it. This suppression is of short duration, and frequently the behavior recurs in the absence of the punisher.

Punishment is viewed by the behavior management practitioner as two distinct operations. Punishment is accomplished by the *addition* of an aversive stimulus to the environment. Examples are paddling, electric shock, additional homework, and the like. Punishment may also be seen as the *subtraction* (taking away) of a pleasurable item or activity. Examples include loss of extracurricular activities, recess, and the like. Punishment is not to be confused with extinction (see "Extinction").

It can be stated that *some punishments will remove some unacceptable behaviors* (Shea, Bauer, & Lynch, 1989). It has been found, however, that when a punished behavior recurs, it usually does so at a rate higher than before the punishment was originally imposed. Another concern associated with punishment is its potential and actual effect on the physical and emotional health of the child. In some cases, punishment may cause emotional problems. The fact that the punished child identifies the punishment with the punisher rather than with the inappropriate behavior should be of great concern to teachers and parents who, as previously discussed, are models for children. Children who are punished or abused often punish or abuse their children. The results of punishment do not appear sufficient to justify its use as a behavior change agent.

Effects of Consequences

A thorough understanding of the relationships among the four basic consequences of behavior is a primary requisite for the effective application of behavior management principles and techniques.

In general, positive reinforcement increases the target behavior; punishment and extinction decrease the target behavior. Negative reinforcement *may increase or decrease behavior*, depending on the particular target behavior (see Table 3.2).

Generalization, Transfer, and Fading Supports

Generalization, or the transfer of learning, is the process by which a behavior reinforced in one situation will be exhibited in another situation. The generalization process is an essential element of learning. If generalization did not occur, each response would have to be learned in every situation. For example, writing a paragraph in response to a question in social studies class would have to be taught even though the student is able to write a paragraph in response to a science question. One aspect of generalization is the need to discriminate the behavior or event that cues the behavior.

■ *Examples*

A young child learns the name of an animal (dog). He calls a specific dog "dog" and will soon generalize the name "dog" to all four-legged animals within the classification. He will at times label other four-legged animals, such as cats, cows, and crawling brothers and sisters, with the name "dog."

A toddler is reinforced for calling her father "Daddy." She will generalize and call all male figures "Daddy" at an early stage of her development. She may call the letter carrier, an uncle, or others "Daddy." This may result in considerable stress between husband and wife.

If we wish to function successfully in the environment, we must apply the concepts learned in one situation to many and varied situations. For example, as young children we learn honesty, respect for authority, and the basic principles of computation. It is hoped that each year we can generalize this learning to the completion of our income tax returns.

Stokes and Osnes (1989) make several suggestions for teaching students to generalize. They use natural contingencies (i.e., contingencies that commonly occur in the environment as a consequence of a behavior). In addition, training more exemplars may help students to generalize. Reinforcing generalization and self-reports of the target behavior assist in generalization. It is important to remember that just because a student behaves in a desired way in one situation does not mean that generalization of that behavior to other settings has occurred. At least initially, generalization should be programmed consistent with the principles of learning and reinforcement.

Gable and Hendrickson (2003) indicate that strategies for the maintenance and generalization of positive behaviors are an integral part of the functional behavioral assessment and intervention planning process. To increase the usefulness of functional behavioral assessment, it is necessary to broaden its scope to include not only the development of positive and productive behavior but also the facilitation of that behavior by the student over time. They suggest that the complex process of generalization includes both maintenance and generalization.

Maintenance is in place when the behavior occurs over time, after the withdrawal of the intervention. Generalization, on the other hand, is in place when the behavior occurs in a variety of settings. Gable and Hendrickson (2003) suggest that maintenance and management can occur through (a) self-management training, (b) cognitive medication training, (c) self-advocacy training, (d) peer-mediated supports, (e) environmental modifications, (f) periodic booster training, (g) and attributional remediation.

Discrimination

Discrimination is another essential learned behavior. Through discrimination, we learn that we act one way in one situation and another way in a different situation (Axelrod & Hall, 1999). If it were not for the process of discrimination, we would generalize behaviors to a variety of situations in which they would be inappropriate.

■ *Example*

We behave differently in church than we do at a cocktail party (most of us) and differently in class than we do at a football game (although some classes are stimulating and some football games boring). Our behaviors in these situations are reinforced by the rewards we receive.

Discrimination is the result of **differential reinforcement**. Reinforcing a behavior in the presence of one stimulus and not reinforcing it in the presence of another stimulus is differential reinforcement. (Differential reinforcement is discussed in detail in Chapter 6.)

■ *Example*

Teaching a young child to discriminate between the words *cat* and *rat* may be accomplished by listening and reacting to the child's responses. The child is reinforced for the appropriate response only. In this way, the child discriminates between the words *rat* and *cat* when they are presented in the future.

SCHEDULES OF REINFORCEMENT

A **schedule of reinforcement** is the pattern with which the reinforcer is presented in response to the exhibition of the target behavior (Rusch, Rose, & Greenwood, 1988). The schedule of reinforcement that is applied has a significant effect on the behavior change process. The most common types of reinforcement schedules are continuous, fixed ratio, variable ratio, fixed interval, and variable interval.

Continuous Schedules

The **continuous schedule** of reinforcement requires the presentation of the reinforcer immediately after each occurrence of the target behavior (Cooper, Heron, & Heward, 1987). The continuous schedule is most often applied during the initial stage of a behavior change program (Downing, 1990). Frequently, its use will change the behavior rapidly in the desired direction. It is not recommended for long-term use, however, because individuals tend to satiate on this schedule, and initial behavior change gains may be lost. In addition, it presents a very unrealistic and artificial procedure for classroom application.

■ *Examples*

Ms. Bantle wished to increase Deanna's hand-raising behavior during history. To do this, she decided, at least initially, to reinforce Deanna each time she raised her hand. Application of this continuous schedule rapidly increased the target behavior to an acceptable level.

Mr. McCloud was disturbed by Bobby's out-of-seat behavior. He planned an intervention to increase Bobby's in-seat behavior. During the initial intervention, he reinforced Bobby's in-seat behavior each time it occurred. This continuous schedule quickly increased Bobby's in-seat behavior.

Fixed and Variable Schedules

The primary distinctions among fixed and variable (intermittent) ratio and interval schedules are related to the timing and frequency with which the reinforcer is presented. The ratio schedules, fixed and variable, focus on the *completion of specific tasks* before the reinforcer is presented to the child. Reinforcer presentation on the interval schedules, fixed and variable, depends on the exhibition of specific behaviors for *definite periods of time* (Downing, 1990).

Table 3.3 summarizes the schedules discussed in the following sections.

FIXED RATIO SCHEDULES. When a **fixed ratio schedule** is applied, the reinforcer is presented after a specific number of appropriate responses are exhibited by the child.

■ *Examples*

Every time John answers 15 social studies questions correctly, he is given 10 minutes to read a comic book. John's reward (comic book reading) is based on his successful completion of a fixed number (15) of social studies questions.

Every time Sheila reads 5 brief passages in her reading workbook with 80% accuracy, she is allowed to listen to her favorite record album for 5 minutes. In this case, Sheila is on a fixed ratio schedule.

TABLE 3.3 Relationships among the common reinforcement schedules

	Ratio	Interval
Fixed	Child completes 20 problems to receive 10 minutes of free time.	Child is rewarded for remaining in seat for 5 minutes.
Variable	Teacher rewards child, on an average, every third time child raises hand.	Teacher gives child individual attention, on average, every 15 minutes in response to acceptable behavior during the time period.

The fixed ratio schedule usually results in a high rate of response. Consequently, it is most effectively and appropriately applied during the beginning phase of the behavior change process.

VARIABLE RATIO SCHEDULES.   The *variable ratio schedule* is designed to sustain the level of response to reinforcement once the acceptable level of behavior has been attained by means of a continuous or fixed ratio schedule. When the variable ratio schedule is applied, the ratio of the reinforcer presentation varies around a response mean or average. This variability is instrumental in sustaining the appropriate level of response.

■ *Examples*

Mr. Davis has Kerry raising his hand and participating in class discussions. He accomplished this using a fixed ratio schedule. He now wishes to change to a variable ratio schedule. Kerry is placed on a variable ratio schedule of 5 (the reinforcer is presented around a response mean of 5). Kerry may be reinforced the seventh time he raises his hand, the sixth time, the third, the fourth, or the fifth. If this schedule (7, 6, 3, 4, and 5) is averaged, the response mean or variable ratio is 5. The fact that Kerry does not know when Mr. David will call on him to respond (but does know that he will be called on) motivates Kerry to maintain his hand-raising behavior at a high level.

Slot machines (in our experience) operate on a variable ratio schedule. The gambler puts quarters in the slot and is occasionally reinforced with small rewards. This occasional reinforcement keeps the person playing until he or she is broke, but the loser always has the hope that the next pull of the arm will result in the super jackpot.

Inexperienced practitioners are cautioned not to change too early in the behavior change process from a continuous or fixed ratio to a variable ratio schedule. The desired behavior must be adequately established on a fixed ratio schedule before it can be changed to a variable ratio schedule. Many behavior change programs have failed as a result of the practitioner's impatience in making this transition.

FIXED INTERVAL SCHEDULES.   On the **fixed interval schedule**, a specified period of time must elapse before the reinforcer is presented. The reinforcer is presented immediately *after the first response* beyond the specified time period. The following examples should clarify any potential confusion.

■ *Examples*

Debbie does not remain in her seat during language lessons. Mr. Quick has decided to reinforce Debbie on a fixed interval schedule of 10 minutes. Thus, Debbie is rewarded immediately after as well as every time she remains in her seat for 10 minutes during language lessons.

Most people work on a fixed interval (1 week, 2 weeks, or 1 month) pay schedule. They receive their paychecks after the pay period has elapsed.

With fixed interval schedules, the longer the time interval between reinforcements, the lower will be the level of performance. This would suggest that initially during an intervention, reinforcers should be presented at frequent intervals.

VARIABLE INTERVAL SCHEDULES.　　The **variable interval schedule** is similar to the variable ratio schedule. However, the presentation of the reinforcer is based on a behavioral response mean or average. The individual whose behavior is being changed is not aware of when reinforcement will occur. However, the individual does know that he or she will be reinforced for exhibiting a certain behavior.

■ *Example*

Mr. Quick has decided to place Debbie on a variable interval schedule of 10. On this schedule, Debbie will continue to be reinforced for in-seat behavior. She may be reinforced the first time after only 9 minutes of appropriate behavior, the second time after 4 minutes, the third time after 9 minutes, the fourth time after 15 minutes, and the fifth time after 13 minutes. This is a reinforcement schedule of 9, 4, 9, 15, and 13. It is based on a variable interval with a mean or average of 10 minutes.

Again, the behavior manager should be cautious when changing from fixed ratio or fixed interval to variable ratio or variable interval schedules. If this is done too early or too late in the behavior change process, the newly acquired behavior may be extinguished.

The specific schedule to be applied varies with the behavior being changed. For example, if the concern is to keep an individual in his or her seat for a period of time, an interval schedule would be the most appropriate. However, if the behavior is related to the completion of specific numbers or kinds of tasks, a ratio schedule should be applied. The selection and application of the appropriate schedule is part of the art of behavior management. Knowing when and how to apply a specific schedule of reinforcement becomes less confusing with experience.

The use of reinforcement schedules is consistent with fading supports. As the student demonstrates the behavior, reinforcement, or supports become less frequent. This fading of supports is also described as thinning, and is useful in both fixed and variable schedules (Hanley, Iwata, & Thompson, 2001; Roane, Fisher, Sgro, Falcomata, & Pabico, 2004).

Summary Points

- Tangible (primary) reinforcers include food, beverages, and tokens; social (or secondary) reinforcers include praise, games, and smiles.
- Reinforcement should only be given after the target behavior occurs.
- To be effective, reinforcement should occur immediately after the desired behavior.
- When you have just begun a behavior management program, you should reinforce a behavior every time it occurs.
- Once the behavior reaches a satisfactory level, it should be reinforced intermittently.

- Whenever you apply a tangible reinforcer, you must apply a social reinforcer concurrently.
- In positive behavior, a desired event occurs immediately following the behavior.
- In extinction, the reinforcer that is maintaining the behavior is removed.
- In negative reinforcement, a probable or potential adverse situation is removed so the desired behavior occurs.
- Punishment is the least effective behavior management strategy. In punishment, an averse event occurs immediately following the inappropriate behavior.

- Generalization is the transfer of learning.
- Discrimination is the skill through which an individual acts one way in one situation and another way in a different situation.

- Various schedules of reinforcement should be applied during specific stages of behavior management. These schedules may be described as fading or thinning reinforcement.

Projects

1. Make a study sheet that differentiates the five basic principles of reinforcement.
2. Observe a classroom. What principles of behavior management do you see applied? What is the most frequent? Least frequent? Why do you think this occurred?
3. From your own experience, provide examples of generalization and discrimination.

Web Resources

For more information about monitoring behaviors, visit this site:
challengingbehavior.fmhi.usf.edu/monitoring.htm#gen

For more information about negative reinforcement (a confusing concept), visit this site:
www.mcli.dist.maricopa.edu/proj/nru/nr.html

For more information about the behavior change process, visit this site:
www.pacer.org/parent/function.htm

References

Alberto, P. A., & Troutman, A. C. (2002). *Applied behavior analysis for teachers* (3rd ed.). Upper Saddle River, NJ: Merrill/Pearson.

Axelrod, S., & Hall, R. V. (1999) *Behavior modification: Basic principles*. Austin, TX: Pro-Ed.

Cipani, E. O. (1995). Be aware of negative reinforcement. *Teaching Exceptional Children, 27*(4), 36–40.

Cooper, J. O., Heron, T. E., & Heward, W. L. (1987). *Applied behavior analysis*. Upper Saddle River, NJ: Merrill/Pearson.

Downing, J. A. (1990). Contingency contracts: A step-by-step format. *Intervention in School and Clinic, 26*(2), 111–113.

Downing, J. A., Moran, M. R., Myles, B. S., & Ormsbee, C. K. (1991). Using reinforcement in the classroom. *Intervention in School and Clinic, 27*(2), 85–90.

Gable, R. A., & Hendrickson, J. M. (2003). Strategies for maintaining positive behavior change stemming from functional behavioral assessment in schools. *Education and Treatment of Children, 23*(3), 286–297.

Gardner, A. W., Wacker, D. P., & Boelter, E. R. (2009). An evaluation of the interaction between quality of attention and negative reinforcement with children who display escape-maintained problem behavior. *Journal of Applied Behavior Analysis, 42*(2), 343–349.

Hanley, G. P., Iwata, B. A., & Thompson, R. H. (2001). Reinforcement schedule thinning following treatment with functional communication training. *Journal of Applied Behavior Analysis, 34*(1), 17–38.

Kerr, M. M., & Nelson, C. M. (2002). *Strategies for managing problem behaviors in the classroom* (4th ed.). Upper Saddle River, NJ: Merrill/Pearson.

McDaniel, T. (1980). Corporal punishment and teacher liability: Questions teachers ask. *The Clearing House, 54*(1), 10–13.

McSweeney, F. K., & Swindell, S. (2002). Common processes may contribute to extinction and habituation. *Journal of General Psychology, 129*(4), 364–400.

Rasmussen, K. (2006). The effects of fixed-time reinforcement schedules on problem behavior of children with emotional and behavioral disorders in a day treatment classroom. *Journal of Applied Behavioral Analysis, 39*(4), 453–357.

Roane, H. S., Fisher, W. W., Sgro, G. M., Falcomata, T. S., & Pabico, R. R. (2004). An alternative method of thinning reinforcer delivery during differential reinforcement. *Journal of Applied Behavior Analysis, 37*(2), 213.

Rusch, F. R., Rose, T., & Greenwood, C. R. (1988). *Introduction to behavior analysis in special education.* Upper Saddle River, NJ: Prentice Hall.

Shea, T. M., & Bauer, A. M. (1987). *Teaching children and youth with behavior disorders.* Upper Saddle River, NJ: Merrill/Pearson.

Shea, T. M., Bauer, A. M., & Lynch, E. M. (1989, September). *Changing behavior: Ethical issues regarding behavior management and the control of students with behavioral disorders.* Paper presented at the CEC/CCBD conference, "Find the answer for a decade ahead," Charlotte, NC.

Stokes, T. F., & Osnes, P. G. (1989). An operant pursuit of generalization. *Behavior Therapy, 20,* 337–355.

CHAPTER OBJECTIVES

After completing this chapter, you will be able to do the following:

1. Define Response to Intervention (RTI) and its purposes.
2. Explain the underlying assumptions of RTI.
3. Describe the roles of the participants in RTI.
4. Describe aspects of culturally responsive practice.

Response to Intervention

KEY TERMS

Curriculum-based measurement (CBM)

Collaboration

Planning framework

Progress monitoring

Research or scientifically based practices

Response to Intervention (RTI)

Student support team

Tiers of scientifically based intervention

Ms. Lewis, a third-grade teacher, was as frustrated with Ian's writing as Ian was with his writing. Ian was a good reader and could tell elaborate stories. Yet when he sat down with his journal to write sentences containing newly introduced science words, he would leave his seat, sharpen his pencil, or ask to go to the restroom. When cajoled he would write a simplistic sentence that seemed to run all over the page.

In her effort to support Ian, Ms. Lewis brought his case to the Student Support Team. She was convinced that he had a learning disability and needed special help. The team, however, suggested three interventions that research had demonstrated to be successful in cases like Ian's. Ms. Lewis thought that one of these interventions, using a voice-activated writing program, might motivate Ian to truly express himself. A week after teaching Ian to use the program, Ms. Lewis noted that his behavior was changing. His journal entries and sentences were more complex and on subject. Ian was far more motivated to try to put words on paper, and began to attempt to use the word processor. It occurred to Ms. Lewis that not only did Ian not have a learning disability requiring extra help but that he was one of her best writers when the need to hold a pencil was eliminated.

What could have been the outcome of Ian's immediate referral for special education evaluation? What may have been the effects of being labeled as having a learning disability when non-special education accommodations were made available?

Ms. Erickson, the principal of Equality Middle School, was concerned about the wide range of reading skills demonstrated by fifth-graders entering Equality each August. She and the language arts faculty were concerned that students quickly became labeled as "the stupids" if they were less fluent than their peers. The majority of the students who were less fluent came from a primary school in a lower socioeconomic, culturally diverse area of the community. Avoiding the stigma of being poor and not being able to read well was an essential part of the faculty's plan to increase the sense of community among all the students and faculty in Equality Middle School.

Ms. Erickson worked with the principals of the feeder schools to administer a reading screening instrument prior to the end of their students' fourth-grade year. The screening results were to be forwarded to Equality. Students identified as needing significant help were invited to attend a 2-week "Skills Academy" at Equality prior to the beginning of the school year. During the academy, they were instructed in reading strategies and provided a "student sponsor" from the sixth-grade class. The sponsor was to meet weekly with his or her student and provide any tutoring in reading and other subjects, as needed.

After implementing the program, Ms. Erickson was able to concentrate further reading tutorial services to the students who were not successful or did not attend the Skills Academy or refused to or did not work with a sponsor. Ms. Erickson and the faculty found that the program provided a leveling experience for students entering the fifth grade and reduced referrals to the Student Support Team and Special Education.

> *What if Ms. Erickson had simply grouped all the poor readers together instead of using a screening instrument and the Skills Academy? What could have been the impact on the sense of community at Equality Middle School?*

WHAT IS RESPONSE TO INTERVENTION?

The Individuals with Disabilities Education Improvement Act presented an innovative alternative to the manner in which students were referred for evaluation for special education services. The reauthorization of IDEA mandated **Response to Intervention (RTI)**. RTI is described as a procedure to provide earlier help to students at risk for school failure (Fuchs, Mock, Morgan, & Young, 2003). In the 1980s schools implemented Student Support Teams to encourage problem solving among teachers and allied professionals when students were not achieving like their peers. The RTI procedures evolved from these support teams' efforts to work with at-risk students before they are identified as needing special education. In addition to this problem-solving background, RTI can trace its beginnings to "standardized protocols" (Vaughn, Wanzek, & Fletcher, 2007), which were used to provide interventions to prevent reading problems. These interventions follow a path to become more intense and differentiated depending on the student's response to the instruction.

RTI refers to a variety of multi-tiered service-delivery programs in which students receive layered interventions that begin in the general education classroom and become more intense depending on the students' instruction response (Fletcher & Vaughn, 2009).

Fuchs and associates (2003) describe these five actions for implementing RTI:

- Provide students with classroom instruction that is effective. If students are not receiving effective instruction, then such instruction must be implemented before focusing on the child as the source of the problem.
- Student learning is documented and monitored.

- Students who are not responding to the effective instruction that they and their peers are receiving are to be provided with "something more," either from their teacher or another person. Examples include an additional or alternative program, resource room, tutor, or small group instruction.
- Student learning is again documented and monitored related to this "something more."
- Students who are still not responding to these efforts are referred to special education.

■ *Example*

Joey attends fourth grade at a rural K–8 school. He began the school year with a teacher who only taught 3 weeks before becoming disabled and retiring. The principal scrambled to find a replacement teacher, but a series of substitutes flowed through the classroom. Finally in January, Mr. Mitchell, a new, well-prepared teacher arrived in the classroom. He began by assessing the students' skills and found them to have made very little progress since the beginning of the school year. Joey was especially challenged. He was very confused by the new teacher routines and expectations. Mr. Mitchell decided he would "start from scratch" and evaluate each student, even Joey, before referring any student for extra help or special services.

Mr. Mitchell found the students eager to learn and progressing quickly, but Joey continued to struggle in mathematics. The teacher collected samples of Joey's work and did a simple assessment by providing Joey problems showing different aspects of mathematics computation. Then he met with the **Student Support Team** to plan an effective program of instruction.

ASSUMPTIONS UNDERLYING RTI

The assumption underlying RTI is that if a student is not successful with the best support available and possible in a given instructional setting, then the student can and should be given additional assistance, which may include special education (Gresham, 2007). Gresham argues that what a student receives is changed after data demonstrate that the student is making inadequate RTI. In addition, decisions are made only after reviewing objective data and implementing data-based decision-making procedures. Data indicators should be based on indicators of desired behaviors, and the intensity of the intervention should be based on the collection of more and more data.

RTI is not a rigid model. Typically, it involves (a) tiers of specific research-based interventions, (b) screening and **progress monitoring** (ongoing assessment of student learning and behavior in response to instructional goals and objectives), and (c) decision points at which the student is evaluated for special education (Zirkel and Krohn, 2008). The 2006 IDEA Regulations (300.307[a]) require that states use RTI to identify students with learning disabilities. Beyond naming RTI, the regulations do not describe the process for implementation. Determining that students are eligible for services requires that the instructional strategies be specific to the student's needs and data collected on the student's performance. The student's parents are to be engaged in the RTI process.

The evaluation of students for eligibility for special education is discussed in Chapter 1. In this chapter, the aspects of RTI include tiers of intervention, research or scientifically based practices, screening and progress monitoring, collaboration, and culturally responsive practice.

Tiers of Scientifically Based Interventions

Tiers of scientifically based interventions emerged from the use of standard protocols. One of the assumptions of RTI is that at least three tiers of services are provided to students. The first tier, sometimes called primary intervention is high-quality, research-based instruction in the regular classroom. In addition, the first tier includes screening to find those students potentially in need of more help to succeed as well as progress monitoring of those students to ensure that they are learning. Bradley, Danielson, and Doolittle (2007) describe the following tiers as additional supports for students who are not responding to high quality classroom instruction. For example, a second tier, sometimes referred to as secondary intervention, may include 8 to 12 specific, research-based strategies to meet the student's learning needs. The last tier, referred to as tertiary intervention, includes individual services, such as those provided on special education. Information developed through the earlier tier services should provide the information useful to determining whether a student is eligible for special education.

These three tiers are applied to address both academic and behavioral problems. In Tier 1, the academic and behavior systems all address students through preventive, proactive programming. In the second tier, which addresses approximately 15% of the students in a classroom, highly efficient academic and behavioral interventions are implemented to evoke rapid change. The 5% of students who do not respond to Tier 2 interventions receive Tier 3 intensive, individual intervention, as well as high intensity assessment-based intervention over a longer time. The general characteristics of the three tiers are presented in Table 4.1.

TABLE 4.1   Characteristics of Response to Intervention tiers

Characteristic	Tier 1	Tier 2	Tier 3
Focus	All students	Students who aren't profiting from efforts for all students	Students who haven't responded to Tier 1 or Tier 2 efforts
Nature of prevention	Primary	Secondary	Tertiary
Percent of students service	@ 80%	@ 15%	@ 5%
Teacher role	Screening, effective instruction	Specific, small group, short term services	Individualized, longer services that may be delivered by another profession
Progress monitoring	Group comparisons	Small group comparisons	Individual data generated
Nature of programming	Scientifically based and evidence-based instruction for all students	Specialized scientifically based instruction focused on critical components	Intense, individually developed programs

Research or Scientifically Based Practices

The interventions provided in the tiers of services are research or scientifically based. The regulations for IDEA apply the definition of scientifically based research from the No Child Left Behind Act. It states that the research that documents these strategies be rigorous, be systematic, be objective, and provide reliable evidence. The definition maintains that the research should be peer reviewed and rely heavily on traditional research models. Classroom management programs are typically described as "evidence-based," which infers that they were (a) evaluated using experimental design and methodology, (b) demonstrated to be effective, and (c) supported by at least three studies published in peer refereed journals (Simonsen, Fairbanks, Briesch, Myers, & Sugai, 2008).

In terms of managing behavior, Simonsen and associates (2008) contend that there are five critical features of effective, evidence-based classroom management. These features include:

- maximize structure, with explicitly defined carefully arranged classroom space;
- post, teach, review, monitor, and reinforce expectations using active supervision;
- actively engage students in observable ways by increasing the rates of students' opportunities to respond, using classwide peer tutoring, or guided notes;
- using a continuum of strategies to acknowledge appropriate behavior, including specific praise, classwide contingencies, and contracts; and
- use a continuum of strategies to respond to inappropriate behavior, including error correction and feedback.

With these practices in place, most students' behavioral needs can be addressed in Tier 1, or the general education classroom.

■ *Example*

Ms. Shitake was concerned about several of the students in her fourth-grade classroom. An inordinate number of students seem to "drift off" during her social studies lessons. After talking with her professional learning community, Ms. Shitake decided to increase the opportunities for her students to respond. After presenting a segment of information, Ms. Shitake asked a series of multiple choice questions. The students responded by raising index cards that use A, B, or C to represent the answers. Ms. Shitake used students' responses as a basis for more discussion, at times having the students get up and move into groups to defend their answers. The increased opportunities not only gave her a way of engaging the students; it also provided Ms. Shitake with ongoing feedback on whether the students were understanding her presentation.

The Council for Exceptional Children (CEC, 2010) suggests that teachers often think of RTI at Tier 2 for academic issues only. However, small group activities have been successful in helping students increase their successful school behaviors. They suggest that specific instructions in social skills, self-management plans, self-talk, mentoring, and peer tutoring can address students' needs in the classroom. The CEC suggests that one of the most commonly used interventions at this level is check in/check out, in which students carry a point card to classes and accrue points for behavior.

■ *Example*

Several of the ninth-graders were having trouble adjusting to the larger school and using lockers for their possessions and materials. Mr. Hooha, the leader of the ninth-grade instructional team, met with a group of students who had come to the attention of the teachers as having consistent problems in bringing materials to class. He provided students with weekly check sheets that they would give to each teacher at the beginning of class, indicating that they had their materials for the class. Mr. Hooha then described incentives that would be in place, ranging from a free homework pass for a class to accumulating enough points for a school T-shirt. Students quickly responded, and the program was terminated after 6 weeks, with only periodic rewards for all students who brought materials to class.

Intensive individualized intervention plans are developed in Tier 3. At this point, students and teachers may become engaged in a functional behavioral assessment (Chapter 5). The results of this functional behavioral assessment are used to develop an individualized behavior plan (Chapter 6). In addition, further resources may be brought in to support the student. The Council for Exceptional Children (2010) emphasizes that just because students are receiving services at this level, they may or may not be identified with an emotional behavioral disorder. These interventions comprise much of the remainder of this text.

Screening and Progress Monitoring

Most school districts have a "kindergarten roundup," "welcome day," or "visiting day" during which simple assessments are administered to children who will be entering kindergarten. These simple assessments are actually a form of universal screening, or a way of providing some initial information about student needs. Generally, screenings such as these overidentify children as being at risk because of the speed in which the assessment is conducted and the novelty of the situation (Fletcher, Lyon, Fuchs, & Barnes, 2007). This screening is very helpful in identifying students who may need watching. This screening is an initial step in Tier 1 and is followed by progress monitoring.

To support students, it is necessary to know how they are learning. Daly, Glover, and McCurdy (2006) indicated that progress can be measured by the rate at which a student is learning as well as the accuracy of his or her work. They suggest that **curriculum-based measurement (CBM)** is the most common method of monitoring academic progress. CBM answers the question "Is the student learning what is being taught?" Teachers often give quizzes, tests, worksheets, or assignments as a way to measure what is being taught. For example, short term monitoring in the first grade can be used to identify students who may need additional support (Davis, Lindo, & Compton, 2007). Compton, Fuchs, Fuchs, and Bryant (2006) found that monitoring progress during the first weeks of the first grade is predictive of problems in the second grade.

■ *Examples*

During the first week of school Ms. Bodkin worked with the first-graders to follow the classroom routines. Once they were settled, she began working individually with the students, having them print their names, asking them personal information, and having them write letters as dictated. She also asked them to write any words they knew how to read and write. Jamaal, responding to the question, asked, "All of them? I know too many." Ms. Bodkin then asked him to write a story if he wanted. Jamaal responded with three paragraphs about his dog, with a clear beginning, middle, and end. It occurred to Ms. Bodkin that she had misread Jamaal; she had taken his wandering around the room and asking "What can I do now?" as not understanding the schedule. She now understood that he had been finishing everything far more quickly than the other students and that she needed to provide him with a different set of materials to address his skills.

Mr. Ness had been working on punctuation related to conversation in writing class. He taught a lesson and provided guided practice to the correct writing and punctuation in dialogue. He collected the students' paper for review. As he corrected the students' efforts, he sorted them according to errors. He concluded that he hadn't devoted sufficient time to the placement of commas "inside" quotation marks, in that it was the most common error on the students' papers. After reteaching the concept the following day, Mr. Ness showed a brief scene of dialogue from a popular film. He then directed his students to write additional conversation among the characters in the film to conclude their unfinished conversation. When Mr. Ness reviewed those papers, he noted a strong improvement in almost all students' use of commas.

Progress monitoring specific to behavior management is discussed in Chapter 6. On the whole, monitoring behavior is based on observation rather than permanent products.

Collaboration

RTI requires collaboration among general education teachers, special educators, administrators, and related service providers. Mahdavi and Beebe-Frankenberger (2009) emphasize the need for adequate time to work collaboratively as a team. They suggest that **collaboration** begins with working together as equal partners with shared vision, goals, and principles. To encourage collaboration, Stuart and Rinaldi (2009) urge the application of a **planning framework**. The framework begins with grade-level teams identifying a classwide view of the challenges in the classroom. In planning, teachers first consider how and where they can identify evidence-based intervention to support instruction. During the second stage, the grade-level team discusses the type of additional supports and the nature of differentiation needed delivered through small group instruction or more targeted efforts. The last phase, feedback, involves the evaluation of the effectiveness of the intervention. If progress is not being made, the team discusses whether the way in which the student's performance is being measured is appropriate, whether the intervention needs improvement, or whether a new intervention is needed.

Sawyer and Rimm-Kaufman (2007) conceptualize collaboration as a set of communication skills. They contend, however, that not all school environments encourage collaboration, and when discouraged, the cost to individual teachers who attempt to collaborate may be significant. In schools where collaboration is not valued, schedules are inflexible and do not allow time for meetings, and those meetings conducted during the school day may be perceived as taking time away from instruction. The physical structure of the school—long hallways, closed classroom and office doors, no real conference space—may act as a barrier to collaboration. Sawyer and Rimm-Kaufmann found that collaboration in schools is relatively rare and difficult to sustain.

When the vision is shared, however, collaboration is more likely to take place. Sawyer and Rimm-Kaufmann (2007) describe this vision as encouraging teachers to reflect on their practice to enhance each student's learning and each teacher's efforts. In the study, they found that teachers were more likely to collaborate three or four times a month regarding students' individual learning problems and needs for materials and discipline. Teachers were less likely to collaborate on their teaching methods, evaluation, and room organization. Teachers preferred to collaborate with other teachers in the same grades and felt that the principal's involvement formalized and placed controls on the collaboration. The most typical pattern was that teachers collaborated with fellow teachers about student-centered topics approximately once or twice per month.

■ *Example*

Ms. Miller was a new third-grade teacher. She felt that she had been given the class list of all the students that the other teachers had rejected. Ms. Nguyen, a third-grade colleague, walked past Ms. Miller's classroom and noted that Ms. Miller was yelling and taking away recess, which seemed to punish Ms. Miller as well as the students who were not responding to her. Ms. Nguyen invited Ms. Miller to identify the ringleaders and bring information about them to the Student Support Team. Ms. Miller, who had not student taught in a collaborative setting, declined, saying that she had been trained in classroom management and didn't need help. Because of her lack of experience in collaboration, Ms. Miller spent the year struggling with the class.

Culturally Responsive Practices

Schools, classrooms, and allied service agencies are supporting students who represent a wide range of diversity: social class, ethnicity, language, disability, religion, sexual orientation, and special education needs and any combination of these dimensions (Bartalo & Smyth, 2009). One of the first challenges confronting teachers is the need to overcome the deficit thinking that they may have from their personal experiences or lack of experience. Bartalo and Smith emphasize that each student should be seen as an individual and that his or her performance and behavior may vary based on societal expectations related to a particular group. Thus, a one-size-fits-all curriculum, teaching methodology, and assessment strategy are generally ineffective and unfair. It is essential in that the need to accommodate and adjust become the norm in teaching. RTI assumes that teachers and other service providers confront deficit thinking and reframe their practices to support the development of all students.

Gay (2000) describes culturally responsive teaching as teaching to students' strengths and increasing instructional effectiveness by using the cultural knowledge, experiences, and performance styles of diverse students. She contends that in culturally responsive teaching teachers must recognize that students' dispositions, attitudes, and approaches to learning might legitimately be affected by their cultural heritage. Teachers must make learning meaningful, bridging home and school experiences. Teachers must use a range of instructional strategies that are aligned with various learning styles. Through the use of multicultural information, resources, and materials in all subjects, students learn to recognize and celebrate each other's cultural heritage.

■ *Example*

Ms. Alexander knew that she had several students in her class who were Native American members of the Shawnee Remnant. She also knew that the students' parents had not sent them to school for the "Thanksgiving Feast" and were very upset about students making vests out of paper bags and decorating them with symbols. Ms. Alexander decided she would meet with the parents and consult with them regarding "what to do about Thanksgiving." The parents were delighted, and two sets of parents came to the class, talked about the "three sisters," and even conducted a drumming circle with the students.

Guerin (2005) presents several key activities related to culturally responsive practice. She suggests that teachers begin with a clear sense of their own personal cultural identity and learn about the cultural background and experience of the diverse individuals with whom they work. Teachers and service providers must use effective cross-cultural communication and be aware of divergent styles of thinking and learning, Students' needs, preferences, strengths, and experiences should be addressed by incorporating relevant curriculum materials and using multiple modes of teaching. Culturally responsive practices require positive expectations of all students and parents as well as community involvement.

Understanding poverty and the impact of socioeconomic status is another aspect of being culturally responsive to students. Through there are large numbers of low income African American and Hispanic students, the largest number of low income students is white (Bennet, 2008). To meet the needs of students, Bennet suggests we must become aware of the impact of socioeconomic differences and develop rapport and caring attitudes toward all students. The concepts of culturally responsive teaching also apply when working with students living in poverty.

THE TEACHER AND RTI

Teachers play a key role in RTI. The initial matter in which a teacher may be engaged to RTI is to participate in the application of a universal screening instrument. This involves administering a checklist, rating scale, or series of learning tasks to all students to determine those who may be at risk for learning and behavior problems. Davis, Lindo, and Compton (2007) contend that the selection of a screening instrument is key and must include ratings of students' attention and behavior as well as academic skills.

In general, teachers welcome RTI because they do not have to wait a specified period of time for students to fail before the student is provided services (Bradley, Danielson, and Doolittle, 2007). Effective teachers spend more time on instructional activities and have more engaged-time with students (Foorman, 2007). The question in RTI, though, is more complex than simply using effective teaching strategies. Rather, instructional activities must be appropriate for the students and for their academic development.

The National Education Association (2006) suggests that RTI will create new roles for teachers. Teachers may need additional preparation in differentiating instruction, curriculum analysis, evidence-based practices, collaboration, and problem-solving skills. Collaboration is essential; teachers have a critical role in decision making and implementing instruction. In addition, teachers will need to collaborate to address the needs of individuals and small groups and to support each other in collecting and analyzing data.

Whole class instruction appears to decrease when RTI is in place. Small group and individualized instruction is increased. In addition, applying progress monitoring and trying to identify barriers to instructional efforts emerge as necessary. Teachers must work together with other team members to set appropriate goals, develop instruction, and track progress.

Summary Points

- Responsive to Intervention (RTI) refers to a variety of multitiered service delivery programs in which students receive layered interventions that begin in the general education classroom and become more intense depending on students' response to instruction.
- RTI involves (a) tiers of specific research-based interventions, (b) screening and on-going progress monitoring, and (c) decision points at which the student is evaluated for special education.
- Tier 1 is high quality, research-based instruction in the regular classroom.
- Tier 2 includes 8 to 12 specific, research-based strategies to meet the student's learning needs.
- Tier 3 includes individual services, such as those provided in special education.

- Evidence-based practices are evaluated using experimental design and methodology, (b) demonstrated to be effective, and (c) supported by at least three studies published in peer-reviewed journals.
- Curriculum-based measurement is the most common method to monitor academic progress.
- RTI requires collaboration among general education teachers, special educators, administrators, and related service providers.
- Culturally responsive teaching addresses student strengths and increases instructional effectiveness by using the cultural knowledge, experiences, and performance styles of diverse students.
- RTI may require teachers to learn new skills.

Projects

1. Interview a teacher who is engaged in RTI. Ask him or her to describe the role of the teacher as well as what differentiates how teachers are prepared for and whom they serve in this model.
2. Collect materials about RTI from a local school district. How many tiers are involved? What interventions are provided at each tier?
3. Describe a classroom, and then discuss an activity that may be described as culturally responsive. Describe an activity for the same classroom that may reflect a lack of sensitivity.

Web Resources

National Center on Response to Intervention
www.rti4success.org

Center for RTI in Early Childhood
www.crtiec.org

Positive Interventions and Behavioral Support
www.pbis.org

References

Bartalo, P., & Smyth, G. (2009). Teacher education for diversity. In A. Swennon & M. Van der Klink (Eds.), *Becoming a teacher educator* (pp. 117–131). New York: Springer Science.

Bennet, G. (2008). Interrelations of socioeconomic position and occupational and leisure-time physical activity in the National Health and Nutrition Examination Survey. *Journal of Physical Activity and Health, 5*(2), 229–221.

Bradley, R., Danielson, L., & Doolittle, J. (2007). Responsiveness to intervention, 1997–2007. *Teaching Exceptional Children, 39*(5), 8–12.

Compton, D. L., Fuchs, D., Fuchs, L. S., & Bryant, J. D. (2006). Selecting at-risk readers in first grade for early intervention. *Journal of Educational Psychology, 98*(2), 394–409.

Council for Exceptional Children (2010). *RTI for emotional/behavioral disorders shows promise*. Retrieved December 29, 2010, from www.cec.sped.org/AM/Template.cfm?Section=Home&CONTENTID=11297&TEMPLATE=/CM/ContentDisplay.cfm

Daly, E., Glover, T., & McCurdy, M. (2006). *Response-to-intervention technical assistance document*. Lincoln, NE: Nebraska Department of Education. Retrieved January 1, 2011, from www.esu1.org/downloads/RtI/rtitechassist.pdf

Davis, G. N., Lindo, E. J., & Compton, D. L. (2007). Children at risk for reading failure. *Teaching Exceptional Children, 39*(5), 32–37.

Fletcher, J. M., Lyon, G. R., Fuchs, L. S., & Barnes, M. A. (2007). *Learning disabilities: From identification to intervention*. New York: Guilford.

Fletcher, J. M., & Vaughn, S. (2009). Response to intervention: Preventing and remediating academic differences. *Child Development Perspectives, 3*(1), 30–37.

Foorman, B. R. (2007). Primary prevention in classroom reading instruction. *Teaching Exceptional Children, 39*(5), 24–30.

Fuchs, D., Mock, D., Morgan, P. L., & Young, C. L. (2003). Responsiveness to intervention: Definitions, evidence, and implications for the learning disabilities construct. *Learning Disabilities Research and Practice, 18*(3) 157–171.

Gay, G. (2000). *Culturally responsive teaching: Theory, research, & practice.* New York: Teachers College Press.

Gresham, F. M. (2007). Response to intervention and emotional and behavioral disorders: Best practices in assessment for intervention. *Assessment for Effective Intervention, 32*, 214–222.

Guerin, L. (2005). *Enhancing instruction to connect with diverse audiences.* Gainesville, FL: University of Florida, Family Youth and Community Sciences.

Mahdavi, J. N., & Beebe-Frankenberger, M. E. (2009). Pioneering RTI systems that work. *Teaching Exceptional Children 42*(2), 64–73.

National Education Association (2006). New roles for teachers. In *New roles in Response to Intervention: Creating success for schools and children.* Retrieved December 30, 2010, from www.sswaa.org/userfiles/file/NewRolesinRTI.pdf

Sawyer, L. B., & Rimm-Kaufman, S. (2007). Teacher collaboration in the context of the Responsive Classroom approach. *Teachers and Teaching, 13*, 211–245.

Simonsen, B., Fairbanks, S., Briesch, A., Myers, D., & Sugai, G. (2008). Evidence-based practices in classroom management: Considerations for research to practice. *Education and Treatment of Children, 31*(3), 351–280.

Stuart, S. K., & Rinaldi, C. (2009). A collaborative planning framework for teachers implementing tiered instruction. *Teaching Exceptional Children, 42*(2), 52–63.

Vaughn, S., Wanzek, J., & Fletcher, J. M. (2007). Multiple tiers of intervention: A framework for prevention and identification of students with reading/learning disabilities. In B. M. Taylor & J. Ysseldyke (Eds.), *Educational interventions for struggling readers* (pp. 173–196). New York: Teacher's College Press.

Zirkel, P. A., & Krohn, N. (2008). RTI After IDEA: A survey of state laws. *Teaching Exceptional Children, 40*(3), 71–73.

CHAPTER OBJECTIVES

After completing this chapter, you will be able to do the following:

1. Define functional behavioral assessment (FBA).
2. Describe the role of an FBA in intervention design.
3. Conduct an FBA.
4. Recognize the role of establishing operations in designing interventions.
5. Relate FBA to positive behavioral support.

CHAPTER 5

Functional Behavioral Assessment

KEY TERMS

Antecedent-Behavior-Consequence (ABC)
 chart
Functional behavioral assessment (FBA)

Positive behavioral supports
Establishing operations
Waking day interview

Mr. Mercedes was confronted with two essays that did not meet his criteria for passing. The first was from Luis, who simply had written, "This book is really boring. But the teacher is also really boring. Takes one to know one." The second was from John, who had written three paragraphs, each three sentences in length, concluding with "This was a stupid book, and I didn't like it." Both students needed to do an alternative assignment to make up the grade.

How is Mr. Mercedes going to design appropriate alternative assignments? He knows that Luis has been in an accelerated curriculum, and had he not had a complex schedule with his other advanced placement classes, he wouldn't even have been in Mr. Mercedes's class. He knows that John typically uses a scribe to assist him in his writing due to his problems in writing. He knew that assigning the same "rewrite" to the students wouldn't be helpful. How can he identify a strategy to better meet each student's needs? Perhaps if he studied the learning environment and identified features in it that needed change, each student could succeed.

Marco was consistently late. He would saunter in last, make a comment to one or two of the girls who were sitting in the row by the door, plop down in a desk, and make a comment such as "Continue, professor." Being sent out of the room did not discourage the behavior. When his classmates ignored him, his comments only became more outrageous (and funny). Ms. Tyson was ready to lock the door at the conclusion of the bell, but Marco often was an active participant in class discussions, and he learned little sitting in the school office or in the in-school suspension classroom.

How can Ms. Tyson decide how to deal with Marco? What was this behavior actually doing for Marco, and to the class? If Ms. Tyson understood the function of the behavior, perhaps she could design a better way to deal with it.

Functional behavioral assessment is linked explicitly to RTI and designing individualized behavior plans. The student first should receive quality, structured management in the general education classroom (Tier 1) and small group or more specific interventions and supports (Tier II). If he or she continues to demonstrate problems in production or engagement, he or she moves to more individualized programs (Tier III). These individualized programs are developed through functional behavioral assessment. Individualized behavior plans are based on the results of this assessment (Chapter 6).

DEFINING FUNCTIONAL BEHAVIORAL ASSESSMENT

Functional behavioral assessment (FBA) is not, in itself, an intervention. FBA is a process used to identify what are potentially the most helpful interventions (Packenham, Shute, & Reid, 2004). The Individuals with Disabilities Education Act (IDEA 97) requires that when a student with a disability demonstrates a behavior that has a negative effect on his or her learning or the learning of others, the IEP team must consider "strategies, including positive behavioral interventions, strategies, and supports to address that behavior" (20 USC § 1414 (d) (3) (B) (i)). The IEP team takes action in two ways: (a) determining whether the behavior impedes the student's learning or that of other students and (b) developing a plan based on information from a functional based assessment. The Office of Special Education Programs (1999) defines FBA as a process that looks for explanations of the purpose behind the behavior.

Several assumptions are made when applying functional behavioral support. First, it assumes that behavior serves a function (Jordan, 2006). According to Carr (1994) the function or impact of behavior fits broadly into five categories:

- To receive social attention or communicate
- To gain access to tasks or preferred activities
- To escape, delay, or avoid a task or activity
- To avoid someone
- To receive sensory stimulation

The behavioral aspect of FBA comes from its basis in behavioral learning theory. Behaviorism is grounded in an analysis of what maintains the behavior in the environment. As an assessment, FBA serves the purpose of providing information necessary to produce change.

Another assumption of FBA is that behaviors are related to the context in which they occur. An individual's behavior may differ depending on who is nearby, what is occurring, where the individual is located, and what transitions are taking place (Jordan, 2006). Turnbull, Wilcox, Turnbull, Sailor, and Wickham (2001) contend that an FBA has at least three results:

- hypotheses that include operational definitions of the behaviors, descriptions of what occurs before the behavior that predicts the behavior's occurrence and nonoccurrence, and descriptions of the consequences in the environment that maintain the behavior;
- observational data that provide evidence for these hypotheses; and
- a plan for positive behavioral supports.

FBA involves (a) describing the behavior, (b) collecting information about when the behavior does and doesn't occur, (c) collecting data on the student's performance from as many sources possible (d) developing hypotheses about the potential function of the behavior, (e) identifying other behaviors that can be taught and provide the same result for the student, (f) testing hypotheses about the function of the behavior, and (g) evaluating the success of the intervention (Jordan, 2006). An example of these steps of FBA is provided in Table 5.1.

TABLE 5.1 Steps in the Functional Behavioral Assessment (FBA) process

Step	Example
Describing the behavior	Lara, a tenth-grader, sleeps during history class and is in danger of failing due to lack of participation.
Collecting information about when the behavior occurs and does not occur	Lara falls asleep about 10 minutes into the class; the class is at 7:50 a.m.; Lara is awake throughout other classes.
Collect data from as many sources as possible	History class is based in lectures; though there are "discussions," the course is essentially teacher controlled. Lara begins taking notes in history class and appears to "nod off." Lara says she hates history class and that the teacher just talks about old dead guys. The tests are multiple choice and detailed. Lara has failed every test. Lara's homeroom teacher indicates that she is awake and animated during homeroom class meetings immediately before history.
Developing hypotheses about the behavior	History is the first period of the day and requires Lara to attend to a lecture for 50 minutes. Lara may fall asleep because (a) Lara is tired during the "first bell" at 7:50 a.m. and may have difficulty attending to the class due to setting events such as not getting enough sleep, not being a "morning person," or not having breakfast; (b) Lara may be demonstrating "learned helplessness;" she has essentially shut down and having failed every test feels that no matter what she does she'll fail the next test; and (c) observations of other classes indicate that Lara tends to be a kinesthetic learner; the passive lecturing may be a complete mismatch with Lara's learning style. Interviews with teachers of Lara's other classes indicate that she has a "need to do." Lara is described by teachers as a student who needs to know she is doing well. Lara is described by her algebra teacher as a "failure avoider"—this teacher indicated that she has broken the tests into several shorter quizzes so that Lara experiences success.
Identify another behavior that can be taught	Instruction in note taking by generating cognitive maps may both provide more interest and interaction for Lara and help her with study skills.
Testing the hypothesis	Lara and the current history teacher develop a contract that takes into account past failures and provides a way for her to pass the class. The teacher agrees to count the cognitive maps she draws as part of her grade.
Evaluating the intervention	Evaluation is completed through examining Lara's grades, teacher interviews, and interviews with Lara regarding how the intervention is working.

Drasgow and Yell (2001) summarize the legal requirements regarding functional-based assessments and behavior intervention plans by identifying two major points. First, IDEA 97 emphasizes the use of positive behavioral support. This requires that behavior plans teach more appropriate behaviors rather than just eliminating unproductive behaviors. Second, when an FBA has not been completed before a behavioral incident that leads to the student being suspended for more than 10 days or being removed to an alternative educational placement, a functional-based assessment must be conducted and a behavioral intervention based on this assessment must be designed.

An FBA provides the information needed to increase the likelihood that an intervention will be successful. Through an FBA, data are made available that support the hypotheses about the behavior. When an FBA is completed, the teacher should be able to report (a) when the behavior is likely to occur, (b) when the behavior is not likely to occur, (c) the impact the behavior has that encourages it to continue, and (d) what the student should be taught to do as an alternative of the behavior.

CONDUCTING A FUNCTIONAL BEHAVIORAL ASSESSMENT

One of the unique aspects of an FBA is identifying a replacement behavior. After determining the function of the behavior, a new skill should be identified to support the student's educational program. For example, Joey is a 3-year-old preschooler with language delays. When a classmate takes a favorite toy from him, Joey bites. The function of the behavior is desirable for Joey—he reclaims the toy. Recognizing that biting is serving a powerful function for Joey, his teacher observes Joey carefully. When a classmate interacts with him in such a way that Joey would bite, his teacher intervenes and says to Joey, "Say no." The teacher is helping Joey substitute words for actions, which not only helps his social behavior but also helps his language development.

THE STEPS OF FUNCTIONAL BEHAVIORAL ASSESSMENT

The FBA strategy begins very much like any other behavior management plan. As you continue, however, the emphasis shifts.

Step One: Describing the Behavior

As in any behavior management plan, the behavior that is the target of the FBA should be stated as clearly and concretely as possible. For example, rather than describing Joey, the preschooler in our previous example, simply as "aggressive" or "violent," the behavior could be described in this way: "Joey bites classmates when they take his toys or when they have a desired toy or object." Other examples include the following:

- Rather than "Luisa refuses to work," state "When presented with written worksheets, Luisa attempts three or four items and does not continue."
- Rather than "Mei is hyperactive," state "During seat work, Mei taps her pencil, fidgets, and shreds the corners of her paper."
- Rather than "Rochelle is disrespectful," state "When given a request to rework a problem or edit a paper, Rochelle makes comments such as, 'No way,' 'I did it once—not doing it again,' or 'Are you talking to me?'"

TABLE 5.2 Waking day interview for Francis (9-year-old third-grader)

Routine/Event	Behavior
On the bus	Francis wants to sit alone in "his" seat; if someone is already in the seat, he remains in the aisle of the bus, doesn't say anything, and just stands there looking at his seat; the bus driver usually asks the child in the seat to move so that the bus can get going.
Arrival at school	Francis gets off the bus with no problem; goes directly to his classroom.
Entering the classroom	Francis enters the room quietly, doesn't greet his teacher or other students, and spends a lot of time at his cubby making sure his book bag is "all right." When prompted by the teacher, he usually continues to mess with his book bag for 10 to 15 seconds before going to his seat.
"Morning work"	Francis is slow to get started, has to have two sharpened pencils, and will begin work but often approaches his teacher about another student bothering him or looking at him.
Transitions	Francis is slow to pack up; everything must be in order. When told to hurry, he may get angry. When a peer started to clear off his desk for him, Francis pushed the peer hard into another desk, causing a bruise on the student's back.
Lunch	Francis eats at the end of the table, alone; when a student approaches him, he moves. He brings the same lunch every day. When he lost (or forgot—what happened was never determined) his lunch one day, he wouldn't eat anything offered to him, saying that it wasn't his lunch.

A concrete description is needed to ensure that all those involved with the student are describing the same problem. Crone and Horner (2003) suggest beginning with an interview with the teacher or parent. During this behavior a description is sought to answer the questions "What does this behavior look like?" and "What are the frequency, duration, and intensity of the behavior?" Table 5.2 summarizes the description of the teacher's primary concern, Drew's difficulty in completing work.

Step Two: Collecting Information on When the Behavior Occurs and Does Not Occur

Knoster (2000) describes this step as "gathering broad information" (p. 204). It can be completed through interviews, rating scales, referrals, or reviewing records. Each individual who works with the student can describe the nature of their interactions and their general understanding of the behavior. Summary statements for our examples in this stage may include the following:

- Interviews with Joey's teacher and teaching assistant in the preschool classroom suggest that when Joey is unable to get his way with another student, he will bite. The teacher's aide suggests that the behavior usually occurs in the block area and "pretending" area. A review of Joey's preschool records indicated that this behavior has just emerged. His teacher feels that Joey used to play by himself, almost isolating himself, and that the behavior emerged as he began trying to interact with the other students.

- Mei, a kindergarten child, uses Chinese as her first language. She is very shy, and though her English has vastly improved since she came to the United States a year ago, she remains quiet and doesn't volunteer in the classroom. She is very conscious about making mistakes, and she is hesitant to make marks on the paper without the teaching assistant nearby. When the teaching assistant is not available, she will fidget and "mess with" the paper until help is available.
- Rochelle, repeating ninth grade, is described by her teachers as bright yet underprepared. Until her grandmother took custody last year, Rochelle attended school intermittently. She tends to be defensive about her work and makes statements such as "I'm not stupid, you know." Her verbal skills and vocabulary are very strong, and she enjoys challenging the social studies teacher on controversial issues. Ms. Kapp, the social studies teacher, indicates that such discussions are welcome in the classroom and that Rochelle's general information far surpasses the written work she turns in. Ms. Marx, the language arts teacher, indicated that during a unit on poetry Rochelle wrote "incredible" free verse. However, now that the topic is expository essays, Rochelle is "belligerent." "You wouldn't think it's the same child," reported Ms. Marx.

These examples demonstrate that the assumptions we may make about a behavior, even when it is concretely identified, may shift with interview data and records review.

Though it was first developed by Wahler and Cormier in 1970, the waking day interview remains an effective strategy for collecting information about behaviors. This strategy has been successfully used in naturalistic assessment and intervention design that is grounded in FBA. In a **waking day interview**, the natural routine of the day is listed. During each of the routines and events, the interviewer asks for specific examples of the students' behavior in that setting. Patterns in the occurrence of the behavior then can be identified. A portion of a waking day interview is presented in Table 5.2.

Step Three: Collect Data from as Many Sources as Possible

There are two ways to collect information about the behavior for an FBA. An indirect way is to use interviews, records, and behavior rating scales. These methods are removed from the behavior itself (Gresham, Watson, & Skinner, 2009).

Interviews are commonly used to gather information about behaviors. Gresham, Watson, and Skinner (2009) suggest that an interview can (a) help define the behavior, (b) identify antecedents of the behavior, (c) provide preliminary information about its function, and (d) identify possible replacement behaviors. Witt, Daly, and Noell (2000) suggest answering questions such as these:

- What are the problem behaviors?
- Which behavior is the top priority for change?
- What is the student's functioning in comparison to other students in academics? In behaviors?
- What could be a cause of the behavior?
- How do the student's parents react to the behavior?
- Is there a time of day when the behavior is worse? Better?

TABLE 5.3   ABC chart

Antecedent	Behavior	Consequence
Ms. Prudent asks Rochelle to read from the text.	Rochelle says, "Me?"	Ms. Prudent says, "Yes, Rochelle, your turn."
Ms. Prudent waits for Rochelle to begin reading.	Rochelle asks, "Why do I always have to read?"	Ms. Prudent replies, "It's your turn, Rochelle."
Ms. Prudent again waits for Rochelle to begin reading.	Rochelle begins to read, stumbles over a word.	Ms. Prudent provides the pronunciation of the word.
Ms. Prudent waits for Rochelle to begin reading again.	Rochelle glares at Ms. Prudent and states, "Why are you interrupting me?"	Ms. Prudent ignores the statement.
Ms. Prudent asks Rochelle to go on.	Rochelle states, "If you're going to keep interrupting me, why don't you read it?"	Ms. Prudent says, "We're all waiting for you, Rochelle."
Ms. Prudent waits for Rochelle to begin.	Rochelle stands up, slams the book, and says, "You can all keep waiting. I'm out of here."	Ms. Prudent asks Rochelle to sit.
Ms. Prudent asks Rochelle to sit.	Rochelle continues to stand.	Ms. Prudent goes to her desk and writes an "in-school suspension" slip.
Ms. Prudent hands Rochelle the slip.	Rochelle states, "Thanks for getting me out of this asylum" and walks out of the door.	Ms. Prudent asks the class to continue reading independently.

Record review can also provide indirect information in formulating a description about the behavior. These records provide demographics, information about the number of moves or changes in family status, attendance, test scores, and disciplinary contact. Behavior rating scales can also be used, are brief and easy to complete, but rarely provide the detailed information needed for a behavior plan.

Direct methods include recording observations surrounding the problem behavior. One of the most common ways to record an observation is the use of an **Antecedent-Behavior-Consequence (ABC) chart**. This strategy involves recording in three columns what occurs before a behavior, the nature of the behavior, and the consequences. An example of an ABC chart is provided in Table 5.3.

Another simple way to record observations is through a flow log. When using a flow log the observer notes the times when an event or interaction occurs and the nature of the interaction. An example of a flow log is provided in Table 5.4.

O'Neill et al. (1997) have several additional suggestions for observation. They contend that observations shouldn't interfere with normal daily interactions. Direct support staff, teachers, or family members who already work or live with the student may be appropriate observers. Observations should continue until 10 to 15 instances of the behavior have been logged so that patterns may be identified.

TABLE 5.4	Flow log

Context: Block area
Participants: Joey, Maisy, and Michelle

Time	Event
9:03	Joey is playing by himself in the block area, building a "road," placing the rectangular blocks end to end.
9:05	Maisy enters the area. Joey doesn't look up.
9:06	Maisy observes Joey. Michelle enters the area and stands by Maisy. Michelle has a small car in her hand.
9:07	Maisy says to Michelle, "Build a road?" and goes to the shelf to select some blocks. Michelle kneels with the small car in her hand, observing Joey's road.
9:09	Maisy and Michelle cooperatively build a "road." Michelle places her car on it every now and then.
9:11	Michelle turns and puts her car on Joey's "road." Michelle says, "Look Joey, I'm driving.
9:12	Joey pushes Michelle's hand away. Michelle puts the car on the road again, says, "It's your road, Joey."
9:13	Joey grabs Michelle's hand, pulls out the car, and throws the car at Maisy. Maisy cries and runs to the paraeducator. Michelle screams, "You stop it, Joey!"

Step Four: Developing Hypotheses About the Behavior

Knoster (2000) suggests that hypotheses regarding behaviors should be stated in the form of "When this happens, the student does this, in order to get that." In terms of our examples, the hypotheses would be stated in these ways:

- To obtain a desired toy or object from a boy, Joey may bite the student, obtaining the toy without having to use words.
- To manage her anxiety about potentially making a mistake, Mei hesitates, fidgets, and "worries" about her papers until the teaching assistant is available to help her complete it correctly, ensuring that the paper will be completed correctly.
- To avoid appearing less capable than her peers and to demonstrate that she is less well prepared than her classmates, Rochelle makes negative statements regarding her willingness to edit or revise, allowing her to appear angry and "tough" rather than unable to complete the work.

The role of identifying antecedents in developing behavior plans cannot be overlooked. In their study of antecedent versus consequence analysis in predicting behavior, Camp, Iwata, Hammond, and Bloom (2009) found that antecedent events were better predictors of problem behaviors than consequences. Manipulating antecedents may be an initial step in preventing problem behaviors. Teachers must avoid "walking on eggshells," trying to prevent challenging behaviors by eliminating any directive efforts to teach.

This step is the key to FBA. A hypothesis about the "function"—the purpose the behavior serves for the student—is developed. The behavior may help the student avoid an activity. It may help the student get attention. The student may participate in the behavior in order to feel as if he or she is in control. On the other hand, the student may demonstrate a behavior because he or she has not yet learned an alternative. Quinn, Gable, Rutherford, Nelson, and Howell (1998) suggest asking:

- Does this behavior occur because the student is not yet able to perform the appropriate skill or behavior? (a skill deficit)
- Does the student fail to perform the appropriate skill or behavior? (performance deficit; the student finds some value in engaging in an inappropriate behavior, is avoiding a low-interest task, or perceives rules, routines, or expectations irrelevant)

Using the information gathered during the observations, a hypothesis regarding the function of the behavior is generated. This hypothesis predicts the conditions under which the behavior is likely to occur (the antecedents) and the consequences that seem to be maintaining it. For example, when confronted by an academic demand for which she may not be prepared, Rochelle (see Table 5.3) demonstrates verbally aggressive behavior so that she can be removed from the classroom and, in her mind, avoids embarrassment.

Step Five: Identify Another Behavior That Can Be Taught

Gresham, Watson, and Skinner (2009) describe the process of identifying another behavior to be taught as a "competing pathways model" (p. 165). This behavior is based in the hypothesis about the function of the behavior. Given the function of the behavior, given the problem conditions and situations, the desired behavior is identified. Then an appropriate, alternative behavior can be identified. However, to establish this new, more appropriate behavior, the teacher must make sure that the problem behavior is not rewarded and that the appropriate behavior is rewarded. A key aspect of this step is to make a list of changes in the environment that will make the performance of the new, more appropriate behavior more likely than the problem behavior. Examples using our three sample cases follow:

- To obtain a desired toy or object from a boy, Joey may bite the student, obtaining the toy without having to use words. Joey should ask if he can share or play. If Joey approaches a student, the teaching assistant will intervene, stating, "Joey, would you like that toy? Say 'Can I play?'" and praise Joey when he uses his words.
- To manage her anxiety about making a mistake, Mei hesitates, fidgets, and worries about her papers until the teaching assistant is available to help her complete it correctly, ensuring that the paper will be completed correctly. Mei will be rewarded for initiating the paper and then completing aspects of it independently. The research assistant will cue Mei, "Try three, and then ask me."
- To avoid appearing less capable than her peers and demonstrate that she is less well prepared than her classmates, Rochelle makes negative statements regarding her willingness to edit or revise, allowing her to appear angry and "tough" rather than unable to complete the work. Rochelle will be given opportunities to work from a copy that has been edited by the teacher or a peer, providing her with the support she needs to accurately complete the assignment.

Step Six: Testing Hypotheses

Only when the relevance of the behavior is known is it possible to speculate about the true function of the behavior and establish an individual behavior intervention plan. In other words, before any plan is set in motion, the team must formulate a plausible explanation (hypothesis) for the student's behavior. It is then desirable to manipulate various conditions to verify the assumptions made by the team regarding the function of the behavior. For instance, the team working with Rochelle in preceding example may hypothesize that during class discussions Rochelle calls out to get peer attention. Thus, the teacher might make accommodations in the environment to ensure that Rochelle gets the peer attention she seeks as a consequence of appropriate, rather than inappropriate, behaviors.

If this manipulation changes Rochelle's behavior, the team can assume their hypothesis was correct; if Rochelle's behavior remains unchanged following the environmental manipulation, a new hypothesis must be formulated using data collected during the FBA.

ESTABLISHING OPERATIONS AND INTERVENTIONS

Establishing operations are events or aspects of the setting that can make the problem worse, such as diet, medical conditions/illness, sleep, fatigue, or social conflicts (Sugai et al., 1999). An easy way to think about such setting events is that they have an impact on how the student responds in certain situations. For example, even the best students may have difficulty paying attention the day before spring break; a student who already has trouble with math class may have even more significant problems when he or she is having an allergy attack. Freeman (2004) indicates that establishing operations can occur immediately before a problem behavior or days in advance. Though some setting events may be fairly obvious (e.g., a student having trouble staying awake the rest of the day after having a seizure in the morning) others may be more difficult to identify (e.g., parents considering a divorce). Freeman indicates that setting events can be social (e.g., an argument before school), physiological (e.g., forgetting medication or being ill), or environmental (e.g., construction occurring right outside the classroom window.)

FUNCTIONAL BEHAVIORAL ASSESSMENT AND POSITIVE BEHAVIORAL SUPPORT

Though IDEA 97 refers to positive behavioral interventions, strategies, and supports, it provides no definition of positive behavioral (intervention) support (PBIS) (Turnbull et al., 2001). Turnbull et al. provide the following characteristics of **positive behavioral supports**:

- The student is viewed within the systems and environments in which the student received education or related services. The student is not viewed in isolation but, rather, in relationship to the factors that influence the behavior.
- Positive behavioral support strives to provide accommodations in the systems and environments by promoting the student's skills and those of others in the same settings.
- Positive behavioral support emphasizes creating new experiences, relationships, and skills for the student, rather than focusing on the elimination of inappropriate behaviors.
- Positive behavioral supports are long-term efforts, attempting to make changes in the environment, develop skills, and develop behavioral consequences.
- Positive behavioral supports are developed, implemented, and evaluated by a team of educators, family members, the student, and members of the student's social network.
- Planning for positive behavioral supports considers (a) identifying the student and family's desired lifestyle, (b) the social validity of the supports, and (c) the quality of life that may be attained for the student.
- Positive behavioral supports are designed so that they can be implemented in the greatest number of environments possible and in the general education curriculum.

- The purpose of positive behavioral supports is to develop a uniquely appropriate set of strategies so that the student can be independent, productive, and included.
- Positive behavioral supports are grounded in FBA to define the factors that predict and maintain the behaviors and ways to replace those behaviors with more productive behaviors.

Gable, Hendrickson, and Von Acker (2001) suggest that replacement behaviors should be selected with care. The behavior that is to be taught should be in high demand in the student's environment so that he or she is more likely to engage in the behavior. Observing peers may help in the selection of a replacement behavior. Gable et al. also suggest that it may be helpful to select a behavior that the student has demonstrated, though it has occurred rarely. They also recommend looking at skill deficits as an aspect of the behavior; for example a ninth-grader may not complete an assignment because he or she does not know how, or a student may not participate in class because of concerns about his or her speech and language.

According to Fox, Dunlap, and Benito (2001), PBIS is longitudinal and team based, involving school and family. Positive behavioral supports are continually adjusted to meet the student's changing needs and can become an essential factor in successfully including students in general education.

Unlike traditional management interventions that view the individual as the problem and strive to eliminate behaviors, PBIS and FBA view systems, settings, and the lack of skills as part of the problem and work to modify these factors to support the student. From this perspective, long-term strategies are implemented to decrease inappropriate and unacceptable behavior, teach more appropriate behavior, and offer the contextual supports needed by the student for effective outcomes (Warger, 1999). Positive behavioral supports have several advantages, including the following:

- being widely applicable to individuals with disabilities;
- contributing to the knowledge of how to use assessment as a basis for intervention and correct problems in the educational setting; and
- being effective in reducing problem behaviors.

Effective teachers often use many of the elements of PBIS in their daily routines and management strategies. Effective teachers respond to the individual needs of students, alter environments to benefit their students, teach new skills, and respond to positive behaviors exhibited by students.

Effective behavioral support (EBS) is a systems approach to the application of PBIS schoolwide (Lewis & Sugai, 1999). A team works systematically to solve problems and plan. The members of this team receive professional development in the areas of systems change and management principles and practices and the application of research-validated instructional and management practices throughout the school setting. The team works to secure a commitment to the EBS model, review the behavioral supports and practices in the school, and help develop plans to respond to unique student and staff needs.

There are three components to implementing EBS: schoolwide supports, classroom supports, and nonclassroom supports. At the school level, components are consistent with best practices for schools. For example, there is a common approach to discipline, with the emphasis on teaching all students behavioral expectations and routines. Each school has (a) a mission, (b) schoolwide rules and expectations, (c) strategies for teaching and encouraging expected behaviors, (d) strategies for discouraging inappropriate behaviors, and (e) record-keeping practices. Scott and Hunter (2001) state that administrator support and active involvement are essential to the success of a school-wide support system.

The classroom system is an extension of the schoolwide system. The systems overlap in order to (a) facilitate communication among students, staff, and parents, (b) increase the consistency with which behavior is handled in various school settings, and (c) ease transitions as students move from setting to setting. To support students, teachers use:

- advance organizers;
- productive and authentic activities;
- consistent enforcement of school and classroom rules;
- consistent correction of rule violations and social interaction problems; and
- planning and teaching of transition behavior.

Because of the explicit nature of the management in these classrooms, the classroom support system is helpful to students at risk for behavior problems.

Nonclassroom supports are also an extension of the schoolwide system. In addition to responding to the needs of students outside the classroom (i.e., hallways, gym, cafeteria, library, office, bus), instruction is implemented to teach students the expectations for behavior in each setting. The team analyzes the specific settings and activities to assess the routines and physical characteristics of the settings and activities and to design appropriate supports.

For students with significant behavior problems, individual support systems are used to offer immediate, relevant, effective, and efficient responses. Individual support systems are needed by a very small number of students (3%–6%). Students who are in need of individual behavioral support are identified, and an easy procedure for teachers to request and receive assistance is in place. An FBA is conducted, and an individualized behavior support plan is implemented and monitored.

The greatest issue in implementing EBS is school and classroom climate. A significant shift must be made from responding to negative behaviors to supporting positive behaviors.

Schoolwide positive behavioral support has been effective in making positive changes in both student and faculty member behavior. Training, however, has been linked with better results (Bradshaw, Reinke, Brown, Bevans, & Leaf, 2008). In addition, better success has been noted when teachers identify the function of the problem behaviors and use that as the basis for designing an intervention (Packenham, Shute, & Reid, 2004). Positive behavioral support is not a special education activity; general education teachers and the whole staff can be effective in improving school behavior (Maag & Larson, 2004).

EVALUATING THE INTERVENTION PLAN

Gable, Hendrickson and Von Acker (2001) provide several guidelines for ensuring the quality of an intervention. In view of FBA and positive behavioral support, they contend that a quality intervention:

- is consistent with the function of the behavior and is appropriate in the context in which it occurs;
- has been demonstrated to be effective;
- is accepted by the adults responsible for its implementation; and
- is consistent with the skill level and commitment of the individuals who will be implementing it.

An example of an intervention plan is provided in Figure 5.1.

Name Rochelle Rodriquez	Age 16
Grade 9	

Assessment Team:	**Problem Behavior:**
Ms. Kapp, Social Studies Ms. Marx, Language Arts Mr. Sledge, Mathematics Luisa DeCamp, School Psychologist Ms. Marino, Rochelle's grandmother	When confronted with tasks, Rochelle makes negative statements regarding her willingness to participate, edit, or revise.

Setting Events:	**Antecedents to the Problem Behavior:**
1. Rochelle has a history of inconsistent attendance, which has led to her underpreparedness in school-related skills. 2. Rochelle is at least a full year older than her classmates and conscious of her age.	Rochelle is presented with a task or assignment with which she will need additional support in order to be successful.

Behavioral Hypothesis:	**Maintaining Consequences of the Behavior:**
In order to avoid appearing less capable than her peers and demonstrate that she is less well prepared than her classmates, Rochelle makes negative statements regarding her willingness to edit or revise, allowing her to appear angry and "tough" rather than unable to complete her work.	1. Teacher may "back off" and Rochelle takes the work home, completing it one-on-one with her grandmother. When teachers confront Rochelle, she often leaves the room and demands to see the school psychologist with whom she has a strong relationship. Both of these responses allow Rochelle to avoid completing the work.

Expected Outcomes:	**General Approach and Intervention:**
Rochelle will accept support in completing challenging tasks and assignments.	1. After discussing the results of the functional behavior analysis with Rochelle and her grandmother, Rochelle admitted that she was embarrassed at being older than the other students and making mistakes.
Monitoring: 1. The number of aggressive statements Rochelle makes during each week will be counted. 2. The number of times Rochelle walks out on the class during the week will be counted. 3. The amount of tasks Rochelle completes each week will be counted. 4. The number of positive requests for assistance Rochelle makes each week will be counted. 5. The number of times Rochelle leaves the room without aggression for her "5-minute break" will be counted each week.	2. As a general approach, teachers agreed to call on Rochelle when her hand was raised, allowing her opportunities to appear successful to her peers. (Rochelle had complained that she was only called on when she didn't know what was going on) 3. Rochelle agreed to attempt every task, and if she was not successful, to work quietly on some alternative work. When there was a break in the flow of the class, Rochelle could request help from a peer or the teacher. 4. If a task was too frustrating, Rochelle would ask to get a drink, leave the room briefly, and return within 5 minutes. This would be a signal that Rochelle needed private help on the task.

Evaluation:
After one month, Rochelle and Ms. DeCamp will have a private conference to discuss progress. After six weeks, the team will reconvene.

FIGURE 5.1 Behavior intervention plan

Summary Points

- Functional Behavioral Assessment (FBA) is a process that looks for explanations of the purpose behind the behavior in order to plan successful interventions.
- The results of an FBA include a hypothesis that has a definition of the behavior and what maintains it, observational data that provide evidence for hypotheses about the functions of the behavior, and a plan for positive behavioral supports.
- The activities involved in an FBA include information gathering, direct observation, and manipulating variables to test the hypotheses.

- The five steps of FBA include (a) describing the behavior; (b) collecting information on when the behavior does and does not occur; (c) observations; (d) developing hypotheses; and (e) testing those hypotheses.
- Establishing operations are events or aspects of the setting that can affect the behavior and the intervention, including diet, medical conditions, sleep, or social conflicts.
- The key to FBA is the selection of replacement behaviors for the behavior of concern.
- Evaluation of the assessment plan and the intervention increases the likelihood of a successful outcome.

Projects

1. Conduct a waking day interview. List the events/routines in a student's day, and then interview the parent or teacher to identify the student's behavior during each event or routine. What patterns can you identify?
2. Observe a student using an ABC chart. Review your data. Do the data support your first assumptions about the behavior?

3. Complete a flow log on a student. What information does this flow log provide? How is it different from the information provided from an ABC chart?
4. Consider a student with whom you are familiar. What establishing observations or setting events may have an impact on the student's behavior? How could you mitigate these establishing observations?

Web Resources

For more information about Functional Behavioral Assessment, visit these sites: cecp.air.org/fba *www.pacer.org/parent/php/php-c79.pdf*

For more information about positive behavioral support, visit this site: *www.pbis.org/about_us/default.aspx*

For fact sheets about positive behavioral support, visit this site: *www.nasponline.org/resources/factsheets/pbs_fs.aspx*

References

Bradshaw, C., Reinke, W., Brown, L., Bevans, K., & Leaf, P. J. (2008). Implementation of school-wide positive behavioral interventions and supports (PBIS in elementary schools). *Education and Treatment of Children, 31*(1), 1–26

Camp, E. M., Iwata, B. A., Hammond, J. L., & Bloom, S. E. (2009). Antecedent vs. consequent events as predictors of problem behavior. *Journal of Applied Behavior Analysis, 42*(2), 469–484.

Carr, E. G. (1994). Emerging themes in the functional analysis of problem behavior. *Journal of Applied Behavior Analysis, 27*(2), 393–399.

Crone, D. A., & Horner, R. H. (2003). *Building positive behavior support systems in schools: Functional behavioral assessment.* New York: The Guilford Press.

Drasgow, E., & Yell, M. L. (2001). Functional behavioral assessments: Legal requirements and challenges. *School Psychology Review, 30*(2) 239–251.

Fox, L., Dunlap, G., & Benito, N. (2001). Vincent's story: From Head Start to fourth grade. *Beyond Behavior, 11*(1), 5–6.

Freeman, R. (2004). An introduction to positive behavior support (PBS) planning. Retrieved January 5, 2010 from www.specialconnections.ku.edu/cgi-bin/cgiwrap/specconn/main.php?cat=behavior&section=main&subsection=pbs/main

Gable, R. A., Hendrickson, J. M., & Von Acker, R. (2001). Maintaining the integrity of FBA-based interventions in the schools. *The Education and Treatment of Children, 24*(3), 248–260.

Gresham, F. M., Watson, T., & Skinner, C. (2009). Functional behavioral assessment: Principles, procedures, and future directions. *School Psychology Review, 30* (2), 156–172.

Individuals with Disabilities Education Act, 20 USC § 1414 (d) (3) (B) (i).

Jordan, D. (2006). Functional behavioral assessment and positive interventions: What parents need to know. *PACER Center Action Information Sheet,* PHP-C79.

Knoster, T. P. (2000). Understanding the difference and relationship between functional behavior assessments and manifestation determinations. *Journal of Positive Behavior Interventions, 2*(1), 53–58.

Lewis, T. J., & Sugai, G. (1999). Effective behavior support: A systems approach to proactive schoolwide management. *Focus on Exceptional Children, 31*(6), 1–24.

Maag, J. W., & Larson, P. J. (2004). Teaching a general education teacher to apply functional assessment. *Education and Treatment of Children, 27*(1), 26–36.

Office of Special Education Programs (1999). Twenty-First Annual Report to Congress on the Implementation of the Individuals with Disabilities Education Act Washington, DC: Author.

O'Neill, R. E., Horner, R. H., Albin, R. W., Sprague, J. R., Storey, K., & Newton, J. S. (1997). *Functional assessment and program development for problem behavior.* Pacific Grove, CA: Brookes-Cole.

Packenham, M., Shute, R. H., & Reid, R. (2004). A brief functional assessment procedure for children with disruptive classroom behavior. *Education and Treatment of Children, 27*(1), 9–25.

Quinn, M. M., Gable, R. A., Rutherford, R. B., Nelson, C. M., & Howell, K. W. (1998). *Addressing student problem behavior.* Washington, DC: Center for Effective Collaboration and Practice.

Scott, T. M., & Hunter, J. (2001). Initiating schoolwide support systems: An administrator's guide to the process. *Beyond Behavior, 11*(1), 13–15.

Sugai, G., Horner, R. H., Dunlap, G., et al. (1999). *Applying positive behavioral support and functional behavioral assessment in schools.* Technical Assistance Guide 1 Version 1.4.4 (12/01/99), Washington, DC: Office of Special Education Programs Center on Positive Behavioral Interventions and Support.

Turnbull, H. R., Wilcox, B. L., Turnbull, A. P., Sailor, W., & Wickham, D. (2001). IDEA, positive behavioral supports, and school safety. *Journal of Law and Education, 30*(3), 445–503.

Wahler, R. G., & Cormier, W. H. (1970). The ecological interview: A first step in outpatient child behavior therapy. *Journal of Behavior Therapy and Experimental Psychiatry, 1,* 279–289.

Warger, C. (1999). *Positive behavior support and functional assessment.* ERIC/OSEP Digest E580. (ERIC Document Reproduction Service No. ED 434–437)

Witt, J. C., Daly, E. M., & Noell, G. H. (2000). *Functional assessments: A step-by-step guide.* Longmont, CO: Sopris West.

CHAPTER OBJECTIVES

After completing this chapter, you will be able to do the following:

1. Characterize the steps in developing a behavior intervention plan, including
   a. selecting target behaviors, including the function, antecedents, consequences, and establishing operations of the behavior;
   b. collecting and recording baseline data;
   c. selecting the intervention and acceptable behavior to reinforce;
   d. implementing interventions and collecting and recording intervention data; and
   e. evaluating the effects of intervention including adherence.
2. Describe and exemplify the observer reliability process.
3. Define various forms of prompting.

Developing a Behavior Intervention Plan

CHAPTER 6

KEY TERMS

Abscissa points

Adherence

Antecedents of effective management

Baseline data

Counting behavior

Fading

Graphing (charting) behavior

Instructional objectives

Interobserver reliability

Measurability

Observability

Ordinate points

Phasing out

Prompting

Time sampling

George, a junior high student at the John T. Belfast School, appears to be having problems in school. Mrs. Chung, a social studies teacher, notices that George does not participate in class discussions, associate with other students, or take part in extracurricular activities. Mrs. Chung wishes she could help George become involved with his peers. She feels guilty about George's isolation and believes that she has in some manner let him down. The one thing Mrs. Chung has noticed about George is that he likes to draw. He often spends his free time in class working in a sketch pad.

Mrs. Chung has brought George's problems to the Student Support Team for discussion. Several interventions were suggested but the results have been inconsistent. Mrs. Chung and the team have decided that the time has come to refer George for a multifactored evaluation and possible referral for special services. The school principal, Mr. Hummer, recognizing Mrs. Chung's frustrations and George's problems, refers him for evaluation.

The school psychologist, Dr. Honda, reports that George has superior intelligence as measured on an IQ test and that there are no signs of learning disabilities. Mrs. Chung decides to show some of George's drawings to the art teacher, who is impressed with their creative quality. The drawings are shown to the art professor at a local university, who agrees that they are the work of a very talented young person with great potential.

> *Perhaps if Mrs. Chung could apply the steps in the behavior change process, George would become more involved with other students.*

Mrs. Anderson teaches algebra and geometry at Thomas Edison High School. She enjoys teaching and is a conscientious instructor. Her students respect her, she is admired by her colleagues, and the principal refers to her as "my perfect teacher." Mrs. Anderson has been presented the Outstanding Teacher of the Year award twice by the school board. She was voted Teacher of the Year by the state education association. However, Mrs. Anderson has a serious problem—not at school but at home.

Mrs. Anderson is a single parent. She is head of a household that includes three teenagers, ages 13, 15, and 17. Her children take little responsibility for caring for themselves or the house. After Mrs. Anderson has taught school, attended faculty meetings, corrected papers, called parents, changed her bulletin board, prepared monthly reports, and planned for the next day, she goes home to her other job. At home she must prepare meals, wash and iron, clean the house, do the yard work, take out the garbage, wash and fuel the car, shop for food and clothing, care for the dog, and finally care for three teenagers.

> *Perhaps if Mrs. Anderson could apply the steps in the behavior change process, she could change her home situation.*

In this chapter, the specific steps and procedures applied during the behavior change process are discussed and exemplified in detail. Teachers and parents should follow these steps closely: (a) select a target behavior, (b) collect and record baseline data, (c) identify reinforcers, (d) implement intervention and collect and record intervention data, and (e) evaluate the effects of intervention. This chapter also includes a discussion of observer reliability and prompting.

SELECTING A TARGET BEHAVIOR

The initial step in the behavior change process is the identification of the target behavior. The target behavior is the behavior to be changed. A target behavior may be an existing behavior that the teacher or parent desires to increase or decrease or a nonoccurring behavior—that is, a behavior that is not observable in the individual's behavioral repertoire but one to be developed.

In most classroom situations, it is not difficult for the teacher to identify a variety of behaviors needing change (target behaviors). The teacher may recognize the following:

Percy does not communicate verbally.

Jake should increase his reading skills.

Mary should stop yelling in the classroom.

Joseph needs to learn to listen to instructions before he begins an assignment.

Shauna should improve her table manners in the lunchroom.

All these are potential target behaviors that the teacher could identify in the classroom.

It should be remembered that whenever an individual or a group is singled out for observation and study for the purpose of initiating a behavior change program, it is inevitable that several individual and group target behaviors will be identified. All children and adults manifest behaviors that are unacceptable to some other individuals or groups of individuals under certain conditions.

Decisions leading to the selection of a behavior for change should be governed by certain considerations, including but not limited to:

- type and function of the behavior;
- antecedents establishing operations, and frequency of the behavior;
- duration of the behavior;
- intensity of the behavior; and
- overall number of behaviors needing modification.

It is generally recommended that behaviors be addressed one at a time. Implementing several behavior change programs simultaneously frequently results in inefficiency, and otherwise useful interventions prove ineffective.

■ *Example*

Ilion manifests a variety of challenging behaviors. Among the behaviors of greatest concern to his teacher, Mr. Wise, are (a) withdrawal from group activities, (b) eating habits, (c) verbal communication with his classmates and Mr. Wise, and (d) gross motor skills.

Mr. Wise recognizes that a program cannot be initiated to modify all of Ilion's potential target behaviors at one time. Because of the nature of the behaviors, the proposed interventions could be in conflict with one another. Mr. Wise must respond to the following question: Is it more important for Ilion, at this time, to participate in the luncheon discussion (behaviors a and c would be targets), or is it more important to improve his gross motor skills and eating habits (behaviors b and c would be targets)?

In response to this question, Mr. Wise develops the following priority list for Ilion's program:

- First priority: Increase participation in group activities.
- Second priority: Increase verbalization with others.
- Third priority: Increase gross motor skills.
- Fourth priority: Increase acceptance of a variety of foods.

TYPE AND FUNCTION OF THE BEHAVIOR

Identifying the type of behavior is important to determining priorities. Priorities vary with individual student needs and the setting in which the behavior change intervention is applied. However, the objective of all behavior change is to benefit the student (Alberto & Troutman, 1990) or, as stated previously, increase self-discipline or self-control.

With an increase in experience and skill in the behavior change process, the teacher or parent may wish to program more than one individual or group target behavior simultaneously. However, the beginning practitioner should refrain from programming for multiple behaviors. The function of the behavior should also be reviewed when identifying the behavior. At times, providing the student with an alternative behavior may even eliminate the need to intervene. The functions of the behavior may include social attention, escape, tangible reinforcement, physical comfort, and nonsocial reinforcement (Paclawsky, Matson, Rush, Smalls, and Vollmer, 2000). Sometimes identifying the function of the behavior can eliminate the problem.

■ *Example*

Ms. Castillo noted that if she didn't call on Rhea during the mini-lesson portion of the period, the fifth-grader hovered around her before beginning to work on the guided practice. At times, because Ms. Castillo was working with other students, Rhea lost up to 10 minutes of time on the assignment, causing her to frequently fail. When Ms. Castillo finally reached Rhea for her question, she often stated, "I just wanted to check this out with you" or "I wanted to talk to you about this." The questions appeared unnecessary and simply a way for Rhea to connect with her teacher. Ms. Castillo decided to experiment. When Rhea entered her classroom, she made sure that she chatted with her briefly. In addition, during the mini-lesson, Ms. Castillo would ask Rhea as many questions as possible without attracting undo attention to her. Rhea was getting the social attention she needed from Ms. Castillo and no longer hovered around losing instructional time.

FREQUENCY OF THE BEHAVIOR AND ESTABLISHING OPERATIONS

When selecting a target behavior, the practitioner must consider the frequency of the behavior. Some behaviors occur so infrequently that they do not necessitate or respond to a formal behavior change intervention. Of course, the reverse is also true: Some behaviors occur so frequently that they obviously require a behavior change program.

■ *Example*

Ms. Lochman was very concerned about Martin, a member of her class. Six-year-old Martin appeared to be constantly out of his assigned seat. When out of his chair, he would grab other children's work, work tools, and lunches. Using a time-sampling technique, Ms. Lochman collected baseline data on Martin's out-of-seat behavior for 1 hour a day for 5 days. She found that during these observation periods, Martin was out of his seat 17 times an hour on average. (Time sampling is discussed later in this chapter.)

This behavior was so frequent and so obtrusive that it usually brought all productive classroom activity to a halt until Ms. Lochman could control Martin and return him to his seat.

Teachers and parents are confronted daily with behaviors that are responsive to behavior change intervention. Such behaviors include lack of attention to tasks, incomplete assignments, fighting, not cleaning one's room, tardiness to and from school, excessive television watching, neglecting music or dance practice, and independent reading, to name a few.

■ *Example*

Ms. Derry, like many of her peers, does not approve of chewing gum in school. Johnny, a member of her classroom group, was seen chewing gum on the second day of school this year. Ms. Derry grabbed him, removed the gum from his mouth, and stuck it on his nose, where it stayed for the remainder of the day. Ms. Derry then proceeded to make plans for a formal behavior change program. After several hours of planning, she was satisfied with her elaborate scheme for gathering baseline data and applying the chosen intervention. Unfortunately (or fortunately), Johnny never chewed gum in school again (that she observed).

Such a technique for adjusting student behavior does not respect the dignity of the child. Many behaviors, like Johnny's, appear so infrequently that they do not require a formal behavior change program. Examples of such behaviors are the following:

- George's annual 2-minute tantrum;
- Barbara's occasional reading reversal;
- Don's infrequent falling out of his seat; and
- Judy's bimonthly bus-missing behavior.

If a proposed target behavior is both obtrusive and occurs frequently, the teacher should next consider the duration of the behavior.

■ *Examples*

For several weeks, Gerald was very nervous in school. His teacher, Ms. Farley, noted that he was frequently out of his seat, irritable, and ready to burst into tears. She had never seen Gerald in this condition. Ms. Farley attempted to discuss the situation with Gerald, but he rebuffed her.

Ms. Farley decided to establish a formal intervention to decrease the behaviors. However, before initiating the program, she discussed the situation with Gerald's mother. During the conversation, Gerald's mother indicated that she had observed similar behavior at home and was attempting to help Gerald regain his old composure. She thought the behavior was the result of the recent death of Gerald's grandfather. Gerald and his grandfather had been pals; they had always been together in the evenings. The death left a great void in Gerald's daily life. Gerald's mother said that her husband was rescheduling his evening activities so that he and Gerald could spend more time together.

Ms. Farley decided to hold the intervention program in abeyance for another few weeks. Within a short time, Gerald was his normal self. The program was never implemented.

Mr. Parker is Maryann's kindergarten teacher. He thoroughly enjoys his work with Maryann and her 16 classmates. The kindergarten is an interesting and exciting learning place for the children.

During the first few weeks of the school year, Mr. Parker observed that Maryann, although involved in the classroom activities, seldom, if ever, spoke to him, the paraprofessional, or her classmates. He decided to collect some baseline data on the frequency of Maryann's verbal behavior. In cooperation with the kindergarten paraprofessional, an observation schedule was set up to obtain some objective data. Using a time-sampling technique, Maryann's behavior was observed an average of 1 hour a day for 10 days. Data indicated that Maryann spoke only four times a day, on average, while in school. She directed all her verbalizations to one classmate.

Although Mr. Parker was very concerned about the behavior, he did not implement a behavior change program at this time. He had worked with kindergarten children in the past who were shy and quiet and did not begin to interact verbally in the classroom until just before Christmas vacation.

The paraprofessional continued to collect data 1 day each week until mid-December. No change was noted in Maryann's behavior.

Mr. Parker concluded that the behavior had endured too long and that a behavior change program was needed to help Maryann. He conferred with the school's language therapist, who evaluated Maryann. He also discussed the problem with Maryann's mother, who agreed to participate in a home–school behavior change program. The intervention was implemented immediately after the Christmas holidays.

The antecedents and establishing operations of the behavior should also be determined in designing a behavior improvement plan. Antecedents may be seen as the "triggers" for a behavior (Aspy & Grossman, 2007). **Antecedents of effective management** are those interventions that change the environment to prevent a behavior from happening. Examples of antecedents that are easily managed are sitting next to a specific peer, sitting by a window, or presenting a task that a student does not like. However, not all triggers can or should be removed. If a student always acts out during a specific class, it is not effective to simply eliminate that class from the student's schedule.

Establishing operations are often out of the teacher's (and often the student's) control. These may include medication changes, hunger, lack of sleep, or family circumstances. Again, even though the teacher should recognize the role that the event or condition plays in the behavior, excusing ineffective or unconventional behaviors because of the setting event is not helpful to the student's development. Rather, building in coping strategies for the student will be more effective.

The teacher or parent must also consider the intensity of the behavior. Some behaviors, although unacceptable, are relatively mild and unobtrusive. They do not generally interfere with the classroom process or the individual child's overall functioning. Of course, other behaviors, although infrequent, are so intense that they are extremely obtrusive. Not only do they adversely affect the individual's overall functioning, but they also interfere with the classroom program and group process. Such behaviors must be changed.

■ *Examples*

Ricky, identified as having emotional/behavioral disorders, is 7 years old and included in first grade with supports. Ricky has temper tantrums that are unpredictable, and frequent. These tantrums involve lying on the floor with feet and arms flying and verbalizations that are interesting but disturbing combinations of four-letter words. The tantrums last up to 45 minutes, averaging about 25 minutes.

These tantrums destroy the classroom program, frighten the other children, and interfere with Ricky's overall functioning. The behavior must be changed.

Keith is 13 years old and in the seventh grade. Occasionally, he manifests some behaviors that are bothersome but normal for his age group, such as know-it-all behavior, big-shotism, and negativism. These behaviors are of minimal intensity. They are manifested by a wise remark at the termination of a conversation, such as Keith saying "No, I won't" before beginning the directed task. The behaviors are generally ignored by others and have little effect on either the classroom process or Keith's overall functioning.

The final characteristic to be considered in the selection of a target behavior is the type of behavior. Some behavior that is disturbing to some adults and children is really quite normal from a child development point of view. In fact, a child who did not manifest such behavior might be considered abnormal.

■ *Examples*

Paul is a sixth-grader and a straight-A student. When he is asked whether he likes school, his teacher, and so on, he says, "No, I hate it."

As most teachers realize, Paul's behavior is quite normal for a sixth-grade boy.

It is within normal limits and of a kind that does not necessitate a formal intervention program.

Russell is 12 years old and in a junior high school special class. He has an uncontrolled temper and frequently tells his teacher, among other things, to "Go to Hades!" or "Drop dead!" Russell gets into occasional fights with his classmates. These fights are extremely vicious. On two occasions, he has inflicted injury on his opponent.

Russell's behavior is of a type that cannot be ignored. An intervention must be implemented, both for his benefit and for the safety of his peers.

After these variables (type, frequency, duration, intensity, and number) have been considered and a target behavior selected, the teacher must decide the direction of the behavior change process. A behavior may be increased or reduced as a consequence of an intervention. Table 6.1 presents the behavior change directions and examples of each.

TABLE 6.1   Behavior Change Directions

Direction	Example
Increase	Group participation
	In-seat behavior
	Interaction with peers
	Typing skills
	Reading rate
	Number skills
	Study skills
Reduce	Verbal outbursts
	Inattentiveness
	Use of four-letter words
	Food intake
	Smoking
	Talking during study period
	Spelling errors

Behavior change programs, then, are implemented to increase acceptable behaviors or decrease unacceptable behaviors. Teachers can easily select behaviors they wish to increase or decrease. In most instances, however, the practitioner takes the child's manifestation of acceptable behaviors for granted and does not systematically reward such behaviors. More effort should be made to prevent unacceptable behaviors from developing, using the systematic rewarding and maintenance of existing acceptable behaviors. In regard to positive behavioral support, identifying replacement behaviors and increasing their occurrence is an essential part of the behavior change process. Positive behavioral support is discussed in some detail in Chapter 7.

Two other important characteristics of the target behavior are that they be observable (**observability**) and measurable (**measurability**). Behaviors must be readily observable in the environment in which they occur.

■ *Examples*

Ernest, in Ms. Morale's words, is "an unhappy child." Ms. Morale would like to decrease his unhappiness (and increase his happiness). However, when she attempted to observe and quantify Ernest's unhappiness, she abandoned the behavior change program before the baseline data were collected.

Brian seldom participated in organized group activities on the playground. Mr. Spencer wished to increase his level of activity. He recorded Brian's group participation rate on the playground during morning recess. Mr. Spencer easily established Brian's baseline of activity; he could thus directly observe and quantify the frequency and duration of Brian's participation in group activities.

Roy is in Mr. Watson's fourth-grade class. He has perfect school attendance during the first 7 months of the school year. Mr. Watson would like to have Roy maintain his present level of attendance for the remaining 2 months of the school year. Roy is the only student in his class with a perfect attendance record. Mr. Watson and the class praise Roy for his attendance. If Mr. Watson and Roy's classmates have anything to do with it, Roy's perfect attendance will be maintained.

Statements describing the target behavior, the precise intervention, and the criteria for success or acceptability of performance should be written or otherwise communicated in objective and specific terminology. These statements are often referred to as **instructional objectives.** The following objectives are written so that the target behavior and the result of the intervention can be observed and quantified:

Increase the number of pages Emma reads during each 15-minute study period.

Decrease the number of times Marion yells during the first hour of the morning.

Increase the number of times Ken uses the reference books located on the science table.

Decrease the amount of time Sharon puts her thumb in her mouth during the school day.

Increase Benji's skill in recognizing and naming the letters of the alphabet during language development class.

Program objectives should be written as instructional objectives, whether the target behavior is in the cognitive, affective, or psychomotor learning domain. The instructional objective in its written form should respond to the following guidelines:

1. What is the child or group of children whose behavior is being changed expected to do or not to do?
   a. Use action verbs to denote the behavior change process.
   b. List the specific resources and materials to be used by the child during the behavior change process.
   c. Indicate specifically the desired interaction between the child and the environment, including persons and objects.
2. What is the level of performance (in terms of accuracy, duration, and skill) expected of the child?
3. What percentage of time or what percentage of occurrences of the desired behavior is the child expected to perform at the criterion level?
4. How will the anticipated changes in behavior be measured for evaluative purposes? What instrumentation is needed for the evaluation?
5. How long will the proposed intervention program be in force before its effectiveness is evaluated?

The beginning practitioner is advised to use the checklist in Figure 6.1 to assist in the target behavior selection process.

COLLECTING AND RECORDING BASELINE DATA

Quantitative data collected before the behavior change intervention has been implemented is referred to as **baseline data.** The process of collecting preintervention or baseline data is grounded in functional behavioral assessment (FBA), which is discussed in Chapter 5. Baseline data provide the foundation on which the behavior change process is established. These data are also used to determine the effectiveness of the intervention during the evaluation step of the behavior change process.

In the Individuals with Disabilities Education Act Amendments of 1997 (IDEA 97), Congress required that an effort be made to understand the relationship between the individual student's learning and behavior. Knowledge of this relationship was seen as essential to planning the individual education plan (IEP). To respond to this mandate, the IEP team must address both the student's learning and the student's behavior. Thus, the team must conduct a FBA and plan and implement a behavior intervention plan (Buck, Palloway, Kirkpatrick, Patton, and Fad, 2000; Fitzsimmons, 1998).

According to Buck et al. (2000), two major assumptions underlie the mandate in IDEA 97: (a) "Behavioral problems are best addressed when the cause of the behavior is known; and cause can be determined best when a functional assessment of the student's behavior is conducted" and (b) "behavior intervention based on positive intervention strategies are more effective in changing maladaptive behavior than are punitive strategies (e.g., suspension). Such intervention strategies should be well thought out, implemented in a systematic fashion, and evaluated so that changes can be made when needed" (p. 4).

Target Behavior Selection Checklist

1. What is the target behavior to be modified? _____

   _____

   _____

2. Each characteristic of the behavior that should be considered in the target behavior selective process is listed below. An X should be marked by each characteristic as it is considered. The pertinency of these characteristics varies with the specific target behavior under consideration.

(X)	Characteristic	Comment
( )	Frequency	
( )	Duration	
( )	Intensity	
( )	Type	
( )	Direction	
( )	Observability	
( )	Measurability	

3. Restate the target behavior in precise and specific terminology. _____

   _____

   _____

FIGURE 6.1 Sample checklist to assist in the selection of a target behavior

Buck et al. (2000) state three reasons for previous failures that led Congress to mandate change:

1. School personnel often provide inappropriate interventions because they failed to identify the true cause of the disruptive behavior.
2. Behavioral interventions are often implemented haphazardly (e.g., lack of consistency, with little attention to the monitoring and evaluation of implementation).
3. Disciplinary actions in schools have tended toward punitive rather than positive behavioral intervention plans.

The FBA is conducted to gather information about the student's behavior problem. The assessment focuses attention on the underlying motivation for the problem. As suggested by Fitzsimmons (1998), the function or purpose of the behavior often is not inappropriate; rather, the behavior itself is inappropriate. Therefore, to effectively assist the student, the focus of the intervention is on the purpose of the behavior rather than the characteristics of the behavior. For example, the purpose of a student's misbehavior may be to gain attention. Rather than trying to decrease through punishment or deprivation his inappropriate outbursts and interruptions during class, the appropriate intervention may be to provide opportunities for the student to receive consistent, repeated, and legitimate attention during class. An effective intervention plan for this student, then, focuses on both increasing appropriate behavior and decreasing inappropriate behavior.

Fitzsimmons (1998) suggests five steps common to the FBA:

1. Determine whether the problem behavior can be controlled by the usual classroom intervention strategies. If it cannot be controlled in this manner, then conduct an FBA.
2. Translate the behavior problem into descriptive behavioral terms. Define the behavior so that it can be directly observed and quantified.
3. Analyze the student's behavior and other information about the student to determine the possible cause of the behavior.
4. Collect data and analyze the problem behavior by focusing on the behavior itself as well as its antecedents and consequences.
5. Formulate a hypothesis with regard to the problem behavior. The hypothesis will state a possible explanation for the behavior's occurrence. The hypothesis is then tested by consistently manipulating the variables suggested within it over a period of time. In effect, the practitioner is conducting a research study to test the significance of the proposed hypothesis.

A behavior intervention plan should be written and incorporated into the student's IEP. Scott and Nelson (1999), as cited in Jolivette, Scott, and Nelson (2000), suggest a 10-step process for integrating FBA data into the behavioral intervention plan:

1. Determine the function of the behavior. A functional assessment of the behavior is conducted to determine the purpose of the learner's behavior problem.
2. Determine an appropriate replacement behavior. The alternative appropriate behavior(s) should serve to replace the purpose of the inappropriate behavior and be acceptable to others in the learner's environment.
3. Determine when the replacement behavior should occur. Determine when it is appropriate for the alternative behavior to occur, and instruct the learner in the use of the behavior.
4. Design a teaching sequence. As in the instruction of academics, an instruction plan should be developed to teach the learner the alternative acceptable behavior.
5. Manipulate the environment to increase the probability of success. Arrange reinforcers within the environment to increase the probability that the alternative behavior will occur and be positively reinforced.
6. Manipulate the environment to decrease the probability of failure. Arrange the environment to decrease any barriers to the occurrence of the alternative behavior.
7. Determine how positive behavior will be reinforced. Arrange the environment so that the alternative behavior will be reinforced with consistency. In addition, the environment must be arranged so that the alternative behavior will be reinforced, as necessary, with appropriate frequency and, as necessary, with artificial and natural reinforcers.

8. Determine consequences for occurrences of the problem behavior. Design strategies to be implemented when the learner exhibits the inappropriate behavior.
9. Develop a data collection system. Collect data on the frequency, intensity, and duration of both the inappropriate and the alternative behaviors. This system must also include the frequency, intensity, and duration of the problem behavior prior to the implementation of the intervention plan to teach the learner the alternative behavior.
10. Develop behavioral goals and objectives. These are similar to the goals and objectives developed to instruct in academic areas.

The plan should be positive in nature rather than negative. It should emphasize what the student can do rather than what he or she cannot do. It has been generally demonstrated that positive interventions have a more long-lasting effect on student behavior than negative interventions. Both positive behavioral support and FBA are addressed in detail in Chapter 5.

The behavior intervention plan may include manipulation of variables that precede the observable behavior, instructing in alternative forms of appropriate behavior or providing reinforcement for appropriate behavior (Jolivette et al., 2000).

■ *Example*

The behavior change program Mr. Dixon developed for Jean concerned increasing the amount of time Jean remained in her seat during history class. Mr. Dixon collected baseline data for 1 week. The data demonstrated that Jean usually remained in her seat an average of 10 minutes at a time before she was up and about the classroom. This information provided Mr. Dixon with the data he needed to determine the kind and characteristics of the reinforcement schedule to be implemented. To ensure that Jean received immediate reinforcement for staying in her seat, a fixed interval schedule of 7 minutes was used.

The selection of the fixed interval schedule of 7 minutes was not a haphazard choice. It was based on the fact that Jean had demonstrated that she could, on the average, remain in her seat for 10 minutes without interference. Therefore, it was reasonable to select a 7-minute interval because that was a level of performance that Jean could easily attain. Consequently, she could be frequently reinforced for appropriate behavior.

If Mr. Dixon had not collected baseline data but had proceeded on a hunch, he might have selected a fixed interval schedule of 11 minutes. With this interval, there would be a strong possibility that Jean would be infrequently rewarded and that her behavior would not change significantly.

Reinforcement is initiated at a level of performance either above or below the baseline, depending on whether the behavior is to be increased or decreased. For instance, you want to work with a student on increasing the number of words he can read per minute. You know that the student can read 75 words per minute. To start at baseline or above baseline would usually mean waiting too long to get the appropriate behavior, and your behavior change program may not be effective. If, however, you start your reinforcement at a level below baseline—in this case, for example, at 65 words per minute—you have then established a level at which you can provide immediate success for the student and can begin the program on a positive note.

■ *Example*

Ms. Waters has a very active, unpredictable child in her class named Emmet. Emmet is constantly yelling in the classroom, to the annoyance of Ms. Waters and the other members of the group. Ms. Waters initiated a behavior change program but did not collect baseline data since Emmet appeared to yell constantly. She withdrew attention from Emmet each time he yelled and praised him when he was not yelling.

After 2 weeks, Ms. Waters was convinced that no change had occurred in the frequency of the behavior. Emmet seemed to yell in class more frequently. Ms. Waters concluded that "this intervention stuff" only works in textbooks, and she abandoned the project. Emmet is still yelling in class.

It should be stressed that, generally, failure of an intervention lies not in the principles of management but in the application of those principles by the practitioner. In the preceding example, Ms. Waters would have been wise to collect baseline data. She would have been able to evaluate the effectiveness of the behavior change process. Baseline data would have revealed that Emmet yelled in class an average of 21 times a day. When the intervention was abandoned, the behavior was occurring only 18 times a day (Figure 6.2). The behavior was, in fact, changing in the desired direction. However, without appropriate data, 18 yells a day seems very much like 21 when you are immersed in a situation, as in the case of Ms. Waters.

A variety of methods are available for observing and recording baseline data behavior. According to Lennox and Miltenberger (1989), the three categories of methods for collecting functional assessment data are (a) behavioral interviews, rating scales, and questionnaires that depend on information from the individual whose behavior is under consideration or an informant familiar with the individual, (b) direct observation of the target behavior, including its antecedents and consequences, and (c) experimental manipulation of variables in the environment in which the behavior is exhibited. The

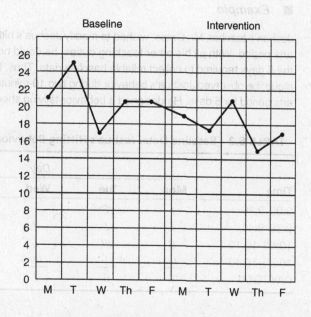

FIGURE 6.2 Frequency of Emmet's yelling behavior before and during the intervention

efficiency of a particular technique varies with the expertise of the practitioner, the characteristics of the behavior, and the setting in which the behavior occurs.

To obtain meaningful baseline data, the practitioner must engage in two activities: counting the behavior and graphing or charting the behavior. **Counting behavior** involves enumerating the number of times the behavior occurs in a given period of time. **Graphing (charting) behavior** involves preparing a visual display of the enumerated behavior in graphic form. These two processes are of paramount importance in the behavior change process.

When the number of occurrences or the average duration of the occurrences of a behavior in a temporal framework are known, the practitioner can select an efficient reinforcement schedule before implementing an intervention. Equally important is the application of the baseline data to the intervention evaluation process. By comparing baseline data with intervention data, the teacher can determine the effectiveness of the reinforcer and the reinforcement schedule. Judgments can be made regarding the responsiveness of the target behavior to the intervention—that is, is the behavior increasing, decreasing, or remaining unchanged?

The recommended method of collecting baseline data is direct observation in the environment in which the behavior occurs. The beginning practitioner is well advised to obtain observation data by means of a time-sampling technique.

A trained observer realizes that it is impossible to observe all the behavior occurring within the environment; neither is it possible to efficiently observe all the occurrences of a single behavior over an extended period. This is particularly true in a busy classroom with many students and a variety of activities occurring simultaneously.

With **time sampling**, the teacher first selects the behavior to be observed and then determines the periods of time that can be devoted to observing that behavior each day during the baseline period. Each occurrence of the target behavior during the observation period is tallied or recorded.

■ *Example*

Joshua's teacher, Mr. Cates, wished to modify Joshua's hitting behavior during the 2-hour language arts period. With all his other teaching duties, he could not observe Joshua the full 2 hours for the 5 days required to collect reliable baseline data. Thus, Mr. Cates used a time-sampling technique; he observed Joshua's behavior during two 10-minute periods for each hour of the language arts period for 5 days. He designed a behavior-tallying sheet to record his observations (Table 6.2).

TABLE 6.2   Baseline Data: Joshua's Hitting Behavior

			Day			
Time	Mon.	Tue.	Wed.	Thur.	Fri.	Time Total
9:00–9:10	/	/		/	/	4
9:30–9:40	/	/	//	/	/	6
10:00–10:10	//	///	/	//	/	9
10:30–10:40	///	/	////	///	//	13
DAY TOTAL	7	6	7	7	5	32

FIGURE 6.3 Joshua's hitting behavior (frequency)

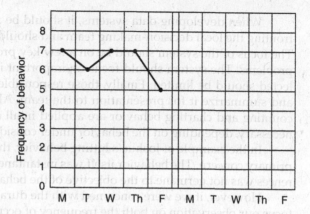

Mr. Cates noted several things as a result of this data-collecting effort:

1. Joshua hit other children a total of 32 times during the observation periods.
2. Mr. Cates observed only one third of the total language arts period—that is, 20 minutes out of each 60 minutes. Thus, in all probability, Joshua hit others approximately 96 times during language arts that week.
3. Joshua hit others, on average, approximately six times a day. However, he hit others less on Friday than on any other day of the week.
4. Joshua hit others more frequently with the passing of each observation period of the day.

During the intervention phase of the behavior change program, Mr. Cates would isolate Joshua for 2 minutes each time he hit another child.

Before initiating the intervention, Mr. Cates transferred the baseline data to a graph to improve his visual image of the behavior (Figure 6.3).

Mr. Cates first made a chart for a 2-week period. His baseline data were entered in the section of the chart reserved for the first week. The remainder of the chart would be used for intervention data. He would enter the number of occurrences of hitting behavior during his observations each day of the intervention phase.

Mr. Cates used the horizontal axis of the chart for the days of the week and the vertical axis for the frequency of the behavior. He plotted the behavior and drew lines between the daily occurrences.

Horner, Sugai, and Todd (2001) state that the use of data is an essential part of developing and implementing a schoolwide system of discipline. They suggest that many teachers and administrators find data to be a "four-letter word" and avoid it if at all possible. A school discipline team's "efficiency, precision, and effectiveness" are improved if its decisions are based on objective data collected on the individual and group problem behaviors it confronts and is responsible for resolving. In addition, data are used to monitor the general patterns of behavior within the school. Horner et al. offer four principles for making data useful in school and classroom: (a) Data should be used for making decisions, (b) data collection and use should emphasize simplicity and efficiency, (c) collected data should be applied to local problems, and (d) data collection and application systems should be designed to be used over time and in a cyclical manner.

When developing data systems, it should be a consequence of the problems confronting the local decision-making team and should focus on resolving those problems. The focus of the system should be on a few key problems rather than a broad range of problems. The system should focus on important issues, and the quantity of data collected should be limited. Finally, those responsible for collecting data should analyze and summarize it for presentation to the team. Although the same basic methods of counting and charting behavior are applied in all cases, certain modifications may be necessary, depending on the behavior under consideration.

In the example of Joshua's hitting behavior, the frequency of the behavior was the primary concern. The behavior itself was instantaneous; thus, the duration of the occurrences was not germane to the objective of the behavior change program.

However, if we were concerned with the duration of Bucky's tantrums, we would focus our observation on both the frequency of occurrence and the duration of each occurrence. In this case, we would collect raw observation data in the manner shown in Table 6.3.

Table 6.3 is a tally log for Monday only, but the tally logs for the remaining 4 days of the baseline period are similar. The teacher, Mr. Wagner, is interested in decreasing both the frequency of the behavior and the duration of the behavior when it does occur. Mr. Wagner has noted in the comments column that the tantrums occur when changes in group activities are taking place, such as at the end of reading period; at the beginning of science; at the beginning of lunch time; and when it is time to go home.

The planned intervention is as follows:

1. Intervene before the transition period and assist Bucky through the potential tantrum period.
2. If a tantrum does occur, isolate Bucky immediately until 2 minutes after the tantrum ceases.

As a result of this baseline data-collecting procedure, Mr. Wagner designed two graphs to visually display the behavior. Figure 6.4 is concerned with the number of tantrums a day. Figure 6.5 represents the average duration of the tantrums.

Regardless of the specific target behavior being charted, the practitioner should remember that the **ordinate points** are generally located on the vertical axis of the chart and the **abscissa points** on the horizontal axis. Ordinate points represent the behavior's

TABLE 6.3 Bucky's Tantrums (Duration and Frequency)

Time			
Begin	End	Total Minutes	Comments
9:31	9:38	7	End of reading
11:03	11:12	9	Beginning of science
12:07	12:17	10	Lunch time
2:30	2:39	9	Time to go home

Total occurrence for day: 4
Average duration: 9 minutes
Day: Monday

FIGURE 6.4 Bucky's tantrums (frequency)

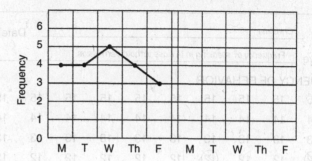

FIGURE 6.5 Average duration of Bucky's tantrums

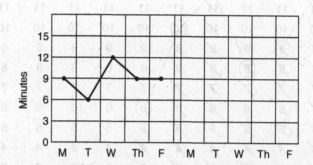

frequency, duration, and percentage of occurrence. Abscissa points represent the hours, days, and sessions of observation (Axelrod, 1983).

To facilitate the data collection and graphing processes, Fabry and Cone (1980) and Shea and Bauer (1987) suggest that practitioners apply self-graphing procedures. Examples of these procedures are presented in Figures 6.6 and 6.7. By using these or similar procedures, the teacher can reduce the time and energy devoted to graphing.

If the practitioner wishes to record only the number of responses or behaviors, the system presented in Figure 6.6 is recommended. In this system, the total number of responses or behaviors exhibited by the student is circled for each day or time period. The circles are connected to form a graph.

In the example in Figure 6.6, Mr. Baden was interested in collecting and graphing data on the number of times Christina speaks without permission during industrial arts class. To begin, Mr. Baden completed the identifying information at the top and bottom of the form. During class, each time Christina spoke without permission, the appropriate number in the day's column was slashed. Next, Mr. Baden circled the highest slashed number for the day. He connected the circled numbers as the days passed and formed the graph in Figure 6.6.

A self-graphing event recording procedure is presented in Figure 6.7. To use this format, list the trial responses in the first column; note the dates in the other columns moving from left to right. As the student responds to each trial, make a slash over the corresponding number for the correct response. At the end of the session, circle the number corresponding to the total number of correct responses. As sessions progress, connect the circles to form a graph.

In the example in Figure 6.7, Mrs. Angie is teaching safety words and phrases to Herm using a predetermined sequence. If Herm responds correctly, the corresponding

Student __Christina__   Date Initiated __9/15/06__

Objective __Frequency of speaking in IA class without permission__

FREQUENCY OF BEHAVIOR

15	15	15	15	15	15	15	15	15	15	15	15	15	15	15	15
14	14	14	14	14	14	14	14	14	14	14	14	14	14	14	14
13	13	13	13	13	13	13	13	13	13	13	13	13	13	13	13
12	12	12	12	12	12	12	12	12	12	12	12	12	12	12	12
11	11	11	11	11	11	11	11	11	11	11	11	11	11	11	11
10	10	10	10	10	10	10	10	10	10	10	10	10	10	10	10
9	9	9	9	9	9	9	9	9	9	9	9	9	9	9	9
8	8	8	8	8	8	8	8	8	8	8	8	8	8	8	8
7	7	7	7	7	7	7	7	7	7	7	7	7	7	7	7
6	6	6	6	6	6	6	6	6	6	6	6	6	6	6	6
5	5	5	5	5	5	5	5	5	5	5	5	5	5	5	5
4	4	4	4	4	4	4	4	4	4	4	4	4	4	4	4
3	3	3	3	3	3	3	3	3	3	3	3	3	3	3	3
2	2	2	2	2	2	2	2	2	2	2	2	2	2	2	2
1	1	1	1	1	1	1	1	1	1	1	1	1	1	1	1

criteria

0	0	0	0	0	0	0	0	0	0	0	0	0	0	0	0

9/15   9/16   9/17   9/18   9/19   9/22   9/23

DATES

Directions:
- Indicate behavior counted.
- Enter criteria line.
- Cross out one number each time the behavior occurs.
- Circle number of times the behavior occurs each date.
- Connect the circles to form graph.

FIGURE 6.6   Frequency data collection and graphing form

number in the day or session column is slashed. At the end of the session, Mrs. Angie counts the number of slashes and circles the appropriate number under the day's column. As the days or sessions progress, she connects the circled numbers to form a graph. The methods of counting and charting behavior presented in this section are the ones used most frequently in the field, probably because of the ease with which the practitioner can visually perceive and evaluate the data and thus determine the status of the behavior at a given point in time.

Student __Herm__   Date Initiated __1/15/06__

Objective __Recognize safety words and phrases__

TRIAL RESPONSES   DATES

		1/15	1/16	1/19	1/20	1/21	1/22	1/25	1/26	1/27	1/28
A	Stop	15	15	15	15	15	15	15	15	15	15
B	Go	14	14	14	14	14	14	14	14	14	14
C	Caution	13	13	13	13	13	13	13	13	13	13
D	Yield	12	12	12	12	12	12	12	12	12	12
E	Don't walk	11	11	11	11	11	11	11	11	11	11
F	Walk	10	10	10	10	10	10	10	10	10	10
G	Keep to right	9	9	9	9	9	9	9	9	9	9
H	Do not enter	8	8	8	8	8	8	8	8	8	8
I	Merge	7	7	7	7	7	7	7	7	7	7
J	No right on red	6	6	6	6	6	6	6	6	6	6
K	Right on red	5	5	5	5	5	5	5	5	5	5
L	4-way stop	4	4	4	4	4	4	4	4	4	4
M		3	3	3	3	3	3	3	3	3	3
N		2	2	2	2	2	2	2	2	2	2
O		1	1	1	1	1	1	1	1	1	1
P		0	0	0	0	0	0	0	0	0	0

Directions:
- Enter objective.
- Place a slash (/) over the number in the dated column for a correct response.
- At the end of the lesson, circle the number in the column that corresponds to the total correct responses (slashes) for the lesson.
- Connect the daily circles to make a graph.

FIGURE 6.7 Self-graphing event recording form

Observer Reliability

To increase confidence in their skills as observers, it is recommended that teachers conduct **interobserver reliability** checks. To do this, a second observer should be invited to observe and record the target behavior. This should be done occasionally during both the baseline and the intervention phases of the behavior change process. It is important that the second person observe the target behavior at the same time under the same circumstances and use the same definition of the behavior as the first observer.

By comparing the results of the two observations, using the following formula, an interobserver reliability percentage or quotient can be calculated. The closer to 100% the quotient is, the greater the confidence the practitioner has in the observation data. For example, Mrs. Sims and Mr. Horner observed Darlene's behavior together for a total of 20 5-minute intervals. Mrs. Sims observed the target behavior 20 times; Mr. Horner observed it 18 times. Using the formula, their interobserver reliability quotient is

$$(18/20) \times 100 = 90\%$$

Kerr and Nelson (2002) refer to this procedure as calculating "point-by-point reliability."

To obtain an interobserver reality quotient for frequency data, divide the frequency reported by the observer with the lesser frequency by the frequency reported by the observer with the greater frequency and multiply the results by 100.

For example, Mr. Luther and Ms. Shanks were both observing Angel's frequency of cursing. They observed during the same time period. Mr. Luther recorded 12 curses; Mr. Shanks recorded 11. Using the formula, their interobserver reliability quotient is:

$$(11/12) \times 100 = 91.66\%$$

Kerr and Nelson (2002) refer to this procedure as calculating "total reliability."

IDENTIFYING REINFORCERS

A behavior change intervention is only as effective as its reinforcer. Regardless of the intervention applied in a behavior change program, if the exhibition of the behavior is not reinforced, the behavior probably will not change. In a behavior change program, all factors may be carefully planned and the intervention precisely implemented, but if the child is not reinforced by the result of his or her behavior, little probability exists for a permanent behavior change.

■ *Example*

Jean's third-grade teacher, Ms. Wildler, developed what she considered to be a foolproof intervention to reduce Jean's off-task behavior. She decided that for each 5-minute period that Jean was on task during language arts period, she would receive a small piece of fruit. Ms. Wildler implemented and monitored the intervention for 1 week. Jean's behavior did not change. During her observation, Ms. Wildler noted that each time Jean received a piece of fruit, she either gave it to another student or dropped it in the wastebasket. Jean did not like the pieces of apple and orange that Ms. Wildler was using as a reinforcer.

Remember: A reinforcer is not necessarily a desirable or undesirable consequence for a child merely because the child's teacher or parent believes it should be (Downing, Moran, Myles, & Ormsbee, 1991; Shea & Bauer, 1987; Smith & Rivera, 1993).

■ *Example*

Mr. Jackson, the ninth-grade teacher at Edville Middle School, was having difficulty getting his third-period social studies class to concentrate on their studies. He decided that he would begin to systematically reinforce their efforts by sending weekly praise notes to their parents.

Mr. Jackson knew that every student liked to have notes of praise sent home. Rod, a class leader, became very agitated when he learned of Mr. Jackson's plan. Rod did not want his parents to know that he enjoyed school. His parents thought he should drop out of school and get a job when he was old enough.

A specific reinforcer is not necessarily desirable to all students.

■ *Example*

Mrs. Karaker, an experienced teacher, maintains a reinforcement menu of at least 10 items for her fifth-grade students. She knows the students have individual preferences and become bored with the same old reinforcer day after day. One student may select a "homework-free day" pass, whereas another student may select an "early dismissal" (15 minutes free at the end of class). The only true test of the effectiveness of a specific reinforcer with a specific child is implementation—that is, "try it."

How can the teacher or parent identify potential reinforcers for the child whose behavior is to be modified? If an FBA (see Chapter 5) has been conducted, then the variables (reinforcers) that maintain or encourage the behavior have been identified and can be manipulated. In other situations, asking the child or the parent, or observing the child, can be used to identify potentially effective reinforcers.

Interview with Child

Interviewing a child to determine what he or she finds reinforcing is frequently productive. The interview should be structured, and the preference list may be used to stimulate discussion. The child is encouraged to express and discuss desires; he or she is asked questions such as "What kinds of things do you like to do?" "What are your favorite toys?" and "What do you like to do more than anything else?" The child's responses will be of great help in attempting to pinpoint those items and activities to be used as reinforcers. In addition, the interviewer has the opportunity to thoroughly explain the behavior change program and answer the child's questions.

The use of the interview technique provides the child with an opportunity to learn to select reasonable and positive reinforcers. Many children initially have difficulty making reasonable selections because of a lack of experience in decision making. In this situation, the interview is in itself a learning experience for the child. The interview technique can be used with small groups as well as individuals.

Interview with Parent or Teacher

An interview with a parent or teacher also can be used in an effort to obtain and rank the child's reinforcers. Although less desirable than a direct interview with the child, the parent or teacher interview can be helpful in determining which reinforcers have been applied successfully and unsuccessfully by others. It also may be used to determine the range of successful reinforcers within the child's response repertoire.

The parent or teacher interview is especially valuable to the behavior management consultant who is trying to determine the level of understanding and acceptance of behavior change techniques by the individual who works directly with the child. The obvious disadvantage in applying this technique is that the parent or teacher's level of sophistication as an objective observer is unknown. It should be recognized that the parent or teacher may not be of real assistance in the selection of potent rewards because of a distorted perception of the child's likes and dislikes. However, the use of the technique can be an excellent learning experience for parents and teachers; frequently, it can sensitize them to the importance of meaningful reinforcers for children.

Direct Observation

The most productive strategy for identifying effective reinforcers is direct observation. According to an old saying, "If you want to see a person do something well, observe the individual doing something he or she enjoys."

Direct observation requires the teacher to observe the child's self-selected activities in a variety of situations, such as on the playground, in the classroom, during structured time, and during free time, and to list those activities the child chooses. These self-selected activities and items can be used during the intervention as reinforcers (Mason & Egel, 1995).

■ *Examples*

Ms. Maron observed that Marvin liked to congregate with his friends during recess to trade baseball cards. She decided to allow the boys to have an additional trading time after they finished their arithmetic lesson. The total arithmetic period was 40 minutes. After 30 minutes, the boys who had finished the assignment could go to a special area of the room and quietly trade cards. The longer Marvin took to complete the lesson, the less time he had to trade cards.

Mr. Dee knew that all 8-year-old boys like to play baseball. Mr. Dee wished to improve Jamie's performance in spelling. He told Jamie that each day that he got 80% of his spelling words correct, he could play catch for 20 minutes on the playground. Mr. Dee was astonished when Jamie did not respond to this reward.

Jamie did not respond for several reasons, and Mr. Dee had failed to take them into consideration. Jamie had visual-perception and gross-motor problems, and these difficulties interfered with his skill in large-muscle activities. It was far more difficult to play catch than to flunk spelling. Mr. Dee's fundamental error was that he did not include Jamie in the reinforcer selection process.

Different children value different consequences. It is nearly impossible to identify any event or item that will serve as a positive reinforcer for all children.

In the end, the potency of a reinforcer selected as a result of using any technique can be determined only by implementation. Many reinforcers, thought to be highly potent, fail to be effective with some children, whereas some reinforcers, discovered only on a teacher's hunch, prove to be most powerful in changing behavior.

A few additional suggestions for the selection and use of reinforcers may be useful:

1. Except for a few basic items such as food and water, no item or activity can be identified with certitude as an effective reinforcer before it has been demonstrated to be effective for a specific child. What is highly reinforcing for one child may not be for another.

2. With overexposure, even the most powerful reinforcer will lose strength and must be replaced. The teacher should provide a variety of reinforcers not only to prevent overexposure but also to satisfy the individual and his or her ever-changing preferences. Many teachers provide a "menu of reinforcers" for their children: On any given day, a variety of items or activities are available to satisfy the diverse needs and interests of the children, who are permitted to select from this menu.

3. The task of observing the effects of existing reinforcers and searching for new reinforcers is a continuous process. A good reinforcement system is an ever-changing blend of established and potential reinforcers.

4. Reinforcers should not be thought of only in terms of tangible items. Many activities and privileges are potent reinforcers. Frequently, teachers use a tangible reinforcer (with a social reinforcer) initially during the behavior change program. Later, they change the reward from the tangible reinforcer to a special activity or privilege (always keeping the social reinforcer). In the final stages of the behavior change process, the social reinforcer used intermittently should be adequate.

Although several methods for identifying reinforcers are discussed in this section, the two procedures most recommended are direct observation and a direct interview with the child. Both have proved effective for identifying reinforcers (Karraker, 1977).

The fact that a child is motivated by a specific reinforcer today does not necessarily mean the child will respond to that particular reinforcer another time. A change in performance may be the signal to initiate a new reward. The fact that Lisa correctly completed 25 addition problems on Monday to play with a puzzle, 27 problems on Tuesday to play with a puzzle, and 28 problems on Wednesday for the same privilege does not mean she will respond in a similar fashion on Thursday. To avoid this situation, a reward menu is recommended. The menu allows the practitioner to systematically vary the rewards a child can work for on different occasions. With proficiency gained through practice in the techniques for changing behavior, the practitioner can predict when it is time to change reinforcers.

Schedules of reinforcement are discussed in Chapter 3; however, it should be reemphasized here that the schedule on which the reinforcement is delivered has considerable influence on the behavior change process.

THINNING REINFORCERS

As stated, a goal of the behavior change process is to teach an individual to respond to appropriate and occasional social reinforcers. Consequently, it is necessary for the practitioner to focus particular attention on phasing out or thinning reinforcers over time. Procedures applied to thinning reinforcers are as follows:

Step 1: Social and tangible reinforcers are presented simultaneously to the individual on a fixed reinforcement schedule. This statement assumes that tangible reinforcers are needed initially in the particular situation. This is not the situation in all cases.

Step 2: Social reinforcers are continued on a fixed schedule, and tangible reinforcers are presented on a variable schedule. Tangible reinforcers are attenuated over time and are finally extinguished. Social reinforcers are presented simultaneously with tangible reinforcers during this step.

Step 3: Social reinforcers are presented on a variable schedule. They are attenuated over time and are finally extinguished as the formal behavior change program is terminated.

■ *Example*

Darlene was having considerable difficulty with her spelling assignments. On average, she was correctly spelling 4 of 10 words on the daily tests. In an effort to help her, Mr. Barea, Darlene's teacher, implemented a behavior intervention.

During the first phase of the program, each time that Darlene improved her score from the day before, she received verbal praise from Mr. Barea and a token worth 5 minutes of free time. She was never reinforced for attaining a score lower than her previous highest score.

When Darlene was consistently and correctly spelling 8 of 10 words, Mr. Barea implemented the next phase of the behavior change program. During this phase, Darlene was reinforced with free time less and less frequently. However, she was verbally praised each time she correctly spelled 8 of 10 words.

In the final phase, Mr. Barea phased out the free-time reinforcer completely and systematically lessened the social praise Darlene received to approximate that of the other students in the class.

PROMPTING

Some children need assistance during the behavior change process. This assistance may be manual or verbal and is called **prompting.** Wolery, Ault, and Doyle (1992) define prompts as "any teacher behaviors that cause students to know how to do a behavior correctly" (p. 37). Prompts may include such activities as guiding a child's hand or foot in the completion of a task, moving the child's head to gain his or her attention, taking a child through a task by repeating precise verbal instruction, providing a verbal model for imitation, and providing printed or three-dimensional material that structures a task (Schloss, 1986). Prompts are used to increase the probabilities of success in a task. Prompting is applicable with several behavior change interventions discussed in Chapters 7 and 8.

According to Martin and Pear (1992), prompts are "supplemental stimuli that control the desired behavior but that are not a part of the desired final stimulus" (p. 126). A parent or teacher may wish to apply various kinds of prompts during the behavior change intervention, including verbal prompts (hints or cues), gestural prompts (motions made without touching the student to facilitate response), environmental prompts (the environment is altered to evoke the desired response), and physical prompts (physically guiding the student to the desired response).

Although prompts of various kinds may be a necessary component of the behavior change intervention initially, they must be eliminated eventually; the child must learn to complete the task independently. This gradual reduction of prompts increases self-management. It is important that the practitioner consider the procedures to be used to fade the prompt before it is implemented.

■ *Example*

Marie, a 6-year-old, was enrolled in a physical therapy program in an effort to remediate her physical coordination problems. One of the objectives of her program was walking a 10-foot balance beam without assistance.

During the therapy program's assessment phase, Marie fell off the balance beam seven times in her effort to walk its length unaided. It was decided that during the initial stages of her motor therapy, Marie would be manually guided by a therapist. He would hold her right hand as she walked the beam.

With manual guidance, Marie learned to walk the 10-foot beam with efficiency within a few days. The therapist decided to fade the prompt (manual guidance) and applied the following schedule during the fading process:

1. The therapist reduced the firmness of his grasp on Marie's right hand.
2. The therapist grasped only one finger of Marie's hand.
3. The therapist positioned his hand in progressive steps approximately 6, 9, and 12 inches from Marie's right hand.
4. The therapist walked beside Marie with his hands at his side.
5. The therapist withdrew to the position he normally assumed to observe a person's efficiency on the balance beam.

EVALUATING THE EFFECTS OF INTERVENTION AND ADHERENCE

Once the new behavior has been established at the acceptable level, the practitioner may question whether the observed changes were a result of the intervention or of an unknown intervening variable. This query cannot be responded to with exactitude. However, a procedure is available to test the effectiveness of the intervention. This is the process of extinction, or of reestablishing the baseline (Baseline 2). The process of reestablishing the baseline in this situation is as follows: If a behavior is thought to be maintained at a specific level by a reinforcer, the practitioner can evaluate the effectiveness of the reinforcer by withdrawing it.

Reestablishing the baseline is not always an effective means of evaluating the potency of a reinforcer. If a behavior has been firmly habituated into the child's behavioral repertoire, it will not respond to extinction.

■ *Example*

Mr. Curtain had established Shirley's hand-raising behavior at an acceptable level. He then wondered whether the reinforcer applied in the intervention phase was the factor that had resulted in her change in behavior. The reinforcer was a smile and verbal praise each time Shirley raised her hand in class.

To check the potency of the reinforcer, Mr. Curtain withdrew it; that is, he ceased smiling at Shirley and praising her when she raised her hand in class. Within a few days, Shirley's hand-raising response began to be extinguished. Because of the decrease in Shirley's hand-raising behavior, Mr. Curtain could assume that the reinforcers (smiles and verbal praise) were instrumental in increasing the hand-raising behavior. He had evaluated the effect of reinforcement on the behavior.

Establishing and then extinguishing a behavior is *not* a standard procedure applied in the behavior change process. However, this technique may assure new students of behavior management that their efforts are effective in changing behaviors. Baseline 2 is used in an intervention at the discretion of the practitioner. However, once a teacher or parent has determined that the reinforcer was instrumental in the behavior change program, it would be a disservice to the child not to reinstate it or not to return to the intervention state.

Meyer and Janney (1989) call for more practical measures of data collecting and thus the evaluation of the outcome of behavioral interventions in the classroom and school setting. Their "user-friendly" measures include (a) the student's schedule of activities, which is evaluated periodically throughout the day, (b) a daily log of student behavior, (c) incident reports, and (d) alternative skill acquisition and excess behavior records. These measures of behavior change are suggested by Meyer and Janney because data collection is less arduous and less intrusive into the ongoing teaching–learning process. These same procedures can be used to supplement the baseline and intervention data collection strategies recommended in this chapter.

Another aspect to be evaluated is the adherence of the behavior plan implementers to the intervention plan. Behavior plan **adherence**, the extent to which a behavioral plan is followed as written, has also been referred to as "treatment integrity." To determine whether an intervention is effective, it has to be consistently applied as described.

■ *Example*

Sonia spent much of the afternoon daydreaming. Ms. Soto, her teacher, discussed her concern about Sonia's lack of attention with her mentor teacher, Ms. Burris. Ms. Burris, after observing the classroom and establishing a baseline of Sonia's behavior, worked collaboratively with Ms. Soto to design a plan. Specifically, Ms. Soto would move Sonia to the front of the room, increase the number of questions she asked Sonia, and increase the number of times she would move closer to Sonia and tap gently on her desk, reminding her to pay attention. After 3 weeks, Ms. Burris asked Ms. Soto how Sonia was doing. Ms. Soto responded, "As lost in space as ever."

Ms. Burris, concerned that the behavior persisted, asked to observe Sonia again. Sonia remained in the back of the room, was posed few questions, and remained in her own world. After the observation, Ms. Soto started the conversation with Ms. Burris: "See—she's still in her dreamland."

Summary Points

- The steps of the behavior change process are (a) selecting a target behavior, (b) collecting and recording baseline data, (c) identifying reinforcers, (d) implementing the intervention and collecting and recording intervention data, and (e) evaluating the effects of the intervention.
- The first step in the behavior change process is the identification of the target behavior.
- Behaviors should be addressed one at a time.
- The objective of all behavior change is to benefit the student.
- In describing a target behavior, the type, frequency, duration, and intensity of the behavior should be described.
- The target behavior and the result of the intervention should be observable and quantifiable.

- Data collected before any effort to change a behavior are baseline data.
- Behavioral interventions should be written and incorporated into the student's IEP. In view of IDEA, they should be grounded in functional assessment and positive behavioral support.
- Reinforcement should be initiated at a level of performance either above or below the baseline, depending on whether the behavior is to be increased or decreased.
- Failure of an intervention is more often related to problems in implementation than in the intervention itself.
- Interobserver reliability increases confidence in the data gathered.

- A FBA identifies the variables that maintain or encourage the behavior. Reinforcers also may be identified by interviewing the student, by interviewing the parent or guardian, or by direct observation.
- Reinforcers should be phased out or thinned over time as the new behavior is established.
- Prompting helps a student learn how to perform a behavior appropriately. Prompts are eventually faded as the student becomes successful at the behavior.
- Data are used to evaluate the effects of intervention.

Projects

1. Observe five students. Identify a potential target behavior for each of the students. After observing the behaviors, discuss their characteristics in terms of frequency, duration, intensity, and type.
2. Collect and record accurate baseline data on two of the behaviors observed.
3. Observe a child in a variety of situations, and develop a list of potential reinforcers for this child.

a. As outlined in the text, interview the same child and develop a second list of reinforcers.
b. Interview the child's parent or teacher and develop a third list of reinforcers.
c. Compare the second and third lists of reinforcers. Can differences be noted between the reinforcers selected by the child and those selected by the child's teacher and parents?

Web Resources

For more information on writing instructional objectives, visit this site:
edtech.tennessee.edu/~bobannon/objectives.html

For more information on the issue of thinning reinforcement, visit this site:
www.connectability.ca/connectability/pages/si_tipsheets/promting-fading.pdf

For information about discrete trials and traditional behavior management programs, visit this site:
www.polyxo.com/discretetrial/schedules.html

References

Alberto, P. A., & Troutman, A. C. (1990). *Applied behavior analysis for teachers* (3rd ed.). Upper Saddle River, NJ: Merrill/Pearson.

Aspy, R., & Grossman, B. G. (2007). *The ziggurat model: A framework for designing comprehensive interven-* *tions for individuals with high-functioning autism and Asperger syndrome.* Shawnee Misson, KS: Autism Asperger Publishing Company.

Axelrod, S. (1983). *Behavior modification for the classroom teacher.* New York: McGraw-Hill.

Buck, G. H., Palloway, E. A., Kirkpatrick, M. A., Patton, J. R., & Fad, K. M. (2000). Developing behavioral intervention plans: A sequential approach. *Intervention in School and Clinic, 36*(1), 3–9.

Downing, J. A., Moran, M. R., Myles, B. S., & Ormsbee, C. K. (1991). Using reinforcement in the classroom. *Intervention in School and Clinic, 27*(2), 85–90.

Fabry, B. D., & Cone, J. D. (1980). Autographing: A one-step approach to collecting and graphing data. *Education and Treatment of Children, 3,* 361–368.

Fitzsimmons, M. K. (1998). *Functional behavioral assessment and behavior intervention plans.* ERIC/OSEP Digest E571, pp. 1–3. (ERIC Document Reproduction Service No. ED 429 420)

Horner, R. H., Sugai, G., & Todd, A. W. (2001). "Data" need not be a four-letter word: Using data to improve schoolwide discipline. *Beyond Behavior, 11*(1), 20–22.

Jolivette, K., Scott, T. M., & Nelson, C. M. (2000). *The link between functional behavioral assessment (FBA) and behavioral intervention plans (BIPs).* ERIC Digest E592, pp. 1–4. (ERIC Document Reproduction Service No. ED 438 662)

Karraker, R. J. (1977). Self versus teacher selected reinforcers in a token economy. *Exceptional Children, 43*(7), 454–455.

Kerr, M. M., & Nelson, C. M. (2002). *Strategies for managing behavior problems in the classroom* (4th ed.) Upper Saddle River, NJ: Merrill/Pearson.

Lennox, D. B., & Miltenberger, R. G. (1989). Conducting a functional assessment of problem behavior in applied settings. *Journal of the Association for Persons with Severe Handicaps, 14*(4), 304–311.

Martin, G., & Pear, J. (1992). *Behavior modification: What it is and how to do it.* Upper Saddle River, NJ: Merrill/Pearson.

Mason, S. A., & Egel, A. L. (1995). What does Amy like? Using a mini-reinforcer assessment to increase student participation in instructional activities. *Teaching Exceptional Children, 28*(1), 42–45.

Meyer, L., & Janney, R. (1989). User-friendly measures of meaningful outcomes: Evaluating behavioral interventions. *Journal of the Association for Persons with Severe Handicaps, 14*(4), 263–270.

Paclawski, T. R., Matson, J. L., Rush, K. S., Smalls, V., & Vollmer, T (2000). Questions about behavioral function (QABF): A behavioral checklist for functional assessment of aberrant behavior. *Research in Developmental Disabilities, 21*(3), 223–229.

Panyan, M. C. (1980). *How to use shaping.* Austin, TX: Pro-Ed.

Schloss, P. J. (1986). Sequential prompt instruction for mildly handicapped learners. *Teaching Exceptional Children, 18*(3), 181–184.

Scott, T. M., & Nelson, C. M. (1999). *Using functional behavioral assessment to develop effective behavioral intervention plans: A ten step process.* Lexington: University of Kentucky Press.

Shea, T. M., & Bauer, A. M. (1987). *Teaching children and youth with behavior disorders* (2nd ed.). Upper Saddle River, NJ: Merrill/Pearson.

Smith, D. D., & Rivera, D. M. (1993). *Effective discipline.* Austin, TX: Pro-Ed.

Wolery, M., Ault, M. J., & Doyle, P. M. (1992). *Teaching students with moderate to severe disabilities: Use of response prompting strategies.* White Plains, NY: Longman.

CHAPTER OBJECTIVES

After completing this chapter, you will be able to do the following:

1. Characterize positive reinforcement.
2. Describe shaping.
3. Understand and exemplify modeling.
4. Define and explain contingency contracting.
5. Describe self-management strategies.
6. Identify and illustrate token economy.

Methods of Increasing Behavior

CHAPTER 7

KEY TERMS

Backward chaining

Cognitive behavior management

Contingency contracting

Contract

Forward shaping (or chaining)

Modeling

Self-management

Shaping

Token economy

Judy, a second-grader, is more socially mature than her peers. This social maturity is a result of her close association with her sister Joanne, who is a fifth-grader. The girls spend most of their time playing together and with Joanne's friends. Judy thinks that second-graders are babies and therefore does not associate with them at recess; she associates with them only when necessary in the classroom. Judy is not only socially mature for her age but is intellectually advanced as well.

Behavior problems are developing for Judy among her peers as well as among Joanne's friends. Joanne's friends often invite her to their homes for parties or to the movies. They do not invite Judy because they think she is too young. As Joanne gets older, Judy is finding herself alone more and more frequently. Not having anyone to play with upsets her greatly.

Maybe if Judy's parents and teachers knew more about behavior management, they might encourage Judy's socialization with her peers.

For the past 2 years, Mr. Peterson has been employed as a part-time basketball coach and recruiter at William Tolbert Community College. He has an excellent reputation as a coach and has developed a winning basketball team. He is a full-time employee of a local high school where he teaches physical education. Because of overstaffing and declining budgets, the college is unable to offer Coach Peterson a full-time position.

Mr. Peterson is worried that additional budget cuts will eliminate his position at the college. He fears he will be replaced by the former basketball coach, who is teaching full time in the physical education department. If so, he believes he is developing a winning basketball team for another coach.

He is so paranoid about the former basketball coach taking his team away from him that it is affecting his coaching and his relationship with the college faculty. Mr. Peterson dwells on one topic in all conversations: "I'm working day and night to build a team for someone else."

Maybe if the physical education department chairperson knew more about increasing behaviors, he would be able to help Coach Peterson be more positive toward his part-time position.

The six most common techniques applied in behavior management interventions for increasing a target behavior are (a) positive reinforcement, (b) shaping, (c) contingency contracting, (d) self-management, (3) token economy, and (f) modeling. These basic methods should be of assistance to the beginning practitioner attempting to establish acceptable behaviors in children. The techniques are applicable with both individuals and groups.

POSITIVE REINFORCEMENT

Positive reinforcement, which is discussed in some detail in Chapter 3, is reviewed in this section. Positive reinforcement is the process of reinforcing a target behavior in order to increase the probability that the behavior will recur. It is known by various labels, including positive attention, approval, social reinforcement, and rewarding. The reinforcer tends to increase the frequency or duration with which the behavior is exhibited in the future. The advantages of positive reinforcement are (a) it is responsive to the child's natural need for attention and approval and (b) it decreases the probability that the child will exhibit inappropriate behavior in an effort to obtain needed attention.

Two rules are essential for the effective application of positive reinforcement. First, when a child is initially exhibiting a new appropriate behavior, it must be positively reinforced each time it occurs. Second, once the target behavior is established at a satisfactory rate, the child's behavior should be reinforced intermittently. A key issue that at times is confused is the focus of the praise. Rather than providing some sort of person-oriented praise (e.g., "You are so smart"), the praise should focus on the process ("You're working hard on that) and product ("Congratulations—you are finished") (Corpus & Lepper, 2007).

A note of caution: Public reinforcement is unwelcome by some children under some circumstances. Individuals may be embarrassed by positive reinforcement in the presence of peers, teachers, parents, and others. In addition, the age and gender of the child may have an impact on the effectiveness of the praise. Corpus and Lepper (2007) reported that among fourth-graders, product and process praise dampened the motivation of girls and had little impact on the motivation of boys. However, among both boys and girls in preschool, person, product, and process praise all increased motivation. In addition, cultural diversity may play a role in the effectiveness of praise. African American and white students, with their cultural emphasis on individualism and success, may respond positively to praise, whereas Asian American and Latina students, with a cultural emphasis on collectivism, may be embarrassed by praise (Suzuki, Davis, & Greenfield, 2008).

According to Filcheck, McNeil, and Herschell (2001), controversy exists regarding the effects of praise on children's behavior. This controversy centers around whether praise or other aspects of general attention (i.e., description and enthusiasm) impact learner behavior. They studied children in Head Start programs to determine the effects on compliance of (a) enthusiastic praise, (b) praise that was not enthusiastic, and (c) nonenthusiastically describing the student's behavior praise. They found that the learners had significantly higher rates of compliance in the nonenthusiastic description condition than in the enthusiastic praise group. Both groups of children responded differently in the three types of conditions. However, children who were disruptive and children who responded typically did not react significantly differently to the three conditions. Finally, Filcheck et al. reported that children who had disruptive behaviors were less compliant than their typical peers.

Larrivee (2002) also suggests that the use of praise by teachers for appropriate student behavior may be detrimental to student development as contributing citizens in democratic society. From her review of the literature, she offers 20 potential perils of praise. These include:

- creating dependence;
- increasing learned helplessness;
- discouraging creativity;
- generating disappointment in those who do not receive praise; and
- increasing doubt about personal abilities.

Larrivee recommends teachers communicate in ways more consonant with the principles underlying democratic leadership and interactive teaching. These alternatives may include talking to students in ways that distinguish (a) between the behavior and the student and (b) between a student's work and a student's worth.

According to Sutherland, Copeland, and Wehby (2001), teacher praise has been found to be an effective strategy for supporting both student learning and behavior. However, they found that in classrooms serving learners with behavioral/emotional problems, teacher praise was quite infrequent. These authors suggested several guidelines for the use of effective praise:

1. Praise should be delivered immediately after the exhibition of the target behavior.
2. Praise should be delivered as unobtrusively as possible to maintain the flow of class activity.
3. Praise should be delivered in a manner that demonstrates that the teacher is sincere.
4. Praise by the teacher should include a statement of the positive behavior for which the learner is being praised.
5. Praise statements should be varied in words and gestures.
6. Praise during the beginning stages of learning a new behavior should be frequent, then should be less frequent as the behavior becomes habituated.
7. Praise is faded when the praised behavior becomes part of the learner's usual manner of behaving.

■ Examples

Michael, a kindergarten student, typically drops his coat and book bag by his cubby when arriving in the morning and bolts to the block area. One day Michael happened to hang his coat. Immediately his teacher said to him, "Michael, I really appreciate your hanging up your coat. That's great!" His teacher continued to congratulate him for putting away his belongings. After a day or two, Michael put away his belongings by himself and said to the teacher, "I hung up my stuff." She again congratulated him. Michael continued to put away his belongings, and his teacher praised him intermittently.

Fourteen-year-old George, a member of the "Wild and Crazy Bunch," likes his math teacher, Ms. Chinn, very much. He enjoys receiving her attention, but sometimes it is a little annoying. This is especially true when Ms. Chinn makes a big show in front of the whole class of his successfully completing a difficult problem. It seems the other members of the "Bunch" hassle him after class when this occurs.

In addition to the use of contingent praise for individual students, several studies support the use of group reinforcement. The "Good Behavior Game," initially developed by Barrish, Saunders, and Wolf (1969), remains an evidence-based practice to increase positive classroom behavior. Extensive randomized field trials have been carried out (Tingstrom, Sterling-Turner, & Wilczynski, 2006).

The Good Behavior Game is often called GBG in the classroom. This classwide effort is designed to create a classroom in which the behavior of each child on the team becomes a matter of concern to all children on that team because the team reward depends on all team members' behavior. The goal is to encourage students to manage their own behavior through group reinforcement and the sense of community.

To begin the game, the teacher posts clear rules for student behavior and gives the students examples of those behaviors. The students are then assigned to two or three diverse groups or teams. Though the original version of the game had a negative perspective (the teacher would randomly make a mark on the board next to the name of a team in which a student was breaking the rules), more recent applications that reinforce positive behaviors have evolved. In developing this proactive application, the teacher:

1. identifies key positive behaviors (working independently, helping another student, clearly engaging in the activity) that are going to be encouraged in the classroom;
2. describes the "Good Behavior Game" in which the class is broken into two or three diverse teams;
3. randomly announces throughout the day that it is "GBG time," names students from the groups, and gives the teams a point for any students who are practicing one of the desired behaviors; and
4. counts up the points at the end of the lesson, period, or day. The team with the most points wins. If teams have equal points, all members of those teams win.

SHAPING

To initiate an intervention for the purpose of increasing a behavior, the teacher or parents need only wait until the child displays the target behavior. When the behavior occurs, it must be rewarded immediately with a potent reinforcer. However, suppose a situation arises in which the level of performance of the behavior is at zero or near zero. What can the teacher or parent do to establish the behavior? There are two alternatives:

1. Wait an undetermined length of time (in some cases, forever) for the behavior to naturally recur.
2. Use a behavior-shaping technique.

Shaping is the systematic, immediate reinforcement of successive approximations of the target behavior until the behavior is established (Shea & Bauer, 1987). It is used primarily to establish behaviors that have not been manifested previously in the individual's behavior repertoire (Kerr & Nelson, 2002). Just as the sculptor shapes and molds an object of art from clay, the practitioner shapes and molds a new behavior from an undifferentiated behavioral response. Shaping also may be used to increase infrequently exhibited behaviors. This technique is applicable to both learning and behavior problems.

The behavior-shaping process includes the following steps:

Step 1: Selecting a target behavior

Step 2: Obtaining reliable baseline data

Step 3: Selecting potent reinforcers

Step 4: Reinforcing successive approximations of the target behavior each time they occur

Step 5: Reinforcing the newly established behavior each time it occurs

Step 6: Reinforcing the behavior on a variable reinforcement schedule

Many of these steps are explained previously in this text. However, some of them require further clarification.

The behavior selected for shaping must be carefully specified. The teacher or parent must be positive that the selected behavior is meaningful to the child in terms of the child's present life context and developmental level.

If the performance level of the target behavior is at zero, the teacher or parent must initiate the shaping process from the child's undifferentiated behavioral manifestations.

■ *Examples*

Tommy's teacher, Ms. Allen, wishes to increase Tommy's communication skills. However, the child enunciates no understandable words. His entire verbal behavior consists of vocal noises, such as screeches, howls, and guttural sounds. The teacher must begin the shaping process with the manifested behavior—that is, vocal noise. She must reinforce successive approximations of intelligible verbal responses.

Jeff, a child with severe disabilities, was having great difficulty interacting appropriately on the playground during circle or ball games requiring running from one specific location to another. When he was required to engage in a game of this type, he ran about at random, dashing here and there, jumping up and down, and in general confusing himself and his playmates.

Mr. Speer, the physical education teacher, wished to modify this behavior. He realized he had to start the change process with the behavior presently being manifested by Jeff. He determined that Jeff did attend to the action of the game and attempted to play by the rules. In this effort to help Jeff, Mr. Speer modified the rules of the game; he established a "new rule" in which all team members ran hand in hand in pairs from one location to another. Jeff was Mr. Speer's partner until he was conditioned to the new running pattern. The game was played by the traditional rules after Jeff developed acceptable skills.

During the behavior-shaping process, the teacher or parent reinforces only those behavioral manifestations that most closely approximate the desired behavior.

■ *Example*

Mr. Jackson designed a shaping intervention to increase the number of assigned math problems that Robert would successfully complete in his workbook during independent study. Robert never completed the 20 problems given for practice. However, baseline data revealed that Robert consistently solved the first 9 problems successfully in each practice section. He simply did not attempt the remaining 11 problems.

During the shaping process, Mr. Jackson reinforced Robert for improvements over his baseline of 9. Robert was rewarded for successfully completing 10 problems, 11 problems, 12 problems, and so on. Robert was never rewarded for completing a quantity of problems below his highest level of accomplishment. Within a short time, Mr. Jackson's intervention data confirmed the fact that Robert was consistently completing the 20 problems successfully. The reinforcer was phased out.

Reinforcing less than the existing baseline results in rewarding behavior that is less desirable than the one you are teaching. For example, if Robert had been completing 10 problems and was rewarded for completing 8, he is learning that 8 is the desired performance level. Remember, *only* the *highest* approximations of the target behavior should be reinforced.

Another important consideration in the shaping process is the teacher or parent's knowledge of how long to provide reinforcement at one level of performance before moving to the next level. Such a movement increases the demands on the child. Determining when to move on is the teacher or parent's greatest dilemma. If reinforcement continues too long at a given performance level, the child's behavior may become so rigidly established that further progress will be difficult. However, if the practitioner insists that the child progress too rapidly from one level to the next, the possibility is great that the new behavior will be extinguished.

Knowing when to progress from one level of performance to the next is of utmost importance. Unfortunately, this knowledge is part of the skill needed for behavior management, and developing it is not easy. The teacher or parent develops this needed sensitivity and skill only with practice and experience in behavior shaping and through knowing the individual child.

The following two examples are presented to clarify the steps in the behavior-shaping process.

■ *Examples*

Ms. Simpkins wished to increase Jim's letter identification skills. Jim could identify 7 of the 26 letters of the alphabet consistently. Before implementing a shaping intervention, Ms. Simpkins determined that stickers were an effective reinforcer for Jim.

During the intervention phase of the behavior change program, Jim was exposed to one new letter of the alphabet at a time. He was to learn each new letter before another letter was presented. Jim was reinforced with a sticker only if he identified the new letter and all previously identified letters. The new letter was always presented last in the daily sequence of letters. After he had learned a letter, it was presented randomly with all the other previously learned letters in the daily session. This procedure was continued until Jim successfully identified all the letters in the alphabet.

TABLE 7.1 Reinforcement schedule for in-seat behavior

Minutes of In-Seat Behavior	Minutes in Reinforcement Area
5	2
5	2
7	2½
8	2½
10	2½
15	3
20	3
25	3
30	3½
45	4
60	4
90	5
120	7½
150	10

Mr. Behe wished to increase Barry's in-seat behavior. Baseline data revealed that, on average, Barry remained in his seat approximately 6 minutes. Mr. Behe had determined through observation that Barry enjoyed listening to his MP3 player. This activity was selected as a reinforcer for acceptable in-seat behavior.

During the intervention, a timer was placed on Barry's desk. He was told that each time he remained in his seat until the timer bell sounded, he would be allowed to go to the reinforcement area of the classroom and listen to his favorite audiobook for a specific number of minutes.

(The reinforcement schedule Mr. Behe used to shape the in-seat behavior is presented in Table 7.1.)

Barry's behavior was shaped with little difficulty. However, during the 20-minute interval between reinforcements, Barry became bored. As a consequence, he remained at the 20-minute interval longer than the teacher had anticipated. At Barry's suggestion, Mr. Behe changed the reinforcer from the MP3 player to jigsaw puzzles.

Shaping may also be referred to as graduated guidance (Kroeger & Sorensen-Burnworth, 2009). Graduated guidance helps you shape behavior by using either a forward or backward chain to master the steps or behaviors in a process, event, or activity. As the student performs a task, the teacher enters with the least intrusive prompt to successfully complete the behavior. The prompt may be a simple point, a verbal prompt, or physical assistance. Through using graduated guidance with **forward shaping or chaining** the student begins the task and gradually receives only reinforcement when a portion of the task beyond that completed independently in the past is finished. In **backward chaining** the task is almost finished, and the steps that the student must complete independently are gradually backed up.

■ *Example*

Mr. McGinnis and Mr. Solomon were responsible for teaching their daughters, Angie and Beth, to make their beds before they left for school in the morning. Mr. McGinnis and Mr. Solomon were very busy in the morning and had little time to teach the task. Mr. McGinnis had a little more time in the morning because he was a professor of behavior management at the local university and left for work later than Mr. Solomon. Both men decided to use shaping.

Mr. McGinnis and Mr. Solomon analyzed the complex task of bed making into the following discrete steps:

STEP	TASK
1.	Remove the pillows.
2.	Pull back the blanket and top sheet.
3.	Smooth the bottom sheet.
4.	Pull up the top sheet and smooth.
5.	Pull up the blanket and smooth.
6.	Fold the top of the top sheet over the top of the blanket.
7.	Put the bedspread on the bed.
8.	Fold back the top one fourth of the bedspread.
9.	Put the pillow on the top of the bed, above the fold in the bedspread.
10.	Place the top one fourth of the bedspread over the pillow.
11.	Smooth and check.

Mr. McGinnis used forward chaining to teach Angie to make her bed. During the teaching process, he and Angie proceeded from Step 1 to Step 11 in order. In the first session, Angie was required to complete Step 1 and was reinforced when the step was completed. After Angie completed Step 1, Mr. McGinnis completed making the bed (Steps 2–11). During the second session Angie completed Steps 1 and 2 and was reinforced, and Mr. McGinnis completed making the bed.

Mr. Solomon used backward chaining to teach Beth to make her bed. He did this because he could reinforce "completed bed making" more frequently and, in addition, the teaching task would be quicker and the bed would look better. During the teaching process, Mr. Solomon and Beth proceeded from Step 11 to Step 1. In the first session, Mr. Solomon completed Steps 1 through 10, and Beth was required to complete Step 11 and was reinforced for making her bed. During the second session, Mr. Solomon completed Steps 1 through 9, and Beth completed Steps 10 and 11 and was reinforced.

Both Angie and Beth learned to make their beds each morning before departing for school. However, Beth appeared to enjoy the learning task more than Angie.

In the progressive shaping intervention, the child is required to engage in a series of steps, each of which is a continuation and progression of the previously learned step or steps. Examples of this intervention are bathing, hand washing, putting on a sweater or socks, and so on.

A chain intervention is composed of two or more separate and distinct steps or skills that are learned and combined sequentially to complete a specific task (Alberto &

Troutman, 1990). Examples of this intervention are tying shoes, polishing shoes, eating, buttoning clothing, and so on.

The following example and conceptual model summarize this discussion of the behavior-shaping process.

■ *Example*

Five-year-old Stephen was nonverbal. His speech teacher selected the initiation of verbal exchanges with his preschool teacher as the target behavior. Baseline data revealed that Stephen's only verbal behavior consisted of babbling, yelling, and screaming. This behavior was frequent when he was in the company of adults he knew. However, he did not consistently emit this behavior in response to queries from others.

Stephen was observed by the speech therapist, who determined that he consistently responded to four tangible reinforcers: pickles, potato chips, prunes, and popsicles.

The behavior-shaping intervention was initiated on a daily basis for 30 minutes during the preschool sessions that Stephen attended at a local school. The effectiveness of the intervention was to be evaluated by means of direct observation of the behavior-shaping sessions and the boy's activities in the preschool classroom with his teacher and playmates.

Shaping began with undifferentiated, inconsistent verbal responses. Within a single school year, Stephen had progressed to initiating some verbal exchanges with others in both the shaping sessions and the preschool class. By the end of the year, he would ask his teacher for milk, juice, cookies, toys, and the like. Although he seldom played with his classmates, he did verbally object to their attempts to confiscate his toys and snacks.

Stephen's ascent up to the behavior-shaping ladder is presented in Figure 7.1. The steps of the ladder are self-explanatory with the possible exception of Steps 3 and 4. During these steps, Stephen consistently used specific verbal noises in place of words. For example, ah was used for the word milk, eh was used for the word no, and the like. Emphasis here was put on converting these emissions into meaningful words.

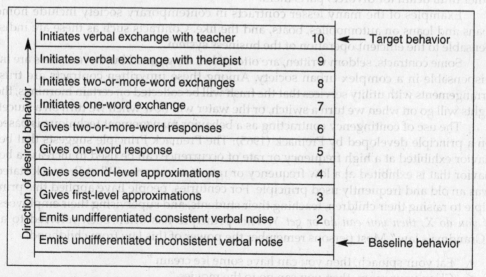

FIGURE 7.1 Behavior-shaping model (Stephen's verbal behavior)

Beilinson and Olswang (2003) applied shaping to teach peer-group entry skills to three kindergarten students with social interaction and communication problems. The children had difficulty both in entering their peer group and in cooperative play. The researchers applied a sequential peer-entry hierarchy or shaping intervention that facilitated the children's movement from low-risk to high-risk interactions with peers in the classroom. The results of the study demonstrated increases (a) in the use of props and verbal statements to enter the peer group, (b) cooperative play, and (c) time spent with peers. The behavior of children post-treatment more closely resembled that of their peers. Though the results of the three cases studied were encouraging, the authors advise caution due to the size of the sample.

CONTINGENCY CONTRACTING

When we consider contemporary emphasis in the media on deferred-payment purchasing, we believe that every child should have some idea of the meaning of a contract. A **contract** is an agreement, written or verbal, between two or more parties, individuals, or groups that stipulates the responsibilities of the parties concerning a specific item or activity. In behavior management parlance, contingency contracting involves organizing events so that the learner gets to do what he or she wishes to do after doing something that the parent or teacher wants him or her to do.

For purposes of this chapter, **contingency contracting** is defined as the process of contracting so that the child gets to do something he or she wants to do following completing something the parent or teacher wants the child to do. We are all parties of contracts in daily living. Some of us are fortunate enough to have a written contract stating the terms of employment. This contract explains what duties we are to perform, for what period of time, and for what compensation. If we perform as specified in the contract, we cannot be fired under normal circumstances. A verbal contract exists between spouses. The terms of the contract state that they will love, honor, and respect one another until death (or divorce) parts them.

Examples of the many lesser contracts in contemporary society include home loans and loans on automobiles, boats, and the like. Contracts such as these are indispensable to the efficient operation of the business system.

Some contracts, seldom written, are often taken for granted but nevertheless are indispensable in a complex urban society. Among these unwritten contracts are trust arrangements with utility services that the trash will be collected on certain mornings, the lights will go on when we turn a switch, or the water will flow when we turn on a faucet.

The use of contingency contracting as a behavior management technique is based on a principle developed by Premack (1965). The Premack Principle suggests that behavior exhibited at a high frequency or rate of occurrence can be used to increase a behavior that is exhibited at a low frequency or rate of occurrence. What Premack stated was an old and frequently used principle. For centuries, people have applied this principle to raising their children, teaching their students, and supervising their employees. *If you do X, then you can do or get Y.* This principle has often been referred to as "Grandma's law." Most persons remember the power of this law from childhood:

- "Eat your spinach, then you can have some ice cream."
- "Clean your room, then you can go to the movies."
- "Cut the lawn, then you can use the car."

TABLE 7.2 X, then Y, statements

X	Then	Y
Sit in your seat 2 hours		Get a 10-minute recess
Complete your term paper well		Get an A
Be a "good" student		Receive a good report card
Volunteer for the football team		Receive recognition from the cheerleaders
Learn a letter of the alphabet		Immediately receive a sticker

- "Do your homework, then you can play computer games."

This same principle carries over to adult life:

- "Write 27 articles and 10 books, then you will be promoted to professor."
- "Don't join the union, then you will retain your job."
- "Don't make waves on the bureaucratic sea of calm, then you will be granted tenure."

Table 7.2 presents a series of X and Y statements found in the classroom.

Within the past several decades, teachers and parents have recognized the significance of individual differences caused by such factors as maturation, general knowledge, locus of control, and experience. Various instructional programs have been developed in response to these differences (Hess, 2003). Contingency contracting is one method that can be used to individualize instruction and behavior control to respond to the child's interests, needs, and abilities; it can be applied to the cognitive, affective, and psychomotor domains of learning. In a study of the truancy behavior of students in an inner-city middle school, Hess, Rosenberg, and Levy (1990) demonstrated that contingency contracting can be applied effectively in conjunction with group counseling.

According to Downing (1990), contingency contracts can be applied to teach new behavior, maintain existing behaviors, decrease inappropriate behavior, and promote enrichment and independent study for both individuals and groups.

The advantages of contingency contracting are many. The method is positive—that is, the child takes an active role in deciding the type and amount of work required. Consequently, personal responsibilities are understood by the child. At regular intervals, the contract is reviewed for the child's reaffirmation. Accountability factors are built into this intervention. The teacher collects empirical data that indicate where the child was, where the child has progressed, and the child's current needs. The teacher can use this information to develop the program, instructional objectives, and developmental objectives with the child.

Self-Brown and Mathews (2003) assessed how classroom structure influences how students are motivated to achieve in mathematics. Using three elementary classrooms, the researchers randomly assigned one of three classroom structure conditions: contingent contract, token economy, or control. In each of the conditions, students set weekly individual achievement goals.

Differences in the goal orientation were assessed by comparing the number of learning goals versus performance goals that students set within and across structure conditions. Students in the contingency contracting group set significantly more learning goals than students in other conditions. No significant differences were demonstrated for performance goals across structures. Within classroom structure conditions, students in the contracting group set significantly more learning goals than performance goals. Students in the token-economy group set significantly more performance goals than learning goals.

Downing (2002) discusses several potential applications for contingency contracting:

- to introduce and teach the learners new behavior;
- to increase the frequency of an existing desired behavior;
- to maintain and support the use and generalization of learner skills;
- to decrease or extinguish learners' existing behavior;
- to facilitate the completion of academic tasks; and
- to document the results of decision making, problem solving, and other interventions.

Downing offers the following step-by-step guidelines for implementing an individualized contingency contract:

1. Identify the area of concern.
2. Describe the circumstances under which the behavior of concern occurs.
3. Analyze the antecedent events that may trigger the behavior and the consequences that may increase the occurrence of the behavior.
4. Determine which, if any, antecedents or consequences might be effective in decreasing the behavior.
5. Develop a hypothesis to explain the student's behavior.
6. Collect and summarize (perhaps in graphic form) the current level of the behavior.
7. Develop behavioral objectives, based on the information or data collected in the previous step, that are specific, observable, and measurable.
8. Identify the unsuccessful interventions that have been applied previously to change the behavior.
9. Develop a list of potentially effective reinforcers that may be effective with the learner.
10. Determine the consequence of the contract for the student if it is a failure. Determine whether there will be negative consequences and whether these will be natural or artificial.
11. Determine who will be involved in agreeing on the terms of the contract and monitoring it.
12. Evaluate the results of the contract.

The teacher serves as contract manager (Hess, 2003), providing facts and explaining the principles. The teacher encourages the child to choose realistic limits. The teacher ensures that both the task and the reinforcer are fair to both parties of the contract (child and teacher).

When contingency contracting is first used with a child, small tasks and small reinforcers are most effective because they allow frequent reinforcement. Lengthy or complex tasks and small reinforcers may defeat the motivational factors inherent in this intervention. If the task is more demanding than the reinforcer is desirable, the learner is not sufficiently motivated to perform. Likewise, the reinforcer should not be greater than the task warrants; otherwise, the instructional objective established for the child is difficult to obtain.

Initially, contracts may encourage and reward approximations of desired behavior. Short work periods are desirable because they permit frequent reinforcement. Low-achieving children usually require immediate reinforcers; consequently, short-term contracts (daily) are most appropriate. Higher achieving children can usually delay reinforcements; therefore, long-term contracts (1 or 2 weeks) are feasible.

The teacher must encourage the child to adhere to the contract for the designated period of time. The child should be cautioned that if the agreed-on task is not performed, the child will not receive the reinforcer. However, if the original contract is too difficult, a new contract must be written for the learner to perform successfully. Every effort should be made to ensure the success of the original contract.

The underlying principle of contingency contracting is constant; the learner, by making decisions concerning personal productivity, develops critical thinking skills, self-control, and the independence that increases productivity.

Two types of contracts are applicable in the classroom setting: verbal and written. Educators have generally found verbal contracts more useful than written contracts. The following are examples of verbal contracts that can be used in the classroom:

- "John, when you have completed eight addition problems correctly, you may play with the puzzles for the remainder of the period."
- "Mary, if you remain in your seat for 15 minutes, you may work in your coloring book for 5 minutes."
- "James, if you come to school on time tomorrow, you may be first in line for lunch."
- "Tom, if you don't hit anyone this morning, you may have an extra milk at lunch."
- "Mike, if you complete your seat work, you may watch *Sesame Street* on television."

Verbal contracts such as these are made daily in the classroom. They work effectively for both the teacher and the child.

Written contracts are more elaborate than verbal contracts. The elaborateness of the written contract depends on the child for whom it is designed. Contracts frequently lose their effectiveness when they include pseudolegal jargon, such as "the parties of the first part," "the parties of the second part," or "henceforth and forevermore." It is recommended that the teacher or parent use the contract format in Figure 7.2 or a similar one. Written contracts, posted or on a student's desk, may also serve as a visual prompt or concrete documentation (Mruzek, Cohen, & Smith, 2007).

Homme, Csanyi, Gonzales, and Rechs (1979) have suggested 10 basic rules for writing a contract for classroom use:

1. The contract payoff (reinforcer) should be immediate.
2. Initially, contracts should call for and reinforce approximations of target behavior.
3. The contract should provide for frequent reinforcers in small amounts.
4. The contract should call for and reinforce accomplishments rather than just obedience.
5. The performance should be reinforced after it occurs.
6. The contract must be fair to both parties.
7. The terms of the contract must be clear.
8. The contract must be honest.
9. The contract must be positive.
10. Contracting must be used systematically as an integral part of the ongoing classroom program.

Date _____

Contract

This is an agreement between _____
(Student)

and _____. The contract begins on
(Teacher)

_____ and ends on _____. It will be reviewed
(Date)   (Date)

on _____.
(Date)

The terms of the agreement are:

Child will _____

_____

_____

Teacher will _____

_____

_____

If the child fulfills his or her part of the contract, the child will receive the agreed-on reward from the teacher. However, if the child fails to fulfill his or her part of the contract, the reward will be withheld.

Student's signature _____

Teacher's signature _____

FIGURE 7.2 Contingency contract

In addition to the preceding rules, the practitioner should consider the following factors when developing and implementing a contract:

1. The contract must be negotiated and freely agreed on by both child and teacher.
2. The contract must include the target achievement or production level.
3. The reinforcer must be consistently delivered in accordance with the terms of the contract.
4. The contract must include the date for review and renegotiation.

One of the major functions of contingency contracting is to get children to the level of development at which they will initiate a contract instead of waiting for suggestions from the teacher.

The key to successful contracting is a negotiation session during which (a) the system of contracting is explained and discussed, (b) the contract is written, and (c) the contract is signed by the child and the teacher. A properly conducted negotiating session is complex

Date ___February 3, 2011___

Contract

This is an agreement between ___Bob Wellrock___ and ___Mr. Bare___. The
                                (Student's name)   (Teacher's name)

contract begins on ___2/9/11___ and ends on ___2/11/11___. It will be
                        (Date)   (Date)

reviewed on ___2/10/11___.
                (Date)

The terms of the agreement are:

Student will ___spell with 90% accuracy the 20 assigned spelling words for Friday.___

Teacher will ___provide a ticket good for admission to the school movie on February 11, 2007.___

If the student fulfills his or her part of the contract, the student will receive the agreed-on reward from the teacher. However, if the student fails to fulfill his or her part of the contract, the reward will be withheld.

Student's signature _____

Teacher's signature _____

FIGURE 7.3 Sample contract

and time consuming, particularly if the teacher has not previously introduced the concept of contracting in the classroom. Both the complexity and the time consumed by the negotiation process decrease as the student and teacher gain experience in contracting. An example of a contract contracts drawn from classroom experience is found in Figure 7.3.

SELF-MANAGEMENT

Cognitive behavior management is a term applied to a group of intervention strategies implemented to instruct learners in self-control. Through these interventions learners become increasingly aware of their cognitive processes and knowledge of how behavior influences academic and behavioral outcomes. The focus is on the evaluation of a learner's behavior and/or academic performance by the learner him- or herself rather than by the teacher (Reid, 1999). According to Swaggart (1998), cognitive behavior management includes (a) observational learning, (b) self-instruction, and (c) self-monitoring. Emphasis in this section is focused on self-monitoring or **self-management**. Observational learning is discussed in the section "Modeling" later in this chapter.

For the student, self-management has three phases (McConnell, 1999):

1. The student asks, "Was I on task?"
2. The student records the answer.
3. The student returns to the task.

Work sheets can be designed for the student to use to record and evaluate his or her responses. The interval used to monitor the target behavior varies according to the needs of the student. The length of the interval will be determined by the frequency, intensity, and duration of the behavior. Interval will also vary with the student's age and developmental level and the setting in which the student is functioning.

McConnell suggests a nine-step self-management procedure:

1. Identify the target behavior. Select a behavior that appears to have the most significant impact on the student's functioning.
2. Define and describe the target behavior so that it can be observed.
3. Collect baseline data and use them to determine the design of the specific intervention to be implemented and to evaluate the results of the intervention.
4. Conduct private and positive conferences with the student. Explain the self-management procedure and its impact on the student's behavior. Discuss the target behavior and baseline data, present and model the appropriate behavior, gain the student's commitment to the self-management intervention, set appropriate goals for the intervention with the student, and select a potentially effective reinforcer.
5. Specify and describe the self-management procedure to be applied.
6. Instruct the student in the use of the self-management procedure to be applied. Provide the student with sufficient practice so that he or she is comfortable with the procedure.
7. Implement the intervention.
8. Monitor the student's implementation of the procedure. Work with the student to improve, if necessary, the effectiveness of the intervention.
9. Conduct periodic follow-up of the student's behavior to ensure that the behavior is being maintained.

In a review of the research literature for a period of three decades, McDougall (1998) found that 240 self-management studies had been published. Only 14 of these focused on students with disabilities in the general school populations. These studies indicated a moderate to strong improvement in student performance after training. The research offers support for the effectiveness of self management in inclusive environments.

Peterson, Young, West, and Peterson (1999) applied and evaluated a programmed generalization intervention in several general education classrooms. They evaluated both the results and the practicality of the intervention. The results suggested that the strategy (social skills training and self-monitoring with teacher match) led to the generalization of improved student behavior in up to six different settings. In addition, the improved behavior was maintained over time. Prevention Plus, a program emphasizing a broad approach for preventing or reducing the antisocial behavior of at-risk youth, was applied with 29 seventh- and eighth-grade students attending a large urban middle school. In the Prevention Plus class, the students were instructed in social skills and self-management procedures.

Using self-management forms, the students attended classes other than the Prevention Plus class. The students' behavior was monitored by both the student and a previously trained teacher. The program used several strategies, including modeling, role playing, behavioral rehearsal, performance feedback, and token economy. Peterson et al. (1999) suggest that, although the study was not experimental, its results are practical.

McDougall and Brady (1998) found self-management procedures to be effective in increasing the fluency of mathematics students in the general education setting. Hutchinson, Murdock, Williamson, and Cronin (2000) found that self-recording, in combination with points and praise and encouragement, increased the on-task behavior and nondisruptive behaviors of a 6-year-old boy diagnosed as emotionally disturbed/behaviorally disordered and on medication. Mathes and Bender (1997) studied the effects of self-monitoring to increase the on-task behaviors of learners with attention-deficit/hyperactivity disorder who were receiving medication. The three 8- to 11-year-old male subjects classified as having emotional/behavioral disorders demonstrated increased on-task behavior when self-monitoring was implemented with medication.

Managing one's behavior without external support is a valued goal of education and critical for achieving success in adult life (Firman, Beare, & Loyd, 2002). Regulating on-task time is essential to success in classrooms, work, and the community. Firman et al. studied a middle school resource room in an effort to investigate the differences in time-on-task between intrinsic and extrinsic forms of self-management. In terms of students with mental retardation, it was found that the more externally assisted procedures resulted in the greatest improvement. However, the less intrusive procedures produced only slightly less effective results. This study suggests that teachers may select less intrusive, more normalized management interventions to help students improve and maintain their behavior.

Snyder and Bambara (1997), using a multiple baseline research design, investigated the effectiveness of a cognitive-behavioral self-management training package on the consistent use of specific classroom survival skills with three seventh- and eighth-grade male adolescents with learning disabilities. The results of the study demonstrated more consistent use of the survival skills by the subjects.

Check in-check out is an evidence-based classwide intervention that supports self-management. Hawken and Horner (2003) suggest that check in-check out is effective because it provides students with increased structure and prompts, support for specific skills, and regular feedback. Each student is provided with a card that demonstrates classwide goals. After a specific time period, the teacher rates the students' response, "checking in" with the student. At the end of the day, the teacher "checks out" with the student, reviewing the day and providing reinforcement according to the classroom plan. Students are also provided feedback and specific praise. Fairbanks, Sugai, Guardino, and Lathrop (2007) used check in-check out as an individual intervention, calling the students who were using the check in-check out cards leaders and the rest of the students' coaches. The coaches were asked to help the leaders earn as many points as possible during the day. At the end of the day, each leader totaled up his or her points and shared the results with the class. If the leaders' total combined points reached a certain level, say 75%, the class earned a reward such as a class game, free choice, simple treat, or pass on homework in one area.

TOKEN ECONOMY

Learning environments vary in the consistency of feedback that they provide for the learner; the more consistent the feedback, the more quickly and easily the individual learns. Learning environments also vary in the degree to which individuals are allowed to set their own work rate. In other words, some environments allow individuals more freedom to work at a self-selected rate than others. Individuals learn more easily and quickly when they are free to set their own pace in working the environment for the desired reinforcer (Ayllon & McKittrick, 1982).

Many children are not able to function appropriately if they must wait an extended time for their reinforcer. In addition, some children have not developed to the level at which social rewards alone are satisfactory reinforcers. In these cases, the use of a **token economy** has proved to be an effective behavior change intervention.

The tokens are usually valueless to the children when originally introduced to them. Their value becomes apparent as the children learn that tokens can be exchanged for a variety of reinforcers, such as being first in the lunch line, earning free time, listening to CDs, watching television, purchasing a favored toy, and so on. This versatility makes the token system superior to many interventions. When the teacher "sells" admission to a movie, use of clay, or the like, the tokens rapidly take on value for the children. When the teacher states the price and asks a child to count out the needed quantity of tokens, the child is engaged in a token economy.

In this manner, the tokens become potent reinforcers. They can be awarded over a period of time for acceptable effort and work. The system allows the teacher to structure the learning environment for positive reinforcement and to provide immediate feedback to the children by administering tokens. Hence, a moderately well run token exchange can promote direct learning regardless of the content of the activity.

These tokens have several advantages over tokens made of rigid, hard materials, such as metal, plastic, and wood. They are made of soft, flexible materials, such as paper, vinyl, or simple pen markings. They are less distracting to have in the classroom atmosphere because they neither rattle nor make noise if dropped on a hard surface. These characteristics eliminate much potential and actual distraction and confusion in the classroom. The tokens are easily glued to a paper, desktop, record card, or chart. They can be permanently affixed to various surfaces to minimize the incidence of misplacement, loss, or theft. However, they must be sufficiently distinctive to prohibit unauthorized duplication.

The following are the basic rules when establishing a token economy system for the classroom:

1. Select a target behavior. (This topic is thoroughly discussed in Chapter 3 and does not warrant further elaboration here.)
2. Conceptualize and present the target behavior to the child or group. It is a well-known fact that an emphasis on "what you can do" is more palatable to children (and adults) than an emphasis on "what you cannot do." Many unsuccessful behavior management practitioners have determined their own failure by introducing a program by saying, "Now you boys and girls are going to stop that noise and fooling around in here. I have this new . . . [and so on]." The children are immediately challenged; they prepare to defeat the teacher and defend their personal integrity.
3. Post the rules and review them frequently.
4. Select an appropriate token.
5. Establish reinforcers for which tokens can be exchanged.
6. Develop a reward menu and post it in the classroom. The children should be permitted to thoroughly discuss and consider the items on the menu. They should be encouraged to make their selections from among the items available. The children should not be permitted to debate the cost (number of tokens) of the various rewards after prices have been established.

7. **Implement the token economy.** Introduce the token economy initially on a limited basis. A complex, sophisticated system as an initial exposure confuses and frustrates the children. Start small and build on firm understanding. Explain the system to the children with great clarity and precision. Be patient and answer all the children's questions. It is better to delay implementation than to create confusion and frustration.

8. **Provide immediate reinforcement for acceptable behavior.** The children will lose interest in the program if the process for obtaining the tokens is more effort than the reward is desirable. Many systems fail because the teacher neglects to dispense tokens at the appropriate time. Rewarding the children immediately reduces frustration and overconcern with the system. When the children are sure they will receive the tokens at the proper time, they can ignore the delivery system and concentrate on their work or behavior.

9. **Gradually change from a continuous to a variable schedule of reinforcement.** As discussed in Chapter 3, quick, unpredictable, or premature changes in a reinforcement schedule can destroy the program.

10. **Provide time for the children to exchange tokens for rewards.** If the token economy is a legitimate class program, make time available during the school day for the exchange. Do not take time from the children's recess, lunch, or free time.

11. **Revise the reward menu frequently.** Children, like adults, become bored with the same old fare day after day.

Rosenberg (1986) studied the effects of daily rule-review and rehearsal procedures on the effectiveness of a token economy with five disruptive and distractible elementary-school students in a resource room program. He found that daily review of classroom rules resulted in an overall time-on-task improvement of 12% and a 50% reduction in disruptive talkouts. Shook, LaBrie, and Vallies (1990) demonstrated the effectiveness of a token economy in the regular classroom with the disruptive behaviors of two boys and one girl ranging in age from 6 to 7 years. Higgins, Williams, and McLaughlin (2001) successfully implemented a data-based token economy with a 10-year-old, third-grade boy with learning disabilities to decrease behaviors such as out-of-seat, talking out, and poor posture. Reid (1999) found the token economy strategy to be effective with learners with attention-deficit/hyperactivity disorders.

In a discussion of token economy reinforcers, Raschke, Dedrick, and Thompson (1987) recommended the use of contingency packages to motivate reluctant learners. The packages are tangible reminders of potential reinforcers. They consist of three-dimensional displays designed specifically to advertise rewards. The packages should be novel, exciting, and age appropriate. Two packages described in detail by Raschke et al. included the "Flip-the-Lid-Robot," a multidrawered container in which each drawer holds various rewards, and "Touchdown Triumph," a football game board designed for adolescents. Raschke (1986) suggested a similar package using available classroom materials (construction paper, sponges, pipe cleaners) to make "delicious" incentives (hamburgers, french fries, ice cream cones) for display in the classroom.

In an effort to increase motivation and lessen the possibility of boredom among fifth-grade students they studied, Anderson and Katsiyannis (1997) developed and implemented a token economy based on an automobile driving and speedway theme. The economy included common items related to driving and auto racing, such as license plates, stop signs, stoplights, speeding tickets, and so on. The authors found the economy to be effective with their students.

Lyon and Lagarde (1997) suggested that teachers develop a "Graduated Reinforcement System" for use with individuals, small groups, and whole classroom groups at the upper elementary and secondary school levels. According to the authors, the system is easy for students to understand, allows the monitoring of both social and academic performance, simplifies record keeping, and eliminates differential points for each target behavior and differential prices for each reinforcer. Points are awarded by levels of performance, and groups of reinforcers are related to these various levels.

Clark (1988) recommended the use of "Behavior Tickets" to extend the token economy outside the classroom. The tickets can be used by involved adults in any class or area of the school in which the student works or plays. When the student leaves the classroom to go to the restroom, lunchroom, playground, or elsewhere, he or she is given a ticket. To earn points, the students must return to class with the ticket in one piece. If the student is caught misbehaving by another teacher, that teacher stops the student, requests the ticket, and tears it into two pieces. Missing tickets are considered to be torn tickets. This technique, according to Clark, has two advantages: (a) The student can be reinforced for appropriate out-of-classroom behavior, and (b) misbehavior can be addressed as soon as the student returns to the classroom. All tickets must be returned to the teacher at the end of the class period or day.

Of course, the system assumes that all adults in the school are trained in the technique and willing to participate. Examples of the point card and tally form to be used for specific behaviors are presented in Figures 7.4 and 7.5. Maher (1989) suggested a "punch-out" card for use as a behavior recording technique. The teacher punches a hole in the card when the student exhibits the appropriate behavior.

Point Card

Student's name _____   Date _____

1	2	3	4	5	6	7	8	9	10
11	12	13	14	15	16	17	18	19	20
21	22	23	24	25	26	27	28	29	30
31	32	33	34	35	36	37	38	39	40
41	42	43	44	45	46	47	48	49	50
51	52	53	54	55	56	57	58	59	60
61	62	63	64	65	66	67	68	69	70
71	72	73	74	75	76	77	78	79	80
81	82	83	84	85	86	87	88	89	90
91	92	93	94	95	96	97	98	99	100

FIGURE 7.4   Point card for specific behavior

Point Tally Form

Student's Name: _____ Date _____

Monday													
Tuesday													
Wednesday													
Thursday													
Friday													

TOTAL

Monday	
Tuesday	
Wednesday	
Thursday	
Friday	
Week	

FIGURE 7.5 Tally form for specific behavior

Punching the card is paired with social and tangible reinforcement, if tangible reinforcement is used.

The teacher, with little difficulty, may plan and implement a multipurpose token economy in the classroom. In this situation, the children earn tokens for a variety of appropriate behaviors as well as academic effort and academic success. Tokens or points can be presented to the child for any or all of the following behaviors:

- being present at the workstation on time;
- having appropriate work tools available for use;
- attending to the instructor's directions;
- exhibiting appropriate social behavior during the work period (raising the hand for attention, remaining at the work station, not talking without permission);
- engaging in the assigned work task during the work period—that is, showing effort;

Point Card for Multipurpose Token Economy

Child _____ Day _____ Date _____

Work period	Readiness	Social behavior	Work effort	Work success	Teacher comments
9:00–9:15			*	*	
9:15–10:00					
10:00–10:30					
10:30–10:45			*	*	
10:45–11:30					
11:30–12:00					
12:00–1:00			*	*	
1:00–1:30					
1:30–2:45					
2:45–3:00			*	*	

*Points for work effort and work success are not available during these periods because of the nature of the activity: opening exercises, recess, lunch, and closing exercises.

FIGURE 7.6   Point card for multipurpose token economy

- correctly or satisfactorily completing the assigned work task; or
- returning work tools to their appropriate place.

Tokens are presented for various appropriate behaviors and withheld for inappropriate behaviors. A point card for a multipurpose token economy is presented in Figure 7.6.

■ *Examples*

Mr. Newman, a junior high school math teacher, was having difficulty with Charlie, who had developed the habit of counting and computing aloud while doing math assignments. At first, this behavior was not a serious problem, but then it began to distract many of the other students.

Mr. Newman decided to implement a token economy system to modify Charlie's behavior. He discussed the system with the class, established a set of rules, and developed a reward menu before implementing this intervention. (The reward menu is presented in Table 7.3.) The token economy was used with the entire class and effectively modified the behaviors of Charlie and his peers. Tokens were initially presented on a fixed interval schedule; as the group progressed, however, a variable interval schedule was introduced. Throughout the program, Mr. Newman conscientiously paired social rewards with the tokens.

TABLE 7.3   Mr. Newman's reward menu

Reward	Time (Minutes)	Cost (Points)
Checkers	10	15
Cards	10	15
Puzzles	15	20
Magazines	18	25
Chess	12	30
Model car kits	10	20
Comic books	5	10
Bingo	15	25
Quiet conversation	10	10

Two physical education teachers were having problems with student participation in class. They were being bombarded with complaints such as headaches, back pain, sore toes, and sore ears. After discussing the token economy system between themselves and with their students, they decided to initiate a program to increase participation. A student delegation aided the teachers in developing the reward menu shown in Table 7.4.

Mrs. Thomas has been attempting to get Mary, her 16-year-old daughter, to share in the housekeeping. Mrs. Thomas has had very little success.

One day, Mary asked whether she and three of her friends could go into the city for dinner and the theater. The big evening was to be in 4 weeks. Mrs. Thomas said yes—if Mary would pay for the trip by helping with the housekeeping. Mrs. Thomas made a list of tasks Mary was responsible for around the house. It included cleaning her room, washing and drying clothes, ironing, washing windows, cleaning the bathroom, helping with the cooking, and so on. Each task was assigned a specific point value. The points could be exchanged for money.

When the time for the trip arrived, Mary had sufficient money for the evening. In addition, she had an improved attitude about helping to take care of the house.

TABLE 7.4   Physical education class reward menu

Reward	Time (Minutes)	Cost (Points)
Getting free time	15	50
Using trampoline	10	40
Shooting baskets	5	30
Acting as activity leader	—	25
Talking with friend	10	40
Playing badminton	10	30
Using trapeze	15	50
Sitting out an activity	—	100

In these three examples, the token economy system proved to be effective in increasing participation. In two of the cases, the teachers changed the reward menu frequently in cooperation with their students throughout the duration of the program. Frequently, the token economy intervention described in this section includes "response cost" procedures. This intervention is defined, discussed, and exemplified in Chapter 8.

MODELING

One of the most common forms of human learning is accomplished through the processes of observation and imitation. All parents and teachers can relate a variety of acceptable and unacceptable behaviors exhibited by their children and students that are imitations of their own (the adults') personal acceptable and unacceptable behaviors. This form of learning at various times and by various theorists and practitioners has been called modeling, observational learning, identification, copying, vicarious learning, social facilitation, contagion, role playing, and so on (Bandura, 1969; Striefel, 1981). In this text, the term **modeling** is used to describe learning by observation and imitation.

As a behavior change method, modeling is the provision of an individual or group behavior to be imitated or not imitated by an individual. This is one of the oldest and most frequently applied methods of changing behavior. Mothers and fathers, husbands and wives, teachers, and principals have been suggesting models to their sons, daughters, spouses, and students for generations:

- "Be a good boy like your brother John."
- "Why can't you be like George, an excellent father, a great lover, and a good provider?"
- "Mary, can't you be a good student like Eileen?"
- "Why can't you behave like the other boys and girls?"

Several state and national organizations exist for the purpose of providing children with acceptable social models. These organizations provide children with either the direct services of a live model or an abstract model inherent in their program and printed materials. Among these organizations are Big Brothers and Big Sisters, Boy Scouts and Girl Scouts, 4-H, and Little League.

According to Bandura (1969) and Clarizio and Yelon (1967), exposure to a model has three effects:

1. *Modeling effect or observational learning.* Children may acquire behavior from a model that was not previously a part of their behavioral repertoire. In this situation, the model performs a behavior that is imitated by the child in substantially identical form. Examples of the modeling effect are teaching a nonverbal child to verbalize in imitation of a model and teaching a child signing skills as a method of communication.
2. *Inhibitory and disinhibitory effects.* Modeling is not confined exclusively to the learning of new behaviors as in the preceding modeling effect. Modeling includes not imitating a model for the purpose of disinhibiting or inhibiting a behavior. For example, a child may observe and not imitate a peer who is punished or ignored for exhibiting a behavior. In this situation, the child may be said to be experiencing the other child's behavior and its consequences vicariously.

3. *Eliciting or response facilitation effect.* In this situation, the model's behavior is employed to facilitate the occurrence of a previously learned but dormant behavior from the child. For example, a child may know that it is appropriate to say "Thank you" when given a cookie at snack time. However, this child may not say "Thank you" as a matter of common practice. Appropriate social responsiveness may be facilitated if all the children who receive cookies previous to this child during snack time say "Thank you."

Before implementing a modeling intervention, the teacher or parent should consider the following factors:

1. Is the child able developmentally and cognitively to imitate the model? Practitioners must be cognizant of the fact that some children are simply not ready to use modeling.
2. Will the child be rewarded for imitating the model? Some children are simply not intrinsically rewarded by performing behaviors that others consider acceptable.
3. Is the model "good"? Caution must be taken when a model is being selected for a child. Remember, what the model does in science class may be quite different from what this individual does in English, in shop, on the playground, at home, or behind the barn.
4. Is the model acceptable to the child? A model who is too good, too bright, too fast, or just plain obnoxious will be rejected by the child.

Modeling techniques can be effectively applied by teachers in an effort to change behavior only when consideration is given to these factors.

■ Examples

Ms. Nyerges is a resource teacher for children identified with intellectual disabilities. Dave and Carl work with Ms. Nyerges in the resource room for 1 hour each day. Until recently, Dave would usually attempt his assigned tasks, whereas Carl would seldom attempt his assigned tasks.

It was determined by Ms. Nyerges that both boys were reinforced by her attention. Therefore, she decided to use her attention as a reward they received for completing their work. Dave was reinforced by Ms. Nyerges's attention. She praised him each time he did his class work, attended to the appropriate stimulus, or completed an assigned task; she ignored Carl's inappropriate behavior.

After several sessions during which Dave's behavior was rewarded, Carl began to imitate Dave to receive Ms. Nyerges's attention. She immediately reinforced Carl whenever he exhibited the appropriate behavior.

The result of this intervention was a dramatic change in Carl's behavior. He is now completing his work to gain approval from Ms. Nyerges.

Mr. Cohen is an instructor of three boys and one girl in a class for children identified with emotional/behavioral disorders. The students' names are John, James, Charles, and Shirley. Of the four students, Charles is the most troublesome. Charles constantly moves about the room, exhibiting feelings of indignation at assignments and disrupting the activities of his classmates and Mr. Cohen. This behavior occurs throughout the school day. Originally, when the behavior occurred, the other children remained busy at their seats. On these occasions, Mr. Cohen would chase after Charles or provide him with attention for the unacceptable behavior he was exhibiting. The acceptable behaviors manifested by Shirley, John, and James were ignored. Lately, Shirley, John, and James have begun to move about the room and exhibit behaviors that disturb Mr. Cohen. They are imitating the behavior of Charles.

One can conclude that Shirley, John, and James are modeling Charles's behavior for the purpose of receiving attention from their teacher.

In both of these examples, the procedure of modeling is effective; in fact, it is effective in developing both appropriate and inappropriate behaviors. The consequence of behavior is again the key factor. In too many classrooms, appropriate behavior is taken for granted. Modeling is a potentially effective preventive technique.

Summary Points

- The six most common techniques used for increasing target behaviors are (a) positive reinforcement, (b) shaping, (c) contingency contracting, (d) token economy, (e) modeling, and (f) self-management.
- Positive reinforcement is the presentation of a desirable reinforcer after the behavior has been exhibited.
- When a child is initially exhibiting a behavior, the behavior must be reinforced every time it occurs. Once the behavior is established, the behavior should be reinforced intermittently.
- Sometimes a behavior cannot be reinforced because it does not occur in the form desired. Shaping is the systematic, immediate reinforcement of successive approximations of the target behavior until the behavior is established.
- In forward shaping or chaining, the first component or step of the behavior is taught first, then the second, and so on. In backward shaping or chaining, the last component is taught first, the second-to-last second, and so on.
- Contingency contracting is the process of contracting so that the child gets to do

something he or she wants to do following the completion of something the parent or teacher wants done.
- When contingency contracts are first introduced, small tasks and reinforcers are most effective. The contract should be adhered to for the specified amount of time.
- One function of contingency contracting is to get the child to participate in creating the contract instead of waiting for suggestions from the teacher.
- Through self-management the student becomes increasingly aware of his or her own cognitive processes and how behavior influences learning outcomes.
- Self-management strategies may include observational learning, self-instruction, and self-monitoring.
- Token economy is a structure for using a token in an exchange system for reinforcers. Point cards also may serve as tokens.
- Modeling refers to learning by observation and imitation. Modeling may increase or inhibit behaviors.

Projects

1. Write two examples of modeling as a technique, one for increasing behaviors and one for decreasing behaviors.
2. Develop and implement a contract for (a) an individual child in a class and (b) an entire class. After

implementation, discuss (a) the advantages of such a system and (b) the challenges presented by the system.

Web Resources

For more information about contingency contracting, visit this site:
slhslinux.cla.umn.edu/Tip%20Sheets/ Other%20Tip%20Sheets/contcon.pdf

For more information about token economies, visit this site:
www.usu.edu/teachall/text/behavior/LRBIpdfs/Token.pdf

For additional self-management strategies, visit this site:
www.specialconnections.ku.edu/cgi-bin/cgiwrap/ specconn/main.php?cat=behavior&section=main&subsection =classroom/self-management

References

Alberto, P. A., & Troutman, C. A. (1990). *Applied behavior analysis for teachers* (3rd ed.). Upper Saddle River, NJ: Merrill/Pearson.

Anderson, C., & Katsiyannis, A. (1997). By what token economy? A classroom learning tool for inclusive settings. *Teaching Exceptional Children, 29*(4), 65–67.

Ayllon, T., & McKittrick, S. M. (1982). *How to set up a token economy.* Austin, TX: Pro-Ed.

Bandura, A. (1969). *Principles of behavior modification.* New York: Holt, Rinehart & Winston.

Barrish, H. H., Saunders, M., & Wolf, M. M. (1969). The Good Behavior Game: Effects of individual contingencies for group consequences on disruptive behavior in a classroom. *Journal of Applied Behavioral Analysis, 2*(2), 119–124.

Beilinson, J. S., & Olswang, L. B. (2003). Facilitating peer-group entry in kindergartners with impairments in social communication. *Language, Speech, and Hearing Services in Schools, 34,* 154–166.

Clarizio, H. F., & Yelon, S. L. (1967). Learning theory approaches to classroom management: Rationale and intervention techniques. *Journal of Special Education, 1,* 267–274.

Clark, J. (1988). Behavior tickets quell misconduct. *Behavior in Our Schools, 1*(3), 19–20.

Corpus, J. H., & Lepper, M. (2007). The effects of person versus performance praise on children's motivation: Gender and age as moderating factors. *Educational Psychology, 27*(4), 487–508.

Downing, J. A. (1990). Contingency contracting: A step-by-step format. *Intervention in School and Clinic, 26*(2), 111–113.

Downing, J. D. (Ed.). (2002). What works for me: Individualized behavior contracts. *Intervention in School and Clinic, 37*(3), 168–172.

Fairbanks, S., Sugai, G., Guardino, D., & Lathrop, M. (2007). Response to intervention: Examining classroom behavior support in second grade. *Exceptional Children, 73*(3), 288–310.

Filcheck, H. A., McNeil, C. B., & Herschell, A. D. (2001). Types of verbal feedback that affect compliance and general behavior in disruptive and typical children. *Child Study Journal, 31*(4), 225–248.

Firman, K. B., Beare, P., & Loyd, R. (2002). Enhancing self-management in students with mental retardation: Extrinsic versus intrinsic procedures. *Education and Training in Mental Retardation and Developmental Disabilities, 37*(2), 163–171.

Hawken, L. S., & Horner, R. H. (2003). Evaluation of a targeted intervention within a schoolwide system of behavior support. *Journal of Behavioral Education, 12*(3), 225–240.

Hess, A. M., Rosenberg, M. S., & Levy, G. K. (1990). Reducing truancy in students with mild handicaps. *Remedial and Special Education, 11*(4), 14–19.

Hess, L. L. (2003). "Contract" isn't a four-letter word. *Momentum,* September/October, 55–57.

Higgins, J. W., Williams, R. E., & McLaughlin, T. F. (2001). The effects of a token economy employing instructional consequences for a third-grade student with learning disabilities: A data-based case study. *Education and Treatment of Children, 24* (1), 99–106.

Homme, L., Csanyi, A. P., Gonzales, M. A., & Rechs, J. R. (1979). *How to use contingency contracting in the classroom.* Champaign, IL: Research Press.

Hutchinson, S. W., Murdock, J. Y., Williamson, R. D., & Cronin, M. E. (2000). Self-recording plus encouragement equals improved behavior. *Teaching Exceptional Children, 32*(5), 54–58.

Kerr, M., & Nelson, C. M. (2002). *Strategies for addressing behavior problems in the classroom* (4th ed.). Upper Saddle River, NJ: Merrill/Pearson.

Kroeger, K. A., & Sorensen-Burnworth, R. (2009). Toilet training individuals with autism and other developmental disabilities: A critical review. *Research in Autism Spectrum Disorders*, 3(3), 607–618.

Larrivee, B. (2002). The potential perils of praise in a democratic interactive classroom. *Action in Teacher Education*, 23(4), 77–88.

Lyon, C. S., & Lagarde, R. (1997). Tokens for success: Using the graduated reinforcement system. *Teaching Exceptional Children*, 29(6), 52–57.

Maher, G. B. (1989). "Punch out": A behavior management technique. *Teaching Exceptional Children*, 21(2), 74.

Mathes, M. Y., & Bender, W. N. (1997). The effects of self-monitoring on children with attention-deficit/hyperactivity disorder who are receiving pharmacological interventions. *Remedial and Special Education*, 18(2), 111–128.

McConnell, M. E. (1999). Self-monitoring, cueing, recording, and management: Teaching students to manage their own behavior. *Teaching Exceptional Children*, 32(2), 14–21.

McDougall, D. (1998). Research on self-management techniques used by students with disabilities in general education settings. *Remedial and Special Education*, 19(5), 310–320.

McDougall, D., & Brady, M. P. (1998). Initiating and fading self-management interventions to increase math fluency in general education classes. *Exceptional Children*, 64(2), 151–166.

Mruzek, D. W., Cohen, C., & Smith, T. (2007) Contingency contracting with students with autism spectrum disorders in a public school setting. *Journal of Developmental Physical Disabilities*, 19, 103–114.

Peterson, L. D., Young, R., West, R. P., & Peterson, M. H. (1999). Effects of student self-management on generalization of student performance in regular classroom. *Education and Treatment of Children*, 22, 357–372.

Premack, D. (1965). Reinforcement theory. In D. LeVine (Ed.), *Nebraska symposium on motivation*. Lincoln: University of Nebraska Press.

Raschke, D. (1986). "Delicious" incentives: A technique to motivate reluctant learners. *Teaching Exceptional Children*, 19(1), 66–67.

Raschke, D., Dedrick, C., & Thompson, M. (1987). Motivating reluctant learners: Innovative contingency packages. *Teaching Exceptional Children*, 19(2), 18–21.

Reid, R. (1999). Attention deficit hyperactivity disorder: Effective methods for the classroom. *Focus on Exceptional Children*, 32(4), 1–20.

Rosenberg, M. S. (1986). Maximizing the effectiveness of structured classroom management programs: Implementing rule-review procedures with disruptive and distractible students. *Behavioral Disorders*, 11(4), 239–248.

Self-Brown, S. R., & Mathews, II, S. (2003). Effects of classroom structure on student achievement goal orientation. *Journal of Educational Research*, 97(2), 106–111.

Shea, T. M., & Bauer, A. M. (1987). *Teaching children and youth with behavior disorders* (2nd ed.). Upper Saddle River, NJ: Merrill/Pearson.

Shook, S. C., LaBrie, M., & Vallies, J. (1990). The effects of a token economy on first grade students' inappropriate behavior. *Reading Improvement*, 27(2), 96–101.

Snyder, M. C., & Bambara, L. M. (1997). Teaching secondary students with learning disabilities to self-manage classroom survival skills. *Journal of Learning Disabilities*, 30(5), 534–543.

Striefel, S. (1981). *How to teach through modeling and imitation*. Austin, TX: Pro-Ed.

Sutherland, K. S., Copeland, S., & Wehby, J. H. (2001). Catch them while you can: Monitoring and increasing the use of effective praise. *Beyond Behavior*, 11(1), 46–49.

Suzuki, L. K., Davis, H. M., & Greenfield, P. M. (2008). Self-enhancement and self-effacement in reaction to praise and criticism: The case of multiethnic youth. *Ethos*, 36(1), 78–97.

Swaggart, B. L. (1998). Implementing a cognitive behavior management program. *Intervention in School and Clinic*, 33(4), 235–238.

Tingstrom, D. H., Sterling-Turner, H. E., Wilczynski, S. M. (2006). The Good Behavior Game: 1969–2002. *Behavior Modification*, 30(2), 225–253.

CHAPTER OBJECTIVES

After completing this chapter, you will be able to do the following:

1. Describe a continuum of interventions.
2. Implement explicit reprimands.
3. Describe performance feedback.
4. Describe the various forms of differential reinforcement and their application.
5. Describe extinction.
6. Characterize response loss.
7. Describe the responsible use of time-out from reinforcement.
8. Describe the rationale against punishment.
9. Discuss desensitization techniques and their applications in the educational setting.

Methods of Reducing Behavior

KEY TERMS

Desensitization

Differential reinforcement

Explicit reprimand

Extinction

Loss of privileges

Response-cost

Time-out from reinforcement

Mrs. Hamilton dreaded coming to school today. It is raining, and her fourth-grade students will have to remain inside during lunch. When the students do not get to go outside for recess, they seem to lose all control. As lunch approaches, they become increasingly disruptive.

On this day, when lunch arrives, Mrs. Hamilton tells the students that they are to engage in silent reading. They can choose any book from the classroom library. With little enthusiasm, each student selects a book. Within 5 minutes, the disruptive behavior begins. Charlie pinches George; Mary reports that Mike is pulling her hair; Fred and Martin are using their desks as drums; Gloria is blowing kisses at Larry; Sharon, Pat, and Carol are giggling; Walter is asleep; Mrs. Hamilton is angry.

Maybe if Mrs. Hamilton knew something about methods of reducing the probability of disruptive behavior, her rainy-day lunch periods could be filled with sunshine.

Mr. Bell dreaded his third-period physical science class. The hands-on experiences that he felt were so important had become difficult due to the behavior of three students who sat in the back of the classroom and toyed with the materials rather than completing the activities. Mr. Bell was ready to resort to lecturing to keep the students from destroying materials, interfering with other students' experiments, or performing their own "experiments."

If Mr. Bell had strategies to decrease unacceptable behavior, he would feel more comfortable providing the hands-on activities he knows to be important.

Throughout the school day, students may demonstrate behaviors that do not support their success in school. In the classroom, students typically have problems in one of two general areas. First, they may have problems with production, missing assignments, not completing tasks, or attempting little of any assignment. Second, they may have problems with engagement, attending to lessons or activities, or demonstrating cooperative behaviors. Increasing production or engagement may require that specific behaviors are reduced. In this chapter, several methods of increasing production or engagement through reducing counterproductive behavior are discussed and exemplified. These are arranged along a continuum, from the least to most intrusive.

A CONTINUUM OF INTERVENTIONS

Even though it may seem difficult to do so, "misbehavior" should be seen as an error. Oliver (2007) draws a parallel between misbehavior and any learning experience. She suggests that just as you would not let academic errors on homework go uncorrected, behavioral errors should not be left uncorrected. She suggests that if behaviors are not caught early, they may only escalate, reducing the student's opportunity to learn and increasing his or her opportunity to continue the behavior.

Simonson, Fairbanks, Briesch, Myers, and Sugai (2008) provide a continuum of strategies to use to respond to behaviors that need to be corrected. This continuum of interventions includes a range of strategies that (a) are evidence based (research has demonstrated that they work) and go from simple to complex. The continuum includes these strategies, which are used to organize this chapter:

- explicit feedback (brief, contingent, specific correction): an informative statement made by the teacher when the behavior occurs, stating the observed behavior and then telling the student what he or she should be doing;
- performance feedback: specifying a level of behavior and providing reinforcement, helping students to see their progress;
- differential reinforcement: reinforcement provided when the student has lower levels of the undesired behavior or higher levels of the desired behavior than previously observed;
- extinction (planned ignoring): paying no attention to the student when he or she demonstrates the undesired behavior;
- response cost: removing a token or privilege when the behavior occurs; and
- time-out from reinforcement: removing the student from a reinforcing environment to a less reinforcing environment when the behavior occurs.

EXPLICIT REPRIMANDS

When you hear the word *reprimand*, you may think of being scolded, yelled at, bawled out, or otherwise verbally chastised for exhibiting an inappropriate target behavior. Reprimands are useful when a child is engaging in behavior that necessitates immediate action because it is potentially harmful to self, others, or property. Reprimands should be used selectively in response to specific behaviors. A reprimand should include a statement of an appropriate alternative to the inappropriate behavior (Piazza, Bowman, Contrucci, et al., 1999). These reprimands should be brief, direct, and explicit. The following are some guidelines for the effective use of an **explicit reprimand**:

- Tell the child exactly what inappropriate behavior is being reprimanded.
- Reprimand the behavior; do not derogate the child.
- Reprimand immediately, calmly, in a firm voice and posture.
- If either the child or others may be harmed by the behavior, remove the child.
- If necessary, back up the reprimand with loss of privileges.
- Encourage the child to behave appropriately and include a statement of the appropriate behavior in the reprimand.
- When it's over, it's over. Do not keep reminding the child of past inappropriate behavior; avoid embarrassing the child in the presence of peers and others. To this end, use nonverbal reprimands: shake your head to indicate "No," point your finger, frown, and so on.
- Always observe the child's reaction to the reprimand to determine whether it is aversive.

■ *Examples*

- "Margie! Turn off the lathe. Do not turn it on again until you have put on your safety glasses and removed that loose scarf from your neck. Please review the safety rules."

- "Donald! Sit up straight and put your feet on the floor while you are typing. Proper posture will help your concentration and prevent back pain and physical discomfort in the future."

- "Mary! Put on your seat belt. It is the law in Illinois and may save you from injury if we have an accident."

- "Herm! Close the windows when you turn on the air conditioner. This will save electricity, which is very expensive."

Research evidence about the effectiveness of reprimands is mixed (Salend, Jantzen, & Giek, 1992). The efficacy of the verbal reprimand appears to be controlled by various conditions. According to Van Houten, Nau, Mackenzie-Keating, Sameoto, and Colavecchia (1982), the effectiveness of a reprimand is increased when (a) combined with nonverbal behavior generally associated with a verbal reprimand (e.g., pointing a finger) and (b) delivered in close proximity to the individual who is the target of the reprimand.

Wheldall (1991) researched the effectiveness of verbal reprimands with four teachers in general education classrooms. He concluded that reprimands should be given privately and within a positive context. In addition, reprimands should be used infrequently, and be specific to the unacceptable behavior.

PERFORMANCE FEEDBACK

Providing performance feedback is similar to correcting academic errors. Students are provided with charts, graphs, or reports that show their performance in specific behaviors that are inconsistent with those the teacher wants to decrease. For example, if the students are having difficulty completing work, the teacher would provide them with evidence about their work completion. Love, Love, and Northcraft (2010) found that positive feedback is far more effective than negative feedback.

Several guidelines address performance feedback. Shute (2008) suggests that the feedback should be formative, nonevaluative, supportive, timely, and specific. Formative feedback is not scolding; it is provided as information so that the learner can make changes. The teacher can provide reinforcement for accurate performance, explanations of correct answers, and examples. Shute also suggests that the teacher must be mindful of the scheduling of the feedback.

■ Example

Ms. Cantu was concerned with the amount of time her fifth-grade students were daydreaming, chatting, and generally "messing around" during her "Stop Everything and Read" sustained reading period. She met with the students and described the need for practice in silent reading and the need to settle down after lunch by reading before beginning the afternoon's activities. Ms. Cantu presented each student with a "pages read" chart and bookmarks. Each day they were to read, place their bookmarks where they had stopped, and mark the number of pages read on their chart. Ms. Cantu did spot reliability checks, pulling three books a day and checking the accuracy of the page posting. Each week Ms. Cantu provided written feedback on the charts and returned them to the students, sometimes rewarding the students who had read the most with a "free homework pass." Silent reading increased dramatically, and the noise and lack of attention almost disappeared.

DIFFERENTIAL REINFORCEMENT

Too often in school and at home, the attention of teachers and parents is focused on the inappropriate behaviors rather than on the appropriate ones that children and youth exhibit. This unfortunate and generally ineffective and inefficient circumstance can be changed by applying differential reinforcement or positive reductive strategies. With the use of this group of strategies for modifying behavior, the practitioner "accentuates the positive" to "eliminate the negative" (Reid, 1999; Webber & Scheuermann, 1991, p. 13).

Differential reinforcement is reinforcement provided when a student engages in (a) low rates of the behavior you wish to change, (b) behaviors other than the behavior you wish to change, (c) a behavior that you want to replace the undesired behavior, or (d) an incompatible behavior (Simonsen et al., 2008). These strategies are often referred to by their initials (Drasgow, 1997; Kerr & Nelson, 1989; Martin & Pear, 1992; Webber & Scheuermann, 1991): (a) differential reinforcement of zero rates of behavior (DRO), (b) differential reinforcement of incompatible behaviors (DRI), and (c) differential reinforcement of lower rates of behavior (DRL). The application of any differential reinforcement intervention requires the teacher to (a) identify and define the unacceptable behavior to be decreased or eliminated and (b) select and define an acceptable replacement behavior to increase.

When using the DRO strategy, the individual is reinforced for not exhibiting the target behavior during a specific period of time. Occurrences of the target behavior are ignored. Of course, the individual is reinforced for exhibiting appropriate behavior in other circumstances.

Brulle and Barton (1992) refer to DRO as differential reinforcement of other behaviors and define it as a schedule in which reinforcement is delivered if the client does not emit the target response for a specific interval.

■ *Example*

Stacey, a student with emotional/behavioral disorders in Mr. Hicks's class, had mild tantrums several times each day. This behavior interfered with Stacey's classroom activities and annoyed the other students and Mr. Hicks.

Mr. Hicks decided to implement a DRO intervention. He took baseline data for a period of 10 school days and determined that Stacey had a tantrum, on average, nine times each day. These occurred approximately every 35 minutes. Mr. Hicks discussed the DRO intervention with Stacey and the other students. He began reinforcing Stacey after each 30-minute period of tantrum-free behavior. When Stacey had a tantrum, it was ignored by Mr. Hicks and her classmates, who were reinforced for ignoring the behavior.

During the following 3 weeks, Mr. Hicks systematically extended the period of time Stacey had to be tantrum free to receive a reward. Within a month, the behavior was eliminated.

Among the behaviors to which DRO may be effectively applied are fighting, cursing (White & Koorland, 1996), name-calling, threatening, talking back, and destroying property. Dipipi, Jitendra, and Miller (2001) successfully applied a combination of differential reinforcement of other behaviors, time delay, and self-monitoring strategies to teach socially appropriate verbal behavior to replace echolalic speech in an individual with mild mental retardation and a seizure disorder. Flood and Wilder (2004) have also applied differential reinforcement successfully to reduce separation anxiety. If a behavior is dangerous to self or others, causes serious destruction, or interferes excessively with the teaching–learning process, it cannot be ignored; an intervention other than DRO must be applied.

At times, it is necessary or desirable to decrease a behavior by systematically reinforcing a behavior that is in opposition to or incompatible with it. Such an intervention is called differential reinforcement of incompatible behaviors (DRI) (Kerr & Nelson, 1989).

■ *Example*

For a major part of the school year, Mr. Weber had been trying to decrease Wallace's random walking about the classroom. All efforts appeared to have been in vain. It seemed that the more effort Mr. Weber put forth to modify Wallace's out-of-seat behavior, the more frequent it became. Evidently, the attention Wallace received from Mr. Weber for being out of his seat was reinforcing.

As a last resort, Mr. Weber decided to attempt the technique of reinforcing incompatible behaviors. To remain in one's seat would be incompatible with walking about the classroom. Mr. Weber decided to positively reinforce Wallace's in-seat behavior and ignore his out-of-seat behavior. Initially, Wallace resisted the program. However, after a short time, the out-of-seat

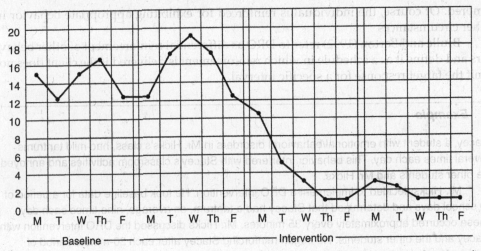

FIGURE 8.1 Frequency of Wallace's out-of-seat behavior before and during the intervention

behavior decreased and was eventually eliminated. Figure 8.1 represents the data collected on Wallace's behavior.

There is no known explanation for the recurrence of Wallace's out-of-seat behavior on the 16th and 17th days of the intervention. One possible explanation is that because the target behavior had not been exhibited for 2 days, Mr. Weber acted as though the behavior had been eliminated. He may have altered his response to either the behavior he was reinforcing or the behavior he was ignoring.

The classroom teacher could probably think of a number of other situations in which reinforcing an incompatible behavior might decrease target behavior.

■ *Examples*

- John cannot be looking at the teacher and looking out the window at the same time.

- Paul cannot be standing in line for lunch and writing on his desk at the same time.

- David cannot be mowing the lawn and watching television at the same time.

Additional examples of the behaviors to which the DRI intervention may be successfully applied are (a) following directions versus noncompliance, (b) name-calling versus using an appropriate or proper name, (c) talking at inappropriate times versus being quiet at appropriate times, (d) off task versus on task, (e) in seat versus out of seat, (f) sleeping in class versus not sleeping in class, (g) being tardy versus being on time, and (h) messy or incomplete work versus neat or complete work.

Another type of differential reinforcement is the differential reinforcement of lower rates of behavior (DRL) (Martin & Pear, 1992; Webber & Scheuermann, 1991). DRL may be applied with behaviors that (a) are habits, (b) do not need to be reduced rapidly, and (c) do not need to be reduced to zero. DRL is applied to gradually reduce the behavior by reinforcing progressively lower rates of the behavior.

■ *Example*

Elmer was a "nail biter." He appeared to be constantly chewing his nails. For his behavior management project in Special Education 430 (Behavior Management in Special Education), Elmer decided to reduce and eventually eliminate his nail biting.

He defined "nail biting" as any time his fingertips came in contact with his lips. During a week of baseline, Elmer found that his fingertips came in contact with his lips, on average, 97 times a day. Elmer decided that during the first week of intervention, he would be rewarded with one MP3 download if he reduced his tips-to-lips contacts to an average of 80 times a day. He attained this goal and was reinforced. The next week he decided to reduce his tips-to-lips contacts to 65 times a day. Elmer was unsuccessful; he averaged 69 tips-to-lips contacts a day and was not rewarded. During the third week of intervention, Elmer remained at the goal of 65 and was rewarded. Elmer continued the program for the next 12 weeks of the semester and was successful in eliminating his nail-biting behavior.

The DRL intervention may be applied to various behaviors, such as attention seeking, completing assignments, responding to a teacher or parent's questions, and hand raising.

When implementing a differential reinforcement intervention, the behavior change program (as discussed in Chapter 6) requires the following steps:

1. Select the target behavior to be changed.
2. Select a positive alternative to the target behavior.
3. Select the appropriate differential reinforcement strategy (DRO, DRI, or DRL).
4. Determine the reinforcers to be used in the intervention.
5. Determine the criteria for success.
6. Implement the intervention.
7. Evaluate the results of the intervention.

According to Webber and Scheuermann (1991), the use of a differential reinforcement strategy allows the practitioner to avoid punishment and its side effects and facilitates the teaching of prosocial behaviors.

EXTINCTION

The discontinuation or withholding of the reinforcer of a behavior that has previously been reinforcing the behavior is called **extinction**. This process, described in detail in Chapter 3, is also known as systematic ignoring (Hall & Hall, 1980a).

■ *Example*

Timmy was constantly attempting to obtain Mr. Calm's attention in class by jumping up and down in his seat, frantically waving his hand, and whispering in a loud voice, "Mr. Calm, Mr. Calm, me, me, I know."

FIGURE 8.2 Frequency of Timmy's attention-seeking behavior before and during the intervention

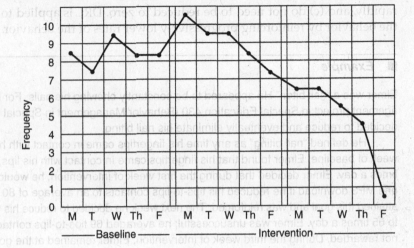

Mr. Calm knew he would have to change his name to Mr. Storm if this behavior did not stop or, at the least, decrease in frequency. To retain his composure and aid Timmy, he reflected on the interactions.

Baseline observation data indicated that Timmy exhibited the target behavior an average of 8 times per day, or 40 times during the 1-week baseline data-collecting phase. During this phase, Mr. Calm also collected data on his personal overt reactions to the unacceptable behavior. He discovered that 90% of the time, he responded to the behavior by either permitting Timmy to answer the question, telling the child to be quiet and sit still, or signaling his disapproval nonverbally. Regardless of his specific reaction, Mr. Calm realized that he was attending to Timmy's attention-seeking behavior.

Mr. Calm devised an intervention whereby he would not reinforce the behavior with his attention and would thus extinguish it. He would respond to Timmy only when he was exhibiting acceptable behavior in response to questions directed to the class.

As indicated in Figure 8.2, the behavior was extinguished within 2 weeks, although brief periods of regression occurred thereafter.

Timmy's behavior (attempts to obtain attention) increased during the days immediately following the implementation of the intervention. This increase in the target behavior appeared to be an attempt by the child to defend his method for obtaining attention against the loss of effectiveness. This phenomenon is known as an "extinction burst." As demonstrated in the case of Timmy, extinction techniques, when properly applied, result in a gradual decrease in the target behavior and its eventual elimination.

Extinction is only as effective as the teacher or parent is consistent and persistent in implementation of the intervention. The most effective approach to extinguishing behavior that has been previously reinforced is ignoring that behavior. This is easier said than done. Most of us are conditioned to the point that we find it difficult to ignore inappropriate behavior. But to ignore a behavior means exactly that—to totally and consistently ignore the target behavior. We are aware that some behaviors are so serious that they cannot be ignored. However, if the individual is not inflicting pain on himself or others or disrupting the ongoing classroom program, then extinction may be the intervention of choice.

The following are some guidelines for those wishing to apply extinction:

- When the target behavior is exhibited, remain impassive; give no indication that you are aware of the behavior.
- Continue your present activity.
- If the behavior persists, turn your back and walk away.

RESPONSE COST

Unlike the vast majority of interventions discussed in this text, **response cost**—often referred to as **loss of privileges**—is a negative behavior management intervention, though its results may be positive When loss of privileges is applied, a portion of the child's present or future positive reinforcers is taken away following the exhibition of the target behavior.

This intervention is most effective when the privilege the child loses is a natural or logical consequence of the inappropriate behavior. For example, if a child refuses to work on assignments during class time, then the privilege of free time is lost. Likewise, if a child is late for the school bus, then he misses it. We recognize that it is not always possible to impose natural consequences; thus, the teacher on occasion must impose an artificial consequence. In an artificial consequence, the relationship between the privilege lost and the behavior exhibited is arbitrary. It exists only because the teacher decides it will exist. Such artificial relationships must be carefully explained to the child.

When using loss of privileges, the teacher has several guidelines to follow:

1. Be sure the child understands the relationship between the target behavior and the privilege to be lost.
2. Be sure the child knows the inappropriate behavior and the consequence of exhibiting it.
3. When possible, use natural or logical consequences.
4. Apply the loss of privilege interventions fairly.
5. Avoid warning, nagging, or threatening.
6. Do not debate the inappropriate behaviors, the rules, or the consequence once these have been established.
7. Do not become emotionally involved. Do not feel guilty when the child loses a privilege. If the child knows the rules and the consequences of the behavior, then he or she has chosen to break the rule and suffer the consequences.
8. Be consistent.
9. Reinforce appropriate behaviors; do not emphasize inappropriate behaviors only.

■ *Examples*

Patricia is head cheerleader at Saint Rudolph's High School. She greatly enjoys leading cheers at basketball and football games. Patricia was tardy for English class about three times a week. Her English teacher, Sister Mary, was very concerned that Patricia would fail the course if her attendance did not improve. Sister Mary talked to the principal, Sister Sharon, and they agreed to deprive Patricia of the privilege of cheering at one game for each time she was tardy for English class. The rule was explained to Patricia and implemented. After missing two games during the next 3 weeks, Patricia's tardiness ended.

Thomas, a salesperson for a major computer software firm, owned a 1990 Mercedes-Benz 535SEL and loved to drive down the interstate highways at 80 miles per hour. He was caught by the highway patrol on three occasions and fined. On the fourth occasion, he lost his driving privilege for 30 days. Thomas still enjoys driving fast but controls this urge.

Kevin, who is 17 years old, was allowed to stay out on Friday and Saturday nights until midnight. He consistently arrived home (and awakened his parents) at 1:00 or 2:00 in the morning. Needless to say, this behavior caused many heated discussions. It was finally agreed by Kevin and his parents that for each minute he was late arriving home, 5 minutes would be subtracted from the curfew time on the next evening he went out with his friends. After losing several hours during the course of the following few weeks, Kevin's behavior improved.

Proctor and Morgan (1991) (replicating the work of Witt & Elliott [1982]) researched the effectiveness of a response-cost raffle. The intervention was applied in a special education resource room to the behavior of four junior high school boys with mild to moderate behavior problems. At the beginning of each class, four slips of colored paper (raffle tickets) were placed on each student's desk. (Each student's ticket was a different color.) When a student exhibited an inappropriate behavior, the teacher removed a ticket and told the student the specific misbehavior. If the student responded negatively, the teacher removed another ticket. If the student continued to exhibit inappropriate behavior and responded negatively after all the tickets had been removed, then he was removed from the room. Five minutes prior to the end of class, the teacher collected all the remaining tickets. Two tickets were marked for a "group" reward. These and the other tickets were placed in an envelope. The teacher conducted the raffle, and the winning student selected a reward (e.g., soda, potato chips, free time) from a reinforcement menu. Or, if the winning ticket was designated as a "group" reward, the winner selected from among the group rewards (e.g., movie, group game, party). The results of this research suggest that the response-cost raffle is an effective and efficient intervention for reducing disruptive and inappropriate behavior.

TIME-OUT FROM REINFORCEMENT

In general, **time-out from reinforcement** is the removal of a child from an apparently reinforcing setting to a presumably nonreinforcing setting for a specified and limited period of time. Time-out is "time away from positive reinforcement" (Powell & Powell, 1982; Simonson et al., 2008). It is not the same as secluding a student (see Chapter 12). According to Cuenin and Harris (1986), the definition of time-out includes two important factors: (a) time-out is contingent on the exhibition of the target behavior, and (b) the student must see a difference between the time-in and time-out environments. Such removal can effectively decrease a target behavior (Hall & Hall, 1980b).

In the 1980s and 1990s time-out was a frequently used behavior management intervention. In a questionnaire survey of preschool teachers and teachers of students with behavioral disorders in Kansas and Nebraska, Zabel (1986) found that 70% of her sample applied some form of time-out in the classroom. Teachers of young children used time-out more frequently than teachers of older children. Ruhl (1985) found that

88% of special education teachers surveyed used time-out with their students. In a similar study, Shapiro and Lentz (1985) found that 85% of school psychologists used time-out procedures. Jones, Sloane, and Roberts (1992) compared the effectiveness of time-out and verbal reprimand ("Don't") interventions on the oppositional, aggressive behavior of three preschool children toward their siblings. Mothers of the children were trained and applied the interventions in the home. The researchers found the immediate time-out intervention to be more effective than the verbal reprimand.

In that time-out has been used for several years, the term has often been misused. Ryan, Sanders, Katsiyannis, and Yell (2007) describe several related strategies that are referred to as "time-out." These break into two groups: inclusion time-out and exclusion time-out. Inclusion time-out refers to planned ignoring (discussed previously in this chapter as a less intrusive intervention), withdrawal of materials, contingent observation, and the time-out ribbon.

Withdrawal of materials is as simple as taking the pencil away briefly from a student who persistently taps the pencil while the teacher is talking. With younger children, the teacher may take away the finger paints of a child who has painted a classmate. Contingent observation is often called "sit and watch." A student who needs a "cool down" period may need to leave the area for a brief time, collecting him- or herself, and then returning. The time-out ribbon (Salend & Gordon, 1987) involves a student wearing a ribbon or other object as long as he or she is being appropriate. If an undesired behavior occurs, the student's ribbon is taken and the student may not use reinforcing areas of the classroom for a brief time.

The second group of time-out interventions that Ryan et al. (2007) discuss is exclusionary. These are restrictive interventions because the student is removed from instructional materials and is not allowed to observe. The application of exclusionary interventions is restricted, and documentation is needed. The student is also denied his or her right to an education while in exclusionary time-out. Exclusionary time-out is referred to in laws and guidelines as seclusion.

■ *Example*

Benji is a very active first-grader. He was having difficulty remaining in his seat and refraining from impulsive grabbing of persons and objects near him. He was also taking and eating his classmates' lunches. His teacher realized that these behaviors were interfering with his classroom progress as well as that of his classmates. She attempted several procedures to help Benji control his behavior. Among these were verbal reprimands, ignoring the inappropriate behavior and reinforcing appropriate behavior, and peer pressure. Observation data revealed that none of these interventions were effective, although the teacher's efforts were sufficient.

A behavior management consultant observed Benji and recommended time-out as a potentially effective intervention. Together, the teacher and the consultant decided that each time Benji left his seat, he was to be moved to a separate table for 2 minutes. This intervention necessitated defining and specifying several factors:

1. Out-of-seat behavior was defined as any time Benji's posterior was not in contact with his chair.
2. When the unacceptable behavior did occur, the teacher's assistant was to escort Benji to a separate table. Benji was to remain 2 minutes; during this time, he had to be quiet.

3. After the time-out period, Benji would return to the group. There would be no discussion or reprimand.

4. Benji's desk and chair were relocated in the classroom to ensure that he would not participate in unacceptable behavior, such as grabbing people and lunches, without leaving his seat.

5. A separate table was placed in the corner of the classroom. A chair was provided nearby for the assistant who was to monitor Benji whenever he was in time-out.

6. The intervention was imposed, and although the behavior did not cease immediately, significant progress was observed during the first months, as indicated in Figures 8.3 and 8.4.

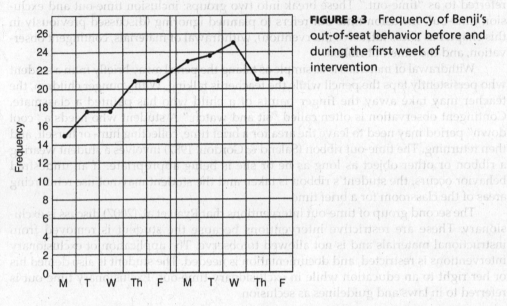

FIGURE 8.3 Frequency of Benji's out-of-seat behavior before and during the first week of intervention

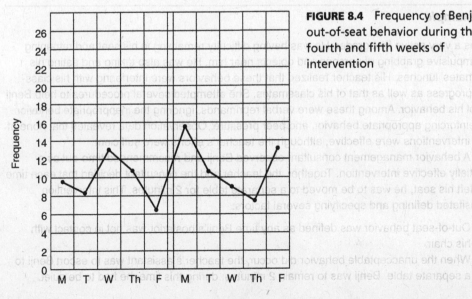

FIGURE 8.4 Frequency of Benji's out-of-seat behavior during the fourth and fifth weeks of intervention

Benji's in-seat behavior increased within a period of several months. However, the separate table remains available for when the undesirable behaviors occur.

The time-out intervention includes the reinforcement of acceptable behavior. A child who is performing or approximating the desired behavior in the classroom should be reinforced for these efforts. The effectiveness of time-out as an intervention is contingent on several factors (Cuenin & Harris, 1986):

- characteristics of the individual child;
- teacher's consistent application of the intervention;
- child's understanding of the rules of time-out;
- characteristics of the time-out area;
- duration of time-out; and
- evaluation of the effectiveness of the intervention.

Characteristics of the Child

The practitioner must know the characteristics of the individual child before implementing a time-out intervention. For the acting-out, aggressive, group-oriented child, time-out may be very effective. Such children wish to be with the group and attended to by the teacher. Consequently, time-out is not rewarding. However, for a withdrawn, passive, solitary child who is prone to daydreaming, time-out may be inappropriate and would be contraindicated. These children may engage in their "own little world" while in the time-out area.

■ *Example*

Richard, an 11-year-old boy in Ms. Jones's physical education class, was constantly arguing and fighting with his teacher and classmates about the rules of a game or how an activity should be conducted. This behavior occurred particularly when he was losing. Observation indicated that Richard truly enjoyed the activities and the company of his peers and Ms. Jones. However, the behavior was obtrusive and had to be eliminated for the sake of the group.

Ms. Jones selected time-out as a potentially effective intervention. Before the technique was imposed, it was decided that each time Richard started to argue or fight during class, he was to be sent to time-out. The time-out was out of view but not out of hearing of class activities. Under these conditions, Richard's disruptions were eliminated very rapidly.

Time-out in this situation was effective because Richard preferred to be with his classmates and teacher rather than in the less stimulating time-out area.

Consistency of Application

If time-out is to be applied as an intervention with a particular child, it must be used with consistency over a predetermined period (Brantner & Doherty, 1983). Frequently, teachers are inconsistent in their application of time-out. As a result, the child becomes confused, and the wrong behavior is reinforced. This situation is analogous to the confusion that results when, on Monday, Wednesday, and Friday, a child is forced to eat green vegetables under pain of death at the hands of Father, but on Tuesday and Thursday, Father is not so insistent. And on the weekend at Grandma's house, the child does not have to eat green vegetables at all.

Child's Understanding of the Rules

Children should know specifically what behaviors are not acceptable in their classrooms. In addition, they should know the consequence of exhibiting the forbidden behaviors. If time-out is to be used as an intervention, the rules for time-out should be communicated to the children; they should be posted and reviewed frequently. The rules assist the teacher in trying to remain consistent and fair in the application of the intervention.

Time-out should never be used whimsically with children—that is, one day a child is sent to time-out for talking in class, the next day for chewing gum, the next day for not completing a homework assignment, and so on. Such misuse will confuse the child and reduce the effectiveness of the intervention.

When time-out is imposed on the behavior of very young children, the teacher is often confronted with an additional problem. Frequently, it is impossible to communicate verbally to such children the rules governing time-out and its imposition. In this situation, it is necessary to initiate the program and demonstrate the intervention through implementation.

Time-out is not a technique that includes lecturing, reprimanding, or scolding before, during, or after the intervention. These techniques, although frequently used in everyday classroom exchanges, can provide unwanted reinforcement to the child. The teacher may wish to include a warning stage in the time-out procedures. When the inappropriate behavior occurs, the child may be redirected to the appropriate behavior. If within 10 or 15 seconds the child does not comply and return to task, then he or she is directed to time-out (Cuenin & Harris, 1986). Twyman, Johnson, Buie, and Nelson (1994) studied the effects of warning procedures to signal a more intrusive time-out contingency—that is, exclusionary time-out with nine elementary school students with behavioral disabilities. In the baseline condition, the students received three warnings before exclusionary time-out was imposed. In the experimental condition, students did not receive any warning prior to exclusionary time-out. They found that the number of exclusionary time-outs remained the same under both baseline and experimental conditions. The use of warnings was related to a decrease in appropriate contingent observation time-out behaviors, but not to the point where exclusionary time-out was imposed. The researchers suggest that warnings prior to the imposition of exclusionary time-out may result in more negative interactions between staff and students.

Time must be taken to explain why time-out is warranted, but the explanation should be brief and explicit. Going to time-out should not be a matter for debate between child and teacher. As the program continues, these explanations need only be reminders of the rules and consequences of exhibiting certain behaviors. Nelson and Rutherford (1983) noted two problems when a child is forced to go to time-out: (a) the physical contact may unwittingly reinforce the child's inappropriate behavior and (b) the teacher simply may be unable to physically control the child.

■ *Example*

Ms. Smith selected time-out as an intervention to decrease Elmo's talking in class. Each time Elmo talked out of turn in class, Ms. Smith would grab him by the arm and drag him to the time-out area. There she would proceed to babble at him (rather incoherently) for about 10 minutes. She would always conclude with the statement "Now, be quiet for two minutes." She would then proceed to stare at Elmo for 2 minutes. At the end of that time, she would say, "Now, get back to your seat."

Ms. Smith's intervention is an example of the improper use of time-out. The results were as expected:

1. Elmo continued to talk out in class because, although he was not particularly interested in Ms. Smith's lectures, he was pleased with his classmates' reactions to her behavior.
2. Ms. Smith's classroom group certainly enjoyed the circus.
3. Ms. Smith suffered from nervous tension.

Characteristics of the Time-Out Area

Care must be taken in the selection of the time-out area. Teachers should avoid selecting an area that may appear nonreinforcing but is in effect reinforcing to children. For instance, placing a child in the corridor for time-out may be extremely reinforcing. In the hallway, the child has an opportunity to communicate with everyone who passes. In addition, the child is provided with an opportunity to get out of the classroom and assignments.

Another commonly used but generally ineffective area for time-out is the principal's office. The office has been demonstrated to be one of the most stimulating and reinforcing areas in the school for the majority of children. In the office, the child has an opportunity to observe piqued parents, out-of-sorts mail carriers, and anxious administrators in their natural state. In addition, the child has opportunities to pick up the latest school news and gossip for dissemination among peers and teachers.

Some administrators do not understand the concept of time-out, and on occasion the child is given various clerical tasks to perform in the office, such as stapling, folding, carrying messages, and making announcements. The child who is in time-out just happens to be available when a body is needed to do something; the reason for the child's presence in the office is not considered when the task is assigned. An investigation of the use of the office for time-out would probably reveal that it is a far more attractive alternative for the child than sitting in the classroom reading, writing, or doing math problems. The time-out area should be (a) away from high traffic, (b) away from doors and windows, (c) out of the other children's view, and (d) within view of the observer.

Duration of Time-Out

Time-out loses its effectiveness as an intervention if a child is left in the setting for too long or not long enough (Pletras & Hackenberg, 2000). Time-out should be limited to approximately 2 minutes after the child has quieted. Four or 5 minutes in time-out should be a maximum except under extraordinary circumstances. Never should a child remain in time-out for more than 10 minutes. Consistency in the duration of the time-out period is essential. It is strongly recommended that the teacher use an inexpensive, bell-type egg timer to ensure that the time limit of time-out is not violated. The timer alerts both teacher and child to the exact moment the time-out period expires. In addition, it reassures the child that the teacher is being fair in the application of the intervention.

Ryan et al. (2007) identified some common problems in using time-out in the classroom. First, for time-out to be effective, the students must want to be in the classroom. If the classroom or the activity is not rewarding, removing the student does not remove reinforcement. A second reason is that the student may inadvertently be reinforced by time-out. The student may be able to at least temporarily escape an assignment or task. Teachers may also inadvertently allow students in time-out for a longer period of time than necessary because they are engaged in teaching rather than monitoring the removed student.

DESENSITIZATION

Desensitization, the process of systematically lessening a specific, learned fear or phobic reaction in an individual, is a therapeutic technique developed by Wolpe (1961).

The desensitization method consists of repeatedly presenting to the imagination of the deeply relaxed patient the feeblest item in a list of anxiety-evoking stimuli until no more anxiety is evoked. The next item of the list is presented and so on until, eventually, even the strongest of the anxiety-evoking stimuli fails to evoke any stir of anxiety in the patient. It has consistently been found that every stage of stimulus that evokes no anxiety when imagined in a state of relaxation will also evoke no anxiety when encountered in reality.

As indicated by Wolpe (1982), the process of desensitization has been demonstrated to be an effective technique when applied to individuals with fears and anxieties related to public speaking, school attendance, participation in large groups, water, animals, heights, flying, test taking, and the like.

The process of systematic desensitization involves three phases or steps:

1. training the subject in deep muscle relaxation;
2. constructing an anxiety-evoking hierarchy of stimuli; and
3. counterposing relaxation and the anxiety-evoking stimuli.

Teachers and parents should study other sources and obtain the services of a behavior therapy consultant before implementing a desensitization intervention.

Kravetz and Forness (1971) reported an experiment with a 6½-year-old boy who was unable to verbalize in the classroom. Psychiatric and medical reports did not reveal any known reason for his not talking in the classroom. The child's school progress was poor; however, test results indicated that he had above-average potential. A desensitization intervention of 12 sessions (2 per week) was implemented to reduce the child's fear of speaking in class.

Deffenbacher and Kemper (1974) applied systematic desensitization in a program to reduce test-taking anxiety in 28 junior high school students. The group was composed of 12 girls and 16 boys. All the students had been referred by a counselor, their parents, or a teacher. The desensitization treatment consisted of 8 sessions (1 per week) in groups of two to five students. The intervention effectively reduced test-taking anxiety. Kennedy and Doepke (1999) used a similar intervention to treat test anxiety of a female college student.

Desensitization is a potent intervention that can be applied in a modified form by the teacher in the classroom. However, if desensitization is to be applied in the classroom, the following conditions must exist:

1. The teacher must have a positive interpersonal relationship with the child. The child must trust the teacher and be free to express his or her fear in the teacher's presence.
2. The teacher must construct an anxiety-evoking stimulus hierarchy.
3. The teacher must be willing (and have adequate time) to accompany the child in the progression from the least to the most anxiety-evoking stimulus in the hierarchy.

Under normal classroom conditions, the desensitization process is time consuming. The teacher must be consistent and patient in the application of this intervention. It may be necessary to repeat some of the specific anxiety-evoking situations until their effect on the child has been eliminated.

■ *Examples*

David, a 5-year-old boy in Ms. Philly's class for children with behavior challenges, was afraid of dogs. Whenever the boy saw a dog, he would crawl under the nearest object or person and scream until the animal disappeared from view. This behavior made it impossible for David to go out on the playground during recess with his peers, to walk to and from school, or to play outdoors in his neighborhood.

Desensitization was suggested as a possible intervention. Ms. Philly thought it was an excellent idea but suggested that implementation be deferred until she knew David better. A stimulus hierarchy was constructed, but the intervention was held in abeyance until 3 months after the beginning of the school year.

The following anxiety-evoking stimulus hierarchy was used to reduce David's fear of dogs:

1. Pictures of dogs were hung on the walls of the classroom. The pictures were initially placed as far away from David's desk as possible. As desensitization continued, they were moved closer to David.
2. Pictures of dogs were observed by David in motion pictures and filmstrips.
3. Pictures of dogs were affixed to David's desk and notebook covers.
4. David observed dogs playing in the schoolyard from his classroom window.
5. David observed dogs playing in the school yard from the door of the school.
6. David observed dogs playing in the school yard as he stood at a distance that was systematically decreased.
7. David permitted dogs to walk past him in the school yard.

At no time during the desensitization process was David encouraged to touch or pet a dog. This precaution was taken simply because some dogs do bite some children.

During the desensitization process, Ms. Philly removed David from an anxiety-evoking situation whenever he manifested the slightest discomfort. The lessening of David's fear permitted him to tolerate dogs and to increase his interactions with his peers in the schoolyard and neighborhood.

Keith, an 8-year-old third-grade student, was enrolled in summer camp. Keith had a fear of water. Swimming lessons were part of the camp program. Although swimming was not mandatory, it was encouraged. At the first suggestion of swimming or going to the pool, Keith would have a temper tantrum of considerable magnitude.

It was decided that Keith should overcome this irrational fear. The staff concluded that systematic desensitization would be an effective intervention.

The following stimulus hierarchy was constructed and applied during desensitization:

1. Swimming was announced to the group and discussed with Keith's peers. Keith did not attend swimming lessons but watched his peers—who were very happy and excited—get on the bus and depart for swimming.
2. Keith rode the bus to the pool and waited outside the building.
3. Keith rode the bus to the pool and waited outside the locker room.
4. Keith entered the locker room, put on his trunks, and remained in the locker room.
5. Keith, in trunks, observed the lesson from the pool observation room.
6. Keith observed the lesson from the poolside (approximately 10 feet from the water).
7. Keith observed the lesson from the edge of the pool.
8. Keith observed the lesson while sitting on the edge of the pool with his feet in the water.
9. Keith stood in the pool with his hands on the edge of the pool.
10. Keith walked in the shallow end of the pool with his hands on the edge of the pool.

Throughout this procedure, Keith was accompanied by his counselor, who provided positive reinforcement. As a result of this process and within 3 weeks, Keith began his swimming lessons. After 3 years, it was noted that the fear had not returned. Keith is an excellent swimmer.

Koegel (2004) applied three experimental designs in research on the use of desensitization on the hypersensitivity to auditory stimuli in three young children with autism. He found desensitization effective in reducing sensitivity to environmental sounds such as the vacuum cleaner, blender, toilet flushing, and others.

Summary Points

- Differential reinforcement is the reinforcing of an appropriate behavior that is to be increased or exhibited. Differential reinforcement simultaneously extinguishes an inappropriate behavior that is to be decreased or eliminated. Zero rates of behavior, incompatible behaviors, or lower rates of behaviors may be differentially reinforced.
- Extinction is the discontinuation or withholding of the reinforcer of a behavior that has previously been reinforcing the behavior. Some behaviors, however, are so serious that they cannot be ignored.
- Explicit reprimands are specific, immediate, firm statements made on the exhibition of an undesirable target behavior.

- Reprimands are useful when the student is engaging in a behavior that requires immediate action because it is potentially harmful to self, others, or property.
- Loss of privileges, or response cost, is most effective when the loss is a natural or logical consequence of the undesirable behavior.
- Time-out is a controversial intervention that removes students from educational opportunities. The decision to use time-out should be a discussion by the student's IEP team and should be carefully documented and evaluated.
- Desensitization presents a series of experiences to lessen the fear or anxiety related to a specific experience or event.

Projects

1. Joanie, a third-grader in Mr. Jewel's class, frequently asks, "What time is it?" She does this about 15 times a day. Mr. Jewel considers this to be attention-getting behavior and wishes to eliminate it. He usually responds to Joanie's request by telling her the time. Using the example of Joanie, (a) design four interventions for eliminating the behavior using the intervention strategies listed below and (b) discuss which of the interventions you think will be the most effective and the least effective.
   a. differential reinforcement
   b. reprimand
   c. extinction
   d. time-out

2. Using the Internet, explore the position of each of the following professional organizations on the use of punishment; then construct a table comparing the stance of these organizations:

   The Council for Exceptional Children
   www.cec.sped.org//AM/Template.cfm?Section=Home

   National Association for School Psychologists
   www.nasponline.org

   National Education Association *www.nea.org*

   United Teaching Profession *www.utp.org*

   American Federation of Teachers *www.aft.org*

Web Resources

For a debate about the use of time-out rooms, visit this site:
www.aft.org/pubs-reports/american_teacher/mar03/speak-out.html

For a discussion of logical consequences and discipline, visit this site:
www.responsiveclassroom.org/pdf_files/10_3nl_1.pdf

For a review of differential reinforcement, visit this site:
www.autismnetwork.org/modules/behavior/dr/faq.html

References

Brantner, J. P., & Doherty, M. A. (1983). A review of time-out: A conceptual and methodological analysis. In S. Axelrod & J. Apsche (Eds.), *The effects of punishment on human behavior* (pp. 87–132). New York: Academic Press.

Brulle, A. R., & Barton, L. E. (1992). The reduction of maladaptive behaviors through DRO procedures: A practitioner's reference. *ICEC Quarterly, 41*(4), 5–10.

Cuenin, L. H., & Harris, K. R. (1986). Planning, implementing, and evaluating time-out interventions with exceptional students. *Teaching Exceptional Children, 18*(4), 272–276.

Deffenbacher, J., & Kemper, C. (1974). Systematic desensitization of test anxiety in junior high school students. *The School Counselor, 21,* 216–222.

Dipipi, C. M., Jitendra, A. K., & Miller, J. A. (2001). Reducing repetitive speech: Effects of strategy instruction. *Preventing School Failure, 45*(4), 177–181.

Drasgow, E. (1997). Positive approaches to reducing undesirable behavior. *Beyond Behavior, 8*(2), 10–13.

Flood, W. A., & Wilder, D. A. (2004). The use of differential reinforcement and fading to increase time away from a caregiver in a child with separation anxiety disorder. *Education and Treatment of Children, 27*(1), 1–8.

Hall, R. V., & Hall, M. C. (1980a). *How to use planned ignoring.* Austin, TX: Pro-Ed.

Hall, R. V., & Hall, M. C. (1980b). *How to use time-out.* Austin, TX: Pro-Ed.

Jones, R. N., Sloane, H. N., & Roberts, M. W. (1992). Limitations of "Don't" instructional control. *Behavior Therapy, 23,* 131–140.

Kennedy, D. V., & Doepke, K. J. (1999). Multicomponent treatment of a test anxious college student. *Education and Treatment of Children, 22*(2), 203–217.

Kerr, M. M., & Nelson, C. M. (1989). *Strategies for managing behavior problems in the classroom* (2nd ed.). Upper Saddle River, NJ: Merrill/Pearson.

Koegel, R. L. (2004). A systematic desensitization paradigm to treat hypersensitivity to auditory stimuli in children with autism in the family context. *Research & Practice for Persons with Severe Disabilities, 29*(2), 122–134.

Kravetz, R., & Forness, S. (1971). The special classroom as a desensitization setting. *Exceptional Children, 37,* 389–391.

Love, E., Love, D., & Northcraft, G. (2010). Is the end in sight? Student regulation of in-class and extra-credit effort in response to performance feedback. *Academy of Management Learning & Education, 9*(1), 81–97. Retrieved from Business Source Complete database.

Martin, G., & Pear, J. (1992). *Behavior modification: What it is and how to do it* (4th ed.). Upper Saddle River, NJ: Prentice Hall.

Nelson, C., & Rutherford, R. (1983). Time-out revisited: Guidelines for its use in special education. *Exceptional Education Quarterly, 3,* 56–67.

Oliver, R. M. (2007). *Key issue: Improving student outcomes in general and special education with effective classroom management practices.* Washington, DC: National Comprehensive Center for Teacher Quality.

Piazza, C. C., Bowman, L. G., Contrucci, S. A., Delia, M. D., Adelinis, J. D., & Goh, H. L. (1999). An evaluation of the properties of attention as reinforcement for destructive and appropriate behavior. *Journal of Applied Behavioral Analysis, 32*(4), 437–439.

Pletras C. J,. & Hackenberg, T.D. (2000). Time-out postponement without increased reinforcement frequently. *Journal of Experimental Analysis of Behavior 74*(2), 147–164.

Powell, T. H., & Powell, I. Q. (1982). Guidelines for implementing time-out procedures. *The Pointer, 26,* 18–21.

Proctor, M. A., & Morgan, D. (1991). Effectiveness of a response cost raffle procedure on the disruptive classroom behavior of adolescents with behavior disorders. *School Psychology Review, 20*(1), 97–109.

Reid, R. (1999). Attention deficit hyperactivity disorder: Effective methods for the classroom. *Focus on Exceptional Children, 32*(4), 1–20.

Ryan, J. B., Sanders, S., Katsiyannis, A., & Yell, M (2007). Using time-out effectively in the classroom. *Teaching Exceptional Children, 39*(4), 60–67.

Ruhl, K. (1985). Handling aggression: Fourteen methods teachers use. *The Pointer, 29,* 30–33.

Salend, S., & Gordon, B. (1987) A group time-out ribbon intervention. *Behavioral Disorders, 12,* 131–136.

Salend, S. J., Jantzen, N. R., & Giek, K. (1992). Using a peer confrontation system in a group setting. *Behavioral Disorders, 17*(3), 211–218.

Shapiro, E. S., & Lentz, F. E. (1985). A survey of school psychologists' use of behavior modification procedures. *Journal of School Psychology, 23,* 327–336.

Shute, V. J. (2008). Focus on formative feedback. *Review of Educational Research, 78,* 153–189.

Simonson, B., Fairbanks, S., Briesch, A., Myers, D., & Sugai, G. (2008). Evidence-based practices in classroom management: Considerations for research to practice. *Education and Treatment of Children, 31*(3), 351–380.

Twyman, J. S., Johnson, H., Buie, J. D., & Nelson, C. M. (1994). The use of a warning procedure to signal a more intrusive timeout contingency. *Behavioral Disorders, 19*(4), 243–253.

Van Houten, R., Nau, P., Mackenzie-Keating, S., Sameoto, D., & Colavecchia, B. (1982). An analysis of some variables influencing the effectiveness of reprimands. *Journal of Applied Behavior Analysis, 15,* 65–83.

Webber, J., & Scheuermann, B. (1991). Accentuate the positive . . . eliminate the negative. *Teaching Exceptional Children, 24*(1), 13–19.

Wheldall, K. (1991). Managing troublesome classroom behavior in regular schools: A positive teaching perspective. *International Journal of Disability, Development and Education, 38*(2), 99–116.

White, R. B., & Koorland, M. A. (1996). Curses! What can we do about cursing? *Teaching Exceptional Children, 28*(4), 48–52.

Witt, J. C., & Elliott, S. N. (1982). The response-cost lottery: A time efficient and effective classroom intervention. *Journal of School Psychology, 20*(2), 155–161.

Wolpe, J. (1961). The systematic desensitization treatment of neuroses. *Journal of Nervous and Mental Diseases, 132,* 189–203.

Wolpe, J. (1982). *The practice of behavior therapy* (3rd ed.). New York: Pergamon Press.

Zabel, M. K. (1986). Time-out use with behaviorally disordered students. *Behavioral Disorders, 12*(1), 15–21.

After completing this chapter, you will be able to do the following:

Recognize characteristics of prosocial classroom management.

Identify strategies to employ the Universal Design for Learning.

Describe the principles of Quality Schools and the Circle of Courage.

Understand the application of the expressive media in behavior management.

Explain the application of the behavior influence techniques in the management of behavior.

CHAPTER OBJECTIVES

After completing this chapter, you will be able to do the following:

1. Recognize characteristics of prosocial classroom management.

2. Identify strategies to employ the Universal Design for Learning.

3. Describe the principles of Quality Schools and the Circle of Courage.

4. Understand the application of the expressive media in behavior management.

5. Explain the application of the behavior influence techniques in the management of behavior.

Prosocial Classroom Management

KEY TERMS

Behavior influence techniques
Circle of Courage
Classroom Conferencing

Expressive media
Quality Schools
Responsive Classroom

Jack is a 13-year-old seventh-grader who performs above grade level in all subjects. However, his social behavior is creating difficulties for Jack, his classmates, and teachers. He is ignored by some students, overtly rejected by others, and used as a scapegoat by a few.

Jack believes that he is unacceptable to (unwanted by) his peers. He appears to believe that others are making fun of him or rejecting him when they are being overtly friendly. When Jack feels he is being rejected, he immediately attempts to escape his discomfort. He escapes by putting his head down on his desk, remaining in the restroom, and even has left the school building.

What can Mr. Bird, as a teacher, do to support Jack in developing more acceptable ways of expressing his discomfort?

Freiberg and Lamb (2009) ask a poignant question: Do we want to raise compliant, passive children and youth or self-disciplined individuals with initiative? They argue that rather than the teacher-centered management that is often in place, in order to support students' social-emotional growth, a shift to person-centered management must take place. Classroom climate is at the core of this discussion. In this chapter we discuss ways to develop a prosocial classroom climate—a classroom in which students are self-disciplined and want to achieve. We describe the rationale and application of the Universal Design for Learning, which levels the instructional playing field for all students. In addition, we provide several models of positive classrooms for your consideration.

Gable and Van Acker (2004) suggest that educational personnel have demonstrated increased concern over the aggressive and antisocial behavior of children and youth. There is a real need to develop and apply more effective interventions for decreasing and eliminating violent aggressive behavior. They suggest that assessment as well as intervention must focus on both internal and external influences of the behavior of children and youth. Intervention should include cognitive, affective, and behavioral dimensions of the behavior problem exhibited by the learner. They recommend a multi-faceted approach as suggested in this chapter.

PROSOCIAL CLASSROOM MANAGEMENT

Prosocial classroom management supports the individual, and in doing so enhances the community of learning in the classroom. Freiberg and Lamb (2009) suggest four dimensions of shifting to a prosocial, person-centered classroom climate. These include:

- an emphasis on teacher's caring for students and valuing them as people;
- efforts to help students attain a strong sense of belonging to the school, their classroom, and their peers;
- a positive climate, in which students feel safe and trust their peers and teachers; and
- self-discipline, in which students learn shared respect and responsibility, recognizing the possible outcomes of their behaviors.

Person-centered classrooms are very different from teacher-centered classrooms. Self-discipline takes precedence over teacher control. All students are an integral part of the classroom community and collaboratively develop rules that form a compact among teachers and students. The rewards in these classrooms are intrinsic, with students sharing in the classroom responsibilities (Freiberg & Lamb, 2009).

Though the teacher shares responsibility for the classroom, a key aspect is his or her social-emotional competence. Teachers who have high social-emotional competence recognize and try to understand students' actions, motives, and emotions. In addition, he or she is a strong role model, demonstrating how to handle situations in a self-disciplined way in which everyone profits. Such teachers tend to be more proactive, more readily connecting to students with enthusiasm (Jennings & Greenberg, 2009). These teachers are comfortable establishing warm and supportive relationships while setting limits and guiding students as well as using skill building and prevention rather than controlling negative behavior through coercion or punishment.

Relationships with teachers can have a long-lasting effect on students. Students who consistently have poor relationships with their teachers act out more, enjoy school less, and are more hostile. Yet Howes, Phillipsen, and Peisner-Feinberg (2000) argue that students with challenging behaviors are destined to have poor relationships with their teachers. Though some teachers may perceive a child with problems as someone with whom they cannot have a positive relationship, others accept the task of constructing a positive relationship not only in spite of the child's behavior but because of it.

Providing social-emotional support is a primary role for teachers. Buyse, Verschueren, Doumen, Van Damme, and Maes (2008) reported the children with behavior problems in the classroom tend to become engaged in a negative cycle, in which their behavior influences the quality of the relationships with teachers, which then has a negative effect on the students' social-behavioral development. Teachers' emotional support can act as a protective factor by breaking the link between the behavior problem and the stressor of poor teacher relationships.

One aspect that can support students with behavior problems in developing and maintaining a relationship with the teacher is classroom conferencing.

Classroom Conferencing

McIntyre (1996) describes a method of classroom conferencing specifically designed for teachers of students with behavioral problems. The long talk is an easily implemented classroom conferencing procedure and is especially responsive to a variety of interpersonal interaction and counseling styles. The long talk is applied to help students analyze their behavior and develop better self-control.

The steps in **classroom conferencing** are to (a) meet, (b) review, (c) discuss respect, (d) discuss typical behavior, (e) devise another response, and (f) reconvene. The teacher should meet privately with the student as soon as possible after the behavioral incident. During the conference, the student is requested to review the incident. The teacher should clarify the student's perception to ensure that both student and teacher are discussing a common perception. The teacher may make corrections in the student's perception on the basis of first-person knowledge of the incident. Next, the teacher and student discuss respect to clarify what actions and feelings resulting from the incident were right and wrong and whose rights and privileges were violated. Student and teacher discuss typical behavior during the next step of the conferencing process. The student is helped to see the inappropriateness of the behavior and is informed that it is unacceptable.

In the fifth step, student and teacher devise another response. The student is requested to suggest alternative ways of responding in similar situations in the future. All suggested alternatives are accepted and written on paper. The student is asked to select the alternative he or she will use in the future. The alternative's use in various situations is discussed. The pros and cons of the alternative are discussed. If the alternative that the student selects is unrealistic, he or she is requested to select another. Student and teacher discuss why the first alternative is unrealistic. The teacher may assist students who are unable to generate alternatives.

In the final step, student and teacher reconvene to review student progress and performance and engage in further planning, as necessary. Behavior change takes time, and a series of conferences is often necessary.

ENHANCING POSITIVE CLASSROOM MANAGEMENT THROUGH UNIVERSAL DESIGN FOR LEARNING

Universal Design for Learning (UDL) is a means for providing effective instruction in diverse classrooms. When applying UDL you are providing several flexible options for (a) presenting or providing access to what is to be learned, (b) planning and implementing learning tasks, the how of what is to be learned, and (c) engagement, interest, and motivation, the why of learning (National Center on Universal Design in Learning, 2009). These three variables form the principles of UDL.

Principle 1: Provide Multiple Means of Presentation

This principle is grounded in the understanding that students perceive and understand information in different ways. These ways may be as easy as visual or auditory preferences. Or they may be more complex, such as levels of language or abstraction. Teachers should provide information through different modes (visual, auditory, touch) and formats. If, for example, you always write and talk, students are automatically provided with two means of representation: visual and auditory.

■ *Example*

Ms. Garza had a very diverse class of seventh-graders, many of whom were English language learners. She recognized that the students all were able to comprehend the information in her math class if it was presented in such a way that everyone could understand. Ms. Garza always opened the class by reviewing the agenda that she had posted on the white board. Some students, however, were given individual copies of the schedule that they read as she reviewed the agenda and used as a check sheet for completion of each section of the lesson. As she worked through the presentation in the book, Ms. Garza passed out a set of guided notes that provided a clear, explicit definition of each of the new terms. Ms. Garza always made sure she had adequate materials when she demonstrated a concept using manipulatives so that students who needed to engage with manipulatives were able to do so.

Presenting in English to English speakers and French to French speakers is an oversimplification of this principle. Language also varies in complexity and level of abstraction. There also may be a difference in what students can understand and describe and what they can read. Showing students a graph may actually clarify a concept for only half of the students in the classroom.

■ *Example*

Mr. Blue recognized that his fourth-grade science students varied a great deal in their personal experiences with the content he was teaching. To make the information available to everyone, he began each lesson by listing keywords and symbols and their definitions. As he discussed each of the keywords, he asked the students to provide examples in their own lives. In describing cyclonic action, he asked one of the students to describe "dust devils" that he had seen on the desert. By allowing Luis to describe the way in which it "spun around like the clock, with a hollow middle," Mr. Blue was able to let a student who often struggled in the classroom demonstrate leadership.

Principle 2: Provide Multiple Means of Expression

As you think about this principle, think about action. Pencil and paper provide very limited ways for students to express themselves. Physical action not only can engage students, but it also can help with the fidgeting and movement needs of students who have problems with extended attention. As long as the student is able to express comprehension of the content, learning can be assessed. Rather than writing a response, a student may be allowed to act it out. Students who struggle with fine motor skills may need to continue to print rather than learning cursive or use of a computer for word processing. (The use of media is addressed later in this chapter.)

■ *Example*

Ms. Wolfe's second grade was completing a unit on insects. She met with the group with a chart that included several options for "showing what you learned." This project was going to serve as both the assessment and the culminating activity of the unit. She described each option and asked the students to first decide if they were going to work independently or if they were going to work with a partner. If they chose a partner, both would have to agree on the project and work together to its completion. Her chart included these options:

- Write 15 true-false statements about insects and their life cycle.
- Using materials at the art table, construct a four-step model of the insect life cycle.
- Using clay, make an insect and label its body parts.
- Draw a picture of an insect. Cut out the names of the body parts from the word sheet and label the picture.
- Using the computer, find images of five insects you have seen personally. In either words or pictures, show the life cycle of one of these insects.

Principle 3: Provide Multiple Means of Engagement

The emphasis of this principle is to find ways to interest and intrigue the students. The teacher's effort at engagement is intentional; plans should include ways to reconnect students who are drifting off, distracted, focusing on minute parts of the lesson, or bored. In addition, teachers work with students to increase their persistence and self-determination.

Burgstahler (2007) suggests that there are several indicators that teachers are using UDL. These include:

- a class climate that respects diversity and inclusiveness;
- regular, effective interactions between teachers and students, with an emphasis on students with different values and skills filling different roles in group efforts;
- ensuring that all activities and materials are physically accessible to all students;
- using many instructional methods that are accessible to all students, providing students with options such as collaborative learning opportunities, hands-on activities, software, fieldwork, or art projects;
- ensuring that course materials are interesting, flexible, and accessible for all students;
- frequent feedback;
- ongoing assessment; and
- planned accommodations so that everyone has an opportunity to succeed.

SCHOOL STRUCTURES: QUALITY SCHOOLS, THE CIRCLE OF COURAGE, AND THE RESPONSIVE CLASSROOM

According to Glasser (in Nelson, 2002) a major problem with current schools is the emphasis on students repeating what they are told rather than teachers helping students develop critical thinking skills. Rather than acquiring knowledge, students should be applying knowledge to solve problems. Glasser believes that the foundation of good education is engaging students in encouraging dialogues while checking for understanding and growth. A core aspect of this dialogue is a strong relationship with a teacher who is able to engage students in conversation about what is being learned.

In Glasser's **Quality Schools** (1998), the emphasis is on competence for all students rather than competition. Criticism is considered dangerous to students' development. If students experience what Glasser refers to as "the seven deadly habits" (Nelson, 2002, p. 98) of criticism (blaming, complaining, nagging, threatening, punishing, and punishing by rewards), then they become disconnected from school.

Greene (2004) describes the characteristics of Quality Schools in these ways:

- There are relationships among students, faculty, and staff that are built on trust and respect, helping each other, supporting competence, and encouraging everyone.
- Continuous improvement is constantly monitored through concurrent and self-evaluation.
- All students are engaged in ways to demonstrate their competence and continuous improvement.
- In addition to all students demonstrating their competence, some students move beyond competence to quality learning, in that they are more involved, demonstrate deeper competence, or are more creative.
- Students, faculty, and staff recognize the need for intrinsic motivation and that control needs to be eliminated.
- School is a joyful place, with an energy for learning. The students, faculty, and staff feel connected to each other and work to do their very best.

■ *Example*

Kyle, a 10th-grade student at Greenwood High School, had superior academic potential. However, he was failing several subjects. It became evident that Kyle's future relative to graduation and college was being affected by his behavior.

Mr. Germaine, Kyle's favorite teacher, decided he must help the young man. He did not want Kyle to jeopardize his future. In their first session, it was found that Kyle would not work in any subject areas if he did not like the teacher. If the teacher was too demanding, unfriendly, and so on, Kyle just gave up—he refused to study. Kyle recognized that his behavior was harmful only to himself. He and Mr. Germaine developed a plan of action.

During the next few months, they met regularly to monitor Kyle's progress. Kyle learned to accept responsibility for his behavior. His grades improved dramatically.

The **Circle of Courage**, developed by Brendtro, Brokenleg, and Van Bockern, (2002), encompasses four core values: belonging, mastery, independence, and generosity.

Based in Native American culture, each of these values includes a course of action for the relationship between students and teachers:

- *Belonging* suggests that everyone should be connected, part of the larger community, so that if one support fails another moves in.
- *Mastery* suggests that someone with more skill is a model for others. In addition, striving to mastery must be grounded in personal growth rather than competition.
- *Independence* suggests that each individual is powerful and should be given opportunities to make choices without coercion.
- *Generosity* suggests that in helping others you have proof of your own worthiness.

The emphasis of the Circle of Courage is depicted on a medicine wheel within which each quadrant represents a value. The emphasis is on reclaiming students and "mending their spirits" (Brendtro et al., 2002). This reattachment occurs through:

- providing cohesive, noncompetitive classroom environments in which each student is a contributing member;
- providing encouragement;
- celebrating individuality and unique talents;
- making expectations clear so that there is an understanding of what to do and how to do it; and
- emphasizing the deed, rather than the doer.

In the Circle of Courage, reclaiming relationships and opportunities for healing are key. The school community should be caring, supporting the individual development of each student.

This therapeutic classroom environment is grounded in getting to know each student as a unique, capable person. The teacher, as the primary caring adult, must believe that all of his or her students can learn and refuse to become angry or hostile with student behavior. Each student's talents and interests should be recognized and used as a way to select instructional methods. Each student should be treated with dignity, with a classroom climate of acceptance of individual differences. Active efforts must be taken to teach problem solving and stress management to students. Perhaps most important, teachers should maintain hope and belief in themselves and their students (Abrams, 2005).

The Responsive Classroom

The **Responsive Classroom** integrates social and academic classrooms. Seven principles guide the teacher:

- Academic and social curricula receive equal emphasis.
- How children learn is as important as what they learn.
- Social interaction facilitates learning.
- Cooperation, assertion, responsibility, empathy, and self-control are critical skills for children.
- The teacher needs to know each student individually, culturally, and developmentally.
- The teacher needs to know each student's family. (Northeast Foundation for Children, 2003)

The teacher implements these principles through several specific practices. Each morning begins with a daily meeting with time for sharing, games, and fun intellectual challenges. All rules are linked with logical consequences and are aimed at preventing problems. These rules are developmentally appropriate, relevant, and grounded in trust between the teacher and the student. Rules are developed collaboratively with students, emphasizing the need to allow everyone to meet learning goals. Contingent praise, described previously in this text, is used, with the teacher commenting descriptively on the student's effort. Language on the whole is positive, emphasizing self-discipline. Students are also taught to notice and internalize productive behaviors through modeling. Classrooms are physically organized to encourage students to be independent, cooperative, and responsible (Rimm-Kauffman, Fan, Chiu, & You, 2007).

The Responsive Classroom emphasizes guided discovery, designing lessons to encourage independence, creativity, and responsibility. Consistent with UDL, academic choice is emphasized, with a variety of learning activities to increase student learning by encouraging teacher-structured choices in students' work. Families are also key, and a partnership is emphasized. Collaborative problem solving is taught and modeled, including a wide range of strategies to resolve problems. Expressive media and role playing as well as other strategies are encouraged. These methods are addressed in the next section of this text.

■ *Example*

Mr. Nguyen decided he was not going to have another year of wasting his ninth-grade homeroom period. With the use of e-mail and the school's e-learning program, it was difficult to use the homeroom period for more than a gripe or gossip session. To combat the negative energy that seemed to emanate from homeroom, Mr. Nguyen met with his ninth-grade homeroom class the first day of class and began by introducing the Morning Meeting. He wanted to be able to share information and get his students to know him and know each other. He called them to the meeting and showed them the agenda he was going to follow:

School business

Personal business (anybody have anything to discuss or share)

Activity (not every day)

Successes

Concerns

Closure

Mr. Nguyen went over the announcements, and then said, "Anybody have any personal business?" The ninth-graders all looked at him dumfounded. So Mr. Nguyen said, "Well, I do. My fourteen-month-old son finally let go of the coffee table last night and walked from my wife over to me. He's on the move now. I'm going to sign him up for track team." The students, surprised, laughed, not having had a teacher tell a story such as this before. Another student finally said, "Well, I have something. I have my learner's permit for driving. Watch out!" The other students laughed and thumped fists with him. Mr. Nguyen moved to his activity, which was asking each student what kind of shoe they would be—if they were a shoe—and to give their reasons. This time he didn't have to go first. At the end of this discussion, Mr. Nguyen had little time to ask for any successes or concerns. He concluded by saying "Let's wish each other a good day." Rather than the student's leaving the room "dissing" each other, they left saying positive things to each other.

EXPRESSIVE MEDIA

The term **expressive media** refers to activities that encourage and permit children to express personal feelings and emotions through creative activities with minimal constraints. Expressive media, applied in an appropriate environment and under competent guidance, can be an acceptable and legitimate means for expressing positive and negative feelings and emotions. Adults frequently reduce personal stresses and frustrations in verbal exchanges with trusted friends and relatives or by means of avocations, hobbies, games, projects, trips, sports, vacations, and so on. For children who are generally less capable in verbal communications and less in control of their personal lifestyle, the expressive media are an opportunity to reduce stresses and frustrations without danger of conflict with others.

The media can provide many benefits for children. Not only are media beneficial in the affective domain, but they also provide a variety of cognitive and psychomotor learning benefits. If the media are to be used as a behavior management technique, the child must be provided with opportunities to find a personally satisfying medium of expression. The individual must be provided with consistent, repeated opportunities to express feelings and emotions through the chosen medium. Examples of media may include:

- puppetry, which may provide a nonthreatening way for students to act out issues and develop solutions to their problems (Caputo, 1995);
- music, which may decrease tension, increase self-expression, engage students with each other, and increase acceptance of each others' performances (Layman, Hussey, & Laing, 2002);
- art productions, which benefit students in communication, socialization, creativity, self-expression, self-exploration, and manipulation of the environment (Williams & Wood, 1977);
- drama, which can assist in the development of decision making, solving problems, facilitating group cohesiveness, allow experimentation with adult roles, and help students conceptualize abstract subject matter (Creekmore & Madan, 1981); and
- pet interaction, carefully monitored and designed to increase self-confidence, develop nurturing skills, improve reality orientation, increase self-esteem, and promote learning to cooperate with others (Murry, 1996).

Some expressive media are easier to use in the classroom than others. These include role-playing, physical activity, writing, and books.

Role Playing

Role playing is a potentially valuable therapeutic intervention for use with children. These techniques are based on the assumption that individuals may gain greater understanding of their behavior if they act out various aspects of their lives (Newcomer,

1980). Warger (1985) and Warger and Weiner (1987) recommend creative drama for children whose play development may be slow as a consequence of a disability. It is an excellent method for enhancing skills critical to learning and developing social skills, and it can be readily individualized. According to Raths, Harmin, and Simons (1978), role playing can assist an individual in the clarification of feelings and emotions as they relate to existing reality in three ways:

1. It can focus on real occurrences. An incident may be reenacted and the participants told to attend to the feelings aroused; or an incident may be reenacted with the participants changing roles and attending to the feelings aroused by these new roles. An individual may be directed to deliver a soliloquy to re-create an emotionally loaded event. Emphasis here is on expressing feelings that were hidden or held back when the event first occurred.

2. It can focus on significant others. The individual may portray a significant person in his or her life about whom a great amount of conflict is felt.

3. It can focus on processes and feelings occurring in new situations. Directions for this type of role playing may be very specific, with the participants provided with special characters and actions; or direction may be vague, allowing the participants to form their own characters.

■ *Example*

Thomas, a 15-year-old tenth-grader, was quite overweight. He was the class scapegoat. His classmates were constantly making fun of his size. They called him "Porky," "Fatso," "Pig," "Slob," "Tubby," and so on. Each day, someone came up with a new name to call him.

Thomas was a sensitive young man, and whenever he was called a name, he withdrew. Frequently, the teacher saw tears in his eyes.

Mrs. Minup was very concerned about Thomas's mental well-being and his classmates' lack of consideration and compassion for Thomas and other children who were different. She believed that role playing might be a method of helping the whole class, including Thomas, gain insight into their behavior.

Without including obesity, Mrs. Minup conducted a series of role-playing activities with the class. The students role-played their reactions and feelings to roles concerned with height, complexion, race, religion, and so on.

As the students began to empathize with the feelings of the characters they were role-playing, Thomas became more accepted and less of a target of their hurtful behavior.

Creative Movement, Dance, and Physical Activities

During creative movement sessions, the child can express past, present, and even future feelings and emotions. These activities encourage the child to externalize personal feelings and begin to deal with them. Movement activities can be conducted with or without music (Hibben & Scheer, 1982). On occasion, voices, hand clapping, feet stamping, recorded environmental sounds, and rhythm instruments are used to facilitate sessions.

■ *Example*

At camp R&R, the staff noticed that the preteen group known as the "cool persons" was the most restrained of all the groups. Children in this group appeared afraid to "let go," to have a good time, or to relax. They appeared concerned about making mistakes in front of their peers.

Ms. Taphorn, a dance enthusiast, suggested that a daily early morning session of creative movement might relax the group and develop cohesiveness. During the sessions, in which Ms. Taphorn and the staff participated, the group became trees, grass, wind, rain, sun, and flowers. They acted out sadness, happiness, joy, sorrow, excitement, fear, and so on.

Within a few days, the "cool persons" were acting as "happy cool persons." The campers began to relax and enjoy each other's company.

In a research brief, Zabel (1988) suggested that available research tends to support physical exercise as an adjunctive therapy. Physical activities have been used to provide both aerobic activity and therapeutic restructuring of the environment (Lane, Bonic, & Wallgren-Bonic, 1983). Group "walk-talks" have demonstrated the production of healthy levels of fatigue and improved peer relationships among adolescents (Lane et al.). Daily jogging programs have decreased disruptive behaviors among behavior-disordered children (Allen, 1980; Hoenig, Shea, & Bauer, 1986). Anderson (1985) reported positive effects from the "A.M. Club," a jogging club for junior high school students with behavioral disorders. Evans, Evans, Schmid, and Pennypacker (1985) studied the relationship between jogging and touch football and specific behaviors in adolescents with behavioral disorders. The data indicated that a decrease in talk-outs and an increase in problems completed were associated with vigorous exercise. Yell (1988) studied the effects of jogging on the talk-outs and out-of-seat behavior of elementary school students with behavioral disorders. A decrease in the inappropriate behaviors following jogging was found in five of six students.

Lopata, Nida, and Marable (2006) suggest the use of progressive muscle relaxation to reduce physical aggression. They suggest developing a script so that you can repeat the same process each time you use the guided activity. The teacher guides the students through a sequence of tensing and releasing. The students begin lying down on their backs with arms out to their sides, out of reach of any other students. They begin by tightening forearms, holding it for 4 seconds, and letting it go. The teacher describes the feeling after the release as "being relaxed." They suggest that using the script earlier in the day may be most helpful.

The Written Word

Few studies have been conducted on the therapeutic benefit of writing as an intervention for children, although writing has been repeatedly demonstrated to be a useful therapeutic intervention for adults. It seems logical that children can express personal feelings and emotions through written communications. By writing and at times sharing with others that which is written, it is possible to externalize personal conflicts and frustrations (Levinson, 1982). According to Dehouske (1982), writing can be a mode of self-expression, self-exploration, and problem solving. Students' stories reveal each student's life view, attitudes, coping skills, and problem-solving strategies. Story writing may be used to help students explore alternatives to social problems.

Two kinds of journaling are typically used in the classroom. One is a dialogue journal, the other a private journal. A dialogue journal is a written conversation between the teacher and student. In addition to allowing the student to "talk" in private with the teacher, the dialogue journal allows students with an ongoing example of an adult's use of written language. Cobine (1995) provides the example that when the teacher uses a specific writing structure in a response, students might later try it themselves. In adopting methods such as comparison, analogy, description, and argumentation, then, students come to write more communicatively and, gradually, more formally.

With a private dialogue-journal, students could write brief notes about their state-of-the-class perspectives. They could question and comment, as well as answer questions and comments that the teacher has written alongside their entries. For instance, if a student notes a barrier to his or her academic progress, the teacher might write a suggestion about an alternative study habit alongside the student's entry. Or, if numerous students share the same perception about a barrier, the teacher might propose a change in classroom protocol. Then the student might write in response to the teacher's proposal or even write a counterproposal. Alongside the student's latest entry, the teacher could again write a comment or question. Since the purpose of a dialogue journal is to provide students with a real audience and thereby enhance their rhetorical awareness, the teacher would respond only to the content of the student's entry, not to grammatical and mechanical errors in the writing; instead, the teacher would lead by example, modeling grammatical and mechanical correctness in his or her own written responses (Burniske, 1994).

Writing for therapeutic benefit is not concerned with any particular format. Concern is focused entirely on content. The written forms may include poetry, stories, essays, articles, books, journal entries, and so on.

■ *Example*

For a teenager, Michael had several serious problems on his mind. Not only was he concerned about himself and his future, but he was concerned about his parents, who were separated and considering divorce.

Michael had great difficulty talking about his problems to anyone, including parents, teachers, and friends. The school counselor suggested that Michael might keep a journal in which he could write to his parents about his concerns and his feelings. The counselor told Michael not to be concerned about spelling, grammar, handwriting, and so on—to just write what he wished. The counselor offered to discuss these writings with Michael if and when Michael wished.

Michael wrote a daily journal. He did not discuss the content with the counselor but did report that it helped him to write about his problems and reread his daily entries.

Bibliotherapy

Bibliotherapy is an indirect intervention that uses the interaction between the reader and literature for therapeutic purposes. It is a tool for helping children deal with their problems through reading literature about characters that possess problems similar to their own (Adderholdt-Elliot & Eller, 1989; Sridhar & Vaughn, 2000). This intervention can be applied with children and youth to encourage them to fulfill their needs, relieve pressures, and improve mental and emotional well-being (Russell & Russell, 1979). McCarty and Chalmers (1997) suggest that bibliotherapy is effective not only in the treatment of behavior problems but also in the prevention of behavior problems.

According to Gladding and Gladding (1991), there are two kinds of bibliotherapy. The first, originating in the 1930s, is a collaborative effort of librarians and counselors. In this form of bibliotherapy, counselors prescribe reading material (suggested by librarians) to individuals who are experiencing emotional difficulties. The individuals respond directly to the materials, and change is brought about through insight, catharsis, or copying the behavior characteristics described in the literature.

The second kind of bibliotherapy is interactive bibliotherapy, which emphasizes that the processes of growth, change, and healing are centered not so much in reading appropriate material as in guided dialogue about the material between the client or group and the counselor. This process involves several phases: identification, catharsis, and insight (Bauer & Balius, 1995; Halsted, 1988). During the first phase (identification), the student identifies with the character(s) in the reading material and recognizes similarities between him- or herself and the character(s). In the next phase (catharsis), the student lives through the situations presented in the reading material and shares feelings with the character(s). Finally, the student develops insight, becoming more aware of the motivations and rationalizations in his or her personal behavior and situation.

Richards, Gipe, and Callahan (1997) recommend holistic literacy lessons to help students with language disabilities enhance their reading comprehension and social understanding. Holistic literacy lessons are designed to connect reading, writing, listening, speaking, and thinking. In addition, they facilitate interpersonal interaction, collaboration, and cooperation among students.

For bibliotherapy to be effective, the child must be able to read, motivated to read, and exposed to appropriate materials. Literature that is selected by the teacher and child, focuses on the child's needs, is at the appropriate level, is realistic, and accurately represents the characters in the story (Cianciolo, 1965) is most effective. Bauer and Balius (1995) suggest a form of bibliotherapy based on storytelling by the teacher or therapist.

Learning activities used to facilitate bibliotherapy include the following:

1. writing a summary of the book for discussion;
2. dramatizing, role-playing, or presenting skits or puppet shows about the message in the literature; and
3. making artworks that represent characters and situations in the literature.

McCarty and Chalmers (1997) see bibliotherapy as including several phases: read, reflect, discuss, and follow-up. First, the student reads the book (or other form of literature). This can be done aloud or silently. Next, the student is encouraged to reflect on the literature. Third, the literature is discussed with the teacher either individually or in a small or large group. Finally, follow-up activities are conducted (i.e., art activities, dramatization, or written responses).

Though more research is needed on the effects of bibliotherapy, Schrank and Engels (1981), in a review of the extant research, concluded that it was an effective intervention. Harms, Etscheidt, and Lettow (1986) suggested the use of poetry as an aid to helping children recognize and explore their feelings and emotions. Poetry is generally brief and concise, and it explores a broad range of topics and events. It can help the child in several ways: creating mental images, responding to varied perspectives, reciting, exploring rhythmic activity, and enacting stories. Children can also express their feelings and emotions by writing poetry.

Sridhar and Vaughn (2000) recommend bibliotherapy for all students to enhance their reading comprehension, self-concept, and behavior. They offer lists of selected books for preschool through second-grade students and second- through fourth-grade students. Prater (2000) is an additional resource, presenting a list of 46 frequently recommended books for the instruction of students about learners with disabilities. McCarty and Chalmers (1997) also list readings focusing on the topics of abuse and neglect, anger, differences, and families. Zambo (2007) suggests that helping students identify characters with whom they can relate may help them become better able to discuss their feelings in a constructive way.

Photography and Videotaping

Kroeger et al. (2004) used a technique called photovoice with students at risk for school failure. The students recorded their lives in photographs and then reflected on what the images said about themselves and their needs. After a discussion of confidentiality and the ethics of photographing other people, students photographed things that mattered to them to describe their lives. They then pasted their favorite photographs in journals and reflected on the photographs. Through these activities, students increased their ownership of the process, reflecting more on their photography and their lives. Through the discussions students had regarding their experiences and thoughts about themselves and school, they were able to discuss their effective and ineffective behavioral strategies. Teachers reported the benefit of having greater insight into the students' lives. Students reported that the discussion group became a community, and their participation in the general classroom also increased.

Falk, Dunlap, and Kern (1996) investigated the effects of self-evaluation by means of videotaped feedback on the appropriate and inappropriate peer interactions of students with externalizing and internalizing behaviors. The students who were identified as emotionally/behaviorally disordered were members of a general education classroom. Consequently, all the experimental sessions included students without identified behavior problems. As a result of the videotaped feedback, substantial increases were found in appropriate interactions for students with internalizing behavioral problems, as were substantial decreases in inappropriate interactions for students with externalizing behaviors.

Lonnecker, Brady, McPherson, and Hawkins (1994) studied the relationships between videotaped self-assessment, self-modeling, discrimination training, and behavioral rehearsal on the cooperative classroom behaviors of two second-grade students with learning and behavior problems. Intervention was effective in helping the students (a) acquire cooperative classroom behaviors, (b) generalize the behaviors to other settings, and (c) maintain the behaviors in both training and generalization settings. In addition, the videotapes reduced inappropriate behavior in the training and generalization settings. Finally, the researchers found a reduction in the variability of the behaviors exhibited by the students.

Holaday (1994) experimented with self-as-a-model videotape viewing to reduce inappropriate behaviors of 26 students from five self-contained classes for students with emotional/behavioral disorders. The students were in experimental (18 students) and control (8 students) groups. Self-as-a-model tapes, 4 to 6 minutes in duration, show the student doing his or her "best" in the classroom. Inappropriate behaviors were edited from the tapes. The tapes are viewed by the student each day for 10 consecutive days. It is expected that during the day, the student will model the "best" behavior on the tape. Although no significant results were found, Holaday asserts that the method does have strong face validity and that further experimentation is needed.

Broome and White (1995) and Parsons (2006), and Graetz, Mastroprieri, and Scruggs (2006) suggest a variety of classroom applications for videotapes:

- providing a permanent record for antecedent-behavior-consequence analysis;
- providing self-monitoring of behavioral strengths and weaknesses;
- evaluating the behavioral strength and weaknesses of others;
- providing reality replay of facial expressions, body language, expressions of feelings, tone of voice, and other hard-to-define performance criteria;
- adding vitality to simulations and role plays;
- reinforcing shared experiences;
- "catching" unobserved challenging and adaptive behavior;
- providing a less intrusive consequence for misbehavior;
- providing parents and others a realistic perspective of student and classroom behaviors;
- providing models of appropriate behavior; and
- practicing job interviews

Teachers are cautioned to use videotape feedback in a nonjudgmental manner with students.

Wilson (2004) described "videotherapy" as a way to help adolescents deal with problems of development such as family issues, making commitments, choice, disabilities, and social concerns. Videos provide students who have difficulty reading with a way to expand their experiences.

Wilson describes four components of using videos. In the first phase, the group views the video and the teacher introduces the basic concepts and conflicts present in the film. As students watch the film together, the teacher works with students in sketching out characters, plot, and insights. In the second phase, students and teachers discuss the film in greater detail, addressing conflicts, personalities, and motivation. Following this discussion, the students create, perform, and videotape a skit that demonstrates their interpretation of events in the video. Finally, the student-produced videos are viewed and analyzed. Wilson suggests that this strategy provided opportunity for communication about social needs with the students, teachers, and parents.

BEHAVIOR INFLUENCE TECHNIQUES

Psychodynamic theorists and practitioners recognize that many of the counseling and expressive media techniques do not immediately change unacceptable behaviors to acceptable behaviors. Techniques of behavior management are needed that can be implemented to interfere with ongoing unacceptable behaviors in the classroom, resource room, school, or playground.

Teachers have a responsibility to interfere with behaviors that:

- present a real danger;
- are psychologically harmful to the child and others;
- lead to excessive excitement, loss of control, or chaos;
- prohibit the continuation of the program;
- lead to destruction of property;
- encourage the spread of negativism in the group;
- negate opportunities to clarify individual and group values, standards, and social rules;
- lead to conflict with others outside the group; or
- compromise the practitioner's mental health and ability to function.

Redl and Wineman (1957) suggested 12 behavior management interventions or **behavior influence techniques** compatible with the psychodynamic framework for the management of surface behaviors. The work of Redl and Wineman has been expanded by Long and Newman (1961, 1965) and Shea, Whiteside, Beetner, and Lindsey (1974). The behavior influence techniques are planned ignoring, signal interference, proximity control, interest boosting, tension reduction through humor, hurdle helping, program restructuring, support from routine, direct appeal, removal of seductive objects, antiseptic bouncing, and physical restraint.

Planned Ignoring

At one time or another, most children engage in unacceptable behavior in an effort to gain the attention of their classmates, teachers, and parents. These unacceptable behaviors are legion in number and may include pencil tapping, body movements, hand waving, whistling, snorting, desktop dropping, book dropping, and so on. Such behavior, although relatively benign, is annoying to others.

Planned ignoring may be used to eliminate many of these behaviors. The teacher using this technique simply ignores the disruptive behavior. No response is made when the behavior occurs. It is generally true that when attention-seeking behaviors are ignored, they become nonfunctional and decrease in frequency. Of course, the child is reinforced when he or she exhibits appropriate behavior (Bacon, 1990).

Signal Interference

A teacher may use a variety of nonverbal techniques to interfere with unacceptable behaviors (Bacon, 1990). Nonverbal techniques or signals, such as eye contact, a frown, finger snapping, toe tapping, book snapping, light flicking, and so on, can alert a child or group to their unacceptable behavior. Often, nonverbal behavior influence techniques help the disruptive child "save face" with his or her peers, and thus the disruption is not escalated. They also save the shy child from unnecessary embarrassment. Conversely, nonverbal signals can be used to reinforce acceptable behaviors in the classroom.

Proximity Control

Very frequently, the proximity of an authority figure (e.g., teacher, parent, police officer) results in the discontinuation of unacceptable behaviors. Even college professors find it useful to walk about the classroom in an effort to reduce the level of conversation and side comments. In addition, proximity can have a positive effect on children experiencing anxiety and frustration. The physical presence of a teacher available to assist has a calming effect on troubled children.

Shores, Gunter, and Jack (1993) suggested that teacher movement in the classroom may effectively control student disruptions by bringing the teacher into closer proximity to all students, thereby increasing the effectiveness of their interactions. Gunter, Shores, Jack, Rasmussen, and Flowers (1995) reviewed the literature and empirical research on the effectiveness of teacher/student proximity control to improve student behavior in general and special education classrooms. They concluded that proximity is generally defined as being within 3 feet of the student and supported with brief interactions with the student. In addition, the proximity of students to other students may have an effect on the control of behavior. It appears that if one student is reprimanded or positively reinforced, this interaction impacts nearby students. Gunter et al. recommend that teachers monitor their movement about the classroom in an effort to increase their proximity to all students. Finally, they recommend that teachers move about the room during seatwork activities.

Interest Boosting

Most persons become bored with routine and difficult tasks. Interest tends to wane with time. The teacher who observes a child losing interest or becoming bored with a task should make an effort to boost the child's interest. This may be accomplished by offering to help, noting how much work has been accomplished, noting how well done the completed part of the task is, discussing the task, and so on. Interest boosting may help the child reorganize a task and mobilize his or her energies to complete it.

Tension Reduction Through Humor

For as long as human beings have been laughing, humor has been used to reduce tension, frustration, and anxiety. Children, quite naturally, become tense when engaged in significant tasks. The prudent teacher will apply humor in an effort to help children relax and place their tasks in perspective when they become frustrated. A joke or humorous comment will frequently reduce tension. Caution must be used to be sure the humor is not harmful to any individual.

Hurdle Helping

Hurdle helping is a technique applied to assist a student who is experiencing difficulty with a specific task. Hurdle helping may simply be an encouraging word from the teacher, an offer to assist with a specific task, or the making available of additional materials and equipment. Help is provided before the child becomes disruptive or simply gives up on the assignment.

Program Restructuring

Occasionally teachers, especially new teachers, are so committed to a lesson, task, or schedule that they will continue regardless of student response. Prudent teachers are sufficiently observant to recognize when a lesson or activity is going poorly; they are flexible. Before the class becomes disruptive or loses all interest, the teacher either restructures the lesson or postpones it until a more appropriate time.

Support from Routine

All persons, including children, like to know their daily schedule. We appreciate being able to plan our day and knowing where, when, why, and with whom we will be at various times. It appears to be especially important to children with behavior problems that they be provided with a schedule and a routine.

The teacher is wise to announce and post the day's schedule in the classroom. Changes in the schedule should be announced in advance if possible. The children should be reminded of future special events. It is equally important to post and review classroom rules. (Rules, schedules, and routines are discussed extensively in Chapter 10).

Direct Appeal

Many times during an unacceptable behavior incident, the teacher can quickly and effectively resolve the problem through direct appeal to the students' sense of fairness. The direct appeal is derived from the following:

1. the teacher's personal positive relationship with the individual or group;
2. the consequences that will result if the unacceptable behavior continues;
3. the effect of the behavior on the student's peers; or
4. the teacher's authority over the student and group.

Many teachers neglect this approach to influencing behavior in favor of more indirect interventions. They neglect to simply and forcefully state, "Stop this behavior because. . . ."

Removal of Seductive Objects

Frequently, misbehavior occurs because the student has available some object of attention that is distracting. Young children bring small toys, games, and other objects to the classroom that distract them. Older children are distracted by books, magazines, combs, keys, and so on. When the teacher finds that these objects are keeping the child from the assigned task, the objects should be confiscated until after class or school. The confiscation should be kind and firm. Discussion is not necessary. It is more effective if children are trained to routinely store such objects in an appropriate place before school and until it is time to use them.

Antiseptic Bouncing

When a student becomes agitated and frustrated with an activity and before he or she is physically or verbally disruptive, it is prudent to remove the student from the work setting (Bacon, 1990). This removal is called antiseptic bouncing. It is viewed as a positive behavior influence technique and not as a punishment. Antiseptic bouncing, properly applied, provides the student with an opportunity to avoid embarrassment, calm down, reorganize thought, and begin the task anew.

Physical Restraint

Perhaps no children are more concerned with their physical and emotional well-being—and perhaps their continued existence—than children who have lost control of themselves in a tantrum. These children feel totally and absolutely helpless. They simply cannot control their physical and verbal behaviors. On such an occasion, physical restraint is not only necessary but a kindness. The child is held until calm. The teacher communicates physically and verbally to the child in a calm voice or whisper. The teacher communicates to the child, "You are safe; I will protect you; I will not let you harm yourself." After the child regains control, the teacher may wish to discuss the incident with the child. Together they may plan ways the child can avoid similar problems in the future.

Because of the controversial nature of restraint and physical contact with children, it is prudent prior to employing them to discuss such methods with the school administrator and ascertain school and district policies with regard to their use. Parental permission must be obtained if physical restraint is deemed necessary to manage a child's behavior. Restraints (ties, belts, jackets) should not be used.

The behavior influence techniques discussed in this section are effective in the control of directly observable behaviors. They should be a part of the behavior management method of all teachers. The techniques are most effective when used consistently.

Summary Points

- Classroom conferencing, sometimes described as a "long talk," involves teacher and student meeting, reviewing what occurred, discussing respect, discussing the typical behavior, developing another response, and reconvening at a later date. These meetings should be held in private.
- In Glasser's Quality Schools, the emphasis is on each individual demonstrating continuous improvement. Competition is downplayed, and respect and engagement are evident in the classroom.
- In the Circle of Courage, four values—belonging, mastery, independence, and generosity—guide interactions between teacher and student.
- Expressive media are supported by the psychodynamic framework. Media may

include, for example, free play, art, music, puppetry, role playing, or dance.
- Teachers have a responsibility to interfere in several situations. However, behavior influence techniques may be adequate for the intervention.
- Behavior influence techniques may include planned ignoring, signal interference, proximity control, interest boosting, tension reduction through humor, hurdle helping, program restructuring, support from routine, and direct appeal. The teacher may also remove objects from a student or briefly remove him or her from the setting. Physical restraint should be used with great care and should be documented when used.

Project

1. Observe a teacher engaging students in several lessons. What behavior influence techniques does he or she seem to use? What are the apparent strengths of these techniques?

Web Resources

For more information on Glasser's Quality Schools, visit this site:
www.wglasser.com/index.php?option=com_content&task=view&id=15&Itemid=30

For more information about the Circle of Courage, visit this site:
www.reclaiming.com/content/about-circle-of-courage

References

Abrams, B. J. (2005). Becoming a therapeutic teacher for students with emotional and behavioral disorders. *Teaching Exceptional Children, 38*(2), 40–45.

Adderholdt-Elliot, M., & Eller, S. H. (1989). Counseling students who are gifted through bibliotherapy. *Teaching Exceptional Children, 22*(1), 26–31.

Allen, J. I. (1980). Jogging can modify disruptive behaviors. *Teaching Exceptional Children, 12*(2), 66–70.

Anderson, E. (1985). A.M. Club. *Teaching: Behaviorally Disordered Youth, 1,* 12–16.

Bacon, E. H. (1990). Using negative consequences effectively. *Academic Therapy, 25*(5), 599–611.

Bauer, M. S., & Balius, F. A., Jr. (1995). Storytelling: Integrating therapy and curriculum for students with serious emotional disturbances. *Teaching Exceptional Children, 27*(2), 24–28.

Brendtro, L., Brokenleg, M., & Van Bockern, L. (2002). *Reclaiming youth at risk: Our hope for the future* (rev. ed.). Bloomington, IN: National Educational Services.

Broome, S. A., & White, R. B. (1995). The many uses of videotape in classrooms serving youth with behavioral disorders. *Teaching Exceptional Children, 27*(3), 10–13.

Burgstahler, S. (2007). *Equal access: Universal design of instruction.* Seattle: DO-IT, University of Washington. Retrieved January 3, 2011, from *www.washington.edu/doit/Brochures/Academics/equal_access_udi.html*

Burniske, R. W. (1994). Creating dialogue: Teacher response to journal writing. *The English Journal, 83*(4), 84–87.

Buyse, E., Verschueren, K., Doumen, S., Van Damme, J., & Maes, F. (2008). Classroom problem behavior and teacher-child relationships in kindergarten: The moderating role of classroom climate. *Journal of School Psychology, 56*(4), 367–391.

Caputo, R. A. (1995). Puppets, problem-solving and rationale emotive therapy. *Beyond Behavior, 6*(2), 15–18.

Cianciolo, P. J. (1965). Children's literature can affect coping behavior. *Personnel and Guidance Journal, 43*(9), 897–903.

Cobine, G. (1995). *Effective use of student journal writing.* ERIC Clearinghouse on Reading, English, and Communication, Digest #99.

Creekmore, N. N., & Madan, A. J. (1981). The use of sociodrama as a therapeutic technique with behavior disordered children. *Behavioral Disorders, 7*(1), 28–33.

Dehouske, E. J. (1982). Story writing as a problem solving vehicle. *Teaching Exceptional Children 15*(1), 11–17.

Evans, W. H., Evans, S. S., Schmid, R. E., & Pennypacker, H. S. (1985). The effects of exercise on selected classroom behaviors of behaviorally disordered adolescents. *Behavior Disorders, 11*(1), 42–51.

Falk, G. D., Dunlap, G., & Kern, L. (1996). An analysis of self-evaluation and videotape feedback for improving the peer interactions of students with externalizing and internalizing behavioral problems. *Behavioral Disorders, 21*(4), 261–276.

Freiberg, H. J., & Lamb, S. M. (2009). Dimensions of person-centered classroom management. *Theory into Practice, 48,* 99–105.

Gable, R. A., & Van Acker, R. (2004). Sometimes, practice makes imperfect: Overcoming the automaticity of challenging behavior by linking intervention to thoughts, feelings, and actions. *Education and Treatment of Children, 27*(4), 276–289.

Gladding, S. T., & Gladding, C. (1991). The ABCs of bibliotherapy for school counselors. *The School Counselor, 31,* 7–13.

Glasser, W. (1998) *The Quality School: Managing students without coercion.* New York: Perennial Books.

Graetz, J. E., Mastroprieri, M. A., & Scruggs, T. E. (2006). Show time: Using video self-modeling to decrease inappropriate behavior. *Teaching Exceptional Children, 38*(5), 43–38.

Greene, B. H. (2004). Rubric for measuring quality school progress. Retrieved December 30, 2004, from www.wglasser.com/gsrubric.htm

Gunter, P. L., Shores, R. E., Jack, S. L., Rasmussen, S. K., & Flowers, J. (1995). On the move: Using teacher/student proximity to improve students' behavior. *Teaching Exceptional Children, 28*(1), 12–14.

Halsted, J. W. (1988). *Guiding gifted readers.* Columbus, OH: Ohio Psychology Publishing.

Harms, J. M., Etscheidt, S. L., & Lettow, L. J. (1986). Extending emotional responses through poetry experiences. *Teaching Behaviorally Disordered Youth, 2,* 26–32.

Hibben, J., & Scheer, R. (1982). Music and movement for special needs children. *Teaching Exceptional Children, 14*(5), 171–176.

Hoenig, G. K., Shea, T. M., & Bauer, A. M. (1986). Jogging and children with behavior disorders: Effects on self-doubting and aggressive behaviors. *ICEC Quarterly, 36*(4), 16–21.

Holaday, M. (1994). Self-as-a-model videotapes: An experimental study with guidelines on how to make videotapes for students. *Beyond Behavior, 5*(2), 19–23.

Howes, C., Phillipsen, L., & Peisner-Feinberg, E. (2000). The consistency and predictability of teacher-child relationships during the transition to kindergarten. *Journal of School Psychology, 38,* 113–132.

Jennings, P. A., & Greenberg, M. T. (2009). The prosocial classroom: Teacher social competence in relation to students and classroom outcomes. *Review of Educational Research, 79*(1), 491–525.

Kroeger, S., Burton, C., Comarata, A., et al. (2004). Student voice and critical reflection: Helping students at risk. *Teaching Exceptional Children, 36*(3), 50–57.

Lane, B., Bonic, J., & Wallgren-Bonic, N. (1983). The group walk-talk: A therapeutic challenge for secondary students with social-emotional problems. *Teaching Exceptional Children, 16*(1), 12–17.

Layman, D. L., Hussey, D. L., & Laing, S. J. (2002). Music therapy assessment for severely emotionally disturbed children: A pilot study. *Journal of Music Therapy, 39*(3), 164–187.

Levinson, C. (1982). Remediating a passive aggressive emotionally disturbed pre-adolescent boy through writing: A comprehensive psychodynamic structured approach. *The Pointer, 26*(2), 23–27.

Long, N. J., & Newman, R. G. (1961). A differential approach to the management of surface behavior of children in school. *Bulletin of the School of Education* (Indiana University), *37,* 47–61.

———. (1965). Managing surface behavior of children in school. In N. J. Long, W. C. Morse, & R. G. Newman (Eds.), *Conflict in the classroom: The education of emotionally disturbed children* (pp. 352–362). Belmont, CA: Wadsworth.

Lonnecker, C., Brady, M. P., McPherson, R., & Hawkins, J. (1994). Video self-modeling and cooperative classroom behavior in children with learning and behavior problems: Training and generalization effects. *Behavioral Disorders, 20*(1), 24–34.

Lopata, C., Nida, R. E., & Marable, M. A. (2006). Progressive muscle relaxation: Preventing aggression in students with EBD. *Teaching Exceptional Children, 38*(4), 20–25.

McCarty, H., & Chalmers, L. (1997). Bibliotherapy: Intervention and prevention. *Teaching Exceptional Children, 29*(6), 12–17.

McIntyre, T. (1996). Entering uncharted waters with tattered sails and a broken compass. In B. Brooks & D. Sabatino (Eds.), *Personal perspectives on emotional disturbance/behavioral disorders* (pp. 232–249). Austin, TX: Pro-Ed.

Murry, F. R. (1996). Animal-assisted therapy: You think you have animals in your class: Animals helping students with EBD. *Beyond Behavior, 7*(3), 10–13.

National Center on Universal Design in Learning. (2009). Principles of UDL. Retrieved January 3, 2011, from www.udlcenter.org/aboutudl/udl-guidelines

Nelson, T. B. (2002). An interview with William Glasser, M. D. *Teacher Education Quarterly, 29*(3), 93–98.

Newcomer, P. L. (1980). *Understanding and teaching emotionally disturbed children.* Boston: Allyn & Bacon.

Northeast Foundation for Children. (2003). *Responsive Classroom level 1 workbook.* Greenfield, MA: Northeast Foundation for Children.

Parsons, L. D. (2006). Using video to teach social skills to secondary students with autism. *Teaching Exceptional Children, 39*(2), 32–38.

Prater, M. A. (2000). Using juvenile literature with portrayals of disabilities in your classroom. *Intervention in School and Clinic, 35*(3), 167–176.

Raths, L. E., Harmin, M., & Simons, S. B. (1978). *Values and teaching.* Columbus, OH: Merrill.

Redl, F., & Wineman, D. (1957). *The aggressive child*. New York: Free Press.

Richards, J. C., Gipe, J. P., & Callahan, T. (1997). The Little Red Hen meets Peter Rabbit: Enhancing the reading comprehension and social understanding of young students with language disabilities. *Teaching Exceptional Children, 29*(3), 71–73.

Rimm-Kaufman, S. E., Fan, X., Chiu, Y. I., & You, W. (2007). The contribution of the *Responsive Classroom* approach on children's academic achievement: Results from a three year longitudinal study. *Journal of School Psychology, 45*, 401–421.

Russell, A. E., & Russell, W. A. (1979). Using bibliotherapy with emotionally disturbed children. *Teaching Exceptional Children, 11*, 168–169.

Schrank, F., & Engels, D. (1981). Bibliotherapy as a counseling adjunct: Research findings. *Personnel and Guidance Journal, 60*(3), 143–147.

Shea, T. M., Whiteside, W. R., Beetner, E. G., & Lindsey, D. L. (1974). *Microteaching module: Behavioral interventions*. Edwardsville: Southern Illinois University Press.

Shores, R. E., Gunter, P. L., & Jack, S. L. (1993). Classroom management strategies: Are they setting events for coercion? *Behavioral Disorders, 18*, 92–102.

Sridhar, D., & Vaughn, S. (2000). Bibliotherapy for all: Enhancing reading comprehension, self-concept, and behavior. *Teaching Exceptional Children, 33*(2), 74–82.

Warger, C. L. (1985). Making creative drama accessible to handicapped children. *Teaching Exceptional Children, 17*(4), 288–293.

Warger, C. L., & Weiner, B. B. (Eds.). (1987). *Secondary special education: A guide to promising public school programs*. Reston, VA: Council for Exceptional Children.

Williams, G. H., & Wood, M. M. (1977). *Developmental art therapy*. Baltimore, MD: University Park Press.

Wilson, G. L. (2004). Using videotherapy to access curriculum and enhance growth. *Teaching Exceptional Children, 36*(6), 32–37.

Yell, M. L. (1988). The effects of jogging on the rates of selected target behaviors of behaviorally disordered students. *Behavioral Disorders, 13*(4), 273–279.

Zabel, R. H. (1988). Research in brief. *Behavior in Our Schools, 2*(3), 9.

Zambo, D. M. (2007). What can you learn from Bombaloo? *Teaching Exceptional Children, 39*(3), 32–39.

CHAPTER OBJECTIVES

After completing this chapter, you will be able to do the following:

1. Describe naturalistic and comprehensive interventions.

2. Discuss group composition and process, discussion groups, and class meetings.

3. Describe and exemplify the several antecedents to effective management.

4. Describe the teacher's role in establishing operations.

5. Define expulsion, suspension, and in-school suspension.

6. Characterize the several biobehavioral interventions.

7. Understand the educator's role in biobehavioral interventions.

CHAPTER 10

Environmental and Biobehavioral Behavior Management

KEY TERMS

Anticonvulsants

Biobehavioral interventions

Cuing

Diet

Environmental interventions

Expulsion

In-school suspension

Naturalistic interventions

Rule

Schedule

Suspension

Transitions

Jack and his gang were loitering near the front door of Hooverville High School planning their Monday morning activities. By general consensus, their target for the day was to be Marcie Meek. Jack conducted a discussion during which the group of five boys decided how to make life miserable for Marcie. Every time she was called on during class, they would grumble and sigh.

Jack and the gang were of considerable concern to the whole school population, especially to Mr. Willis, assistant principal for discipline. It appeared that Jack and his friends selected a different student or teacher each day as a target for their hostility. Each of the boys had been referred to Mr. Willis several times during the year for disciplining. He had punished them, individually and as a group, many times without success. He had even called their parents. Although the group's behavior was disruptive, they were rarely suspended.

Mr. Willis worked with the ninth-grade language arts teacher to have a series of classroom meetings. The problem of the boys' bullying was discussed. Jack and the group argued that it was just "fun." The other students confronted them about how it was getting "old." One student suggested that from now on when one student was targeted, the entire group would respond by saying "Stop it." The class decided on the solution to begin solidarity with the victims. Mr. Willis was hopeful; the whole ninth-grade class had never decided as a group that a behavior was not to be tolerated. Perhaps most important, members of the football team also determined it was going to stop. After a week of

Jack and the gang being told "Stop it," the fun of selecting a target became less evident. No one laughed, and few failed to ignore the perpetrators beyond saying "Stop it."

Mr. Willis knows that the group's behavior must be redirected. He also understands that unless he has peer support, the bullying will continue. The class meeting provided a means to motivate the students to think as a group with values.

Six-year-old John was being observed by the first-grade teacher, Mrs. Prime. As she observed John, he climbed over the worktable, ran to the toy box, and threw several blocks, trucks, and dolls on the floor. Next, John ran around the room, touching each child and the four walls.

After this, he returned to his seat at the worktable, grabbed his crayon, and scribbled on his worksheet for about 10 seconds. While he was scribbling, John was wiggling in his chair and tapping his feet. Suddenly, John fell to his hands and knees and began crawling to the toy box. He climbed into the box and threw the remaining toys on the floor. Having accomplished this, he returned to the worktable. John's hyperactive behavior continued throughout Mrs. Prime's 1-hour observation session.

That afternoon, in discussion with John's mother and preschool teacher, Mrs. Prime learned that John's behavior during the observation session was typical of his behavior at home and in preschool. Both the preschool teacher and John's mother reported using a variety of interventions without success. John appeared unable to control his activity; he appeared driven.

Mrs. Prime knows that she must have some assistance if John is to attend her first-grade class. He simply cannot succeed in school unless his behavior changes.

In this chapter, a variety of behavior management interventions derived from environmental and biobehavioral perspectives are reviewed and exemplified. Following a discussion of naturalistic interventions, environmental behavior management interventions such as group composition and processes, the classroom setting, and class meetings are described. Antecedent-based interventions and in-school suspension, suspension, and expulsion are discussed.

The second section of this chapter is devoted to a discussion of biobehavioral strategies, such as medication and diet. This section concludes with discussion of the educator's role in these interventions. It should be noted that, for the most part, environmental interventions focus attention on the manipulation of groups and the learning environment rather than on individual students. Several environmental and biobehavioral interventions employed by professionals in the medical and mental health disciplines are not presented in this chapter because of their complexity and the training requirements necessary for implementation.

NATURALISTIC INTERVENTIONS

With the shift to functional behavioral assessment (FBA), **environmental interventions** have gained more attention. The focus of an FBA is on environmental events. Rather than viewing behaviors as the result of something within the child, FBAs and the environmental interventions that may result see behavior as a way of responding or communicating in the environment (Horner & Carr, 1997).

Naturalistic interventions are focused on interactions between the student and the people that have the greatest opportunity to interact with the child. Barnett and Carey (1993) suggest that naturalistic interventions are based on naturally occurring interactions between the parent, teacher, or peers and the student. The interventions should be able to be adapted to the individual styles of the parent or teacher within the settings in which the problem behaviors occur. Barnett and Carey further clarify that naturalistic interventions are incorporated into routines or unobtrusively change the experiences that occur within the school or home. Because the interventions are built into the day, generalization of the behavior is more likely.

Naturalistic interventions have been used in the home and in classrooms. Because of the recent emphasis on standards-based instruction, typical classroom interactions are not limited to large or small group core academic tasks. With the blending of inclusion and standards-based instruction, it is essential to teach play and social skills where they naturally occur, on the playground (Koegel, Openden, Fredeen, & Koegel, 2006).

■ *Example*

Austin, a fifth-grader, had a difficult time finding a place to sit during lunch. He would stand with his tray, move toward one table, then hesitate again. By the time he had decided on his spot, the table had been filled. Ms. Cruces, his teacher, had talked about going directly to a place when he turned in work in the classroom, but he still hesitated. She decided to join him in the room and subtly give him a cue. He picked up his tray, and Ms. Cruces was standing there nonchalantly at the end of the line. She cued him, "Go right over and sit by Luis and Mirabeau." He did so and, after listening for a few moments, timidly joined the conversation. Ms. Cruces's attempts in the classroom had not been effective; dealing with the behavior where it occurred was.

One way to look at naturalistic interventions is as incidental teaching. Incidental teaching has been long used as a way to improve peer relations and social skills (Brown, Odom, & Conroy, 2001). Brown and Odom (1995) describe incidental teaching as occurring during brief, unstructured activities in which students and peers are involved with materials or activities that interest them. In early childhood classrooms, these activities can include working at learning centers, playing outside, meals and snack, and transitions. With older students, these activities can include transitions, group work, classroom meetings, or discussions. During incidental teaching, adult and peer models provide appropriate social and behavioral models. Teachers may encourage or prompt peers as well. The strength of incidental teaching is that it can become a fluid part of the day, giving students opportunities more often than if they were required to sit for instruction with a teacher.

Another aspect of naturalistic interventions is that they are comprehensive. Comprehensive interventions "produce rapid, durable, generalized reduction in problem behaviors while improving the individual's success" (Horner & Carr, 1997, p. 108). An intervention is considered comprehensive when it (a) meets several needs for the student,

(b) is based on an FBA; (c) is used throughout the day, (d) includes several procedures (such as changes in classroom structure, instruction, or consequences), and (e) uses procedures that are consistent with the values, skills, and resources of the individuals applying the intervention. The comprehensive interventions approach makes it necessary for interventions to be "a mile wide and a mile deep" (Quinn & McDougal, 1998, p. 201).

Two "mechanisms" (Horner & Carr, 1997) are in place in regard to comprehensive interventions. The first, establishing operations, is discussed in Chapter 5. Establishing operations include events that influence problem behaviors, such as headaches, allergies, hunger, or a previously difficult situation. Considering these establishing operations is part of a comprehensive plan for supporting a student. The second mechanism is choice. Personal choice can be key in decreasing problem behaviors. In addition, using preferred activities may reduce behavior problems. Horner and Carr (1997) conclude that teaching students with disabilities to make choices and incorporating choice options into daily schedules may be useful elements of comprehensive interventions.

Naturalistic interventions are a contrast to much of what takes place in classrooms. Because the intervention is linked directly to the behavior, generalization is built in. In addition, naturalistic interventions allow students to practice in the context of where the behavior will occur. A limitation of naturalistic interventions, however, is that some skills may be learned more quickly with direct intervention. Some students may need specific instructions in order to learn a skill or skill sequence.

■ *Example*

Travis is a 7-year-old first-grader who is very shy and has difficulty entering play situations on the playground. His teacher, Ms. Azure, is concerned that he seems to want to play but is always on the fringe. Ms. Azure spoke with Chloe and Anthony, two students who were able to enter play situations easily and were open to most children in the class. She asked if they would invite Travis into their games.

The first day of the intervention, Chloe and Anthony paused in their chasing game and asked Travis, "Wanna play?" He shrugged and ran a bit, but then again fell to watching them when they joined other children. Ms. Azure congratulated all three children for playing together so nicely and encouraged them to do so again the next day. Chloe and Austin again invited Travis, and he entered the game more readily. After 2 weeks Travis would walk in line behind Chloe and Austin as the class left for recess, and he then joined in their games without hesitation. Ms. Azure was pleased that the intervention had worked; her earlier conversations with Travis to go play had been ineffective.

ENVIRONMENTAL INTERVENTIONS

The prosocial classrooms described in Chapter 9 are obviously comprised of groups of students. The interventions at Tier 1 and Tier 2 occur as whole group or small group activities (Chapter 4). Groups, however, can make or break any management system. Two topics must be considered in the selection and imposition of these management techniques: group composition and group processes.

Group Composition

Grouping children on the basis of school records and admission data is a difficult task. It is a process that of necessity involves the cooperation of all persons familiar with the children.

Among the variables to be considered during the grouping process are (a) age, (b) sex, (c) interests, (d) disabling conditions, if any, (e) personality traits, (f) the degree, intensity, and kind of behavior problems, if any, and (g) group experiences and skills. When grouping children, an effort is made to avoid extremes in group composition while at the same time attempting to form a "balanced" group. In the organization of groups, the adult members of the group, such as the teacher and paraprofessional, are considered group members. Rockwell and Guetzloe (1996) suggest that the dynamics within a group are affected by the number of students in the group, the severity of their disabilities, and their social and academic compatibility.

Kutnick, Ota, and Berdondini (2008) suggest that though students spend most of their time in groups, these groups can either promote or inhibit learning. In their observations of classrooms, they found that group size may range from pairs to small groups (4–6 students), large groups (10–15), or a whole class. A group's purpose may include learning, social development, or collaboration. At times, groups "happen" as a function of the available furniture or materials. Kutnick et al. documented in their study, however, that students who have close relationships with each other and whose teachers practice social motivation learned more during group activities.

Students appear to learn better in groups when:

- members have close relationships that support and encourage learning (Howes & Ritchie, 2002);
- cooperative and collaborative learning activities are used (Johnson & Johnson, 2003);
- students trust each other;
- students have the communication skills needed to collaborate; and
- an individual is not placed in a group that lacks a like-sex peer.

Grouping is a difficult process because the staff must deal with intangible variables that defy precise measurement. However, the group can have a positive impact on student behavior. Using a nonintrusive management technique to control acting-out behavior, Stainback, Stainback, Etscheidt, and Doud (1986) reaffirmed the belief that peer modeling affects student behavior. They studied the differences in the acting-out behavior of a student in a well-behaved group and in a disruptive group. They noted a significant decrease in acting-out behavior in the well-behaved group.

Group Process

Rockwell and Guetzloe (1996) urge educators to become familiar with the stages of group development and their implications for the management of instructional activities in classes for learners with behavior problems. Their suggestions are based on the work of Maslow's (1962) hierarchy of basic human needs and the developmental stages of Erikson (1963).

According to Rockwell and Guetzloe (1996), students with behavioral disorders begin the school year at Stage 1 of the group developmental process. At this stage, the students focus on satisfying physiological needs and establishing a sense of safety and trust. These needs must be met before the group can move to the next stage. Deviant behaviors at this stage include tantrums, low-frustration tolerance, fighting, power struggles, and verbal and physical aggression.

Stage 2, according to Rockwell and Guetzloe (1996), begins when most of the members of the group are responding appropriately most of the time. The group members focus on the need for belonging to the group and socialization activities. Group thinking appears to shift from "me against them" to "us against them." Aggression decreases dramatically, and assistance to others in the group becomes spontaneous. During Stage 3, there are fewer and fewer conflicts. Students are now capable of problem solving. The group process focuses on developing self-respect, respect for others, and self-actualization.

The group process itself can be of therapeutic benefit to some children. Loughmiller (1965) used self-governing, problem-solving groups in the camp setting. Also applicable in the school setting, these groups are set up to expose students to a wide range of successful interpersonal experiences. These experiences encourage participation, responsibility, and cooperation in activities.

In this intervention, children and teachers are responsible for their daily activities within predetermined limits established by the administration. The members find themselves in a situation in which majority rule prevails. Each individual is responsible for his or her personal behavior and for the behavior of the group (Shea, 1977).

Some limits on the group's behavior and activities are imposed by an administrator or other nongroup authority figure rather than by the teacher, who is a member of the group. However, the group members may impose, by means of majority rule, additional limits on behavior and activities. The limits imposed by the administrator are few in number and are concerned with dining and work schedules, attendance at assemblies, transportation, health, safety, and the like. These limits must be imposed if the administration is to meet its responsibilities to the members of the group.

Any social cosmos requires certain routines (Morse & Wineman, 1957). Without routines, limits, and prescribed ways of behaving, anarchy would result, and the group would disintegrate. Thus, the group, as a group, decides (a) the limits to be set on social interaction, (b) how extreme behaviors are to be managed if they occur, (c) how activities and schedules of events are to be developed and executed, (d) who is to be responsible for various phases of daily living, and (e) how problems and conflicts are to be resolved.

The problem-solving process becomes a part of the group's daily life. When conflicts or unfamiliar problems occur that prohibit the group from attaining its immediate goals, problem solving is initiated. During the problem-solving process, the group attempts to develop alternative solutions to the circumstances confronting it. The members have two major tasks: (a) identifying and clarifying their problem and (b) discussing (evaluating) and agreeing on one or more solutions to the problem. The agreed-on solution can be imposed either immediately or in similar situations in the future. In addition to these tasks, the members of the group must deal with the positive and negative social–emotional behaviors that naturally occur during the problem-solving process.

Discussion Groups

Anderson and Marrone (1979) described the use of therapeutic discussion groups in public school classes for students with emotional problems. As a result of 12 years of experience with more than 6,000 children, they concluded, "We cannot imagine a program for emotionally handicapped students that would not fit the proven, cost-effective methodology of therapeutic discussion groups in the classroom" (p. 15).

After a period of experimentation during which students were involved in individual therapy, therapeutic discussion groups, or nontherapeutic treatment, it was concluded that the group model benefited the children and teachers in several ways. Teachers benefited by receiving support through teamwork with mental health professionals. In addition, they received training in psychodynamic theory and techniques that enhanced their understanding of student behavior. For students, the group provided structured time for communication and affective education. The goal of the therapeutic discussion groups was to change behavior. Through the group, appropriate student behavior could be reinforced and empathy, concern, and caring encouraged. Group discussion also increased the opportunities for early intervention with children who had potential problems. Group techniques were applied successfully with psychotic, passive-aggressive, and depressed children.

When implemented, group sessions of 30 to 60 minutes are conducted weekly with the psychologist or psychiatrist, teacher, paraprofessional, and social worker present. The group sits in a circle, and meeting length varies according to the age and needs of the children. Pre- and postmeeting sessions are conducted by the mental health consultant with the teacher to evaluate the session and to discuss concerns, needs, and behaviors of the children. Group sessions then become a standard part of each student's program.

Anderson and Marrone (1979) suggest the following group discussion guidelines:

1. Children may speak on any topic. Physical aggression and obscene language are inappropriate.
2. Confidentiality is stressed.
3. Discussion may be initiated or facilitated by centering on a specific student interest, need, positive behavior, or similar topic.
4. After several weekly meetings, when the team has an understanding of each student's needs, the following therapeutic progression is applied:
   a. Help each student recognize his or her ineffective behaviors.
   b. Help the student explore and recognize the feelings behind the ineffective behaviors.
   c. Identify the source of the feelings.
   d. Connect these feelings with the student's actions and their consequences.
   e. Facilitate the student's commitment to change.
   f. Plan alternative behaviors with the student.
   g. Support the student's efforts to change.
   h. Recognize the new behavior and encourage it.

Several prerequisites apply to successful implementation of groups in the public schools. Anderson and Marrone (1979) maintain that a belief in the use of therapeutic discussion groups and administrative support are essential. The program also must have a competent mental health consultant (psychiatrist, clinical psychologist, case worker, counselor) who accepts the team concept.

Class Meetings

Class meetings can be instituted as part of the normal classroom procedure. Meetings can be called to deal with the common problems of living and learning in a group setting. Over time, the members of the class learn, with guidance, to seek solutions to problems through verbal transactions with peers and the teacher. During class meetings, members grow in understanding of themselves and others. They learn to conceptualize problems from another's point of view. Coleman and Webber (1988) recommended working with adolescents in groups to reduce teacher-student conflicts and to enhance student self-control. Frey and Doyle (2001) encourage the use of classroom meetings in the elementary school setting to enhance the problem-solving and communication skills of general and special education students. Meetings facilitate the development of a classroom climate in which students learn social skills. The emphasis is on peacefully resolving conflicts and problems.

Three kinds of meetings for classroom application have been suggested by Harth and Morris (1976) and Morris (1982): open meetings, problem-solving meetings, and decision-making meeting.

OPEN MEETING.   This type of meeting is called to permit an individual to express covert feelings. The individual is given an opportunity to state to the group the frustrations and feelings that the individual believes are the result of another member's actions. This other member may be a peer or the teacher. Any member of the group may request an open meeting. The session is generally conducted by a peer.

■ Example

Billy's ninth-grade class was responsible for planning and conducting the all-school assembly for the holidays. It was the most important activity of the school year for the class. Each member of the class had a role to play in the program.

Unfortunately for Billy, he was absent from school on the day his class planned the program. Neither the teacher nor his fellow students remembered to assign a function to Billy. Consequently, he was very frustrated and angry. He was angry with his peers and the teacher. He was hurt and sad because he was forgotten. After all, it was not his fault that he got the flu and his mother made him stay at home.

Billy's teacher, Mr. Jetro, had always suggested to his students that if they had a concern about the group, they should request a class meeting. At the meeting, they could express and discuss their concern with the group.

Billy asked Mr. Jetro for a meeting. At the meeting, he stated his personal concerns. As a result of his action, Billy not only was assigned a role in the assembly but also was given an apology by the program chairperson and teacher for their oversight.

PROBLEM-SOLVING MEETING.   This type of meeting focuses primarily on potential problems. It may be called by any member of the class. Topics include such items as tardiness, disorganization, lack of follow-through on previous commitments, group responsibilities, distractions in the classroom, lack of time to complete assignments, and the like. During the meeting, a solution to the problem is sought by the group. The agreed-on solution is implemented.

■ Example

Mr. Kaat always tells his senior honors German classes that if they are honestly overburdened by the class assignments, they may request a class meeting to discuss the problem. On one particular occasion, Mr. Kaat assigned the class a 10-page translation and a term paper just 3 days before midyear examinations. The students believed that they were severely overburdened and would, as a result, do inadequate work on the translation, the term paper, and the examination. They were also concerned about having sufficient time to prepare for their other examinations.

A problem-solving meeting was called at which a more realistic schedule was agreed to by Mr. Kaat and the class.

DECISION-MAKING MEETING.   This type of meeting focuses primarily on program and curriculum decisions. It gives the program direction: What is to be done? How is it to be accomplished? Where? When? Who is responsible? Why? The decision-making meeting is an excellent medium for involving all members of a class in the curriculum planning.

■ *Example*

Mrs. Picoff was faculty adviser for the Blaskit Island High School Future Educators Association. She was very concerned about the group's future because of lack of interest on the part of the members. The principal had told her that he was considering disbanding the group because they did not plan or complete any projects of benefit to the school or community.

Mrs. Picoff called the officers and members of the group together for a problem-solving meeting. At the meeting, she presented the problem confronting the group. As a consequence, the members planned an annual schedule, assigned responsibilities to various members, and established a feedback mechanism to ensure that each person met his or her responsibilities.

Class meetings are designed to find practical solutions to real problems. In addition, the class meeting intervention has significant potential as a preventive technique if consistently and appropriately applied. Ziont and Fox (1998) presented practical guidelines for teachers wishing to facilitate group classroom meetings. They suggested that meetings be used to provide information to students on getting along with others, communication skill enhancement, improving interpersonal relationships, and a variety of current topics (living in addictive and disorganized families, divorce, abuse, stepfamilies, death and dying, living with HIV/AIDS, suicide, and violence and crisis). Group meetings may be implemented as a vehicle to facilitate behavioral therapy and bibliotherapy. (These interventions were discussed in previous chapters.)

Edwards and Mullis (2003) suggested classroom meetings to encourage a climate of cooperation among students. Meetings are implemented to facilitate the teaching of the academic, social, and emotional skills needed by students to function successfully in school, home, and community. Meeting components include the following:

- *Appreciation and compliments.* In this voluntary phase, students are encouraged to express their appreciation or offer a compliment to another person.
- *Peaceful conflict resolution and problem solving.* The instructor works with students to develop conflict-resolution and problem-solving skills needed for effective meetings. As the students gain skills, this component is gradually phased out or becomes a review.
- *Problem solving.* Students apply the conflict-resolution and problem-solving skills they are learning.

- *Old business.* Students revisit previously discussed conflicts and problems and report on progress. If problems remain, other potential solutions may be suggested.
- *New business.* Students and instructor may present and discuss existing and future classroom activities and concerns.
- *Classroom encouragement activities.* The instructor offers encouragement to the group, through short and personal notes, signs of affirmation, or show and tell.

Antecedents of Effective Management (Organizing for Instruction)

The effective classroom is planned and organized to facilitate instruction and behavior management (Montague, Bergerson, & Lago-Delello, 1997). Prior to beginning the school day or year, the teacher must take into consideration a broad range of factors to enhance the probability that learning will occur in the classroom. Among those factors that must be given consideration are space utilization and storage, including procedures for the use of classroom and nonclassroom space, facilities, materials, and equipment. The teacher must develop procedures for individual and small- and whole-group activities, beginning and ending the school day or period, transitions, housekeeping, interruptions, visitors, fire drills, and various other activities. The teacher must consider classroom rules for behavior and develop schedules to support task engagement. Cues or prompts to be used in the classroom should also be planned.

Stephen W. Smith, in an interview with Brownell and Thomas (2001), suggested that the best way to eliminate problem behaviors in the classroom is to take a proactive approach to classroom management. Being proactive necessitates that many professionals revisit their views about punishment and consider strategies to build more positive, proactive environments in which the opportunities to misbehave are diminished. Effective classroom environments require a positive culture that reinforces values, such as respect and fairness, and that makes students feel welcome and successful. This is a daily priority for teachers who are concerned and care about their students.

In a discussion of the caring classroom environment, Wentzel (2003) suggests that teachers must understand the students' personal goals in order to motivate them. Teachers should understand the degree to which students' goals are valued by teachers and peers. In the caring classroom, it is critical that both teachers and peers support and promote expressions of positive social behavior. This support is critical to students' adoption and pursuit of positive social goals. According to Wentzel, regardless of race, ethnicity, gender, or other aspects of the student's developmental context, the underlying process that contributes to social adjustment are similar. The significance of the impact of these factors varies as a function of minority status.

Brown (2003) discussed gaining students' cooperation in urban classrooms. He suggested that this involves establishing an environment where teachers address students' cultural, ethnic, social, emotional, and cognitive needs. Urban teachers reported the need for a smoothly operating classroom in which teachers' actions are fluid and dynamic. Teachers demonstrated an awareness of a variety of management principles in order to create a cooperative and academically productive classroom. Teachers' efforts toward a comfortable learning environment often overpowered the use of effective curricular and instructional interventions. The teachers demonstrated interest in and mutual respect for students. They also elicited student cooperation through explicitly stated expectations for acceptable behavior and academic growth.

Culturally responsive classroom management requires that the teacher understand his- or herself, the students, and the instructional context (Weinstein, Curran, & Tomlinson-Clarke, 2003). Weinstein et al. suggest that students must recognize that they are cultural beings with personal beliefs, biases, and assumptions. In addition, teachers must acknowledge these differences, among others, and understand the manner in which schools reflect and support society's assumptions. They suggest that teachers should:

- develop a physical environment that supports academic and social goals;
- establish behavioral expectations;
- communicate in a culturally consistent manner;
- establish a caring classroom;
- engage families; and
- implement appropriate and effective intervention strategies with students with challenging behaviors.

The more thoroughly classrooms and programs are planned, the greater the probability of success for both children and teacher. Though the majority of behavior management research focuses on the effects of manipulating the consequences of behavior, Wheldall (1991) reports some positive results from research that focuses on the effects of manipulating the antecedents of behavior. Munk and Repp (1994) did a review of the research literature on instructional variables that may decrease behavior problems in the classroom. The focus of their review was on positive or nonaversive strategies for reducing and preventing problem behaviors. The review centered on the antecedents of instruction. They suggest some variables that may decrease problem behaviors: (a) student choice of task, (b) variation in tasks, (c) instructional pace, (d) interpersonal tasks that occur frequently, (e) partial- versus whole-task training, and (f) decreasing task difficulty.

Engagement in learning increases when tasks (a) are authentic, (b) give students ownership, (c) provide opportunities for collaboration, (d) permit diverse forms of talents, and (e) are enjoyable (Newmann, 1991; Newmann, Wehlage, & Lamborn, 1992). The remaining material in this section is devoted to an overview of the antecedents to effective instruction and classroom management. The suggestions presented are general and must be modified to respond to the needs of a particular classroom situation.

SPACE, MATERIALS, AND EQUIPMENT.   Teachers begin the school year by planning for the use of the space, materials, and equipment that they have been assigned. They must give consideration to the use of the space shared with others, such as hallways, lunchroom, playground, library, and music room (Evertson et al., 1981).

WALLS, CEILINGS, AND BULLETIN BOARDS.   These are valuable spaces that can be used to display a variety of materials, such as schedules, rules, seasonal and topical items, calendars, study assignments, housekeeping assignments, charts, maps, and so on. It is prudent not to overdecorate; space should be reserved for student work and current items. Students can profit from helping to plan displays for bulletin boards. Material displayed on walls, ceilings, and bulletin boards should be changed periodically so that students will not become desensitized to it.

FLOOR SPACE.   The use of floor space will vary with the size of the room, the number of students and their characteristics, and the activities to be conducted. The room must be arranged to ensure that the teacher can observe all areas in which students will be working and that the students will be able to see the teacher and work materials that the teacher is using for instruction. Student desks and tables should be arranged away from high-traffic areas. If tables are used instead of or in addition to desks, then space for storage of student materials must be planned. Space must be planned for individual and small- and whole-group activities. If learning centers (reading, mathematics, science) are used, then space must be planned to include these areas. Centers that generate a high degree of activity and noise should not be located near centers that require a high degree of student concentration. All needed materials and equipment should be located in the appropriate center.

The teacher must plan where common items, such as plants, pet cages, fish tanks, bookcases, and storage cabinets, will be located in the classroom. The teacher's desk, files, and other equipment must be located where they are easily accessible yet do not interfere with activities. Every effort should be made to maintain traffic lanes in the classroom; this will prevent confusion as students move about the room. If the classroom is serving students with physical disabilities or visual impairments, free traffic lanes must be maintained and space organized to ensure accessibility.

STORAGE SPACE.   Various kinds of supplies, materials, and equipment are used in the classroom: everyday supplies and materials, infrequently used supplies and materials, student supplies and materials, and teacher supplies and materials, as well as the personal items of students and teacher. The teacher must plan for their storage and use.

Everyday supplies and materials, such as pencils, paper, and chalk, should be stored in an easily accessible location. The teacher may wish to locate these items where they are available to students. Students' instructional materials, such as texts, workbooks, dictionaries, and study guides, may be stored in students' desks, bookcases, or filing trays and cabinets. Infrequently used items, such as seasonal and topical materials, should be stored in the rear of cupboards. Audiovisual equipment should be stored in a safe place. Students should have a private place to store personal items, such as clothing, gym shoes, lunch boxes, and prized possessions. The teacher must have private space for his or her personal items as well as personal instructional materials and equipment. It is essential that the personal and private space of all—students and teacher—not be violated.

PROCEDURES.   The teacher is responsible for developing a variety of procedures to support student learning and positive behavior. The teacher must be sure that these procedures are compatible with school policy.

1. *Student use of classroom space and facilities.* Procedures should be established to facilitate the care of students' desks and storage areas. Procedures are established for the number of students permitted in various areas of the room at one time and for the use of the drinking fountain, sink, pencil sharpener, restroom, or other shared facilities. Procedures for the use and care of common and personal instructional materials must be developed, and procedures should be made with regard to students' and teachers' personal space and possessions.
2. *Student use of nonclassroom space and facilities.* Procedures should be developed for the use of nonclassroom space and facilities, such as restrooms, drinking

fountains, offices, library, media room, resource rooms, labs, or other areas. Procedures must be developed for students leaving the classroom and moving throughout the building. Playground or lunchroom procedures should be developed.

3. *Whole-group, small-group, and individual activities.* Procedures for a variety of individual and small- and whole-group activities must be established by the teacher. Procedures are developed for the conduct of discussions, the answering of questions during class, talking among students, out-of-seat behavior, and so on. Students should be instructed about the cues and prompts the teacher will use to attain student attention. Procedures are developed for making assignments to work groups, assigning homework, distributing supplies and materials, turning in work, returning assignments, and completing missing assignments. Students should know what they are expected to do when they have completed a task and have unscheduled time available.

Small-group activities require procedures. Students must know the cues the teacher uses to begin and end small-group activities, what materials to bring, and behavioral expectations. Students who are not in a particular small group must know what is expected of them during other students' small-group activities. Students working individually must know how to obtain their work, where they are to work, what work to do, how to signal for assistance, and what to do when their work is complete.

Teachers are prudent to establish standard procedures for beginning and ending the school day or period. It is important to begin and end the day on a positive note. Students should know what behaviors are appropriate and inappropriate during this time. Students should also know the procedures for reporting after an absence, tardiness, and early dismissal.

Procedures are developed for the selection and duties of classroom helpers. These activities should be shared by all students. Finally, procedures should be established for conduct during classroom interruptions and delays; for fire, tornado, and earthquake drills; and other infrequent and unplanned occurrences.

4. *Rules.* According to Joyce, Joyce, and Chase (1989) a **rule** is "the specification of a relation between two events and may take the form of instruction, direction, or principle" (p. 82). The role of rules in a prosocial classroom is discussed in Chapter 9. Students follow rules to obtain both extrinsic (e.g., grades, points, free time) and intrinsic (e.g., getting the correct answer, self-satisfaction) consequences. Rules are usually designed to apply to those activities and occurrences that are not governed by classroom and nonclassroom procedures.

Though we described the need for collaboration in developing rules in Chapter 9, following steps in their development may be helpful. Rules are best developed through the collaborative efforts of student and teacher (Murdick & Petch-Hogan, 1996; Thorson, 1996). Student involvement leads to student ownership. Rules should be posted in a highly visible location, and, when first put in place, reviewed often.

Rademacher, Callahan, and Pedersen-Seelye (1998) suggested a five-step procedure for planning effective classroom rules:

1. Create rules and procedures based on cooperative and productive learning behaviors.
2. Identify specific student behavior.

3. Define teacher responsibilities for rule compliance.
4. Establish a logical positive and negative consequence for compliance.
5. Develop communication among teacher, student, and parent.

Effective rules are acceptable to both students and teacher. Effective rules begin with a verb, stating the desired behavior. The focus of rules should be observable behaviors that are associated with well-established classroom procedures. Rules should be related to work and safety and should be general enough to apply to many situations and settings.

Rademacher et al. recommend the following rules for positive classrooms:

1. Enter the classroom quietly.
2. Begin work on time.
3. Stay on task.
4. Complete work on time.
5. Follow directions.
6. Listen while others speak.
7. Use appropriate language.
8. Keep hands, feet, and objects to self.

Teachers should give students repeated examples of the behaviors demonstrated when following rules. The function of a rule is to encourage appropriate behavior and prevent inappropriate behavior. Teachers are responsible for enforcing classroom rules to support learning rather than "catching" students behaving inappropriately.

Brady, Forton, Porter, and Wood (2003) also suggest that teachers model the behaviors they wish students to exhibit. Simple, clear, direct, nonjudgmental language encourages respect. When a correction is made, the focus should be on the specific behavior and not the child.

Because there is no agreed-upon number of rules for school or home, Seid (2001) suggests three steps to support a caring, peaceful environment. First, set priorities that focus generally on the safety, health, appropriate behavior, rights, and values of the school or family. Next, tailor the message; set rules that make sense to the child and respond to the adults' priorities. Finally, ensure cooperation by explaining to the children the reason for the rule and the consequence for breaking the rule. Children should also be made aware of the positive consequences for obeying the rule.

CUING.   **Cuing** is the process of using symbols and gestures to communicate essential messages between individuals. Cuing reduces interruption in classroom activities and is a proactive, preventive intervention (Slade & Callaghan, 1988).

Various cues can be used in the classroom. Such cues are most effective if developed collaboratively by students and teacher at the beginning of the year. Examples of cues include:

- students writing their name on the chalkboard when help is needed;
- students posting a card when an activity is completed; and
- teachers turning the lights on or off to signal the beginning or ending of activities.

Teachers may use body language—hand signals, smiles, or frowns—as cues (Rosenkoetter & Fowler, 1986). Cues should not take the place of verbal communication, but they can be creative ways of informing students about what is happening in the classroom.

TRANSITIONS.   **Transitions** are the movement from one activity to another. Smooth transitions increase instructional time and help students develop self-management skills. There is a relationship between classroom procedures and transitions; the more everyday tasks can be standardized, the less disruption they cause students (Cangelosi, 2000). Teachers can use a variety of strategies to decrease the disruption caused by transitions:

- Teachers model appropriate ways of making transitions, have students practice, and then give them feedback (Olson & Platt, 2000).
- Provide visual or auditory signals to alert students that a transition is coming (e.g., giving a 5-minute warning) (Smith, Polloway, Patton, & Dowdy, 2001).
- Circulate among students during transitions to help students prepare for the next task and reduce disruptions (Burden, 2003).
- Provide incentives for smooth transitions (Olson & Platt, 2000).

Sainato (1990) reviewed the research literature on interventions to facilitate transitions in special preschools for children with disabilities. Her focus was on factors that increased the effectiveness and efficiency with which children moved from one activity to another during the school day. Effective transition skills are essential for success in inclusive environments. The literature on three groups of antecedents to transitions were analyzed:

- environmental arrangements, including schedules, staff assignments, and room arrangement;
- antecedent interventions, including instruction, time, and task; and
- peer-mediated procedures.

SCHEDULES.   Scheduling is an important teacher function. Rosenshine (1977) found that student learning increases when teachers allocate considerable time for instruction and maintain a high level of task engagement. To develop an effective **schedule,** two important variables are considered: allocated time and engaged time (Shea & Bauer, 1987). Englert (1984) describes allocated time as the amount of time scheduled for a specific subject or activity. Engaged time is the amount of time the students are actually participating in the subject or activity. To increase engaged time, teachers must plan the schedule with care, begin and end activities on time, facilitate transitions from activity to activity, and assign scheduled activities as a first priority rather than engaging in spontaneous, alternative activities.

Scheduling is a dynamic process—a continuous and creative activity (Gallagher, 1988; Murdick & Petch-Hogan, 1996). Schedules must be revised throughout the school year in response to emerging student needs and changing behaviors as well as the demands of the curriculum. Two important kinds of scheduling are overall program scheduling and individual program scheduling. Schedules are based on individual and group priorities. After the teacher determines priorities, available time, personnel, and materials must be fitted into those priorities.

Another variable considered when developing schedules is the length of time of the activity periods. As a rule, it is more effective to begin the school year with brief activity periods and gradually lengthen them as the year progresses; the students then learn the schedule and become involved in the learning process.

Clees (1995) evaluated the effectiveness of students' self-recording of teachers' expectancies. Four middle-school students (two males, two females) with disabilities (three learning disabled, one behavior disordered) were included in the study. They were given a schedule with headings for three general education classes, one special education class, and locker time. Under each heading were listed the expected behaviors for that period. Among the expectations listed on the schedule are the following:

- bring necessary materials to class;
- begin class on task;
- turn in completed assignments;
- complete all classwork; and
- write assignments in assignment book.

The study investigated the differences between student behavior during two conditions: (a) carrying the schedule without self-recording and (b) carrying the schedule and self-recording whether teacher expectancies were met. Carrying the schedule without self-recording had no discernible effect on student behavior. Self-recording, however, was effective across students in increasing the percentage of expectations met.

EXPULSION, SUSPENSION, AND IN-SCHOOL SUSPENSION

Recently, disciplinary removal through expulsion, suspension, and in-school suspension has been discussed in the literature as it applies both to students with disabilities and to regular students. Considerable controversy surrounds the use of these behavior management procedures (Bacon, 1990; Editor, 1995; Lieberman, 1996). Several court decisions impact on their use with regular and special education students (Yell, 1990).

Hindman (1986) and Center and McKittrick (1987) define **expulsion** as the removal of a student from school for more than 10 days and **suspension** as the removal of a student from school for no more than 10 days. **In-school suspension** is the removal of a student from regular or special education class but not from school.

Generally, as long as students' constitutional rights are not infringed upon (*Tinker v. Des Moines Independent Community School District*, 1969) and discipline is meted out with procedural due process (*Goss v. Lopez*, 1975), school officials' handling of student disciplines has not been altered through the judicial process (Bartlett, 1988a, 1988b). This is true for students in the regular class and general school population. However, as a consequence of various court decisions, it is not always true for students in special education (Shea, Bauer, & Lynch, 1989).

The implementation of expulsion with students with disabilities is limited by Public Law 94–142 (Morris, 1987; Yell, Rozalski, & Drasgow, 2001). Except in circumstances in which the student is a threat to the life and well-being of self or others, students with disabilities may be expelled or suspended only if the following criteria are met: (a) the procedures are included as disciplinary options in the student's individualized education plan, (b) the procedural requirements of Public Law 94–142 are adhered to, and (c) the use of the procedures does not result in a permanent cessation of educational services (Grosenick et al., 1982). In most circumstances, expulsion is considered a change in educational placement and cannot be imposed on students with disabilities.

Morrison and D'Incau (2000) studied the developmental and service trajectories that preceded the recommendation for expulsion from school of students with disabilities. The 41 students in this qualitative study were a diverse group and included students with speech disorders, learning disabilities, or emotional/behavioral disorders. The students were from a single school district and included males and females, various ethnic groups, and various ages. Morrison and D'Incau found that special education eligibility may serve as a protective factor in the expulsion process because expulsion charges were frequently dropped.

According to the U.S. Supreme Court, suspension is considered to be not only a necessary tool to maintain order in school but also a valuable educational device. Short-term suspension is permitted if the behavior for which the student is suspended is not directly linked to the disability. In this situation, the suspension is not considered a change in educational placement. However, the linkage between the disability and the behavior must be established or not established prior to the imposition of the suspension unless the student is dangerous to self or others. However, the general 10-day rule applies, and parents must be notified and agree to the suspension.

Center and McKittrick (1987) offer guidelines for those establishing school policy on expulsion and suspension. Policy should include clearly defined expectations for student behavior. Behavioral expectations are generally presented in a policy handbook that is made available to administrators, teachers, parents, and students. The handbook should include the rules, the consequences for violation, and the student's due-process rights. A standard procedure should be developed and implemented consistently in all cases in which expulsion and suspension may be considered as disciplinary options. The imposition of these disciplinary procedures is a team process and should never be done unilaterally.

Morgan-D'Atrio, Northup, LaFleur, and Spera (1996) conducted two studies on the use of suspension in a large urban public school (1,150 students). The first study was concerned with the extent of disciplinary problems in the school, the use of suspension as a disciplinary strategy, and the procedural integrity of the school's disciplinary policy. They found that 65% (745) of the students were referred to the principal's office for discipline during the 1993–1994 school year. A random sample of 150 students was studied. The sample represented a total of 979 disciplinary referrals. Referral ranged from 1 to 43 per student with a mean of 6. Of the 150 students, 94 (62%) were suspended at least once. Reasons for suspension included cutting class, tardiness, disobedience, not attending time-out room, fighting, profanity, disrespect, disturbing the classroom, leaving campus, leaving class, and others. Of the 94 suspended students, 39 (42%) were suspended once and 55 (58%) more than once. With regard to the integrity of the school disciplinary policy, it was found that 45% of the actions taken did not correspond with any of the disciplinary consequences in written school policy. About 20% of the suspensions actually violated school policy.

The purpose of the second study was to ascertain the extent of academic deficits, social skills deficits, and other adjustment problems within the sample of students with recurrent suspensions and to determine the extent of individual differences among that group. The sample included the high school students from the first study and an additional sample from a middle school with approximately the same demographics. Twenty-four randomly selected students were studied. The results of this study were that 22% of the students had social skills deficits, 30% had social skills and academic deficits, 22% had academic deficits, and 26% had no deficit. The deficits of the middle school students were not significantly different. The authors, while recognizing the limitations of the studies, suggested that "it may be a prudent investment of time and resources to practice a more prescriptive approach to the development of treatment alternatives to suspension that can at least begin to answer the classic assessment question of what treatment for what problems for which students" (Morgan-D'Atrio et al., 1996, p. 199).

In their study of out-of-school suspensions, Mendez and Knoff (2003) found an overrepresentation of African American males, beginning in elementary school and continuing through high school. African American females were also suspended at a higher rate than either white or Hispanic females at all levels. In general, Mendez and Knoff found a strong relationship between race, gender, school level, and suspension. At all levels, suspensions were for relatively minor infractions (e.g., disobedience, disruption, fighting, noncompliance, profanity, disrespect). African American males were overrepresented in suspensions for almost all types of infractions. Students at greatest risk for suspension were African American males in middle school.

Farmer (1996) describes the search for alternatives to suspension in a middle school in which more than 3,000 disciplinary referrals resulted in 1,300 placements in in-school suspension and over 400 out-of-school suspensions during a single school year. The teachers and administrators, as a result of frustration with the present disciplinary policies and procedures, designed an alternative. The new system included (a) an honor-level discipline system that emphasized student responsibility and (b) proactive discipline behavior and assistance for students to assume responsibility for their behavior.

In-school suspension has not been tested in the courts, and its use with students with disabilities is becoming more frequent in schools. Center and McKittrick (1987) suggest that school policies established for expulsion and suspension be used for in-school suspension.

In-school suspension has several advantages over expulsion and suspension:

- It eliminates the probability that the student will be unsupervised during the school day.
- As a form of segregation from the general school population, it decreases the probability of disruption in the school.
- With an effective learning program, it can be a useful educational experience.

Those wishing to implement an in-school suspension program must develop policies, curriculum, and management guidelines. The following is a summary of policies suggested by Center and McKittrick (1987):

- The 10-day rule should be applied.
- Age range among students should be no more than 3 years or three grades.
- A maximum enrollment should be set, perhaps 12 to 15 students. An experienced and qualified teacher should be assigned to each group.
- Specific criteria should be set for student assignment to the program.
- Placements should be for a predetermined and specific period of time. The placement period should be uniform for particular offenses.
- Placement should begin on a specific day of the week.
- Students should be required to meet specific criteria for return to their regular school program.
- Failure to successfully complete in-school suspension should result in a hearing to consider other disciplinary procedures.
- Policy should be established for multiple placements within a school year.
- Acceptance or continuation of participation in other school programs (special groups, cocurricular activities, special studies) should be contingent on successful participation in the program.

In-school suspension should not be viewed as simple detention. Students should not be allowed to sit passively for several days and then return to their regular program. In-school suspension should be a valuable learning experience. The issue is to address the student's behavior, not to "give the teacher a break."

There are two general approaches to curriculum in the in-school suspension program. In the first approach, the student may continue studying his or her regular curriculum. This approach is difficult and requires the regular and in-school suspension teachers to coordinate their activities. It is particularly difficult in the secondary school, where a student may be instructed by many teachers. This approach requires the in-school suspension teacher to be familiar with a broad range of curricula.

The second approach to in-school suspension curriculum is the stand-alone curriculum, which includes two options: (a) the learning skills program and (b) the functional academics program. In the learning skills program, the student studies generic learning strategies, such as listening skills, reading skills, study skills, and time management. In the functional academics program, the student studies daily living skills or work skills (e.g., budgeting, interviewing for a job, using credit, maintaining home and auto).

The in-school suspension program must include a behavior management program. Management should be positive and emphasize appropriate interpersonal and work skills. The effectiveness of any in-school suspension program is greatly dependent on the teacher assigned to the program. The teacher must be a highly skilled instructor and behavior manager and must be able to relate positively and productively with students.

In-school suspension is often used with other interventions (Bacon, 1990). In a comparison of the effects of in-school suspension combined with counseling and in-school suspension used alone, Hochman and Woerner (1987) found that students solely in in-school suspension were 13 times more likely to return to in-school suspension and 15 times more likely to be referred to the principal's office. According to Miller (1986), the attendance of adolescent truants improved in an intervention that combined in-school suspension with counseling, bibliotherapy, writing therapy, and contingency contracting.

Stage (1997) conducted a study of the effects of three types of in-school suspension on disruptive classroom behavior and the impact of management strategies on assignment to in-school suspension. Thirty-six students with behavioral disorders enrolled in a residential school were studied. The students ranged in age from 12 to 17. Three types of in-school suspension were imposed:

- a time-out procedure whereby the student was sent to a vacant classroom for one class period (exclusion time-out);
- a longer time-out with the requirement to complete an academic assignment; and
- an in-school suspension with a counseling procedure.

The researchers reported no apparent effects of in-school suspension on disruptive classroom behavior since there were no systematic differences in disruptive behavior in the in-school suspension phase of the study. The rate of student disruptive behavior remained rather constant across all phases of intervention, suggesting that no type of in-school suspension, as defined in this study, is more effective than another. It is suggested that the teacher's use of aversive contingencies in the classroom served to create conditions for students to wish to escape (i.e., enter in-school suspension). No direct or indirect evidence that a coercive behavior cycle was in place was found. The authors suggested that the effectiveness of in-school suspension may rely on sufficient positive social reinforcement within the ongoing classroom environment.

BIOBEHAVIORAL INTERVENTIONS

In this section, several **biobehavioral interventions** are discussed. In the majority of these interventions, the educator plays an important role that is supportive to medical personnel. Consequently, an analysis of the educator's functions in referral, collaboration and reporting, the modification of classroom structure and curriculum content, the obtaining of permission to administer medication, and the safeguarding and administering of medication is presented as a conclusion to the discussion of the biobehavioral behavior management interventions.

In addition to the educator's "need to know," the biobehavioral techniques are reviewed because some of the behavior problems of children may be a direct result of biobehavioral or biobehavioral-environment interactions. In addition, the social-emotional (secondary) effects of many biobehavioral disabilities on the individual's lifestyle are of direct concern to educators.

The biobehavioral frame of reference implies that the source of an individual's behavior problem is an organic defect. There are two known causes of biobehavioral defects in unborn and newborn children: environment and heredity. Environmental factors of special importance to the health of the child are maternal factors (e.g., metabolic disorders, maternal age, number and frequency of pregnancies) and factors that affect the mother during pregnancy (e.g., viral diseases and infections, venereal disease, drugs, alcohol, tobacco, diet, injuries). In addition, the larger environment may have an effect on the child as a consequence of pollution, radiation, and the like.

Heredity, or the transmission of the characteristics or traits of the parents to the child, is a factor in some birth defects. Hereditary characteristics are transmitted from parents to child by chromosomes. Chromosomes are present in every human cell, including the ovum and sperm. Chromosomes are composed of genes—the units of heredity. The inherited characteristics of a child are determined by the composition and manner in which the gene-carrying chromosomes from the parents combine at the time of conception. Approximately 4,000 disorders are known to be caused by genetic defects. Among them, the most commonly known disorders are Down syndrome, sickle cell disease, cystic fibrosis, and hemophilia. Because genetic disorders are permanent, chronic, and complex, they tend to evoke labeling. As a consequence, they impact on the lifestyle of both the individual and the family (Costello, 1988).

Chemical regulation includes such familiar interventions as medication and diet. Corrective surgery is frequently effective in reducing the debilitating effects of clubfoot, cleft lip and palate, and some vision, hearing, and speech problems, among others. Cosmetic surgery is a valuable aid in reducing the effects of observable deformities on the individual. Rehabilitation and training services have a significant positive impact on the lives of people with mental retardation, visual and hearing impairments, speech disorders, physical disabilities, learning disabilities, or emotional/behavioral disorders.

Diet

Dietary management of behavior problems in children has been practiced since the 1920s (Cormier & Elder, 2007). Feingold's (1973, 1985) work during the 1970s is perhaps the best known. He hypothesized that naturally occurring salicylates and artificial food additives may cause the hyperkinetic syndrome in children who have a genetically determined predisposition.

Feingold claims that 48% of his patients were effectively treated by **diet** control and that symptoms can reappear within a few hours if the diet is broken. Cook and Woodhill (1976) supported Feingold's claim in a clinical study of 15 hyperkinetic children. The parents of 10 children were "quite certain" and those of three others "fairly certain" that their child's behavior improved with the diet and relapsed when the diet was broken. Cook and Woodhill cautioned against the generalization of their finding because the sample was limited and the study did not meet rigorous research standards. In a recent study, Bateman, Warner, and Hutchinson (2004) studied the relationship of diet and behavior in 277 preschool children, reporting that the diet was beneficial to the children. Eigenmann and Haenggeli (2004) question this research and conclusions, stating that these diets should not be used to reduce hyperactivity.

Weiss et al. (1980) conducted a challenge study of 22 children with regard to behavioral response to artificial food colors. Of the 22 children, 20 displayed no convincing evidence of sensitivity to the color challenge as reported by their parents. Swanson and Kinsbourne (1980) studied the effects of food dyes on children's laboratory learning performance. In the study, 20 children were classified as hyperactive, 20 were not. Both groups were challenged with food dyes. The performance of the hyperactive children was impaired on the days they received food dyes. Performance of the nonhyperactive children was not affected.

In a review of the pertinent empirical investigations with regard to the Feingold diet, Baker (1980) concluded that the differential results reported by Feingold, parents, and others using the diet may be due to variables other than the eliminated substances. He found that in properly controlled studies, the positive effects of the diet evaporated. At this time, the debate remains unsettled as to whether a diet intervention is truly effective. In a review of the research, Pescara-Kovach and Alexander (1994) concluded that there is no connection between food additives and behavior. They suggest that there is a need to educate the public about these findings.

Other efforts have been undertaken to manage behavior through changes in intake. changes in intake that have been tried in the effort to manage behavior. A sugar elimination diet has been examined, with the question emerging as to whether the activity levels of the students caused the need for a high sugar intake or the sugar intake increased the hyperactivity (Wolraich, 1996). In a carefully controlled study, Wolraich, Wilson, and White (1995) found that refined sugar had no impact on a student's hyperactivity, attention span, or learning. They argued that parents' expectations and increased sense of "doing something" about the student's behavior may have been related to the "improved" behavior reports. Fatty acid supplements have also been evaluated, and well-designed studies have noted no impact of the supplement on student behavior (Rojas & Chan, 2005).

One of the latest diets to emerge is the gluten-free/casein-free diet. Mulloy, Lang, O'Reilly, Sigafoos, Lancioni, and Rispoli (2010) reported that this diet is based on the assumption that the gastrointestinal tracts of individuals with autism spectrum disorder have inadequate production of gluten (found in wheat products) and casein (found in milk products) digesting enzymes. The peptides from these substances leak into the bloodstream, crossing the brain-blood barrier and attaching to neuroreceptors. Their carefully controlled study demonstrated no significant change in behavior among children on this diet. Elder et al. (2006) conducted another trial, and again no changes were noted. Parents argue that the diet has an impact. Mulloy et al. argue that with the lack of evidence and the problems of stigma, attending to the diet and diverting resources away from other instructional efforts, and bone development problems, the diet should only be used if medical professionals confirm allergies or intolerances to gluten or casein.

Medication

Though the impact of medication on behavior has been documented since the 1930s, the use of medication with children and youth has grown most rapidly during the past two decades (Ryan, Reid, & Ellis, 2008). In 2005, 6.1% of all boys and 2.6% of all girls between the ages of 6 and 19 were taking a stimulant to treat attention-deficit/hyperactivity disorder (Castle, Aubert, Verbrugge, Khalid, & Epstein, 2007). It would be a rare classroom that does not have at least one student with prescriptive medication for attention-deficit/hyperactivity disorder (ADHD), allergies, seizure disorder, or some other medical need. Though children may be prescribed a wide range of medications, the most frequent are stimulants, antidepressant/antianxiety medications, anticonvulsants, and allergy/asthma treatments.

According to the American Academy of Child and Adolescent Psychiatry (AACAP, 2006), medications are primarily prescribed for the treatment of bed-wetting, anxiety, ADHD, obsessive-compulsive disorder, depressive disorders, eating disorders, bipolar disorder, psychosis, autism, severe aggression, and sleep problems. The use of medication should always be within a comprehensive treatment plan (AACAP). Medication is not a "quick fix."

Teachers often have little information about the use of medication with children (Ryan, Reid, & Ellis, 2008). Yet if teachers are not active participants in providing feedback to parents and doctors, medication may not address the student's classroom needs. Though schools often have policies for administering and storing medication, many do not have clear directions for monitoring the student's response to those medications. The AACAP (2006) recommends that multiple outcome measures should be used and that information should be gathered from both parents and teachers.

STIMULANTS FOR ATTENTION-DEFICIT/HYPERACTIVITY DISORDER. Stimulants are the most commonly used psychiatric medications in children and adolescents and are most often used with individuals with ADHD (Wilens, 2002). These medications have been demonstrated to increase focus and attentiveness. A concern arises, though, in the prescription of stimulants. Preen, Calver, Sanfillippo, Bulsara, and Holman (2007) found that pediatricians were more likely to prescribe methylphenicate more often, medicate a larger proportion of boys, and prescribe for younger children. Psychiatrists, however, relied more on combined medications or higher doses. With this variation in practice, parents may receive conflicting messages when going from one medical professional to another.

The most common medications—methylphenidate (Ritalin®) and dextroamphetamine (Dexedrine)—are short acting, with children and youth demonstrating changes in their behavior within 30 minutes of taking the medication. The peak of the medication's effectiveness is usually between 1 and 4 hours after administration. Because of this short-term effect, many parents are opting for slow-release versions of these medications, the effects of which usually last from 2 to 6 hours. Other medications used include pemoline (Cylert®) and combined amphetamines (Adderall®). Cylert takes effect within 1 or 2 hours and may last up to 8 hours, and Adderall typically works in 45 minutes and lasts 6 to 8 hours (Wilens, 2002). The Daytrana® patch provides controlled release of methylphenidate for 2 hours after its application to the hip area and continues for an additional 3 hours after its removal 9 hours later (Lerner & Wigal, 2008). These medications work with individuals with ADHD by restoring the delicate levels of neurotransmitters in the brain. The "paradoxical effect" (calming produced by a stimulant) is caused by boosting serotonin levels in the brain, reducing restlessness, impulsivity, and difficulty concentrating (Gainetdinov et al., 1999). In addition, all these stimulants should be used with care in that they are

TABLE 10.1 Most Common Medications Used with Children to Manage Behavior

Medication	Generic	Age Approved	Side Effects
Stimulants for Attention-Deficit/Hyperactivity Disorder			
Adderall®	Amphetamine	3+	Decreased appetite; sleep disturbance; development of tics
Adderall XR® (extended release)	Amphetamine (extended release)	6+	Decreased appetite; sleep disturbance; development of tics
Concerta®	Methylphenidate (long acting)	6+	Decreased appetite; sleep disturbance
Daytrana®	Methylphenidate (patch)	6–12	Decreased appetite, sleep disturbance, rare skin rash
Dexedrine®	Dextroamphetamine	3+	Decreased appetite; sleep disturbance
Ritalin®	Methylphenidate	6+	Decreased appetite; sleep disturbance; flat affect
Obsessive-Compulsive Disorder and Anxiety			
Anafranil®	Clomipramine	10+	Fatigue, headache, dizziness
Luvox (SSRI)®	Fluvoxamine	8+	Fatigue, headache, dizziness
Zoloft (SSRI)®	Sertraline	6+	Fatigue, headache, dizziness
Anticonvulsants			
Depakane®	Valproic Acid	any age	Tremors, seizures, depression
Tegretol®	Carbamazepine	any age	Tremors, seizures, depression
Asthma and Allergy Medications			
Inhalers	Inhaled corticosteroids	6+	Long-term use may slightly delay growth
Xolair	Omalizumab	12+	Injections every 2 to 4 weeks; injection site rash or swelling
Over-the-Counter Oral Antihistamines	Loratadine, cetirizine, clemastine, diphenhydramine	Child versions available	Dry mouth, drowsiness
Over-the-counter decongestants	Pseudoephedrine	Child versions available	Irritability, fast or irregular heartbeat, dizziness, insomnia, headaches, anxiety

Sources: Summarized information from Mayo Clinic, 2010; National Institute of Mental Health, 2010; Ryan, Reid, & Ellis, 2008.

Schedule II medications—that is, medications with a strong potential for abuse and addiction though medically acceptable (National Institute of Mental Health, 2010).

ANTICONVULSANTS.   Anticonvulsants are used to treat children whose behavior and learning problems are complicated by seizures. Trade names for these medications include Dilantin®, Mysoline®, and Depakanec®, among others. These medications require careful monitoring by the teacher, doctor, and parent. Teachers may be expected to keep a behavior and seizure log for the child.

Allergy and Asthma Treatments

Asthma is the most common chronic disease in children (Bacharier et al, 2008). "Second-hand" tobacco smoke is one of the strongest risks for developing allergies and asthma symptoms during childhood. Air pollution and traffic have also been related to asthma and allergies in children. Unfortunately, the primary way of dealing with asthma and allergies is to eliminate triggers (Bacharier et al.). Children may take daily medication or use a controlled release inhaler.

Snider, Busch, and Arrowood (2003) assessed 200 general and 200 special educators' knowledge, opinions, and experiences related to ADHD and its treatment with medication. They found that teachers had scant knowledge about ADHD and the use of stimulant medication. In general, teachers had a positive opinion with regard to the effects of medication on the school-related behavior of children; special educators were more positive than general educators. The authors suggested that teacher education programs include additional information on ADHD and its treatment, including medication, behavioral assessment, diagnosis, and empirical research. Vereb and DiPerna (2004) also explored teachers' perception, reporting that teachers' preparation was positively correlated with knowledge of ADHD and the acceptability of behavior management interventions.

Educator's Role in Biobehavioral Interventions

The educator plays an important supportive role to medical personnel in the application of biobehavioral interventions. Howell, Evans, and Gardiner (1997) suggested several guidelines for teachers of students taking stimulant medications. These guidelines for obtaining optimal benefit from medication include the following:

- Ensure that the decision to use medication is made appropriately.
- Establish direct communication among all concerned parties.
- Plan who will receive the medication and how the medication will be administered.
- Promote student responsibility for personal behavior.
- Alert student to the potential for change as a consequence of medication.
- Help student explain to others about medication.
- Provide student with appropriate and positive reminders to take medication.
- Set realistic goals for behavior change.
- Teach student prosocial behaviors to replace inappropriate behaviors.
- Monitor the effects of medication on academic behavior, social interactions, and adverse side effects.

The supportive role includes (a) referral, (b) collaboration with and reporting of observations to the medical professional, (c) modification of classroom structure and curriculum content to meet the needs of the child, (d) obtaining permission to administer medication, and (e) safeguarding and administering medication to the child in school.

REFERRAL.   The educator is not in a position by experience, training, or function to refer a child directly to a medical professional. Neither is the educator in a position to suggest to a medical professional the prescribing of medication for a specific child. In addition, the educator should not attempt to coerce parents to accept any particular biobehavioral treatment.

It is proper for teachers to inform parents of a child's problems. The school initiates contact with medical personnel on behalf of a particular child only with parental consent. It is suggested that an educator not directly involved with the child in school serve as a contact person and intermediary between the teacher and parents during the referral process (Report of the Conference on the Use of Stimulant Drugs in the Treatment of Behaviorally Disturbed Young Children, 1971).

COLLABORATION WITH AND REPORTING OF OBSERVATIONS TO THE MEDICAL PROFESSIONAL.   A primary role of the teacher in biobehavioral interventions is the provision of current and objective feedback to the medical professional on the observable effects of the treatment on the child's behavior and learning (Wilson & Sherrets, 1979). The effects of medications on a particular child cannot be predicted with exactitude. Thus, meaningful feedback to the prescribing medical professional will assist in maximizing the positive effects of medication. The teacher, a trained observer who is with the child throughout the day, is in an excellent position to observe the effects of the medication and report, through proper channels, to the medical professional.

MODIFICATION OF CLASSROOM STRUCTURE AND CURRICULUM CONTENT.   During the biobehavioral treatment process, especially during the beginning weeks, the child's behavior and learning styles may change radically. Consequently, it will be necessary for the teacher to modify, as necessary, both classroom structure and curriculum content to respond to the child's needs. Classroom structure may have to be increased or decreased to permit the child to adjust to his or her "new" behavior. The curriculum may have to be changed to allow the child to learn the knowledge and skills neglected during the "lost" years.

OBTAINING PERMISSION TO DISPENSE MEDICATION.   The educator must obtain permission to dispense medication in the school when medical personnel are not available. A child should not be dismissed from school because medical personnel are not immediately available to administer medication. In some circumstances, teachers may dispense medication with proper permission. However, school personnel must investigate and adhere to their state's laws and regulations governing the dispensing of medication in the schools. In some cases, the school may need legal advice. A permission form suggested by Renshaw (1974) is shown in Figure 10.1.

Bauer, Ingersoll, and Burns (2004) conducted a national survey of school counselors and medication, school policies, and counselor education. They found that medication was widely used with children, but they also reported concerns with administration of medication in school. Price, Dake, Murnan, and Telljohann (2003) reported that in their large study (385 school secretaries), 69% reported dispensing medication. Of these secretaries, 25% received no training. Most of the secretaries (63%)

Date _____

Child _____ DOB _____

Address _____

Telephone (home) _____ Parent daytime _____

Teacher _____ Grade _____

Physician's direction:

Please administer to _____,

    Medication and dose _____

    Route _____

    Time/frequency _____

Please monitor for these side effects _____

_____

Physician's signature _____ Date _____

Physician contact information _____

PARENT PERMISSION

I hereby consent for my child to be administrated the above medication by a designated individual.

Signature _____ Date _____

FIGURE 10.1 Medication form

Source: From *The Hyperactive Child,* by D.C. Renshaw, 1974, Chicago: Nelson-Hall. Copyright 1974 by Nelson-Hall. Used with permission.

administered medication 5 days a week. The most common medication they administered included medication for ADHD, asthma, or antibiotics. The authors urge school districts to employ more nurses, review and establish policies with regard to the administration of medication in school, and if school nurses delegate the administration of medication, they should understand the risk of liability.

SAFEGUARDING AND ADMINISTRATION OF MEDICATION.   Ryan, Reid, and Ellis (2008) reported that, in their study of special educators, over 60% of the schools had specific guidelines about the administration of medication. However, about half of the teachers

Medication Log					
Child's Name	Date	Time	Medication	Person Dispensing	Notes

FIGURE 10.2   Medication log

reported that they were not adequately informed about students and their prescription medications. When medication is dispensed in the school, the following guidelines must be used:

1. Proper permission forms, completed by parents and medical professionals, should be obtained and filed in the child's record folder (see Figure 10.1).
2. All medications should be stored in a central location. This facility should be clean, ventilated, and lighted and should contain a locked cabinet. A water tap is needed. A refrigerator is necessary for some medications.
3. All medications must be properly labeled with the child's name and the medical professional's name. The label should include directions for use.
4. All medications, including new prescriptions and refills, received from and returned home should be logged in and out of the school. Medication should be inventoried frequently. One individual from the school's faculty or staff should be appointed to inventory the medication and function as a contact person in all communications with parents and medical professionals in relation to medication.
5. A responsible adult must be present when a child takes medication.
6. A log, to be filled in each time a child takes medication, should be affixed to the wall in the medication center. This form is presented in Figure 10.2. The completed forms should be retained in a file.

Summary Points

- Naturalistic interventions (incidental learning) become a fluid part of the day. Naturalistic interventions increase student opportunities beyond having to wait for the teacher.
- Comprehensive interventions produce rapid, lasting, generalized reduction in problem behaviors by taking place in several settings concurrently and working on an array of behaviors.
- Designing instructional groups is a difficult process due to the large number of factors that must be considered.
- Class meetings can be instituted as part of regular classroom procedures and can be used to deal with common problems of living and learning in a group setting.
- The more thoroughly the classroom setting and procedures are planned, the greater the probability of success for students and teacher.
- In addition to the physical space, classroom and nonclassroom procedures must be in place so that students learn and behave effectively. These procedures include the development of classroom rules.
- Cuing is an effective way of preventing behavior problems by providing a sign or signal before the disruption begins.
- Transitions can be facilitated by environmental arrangements, peers, and procedures.
- Expulsion is removal of the student for more than 10 days; suspension refers to such removal for less than 10 days. There are specific limits to the ability of schools to suspend and expel students with disabilities, related to the individualized education plan, and nature of the student's disabilities.
- In-school suspension is often used to decrease disruption in the school by segregating students from the school population. Learning programs must be in place in in-school suspension programs.
- In biobehavioral interventions, teachers typically play a role supportive of the medical professional and other medical personnel.
- Diet remains a controversial biobehavioral intervention, with various studies presenting contradictory results. On the whole, no consistent, substantive evidence affirms that diet control manages behavior.
- Medication is an effective support for some students but should be used only after extensive interventions have been implemented unsuccessfully.
- Stimulants are the most commonly used medication for behavior management of children and youth.
- The teacher's role in biobehavioral interventions includes referral, collaboration and reporting, modifying the classroom structure to meet the student's needs; obtaining permission to administer medication, and safeguarding the administration of medication.

Projects

1. Observe a classroom at the beginning of the day. What routines and procedures are in place? How are transitions facilitated? What cues does the teacher use? What rules are in place?

2. Request information regarding administering medication from two local schools. What policies and procedures are in place? Who may administer medication? What precautions are taken with administration and storage of medication?

Web Resources

For further information about medication, visit these sites:

www.nimh.nih.gov/health/publications/mental-health-medications/complete-index.shtml
www.nlm.nih.gov/medlineplus/asthmainchildren.html
www.aacap.org/cs/root/facts_for_families/obsessivecompulsive_disorder_in_children_and_adolescents

For further information about developing classroom rules and procedures, visit these sites:

www.nea.org/tools/lessons/5325.htm
newteachersupport.suite101.com/article.cfm/effective_classroom_management

References

American Academy of Child and Adolescent Psychiatry (AACAP). (2006). *Psychiatric medication for children and adolescents. Facts for Families, 21.*

Anderson, N., & Marrone, R. T. (1979). Therapeutic discussion groups in public school classes for emotionally disturbed children. *Focus on Exceptional Children, 12*(1), 1–15.

Bacharier, L. B., Bone, A., Carlsen, K. H., Eigemann, P. A., Frischer, T., Goetz, M., et al. (2008). Diagnosis and treatment of asthma in childhood. *Allergy, 63,* 5–34.

Bacon, E. H. (1990). Using negative consequences effectively. *Academic Therapy, 25*(5), 599–611.

Baker, R. W. (1980). The efficacy of the Feingold K-P diet: A review of pertinent empirical investigations. *Behavioral Disorders, 6*(1), 32–35.

Barnett, D. W., & Carey, K. T. (1993). Naturalistic intervention design for young children: Foundations, rationales, and strategies. *Topics in Early Childhood Special Education, 13*(4), 430–455.

Bartlett, L. (1988a). *Doe v. Honing* and school discipline. *Behavior in Our Schools, 2*(3), 10–11.

Bartlett, L. (1988b). To expel or not to expel: Discipline of special education students from a legal perspective. *Behavior in Our Schools, 2*(2), 14–16.

Bateman, B., Warner, J. O., & Hutchinson, E. (2004). The effects of a double blind placebo controlled, artificial food colourings and benzoate preservative challenge on hyperactivity in a general population sample of preschool children. *Archives of Disabled Children, 89,* 506–511.

Bauer, A. L., Ingersoll, E., & Burns, L. (2004). School counselors and psychotropic medication: Assessing training, experience, and school policy issues. *Professional School Counseling 7*(3), 202–211.

Brady, K., Forton, M. B., Porter D., & Wood, C. (2003). *Rules in school.* Greenfield, MA: Foundation for Children.

Brown, D. E. (2003). Urban teachers' use of culturally responsive management strategies. *Theory into Practice, 42*(4), 277–282.

Brown, W. H., & Odom, S. L. (1995). Naturalistic peer interventions for promoting preschool children's social interactions. *Preventing School Failure, 39,* 38–43.

Brown, W. H., Odom, S. L., & Conroy, M. A. (2001). An intervention hierarchy for promoting young children's peer interactions in natural environments. *Topics in Early Childhood Special Education, 21*(3), 162–175.

Brownell, M. T., & Thomas, C. W. (2001). An interview with Stephen W. Smith: Strategies for building a positive classroom environment by preventing behavior problems. *Intervention in School and Clinic, 37*(1), 31–35.

Burden, P. R. (2003). *Classroom management: Managing an effective learning community* (2nd ed.). New York: John Wiley & Sons, Inc.

Cangelosi, J. S. (2000). *Classroom management strategies: Gaining and maintaining students' cooperation* (4th ed.). New York: John Wiley & Sons, Inc.

Castle, L., Aubert, R. E., Verbrugge, R. R., Kahlid, M., & Epstein, R. S. (2007). Trends in medication treatment for ADHD. *Journal of Attention Disorders, 10*(4), 335–342.

Center, D. B., & McKittrick, S. (1987). Disciplinary removal of special education students. *Focus on Exceptional Children, 20*(2), 1–10.

Clees, T. J. (1995). Self-recording of students' daily schedules of teachers' expectancies: Perspectives on reactivity, stimulus control, and generalization. *Exceptionalities, 5*(3), 113–129.

Coleman, M., & Webber, J. (1988). Behavior problems? Try groups! *Academic Therapy, 23*(3), 265–275.

Cook, P. S., & Woodhill, J. M. (1976). The Feingold dietary treatment of the hyperkinetic syndrome. *Medical Journal of Australia, 2,* 85–89.

Cormier, E., & Elder, J. H. (2007). Diet and child behavior problems: Fact or fiction? *Pediatric Nursing, 33*(2), 138–144.

Costello, A. (1988). The psychosocial impact of genetic disease. *Focus on Exceptional Children, 20*(7), 1–8.

Editor. (1995). Court: No services needed in short-term suspension. *The Special Educator, 11*(3), 1, 6.

Edwards, D., & Mullis, F. (2003). Classroom meetings: Encouraging a climate of cooperation. *Professional School Counseling, 7*(1), 20–28.

Eigenmann, P. A., & Haenggeli, C. A. (2004). Food colorings and preservatives: Allergies and hyperactivity. *The Lancet, 364*(9437), 823–824.

Elder, J. H., Shankar, M., Shuster, J., Theriaque, D., Burns, S., & Sherrill, L. (2006). The gluten-free casein-free diet in autism: Results of a preliminary double blind clinical trial. *Journal of Autism and Related Disorders, 36,* 413–420.

Englert, C. S. (1984). Measuring teacher effectiveness from the teacher's point of view. *Focus on Exceptional Children, 17,* 1–14.

Erikson, E. (1963). *Childhood and society* (2nd ed.). New York: W. W. Norton.

Evertson, C. M., Emmer, E. T., Clements, B. S., Sandford, J. P., Worsham, M. E., & Williams, E. L. (1981). *Organizing and managing the elementary school classroom.* Austin: Research and Development Center for Teacher Education, University of Texas.

Farmer, C. D. (1996). Empowering discipline: Proactive alternatives to school suspension. *Journal of Emotional and Behavioral Problems, 5*(1), 47–51.

Feingold, B. F. (1973). Food additives and child development. *Hospital Practice, 8*(11), 11–21.

Feingold, B. F. (1985). *Why your child is hyperactive.* New York: Random House.

Frey, A., & Doyle, H. D. (2001). Classroom meetings: A program model. *Children and Schools, 23*(4), 212.

Gainetdinov, R. R., Wetsel, W. C., Jones, S. R., Levin, E. D., Jaber, M., & Caron, M. G. (1999). Role of serotonin in the paradoxical calming effect of psychostimulants on hyperactivity. *Science, 283,* 397–401.

Gallagher, P. A. (1988). *Teaching students with behavior disorders* (2nd ed.). Denver, CO: Love Publishing.

Goss v. Lopez, 95 S. Ct. 729 (1975).

Grosenick, J. K., Huntze, S. L., Kochan, B., Peterson, R. L., Robertshaw, C. S., & Wood, F. (1982). *National needs analysis in behavior disorders working paper.* Columbia: Department of Special Education, University of Missouri.

Harth, R., & Morris, S. M. (1976). Group processes for behavior change. *Teaching Exceptional Children, 8*(4), 136–139.

Hindman, S. E. (1986). The law, the courts, and the education of behaviorally disordered students. *Behavioral Disorders, 11*(4), 280–289.

Hochman, S., & Woerner, W. (1987). In-school suspension and group counseling: Helping the at-risk student. *National Association of Secondary School Principals Bulletin, 71*(501), 93–96.

Horner, R. H., & Carr, E. G. (1997). Behavioral support for students with severe disabilities: Functional assessment and comprehensive intervention. *Journal of Special Education, 31,* 108–109.

Howell, K. W., Evans, D., & Gardiner, J. (1997). Medications in the classroom: A hard pill to swallow? *Teaching Exceptional Children, 29*(6), 58–61.

Howes, C., & Ritchie, S. (2002). *A matter of trust: Connecting teachers and learners in the early childhood classroom.* New York: Teachers College Press.

Johnson, D. W., & Johnson, F. (2003). *Joining together: Group theory and research.* Boston: Allyn & Bacon.

Joyce, B. G., Joyce, J. H., & Chase, P. N. (1989). Considerations for the use of rules in academic settings. *Education and Treatment of Children, 12,* 82–92.

Koegel, R. L., Openden, D., Fredeen, R. M., & Koegel, L. K. (2006). The basics of pivotal response treatment. In R. L. Koegel & L. K. Koegel (Eds.), *Pivotal response treatments for autism: Communication, social, and academic development* (pp. 3–30). Baltimore, MD: Brookes.

Kutnick, P., Oda, C., & Berdondini, L. (2008). Improving the effects of group working in classrooms with young school-aged children. *Learning and Instruction, 18,* 26–35.

Lerner, M., & Wigal, T. (2008). Long term safety of stimulant medications used to treat children with ADHD. *Psychiatric Annals, 38*(1), 43–50.

Lieberman, H. A. (1996). The court corner: Suspension/expulsion: The "10-day rule." *Missouri Innovations in Special Education, 24*(2), 2–3.

Loughmiller, C. (1965). *Wilderness road.* Austin: Hogg Foundation for Mental Health, University of Texas.

Maslow, A. (1962). *Toward a psychology of being.* Princeton, NJ: Van Nostrand.

Mayo Clinic. (2010). *Asthma medications: Know your options.* Retrieved January 8, 2011, from www.mayoclinic.com/health/asthma-medications/APOOOO8

Mendez, L. M. R., & Knoff, H. M. (2003). Who gets suspended from school and why: A demographic analysis of schools and disciplinary infractions in a large school district. *Education and Treatment of Children, 26*(1), 30–51.

Miller, D. (1986). Effect of a program of therapeutic discipline on the attitude, attendance and insight of truant adolescents. *Journal of Experimental Education, 55*(1), 49–53.

Montague, M., Bergerson, J., & Lago-Delello, E. (1997). Using prevention strategies in general education. *Focus on Exceptional Children, 29*(8), 1–12.

Morgan-D'Atrio, C., Northup, J., LaFleur, L., & Spera, S. (1996). Toward prescriptive alternatives to suspension: A preliminary evaluation. *Behavioral Disorders, 21*(2), 190–200.

Morris, P. (1987). The restricted use of traditional disciplinary procedures with handicapped youngsters. In A. Rotatori, M. Banbury, & R. Foxx (Eds.), *Issues in special education.* Mountain View, CA: Mayfield.

Morris, S. M. (1982). A classroom process for behavior change. *The Pointer, 26*(3), 25–28.

Morrison, G. M., & D'Incau, B. (2000). Developmental and service trajectories of students with disabilities recommended for expulsion from school. *Exceptional Children, 66*(2), 257–272.

Morse, W. C., & Wineman, D. (1957). Group interviewing in a camp for disturbed boys. *Journal of Social Issues, 13*(1), 23–31.

Mulloy, A., Lang, R., O'Reilly, M. O., Sigafoos, J., Lancioni, G., & Rispoli, M. (2007). Gluten-free and casein-free diets in the treatment of autism spectrum disorders: A systematic review. *Research in Autism Spectrum Disorders, 4*(3), 428–439.

Munk, D. D., & Repp, A. C. (1994). The relationship between instructional variables and problem behavior: A review. *Exceptional Children, 60*(5), 390–401.

Murdick, N. L., & Petch-Hogan, B. (1996). Inclusive classroom management: Using preintervention strategies. *Intervention in School and Clinic, 31*(3), 172–176.

National Institute of Mental Health (2010). Mental Health Medications. Retrieved January 10, 2010, from www.nimh.nih.gov/health/publications/mental-health-medications/complete-index.shtml

Newmann, F. (1991). Student engagement in academic work: Expanding the perspective on secondary school effectiveness. In J. R. Bliss & W. A. Firestone (Eds.), *Rethinking effective schools: Research and practice* (pp. 58–76). Upper Saddle River, NJ: Prentice Hall.

Newmann, F., Wehlage, G. G., & Lamborn, S. D. (1992). The significance and sources of student engagement. In F. Newmann (Ed.), *Student engagement and achievement in American secondary schools* (pp. 11–19). New York: Teachers College Press.

Olson, J. L., & Platt, J. M. (2000). *Teaching children and adolescents with special needs* (3rd ed.). Upper Saddle River, NJ: Merrill/Pearson.

Pescara-Kovach, L. A., & Alexander, K. (1994). The link between food ingested and problem behavior: Fact or fallacy? *Behavioral Disorders, 19*(2), 142–148.

Preen, D. B., Calver, J., Sanfillippo, F. M., Bulsara, M., & Holman, C. D. (2007). Prescribing of psychostimulant medications for attention deficit hyperactivity disorder in children: differences between clinical specialties. *Journal of Child and Adolescent Psychopharmacology, 17*(2), 195–203.

Price, J. H., Dake, J. A., Murnan, J., & Telljohann, S. K. (2003). Elementary school secretaries' experiences and perceptions of administering prescription medication. *Journal of School Health, 73*(10), 373–379.

Quinn, K. P., & McDougal, J. L. (1998). A mile wide and a mile deep: Comprehensive interventions for children and youth with emotional and behavioral disorders and their families. *The School Psychology Review, 27*(2), 191–203.

Rademacher, J. A., Callahan, K., & Pedersen-Seelye, V. A. (1998). How do your classroom rules measure up? Guidelines for developing an effective rule/management routine. *Intervention in School and Clinic, 33*(5), 284–289.

Renshaw, D. C. (1974). *The hyperactive child*. Chicago: Nelson-Hall.

Report of the Conference on the Use of Stimulant Drugs in the Treatment of Behaviorally Disturbed Young School Children. (1971). *Journal of Learning Disabilities, 4,* 523–530.

Rockwell, S., & Guetzloe, E. (1996). Group development for students with emotional/behavioral disorders. *Teaching Exceptional Children, 29*(1), 38–43.

Rojas, N. L., & Chan, E. (2005). Old and new controversies in the alternative treatment of attention-deficit hyperactivity disorder. *Mental Retardation and Developmental Disabilities Research Reviews, 11,* 116–130.

Rosenkoetter, S. E., & Fowler, S. A. (1986). Teaching mainstreamed children to manage daily transitions. *Teaching Exceptional Children, 19,* 20–23.

Rosenshine, B. (1977). Review of teaching variables and student achievement. In G. D. Borich & K. S. Fenton (Eds.), *The appraisal of teaching: Concepts and process*. Menlo Park, CA: Addison-Wesley.

Ryan, J. B., Reid, R., & Ellis, C. (2008). Special educators' knowledge regarding psychotropic interventions for students with emotional and behavioral disorders. *Remedial and Special Education, 29*(5), 269–279.

Sainato, D. M. (1990). Classroom transitions: Organizing environments to promote independent performance in preschool children with disabilities. *Education and Treatment of Children, 13*(4), 288–297.

Seid, N. (2001). How to set rules your kids won't break. *Parents, 76*(9), 108–110.

Shea, T. M. (1977). *Camping for special children*. St. Louis, MO: Mosby.

Shea, T. M., & Bauer, A. M. (1987). *Teaching children and youth with behavior disorders* (2nd ed.). Upper Saddle River, NJ: Merrill/Pearson.

Shea, T. M., Bauer, A. M., & Lynch, E. M. (1989, September). *Changing behavior: Ethical issues regarding behavior management and the control of students with behavioral disorders*. Paper presented at the CEC/CCBD Conference, Charlotte, NC.

Slade, D., & Callaghan, T. (1988). Preventing management problems. *Academic Therapy, 23,* 229–235.

Smith, T. E., Polloway, E. A., Patton, J. R., & Dowdy, C. A. (2008). *Teaching students with special needs in inclusive settings* (5th ed.). Boston: Allyn & Bacon.

Snider, V. E., Busch, T., & Arrowood, L. (2003). Teacher knowledge of stimulant medication and ADD. *Remedial and Special Education 74*(1), 46–56.

Stage, S. A. (1997). A preliminary investigation of the relationship between in-school suspension and the disruptive classroom behavior of students with behavioral disorders. *Behavioral Disorders, 23*(1), 57–76.

Stainback, W., Stainback, S., Etscheidt, S., & Doud, J. (1986). A nonintrusive intervention for acting-out behavior. *Teaching Exceptional Children, 19*(1), 38–41.

Swanson, J. M., & Kinsbourne, M. (1980). Food dyes impair performance of hyperactive children on a laboratory learning test. *Science, 207*(28), 1485–1486.

Thorson, S. (1996). The missing link: Students discuss school discipline. *Focus on Exceptional Children, 29*(3), 1–12.

Tinker v. Des Moines Independent Community School District, 393 U.S. 503, 89 S. Ct. 733, 21 L. Ed. 2d 721 (1969).

Vereb, R. L., & DiPerna, J. C. (2004). Teachers' knowledge of ADHD, treatment for ADHD, and treatment acceptability. An initial investigation. *School Psychology Review, 33*(3), 421–428.

Weinstein, C., Curran, M., & Tomlinson-Clarke, S. (2003). Culturally responsive classroom management: Awareness into action. *Theory into Practice, 42*(4), 269–276.

Weiss, B., Williams, J. H., Margen, S., Abrams, B., Citron, L. J., Cox, C., McKibben, J., & Ogar, D. (1980). Behavioral responses to artificial food colors. *Science, 207*(28), 1487–1488.

Wentzel, K. R. (2003). Motivating students to behave in socially competent ways. *Theory into Practice, 42*(4), 319–326.

Wheldall, K. (1991). Managing troublesome classroom behavior in regular schools: A positive teaching perspective. *International Journal of Disability, Development, and Education, 38*(2), 99–116.

Wilehs, T. E. (2002). *The stimulant medications for attention-deficit/hyperactivity disorder*. Washington, DC: National Association for Mental Illness.

Wilson, J. E., & Sherrets, S. D. (1979). A review of past and current pharmacological interventions in the treatment of emotionally disturbed children and adolescents. *Behavioral Disorders, 5*(1), 60–69.

Wolraich, M. L. (1996). Diet and behavior: What the research shows. *Contemporary Pediatrics, 13,* 19–29.

Wolraich, M. L., Wilson, D. B., & White, J. W. (1995). The effect of sugar on behavior or cognition in children: A meta-analysis. *Journal of the American Medical Association, 275,* 1617–1621.

Yell, M., Rosalzki, M. E., & Drasgow, E. (2001). Disciplining students with disabilities. *Focus on Exceptional Children, 33*(9), 1–20.

Yell, M. L. (1990). The use of corporal punishment, suspension, expulsion, and timeout with behaviorally disordered students in public schools: Legal considerations. *Behavioral Disorders, 15*(2), 100–109.

Ziont, P., & Fox, R. W. (1998). Facilitating group classroom meetings: Practical guidelines. *Beyond Behavior, 9*(2), 8–13.

CHAPTER OBJECTIVES

After completing this chapter, you will be able to:

1. Describe an integrative framework as a basis of working with parents and families.

2. Describe the benefits of parent and family involvement.

3. Implement an assessment strategy used to support parents in developing ways to change their child's behavior.

4. Implement parent and family collaboration activities involving communication and conferencing.

Working with Parents and Families

CHAPTER 11

KEY TERMS

Attitudes

Behavior

Conference

Daily Report Card

Expectation

Passport

Psychosituational assessment interview

Travel card

Mr. and Mrs. Mitchell arrived at Room 210 of Collinsdale Junior High School promptly at 7:30 p.m. They were to confer with Mr. Boyle, their 13-year-old daughter Eileen's homeroom teacher. This was the first time they had been summoned to conference because of one of their children.

Neither parent was anxious to visit with Mr. Boyle. Eileen's last report card contained two Fs, three Cs, and a B. Her conduct grades were at the bottom of the school's 5-point scale. In addition to the report card, the Mitchells had received a dozen or more negative notes from Eileen's teachers.

They had grounded, bribed, and reasoned with Eileen during the preceding 3 months without effect. The Mitchells realized that without cooperation from their daughter's teachers, they could not successfully help her.

There must be some strategies that would increase the consistency with which the home and school could improve Eileen's behavior and academic performance.

In a summary of selected research on parent involvement, Wherry (2003) cited over 50 studies demonstrating the benefits of parent involvement in the education of their children. The benefits noted ranged from higher grades and test scores to improved attendance, from improved academic performance to improved behavioral performance. Wherry also noted benefits to students, teachers, parents, schools, and community.

In this chapter we'll describe an integrative perspective on parents and families of children with challenging behaviors or disabilities. After discussions of the benefits of collaboration, strategies for engaging parents in supporting behavior change are described.

AN INTEGRATIVE PERSPECTIVE

Parenting any child isn't easy. When that child has behavioral problems or a disability, it is assumed that parents and family are under even greater stress (Helff & Glidden, 1998). The most common interpretation of the adaptation of families to their children with disabilities has been that of grieving through stages of shock, denial, bargaining, anger, and acceptance (Kroth & Otteni, 1985). Even though these stages were often described and were the basis of the way in which teachers and other professionals were prepared to work with parents, there is little empirical evidence that parents do indeed go through the stages of grief when their child is identified as having a disability (Allen & Affleck, 1985; Blacher, 1984).

All families go through a series of cycles. Lambie (2000) described this life cycle in terms of the birth or diagnosis of a child with a disability. These stages include the following:

- The "new couple" stage, during which the couple realigns relationships with friends and family members in view of new common goals.
- The "family with young children" stage, during which the couple moves from caring only for each other to realigning the marriage to care for a child or children. If a child has a disability, the couple faces the additional challenges of getting appropriate help and dealing with the rest of the family.
- The "families with school-age children" stage, during which typical families emphasize providing opportunities for the development of the child. If a child has a disability, the parents must become more actively involved and balance the needs of the family and the needs of their child.
- The "families with adolescents" stage, in which the couple begins to use their children's increased independence to refocus their own lives. When the couple has a child or children with disabilities, this period becomes more stressful as the family comes to grips with the child's limitations.
- The "families launching children" stage, during which the couple develops adult relationships with their children. Families may need to continue to care for or manage living arrangements and supervision for a child with a disability.
- The "families in later life" stage, during which the parents may need to seek new caregivers as they become unable to deal with a child with a disability.

On the whole, families of children with problems or disabilities strive toward normalization. Families can and do positively adapt. Lustig and Akey (1999) reported that social support, a sense of coherence, and family adaptability are important resources for family adaptation. Normalization is the most common adaptation for families of children with disabilities (Seligman & Darling, 1989). However, other adaptations may emerge. One alternative adaptation that Seligman and Darling describe is that of crusadership. Crusading parents engage in activities to increase public awareness or increase services for their child's disability. Another is altruism, in which families who have achieved normalization remain active on behalf of other families. Resignation may also take place, in which parents become resigned to being a "problem family" and become isolated.

This issue of the development of families with members with disabilities is also explored by Ulrich and Bauer (2003). In their description of developing awareness and the impact of transformational experiences, they described these phases in the development of families and parents of children with disabilities:

- *The Ostrich Phase*, in which the parent has little experience with disabilities. Parents may describe their children's problems as being a little slow, going through a phase, or being just like another family member who eventually was successful. This phase ends when the parent recognizes that the child does indeed have a problem.
- *The Special Designation Phase*, during which the parents recognize the existence of a problem and anticipate that a professional can fix it.
- *The Normalization Phase*, during which parents minimize the differences between the child and his or her peers; the child is perceived as a child first and a child with a problem second.
- *The Self-Actualization Phase*, during which the parents understand that the child needs supports and have ideas about how those supports can be provided.

Taunt and Hastings (2002) investigated the positive impact of children with developmental disabilities on their family. In that most studies dwell on the negative, Taunt and Hastings asked about the positive impact of the child on parents, siblings, and extended family. Parents noted a range of positive perceptions and experiences, including:

- positive aspects of the child, such as a happy disposition;
- a changed perspective on life, with new and more meaningful goals and a greater value on people;
- increased sensitivity, tolerance, and awareness;
- support from other families sharing the experience;
- opportunities to learn about disabilities, parenting, and education;
- greater cohesiveness in the family;
- expanded social networks with the opportunity to influence policy makers;
- increased confidence in dealing with others;
- strengthening of religious faith; and
- increased maturity in siblings.

These positive and developmental approaches to families with children with disabilities are representative of an integrative framework. This framework stresses the understanding of human development and behavior within the contexts of interactions in several settings (Bronfenbrenner, 1977). This approach invites consideration of the joint impact of two or more settings on one another. School and home jointly impact on children with behavior problems. The subsystems that are significant when working with children and their families include parent-child, parent-teacher-child, teacher-child, sibling-child, and sibling-parent-child (Shea & Bauer, 1987). Ecological considerations may include:

- nature and requirements of the parents' work;
- neighborhood, health, and community services;
- school and community relations;
- informal social networks;
- patterns of recreational and social life;
- family type (traditional or nuclear family, blended family, extended family, one-parent family);

- delegation of child care to others outside the home; and
- existence and character of explicit and implicit societal values with reference to parenting, children, disability, and behavior.

It is important to remember that although you may interact primarily with one parent—the mother, for example—other family members (father, grandmother, siblings) may have very different perceptions of the child, the behavior, or the disability. Pelchat, Levert, and Bourgeois-Guerin (2009) reported that though mothers and fathers were both working to increase the child's independence and learning, their strategies were quite different. Mothers associate helping the child toward independence by communication and relationships, striving to increase acceptance of the child. For fathers, developmental progress is key. Because of these different goals, mothers and fathers use different strategies when interacting with teachers. Mothers have more adaptive strategies, whereas fathers tend to want goals and plans.

BENEFITS OF PARENT INVOLVEMENT

Though there is a general acceptance that engaging parents and families in the education of their children is beneficial, Baker and Soden (2000) describe a lack of scientific rigor in studies of parent and family involvement. They noted that confusion exists regarding definitions, activities, goals, and proposed outcomes of parent involvement programs and policies. However, Hill and Taylor (2004) define parent involvement as the interactions between schools and parents that increases the opportunity for academic success.

An additional emphasis on parent involvement has emerged through school reform. Teachers and schools are evaluated on the ways in which they communicate with and engage parents. This communication may go beyond traditional invitations and may include ways to engage students in schooling and available health and social services (Seitsinger, Felner, Brand, & Burns, 2008).

Educators and parents must go beyond the notion of parents coming to school to support school activities (Hixson, 1996). However, this involvement can be a challenge. As the U.S. Department of Education (1994) suggests, the reality of families today is that parents and children spend less time together. There is a consistent struggle to balance the demands of family life and work. The Department of Education suggests that parents, as the child's first teacher, can engage in (a) scheduled and supervised daily homework, (b) reading together, (c) using television wisely, (d) maintaining contact with school, (e) offering praise and encouragement, and (f) talking to their teenagers. School should connect with parents, design homework to engage parents, and play a role in supporting children and families.

Henderson and Berla (1994) suggest that not only the student but also school and parents benefit from parent and family involvement. Students benefit through enhanced academic performance and test scores, better attendance, fewer placements in special education, positive attitudes and behavior, higher graduation rates, and increased enrollment in postsecondary education. Schools benefit through improved teacher morale, higher ratings of teachers by parents, more support from families, higher student achievement, and enhanced reputation in the community.

Henderson and Mapp (2002) provide detailed information related to the impact of parent and family involvement:

- In schools where teachers reported high levels of outreach to parents, test scores grew at a rate 40% greater than in schools with fewer reports of outreach.
- Students with involved parents are more likely to have higher grades and test scores, pass their classes, attend school regularly, demonstrate appropriate behavior, and graduate and go on to further education.
- Student achievement increases directly with the amount of parent involvement.
- The more families support their children's learning and educational progress, the more their children tend to do well in school throughout their school career.

ASSESSMENT STRATEGIES

When engaging parents specifically around behavior, teachers and professionals should start by gathering assessment information. Blackham and Silberman (1980) have suggested four methods for obtaining data on parent-child interactions and problem areas:

1. Direct observation of the child and other family members in the home
2. Direct observation of the child and other family members in the clinic or school setting
3. Parental observation of the child's interaction within the family at home and the reporting of the resultant data to the educator
4. A personal interview with the parents and child

As a result of the administrative organization of the school, the first two methods are generally not feasible—that is, the teacher is usually unable to observe parent-child interaction in either the home or the school. A possible exception may be in school- and home-based preschool programs. The third and fourth methods are most practical and can be implemented by means of the psychosituational assessment interview.

It is important to remember, however, that teachers are not counselors or therapists. The student is your focus. The purpose of assessment is not to identify parent needs but to find ways to help parents support the student's learning.

Psychosituational Assessment Interview

The **psychosituational assessment interview** is primarily an information-gathering technique. The interview focuses on obtaining from the parent or parents descriptive data about the child's behavior and the circumstances surrounding it.

The psychosituational interview technique was designed by Bersoff and Grieger (1971) and applied by Shea, Whiteside, Beetner, and Lindsey (1974). The purpose of the interview is to analyze the unacceptable behavior and uncover the antecedents and consequences that elicit, reinforce, and sustain it. This information about the child is obtained from the parent or parents and contributes to decisions concerning interventions to modify the behavior.

The interview can help determine the extent that the behavior is reinforced and maintained by the environment. In addition, the interview can help determine the extent to which the behavior may be modified by the manipulation of the environment. The primary aspects of the settings in which the behavior occurs are analyzed. These aspects include (a) the child's behavior, (b) the environmental variables surrounding the behavior, and (c) the attitudes and expectations of the parents.

Behavior refers to the actual behaviors for which the child was referred, including the antecedents and consequences of that behavior (teacher, parent, or peer actions and reactions). *Environments* and *situations* refer to the specific places and circumstances in which the behavior occurs, including the presence of significant others. **Attitudes** refers to the beliefs and feelings of the person referring the child.

A parent's concern about a child's behavior may be based on irrational ideas and attitudes that lead to unwarranted expectations, demands, and feelings, all of which may result in inappropriate actions toward the child as a consequence of exhibiting the behavior. **Expectation** has a dual meaning: It refers to the specific performance that the adult would like the child to achieve (short-term goals) and to the long-range aspirations that the adult has for the child.

The four major tasks to be accomplished during the interview are (a) defining the target behavior(s), (b) describing specific situations in which the behavior occurs, (c) uncovering the antecedents and consequences that seem to sustain the behavior, and (d) detecting any irrational ideas, if any, that make it difficult for the parent or parents to objectively understand, accept, and modify the behavior.

Defining the target behavior involves analyzing the frequency, intensity, and duration of the behavior. Obtaining information about the specific situations in which the behavior occurs helps the interviewer plan the intervention. By exploring the antecedents and consequences of the behavior the parent becomes aware of the role he or she plays in the behavior.

Finally, the interviewer must be aware of the parents' irrational and unrealistic ideas about the child. The parent may see the child as more competent than what is being seen at school. When the child's behavior at school is described, the parent may be offended, surprised, or doubtful. Parents may also have unreasonable expectations of the child. These ideas are usually expressed in "ought" and "should" terms. A parent may say, "He should be able to sit longer" or "He ought to know better." Parents may also feel anger, which may lead to guilt and anxiety on the part of the parents that may further interfere with parent-child interactions. A common unrealistic idea is that the child is choosing to behave as he is and should simply stop. The failure to accept things as they exist inhibits rational problem solving.

It is recommended that, if possible, both parents be present at the interview. A joint interview is desirable because differing perceptions and inconsistencies in parental behavior management strategies can be uncovered. It also allows the interviewer to gauge the amount and frequency of mutual support that the parents provide to each other.

The interview may be a single session or a series of sessions. If the interviewer is concerned primarily with obtaining data in an effort to design an intervention that includes parental participation, two or three sessions may be sufficient. However, frequently the strategy can be applied in an ongoing intervention program. To assist the parent, the interviewer may suggest that the parents gather behavioral data. A form for this purpose is presented in Figure 11.1, along with instructions for completing the form. The following are specific interviewer tasks:

1. Establish rapport with the parent or parents, by greeting them warmly and making them physically comfortable.

2. Have the parents specify the target behavior(s)—that is, the specific behavior(s)—that is disturbing to them. Explore the frequency, intensity, and duration of the behavior. Ask "What exactly does the child do that you find unacceptable or bothersome?" "In the course of an hour (day), how often does this happen?"

3. Have the parents delineate the specific situations and environments in which the behavior occurs. Establish where the behavior takes place and who is present when the behavior occurs.

4. Explore the contingencies that may stimulate and sustain the behavior. Determine what happens immediately before and after the behavior occurs—that is, the antecedents and consequences of the behavior. Ask what happens before, after, and during the behavior. What is the reaction of other nearby people to the behavior and the child?

5. Attempt to determine the ratio of positive-to-negative interactions between the child and the parents. Ask "Describe a situation when you and your child had a great time together." "What happens when the child accomplishes something or does a good job?" "What happens when the child doesn't act the way you wish?"

6. Explore the methods—positive and negative—the parents use for behavior control. Ask "How do you deal with the behavior?"

7. Determine to what degree the parents are aware of how praise or punishment is communicated and its effect on the child's behavior. Ask "Does the child know when you are angry?" "Does the child respond to body language indicating that you would like him to stop his current behavior?"

8. Explore the manner in which expectations and consequences are communicated by the parents to the child. Ask "Are there clear rules that you expect the child to follow?" "What are some of these rules?" "Does the child know what he or she is expected to do?"

9. Detect irrational and unrealistic ideas that make it difficult for the parents to understand, accept, or modify the child's behavior. Be alert for and explore irrational ideas that may be expressed by the parents. Restate irrational ideas but avoid reinforcing them.

10. Conclude the session by restating the unacceptable behavior and presenting the desirable behavior. You may suggest that the parents keep a log of the child's behavior. (Refer to Figure 11.1.) Explain to the parents how the log should be used. You may suggest one or two techniques for changing the behavior and make arrangements for a subsequent meeting.

A positive way in which to engage parents is the family assessment portfolio (Thompson, Meadan, Fansler, Alber, & Balough, 2007). This portfolio is essentially a scrapbook that focuses on the child and his or her family. Thompson et al. urge parents to help the child with the portfolio, keeping the text in the child's voice. Though they suggest developing a DVD, this may be beyond the technology available to many families. A simple scrapbook or even a fill-in-the-blank packet can provide you with information such as (a) the people with whom the child lives (b) extended family, friends, or community members, (c) any health issues that may have an impact on behavior, (d) the child's strengths and areas for growth, and (e) how the child interacts with the adults and children around him. The scrapbook should end with setting the stage for further communication. Through this portfolio, parents and child can provide critical information to the teacher about the student.

Behavior Log Form

Target behavior _____

Child _____

Observer _____

Date (2)	Time		Antecedents (4)	Consequences (5)	Applied Interventions (6)	Comments (7)
	Begins (3)	Ends (3)				

INSTRUCTIONS

(1) Complete the top portion of the form, that is, the behavior to be observed, the child's name, and the observer's name.

(2) Write *day* and *date* of the first time the behavior occurred in first column: for example, M/8/3 or Th/11/13.

(3) Upon each occurrence of the behavior, write the time it begins and ends in the second and third columns, respectively. If the behavior is very short, write the time of the occurrence in the second column.

(4) Upon each occurrence of the behavior, write what happened immediately *before* the behavior (antecedents) in the fourth column.

(5) Upon each occurence of the target behavior, write what happened immediately *after* the behavior (consequences) in the fifth column.

(6) In column 6, write what you or another person interacting with or supervising the child did to either *encourage* or *discourage* the behavior. If there was no reaction to the behavior, it should be noted in this column.

(7) In column 7, write any comments you have regarding the occurrence of the behavior that is out of the ordinary. For example, child was tired, grandmother was visiting, bad day in school, marital conflict occurring, and so on.

FIGURE 11.1 Parents' behavior log for home use

IMPLEMENTING PARENT AND FAMILY COLLABORATION ACTIVITIES

In a study of parents' interests and concerns regarding collaboration, Lord Nelson, Summers, and Turnbull (2004) identified three themes of (a) accessibility and availability, (b) breadth of responsibility, and (c) dual relationships. In terms of accessibility and availability, parents wanted professionals to be flexible about the times they are available. In terms of breadth of responsibility, parents preferred professionals who were willing to take action above and beyond their specific duties. Parents agreed with the importance of going beyond the job. In the theme of dual relationships, parents and professionals described a closeness-distance continuum. Some relationships seem to be qualitatively different from the strict parent-professional relationship. They may even include forming a relationship over time long after the professional is no longer responsible for providing services to the parent and child.

Communication is key for all parent and family collaboration activities. Dardig (2005) contends that teachers should begin with a letter or phone call describing you're their understanding that parents are key to their students learning. A personal statement about their philosophy of parent and family involvement, supported through an open, friendly interaction, may break down boundaries with parents who are hesitant to become involved. An e-mail for families with computer access and who frequently use e-mail may be an easy way to reach parents. Even though it may appear unusual with the boom in electronic communication, not all parents use e-mail consistently (or at all); communication provided this way cannot be assumed to reach all parents.

When implementing parent-school collaboration activities, Smrekar and Cohen-Vogel (2001) reported that in contrast to teachers' perceptions, limited parent involvement was not reflected in the parents' interest in the child. Rather, parent involvement of low-income, minority group parents was related to available time, distance or transportation, and child care obligations. Matuszny, Banda, and Coleman (2007) suggest that the teacher should begin the year with an off-campus social event that reflects parent/family culture and respect for social beliefs. Ongoing communication is essential, maintained through phone calls and notes, celebrating positive events. A phone call at the end of the year can help teachers identify what worked and what would increase parent participation.

Engaging parents in urban schools with high populations of students from various cultural, ethnic, and linguistic groups may pose a particular challenge to teachers. Barton, Drake, St. Louis, and George (2004) suggest that in working in high-poverty urban communities, it is important that parents understand the how and why of parent involvement. They contend that teachers must identify urban, culturally diverse, and high-poverty parents, and it is important to identify parents' belief in school involvement. Mutual understanding with parents about negotiating the how and what of parent involvement should be negotiated in order to build parent-teacher relationships.

Benson and Martin (2003) suggest that with the use of seven specific strategies ordinary parent involvement activities can become extraordinarily successful:

1. Focus on the student's success and achievement, drawing on student academic and extracurricular skills to bring parents into the school. Once the parents are in the school other participation can be encouraged.
2. Send personal invitations to events using the correct parent name. Students may write out invitations. A variety of strategies may be used, including mailing invitations, having parents call other parents, sending notices home with students, and such.
3. Involve the extended family to support students, making sure they feel welcome in the school and are invited to celebrate student achievements.
4. Extend frequent invitations to parents for a variety of purposes, such as awarding certificates, organizing events, making invitations, or making phone calls.
5. Use school staff and parent volunteers creatively.

6. Coordinate planning with principals, teachers, aides, parents, students, and community members. To gain support, involve the stakeholders.

7. Pay attention to the small things, such as providing refreshments, using name tags, reimbursing parents for baby sitting, planning events at different times and days, and recognizing parents and staff for their efforts.

Benson and Martin (2003) describe several activities that have been successfully implemented. These activities are provided in Table 11.1.

Darch, Miao, and Shippen (2004) also discuss bringing the parents to the school for positive activities. They describe being proactive and having a yearlong plan. They suggest that clear goals and accommodations for diverse families are essential for strong parent engagement. They suggest a four-phase plan for parent engagement and involvement:

Phase 1:   Prepare by having a positive, proactive philosophy. Conduct a parent interest survey. Use a parent conference planning form.

Phase 2:   Establish parent involvement during the fall months. Assess family needs. Make initial phone contacts with parents. Develop individualized plans and conduct face-to-face meetings.

Phase 3:   Maintain involvement during the winter months. Make periodic phone calls. Use videotapes to introduce yourself or to document positive aspects of the child. Send notes home to parents.

TABLE 11.1   Successful Parent-School Involvement Activities Identified by Benson & Martin (2003) and Dardig (2005).

Parent visitation days, in which parents can observe in the classroom

Parent volunteer programs in which parents can work in the classroom, manage class parties, or make instructional activities

Classroom newsletter

Special events such as ice cream socials, Grandparents or Special Friend Day, fashion shows, parent-child events, cookouts, field days, talent shows, award assemblies

Curriculum fairs to view work and materials

Parents' Computer Day, in which students become their parents' teachers

Coffee with the principal

Parent education workshops

Information days about summer programs

School homework programs

Written communication, such as supplemental reports, happygrams, special certificates, or newsletters

Lending library of parent instructional materials

"Who to call for what" information sheet

Young authors' day

International fair

Read-a-thon or math-a-thon

School committees

Home phone calls

Phase 4:   Help parents plan for the upcoming year. Discuss academic and behavioral requirements of the next grade or school. Identify ways to help the child during the summer. Suggest ways parents can be involved the next year.

Whatever the model, parent communication is key. Several strategies are available to increase communication.

Passport

Courson and Hay (1996) and Schmalz (1987) recommended a home-school notebook for parents and teachers who wished to communicate daily on the behavior of the student in both home and school. The **passport** (Runge, Walker, & Shea, 1975) is an effective technique for increasing and maintaining parent-teacher communication and cooperation.

The passport is an ordinary spiral notebook that the child carries daily to and from home and to and from the classrooms in which the child is instructed. The passport is a medium for communication among parents, special teachers, regular teachers, paraprofessionals, bus drivers, and others concerned with the child's behavior change or academic remediation program. All concerned adults are encouraged to make notations in the notebook.

Before the actual initiation of the program, the passport procedures are explained to the child, who is told that he or she will be rewarded for carrying the notebook and presenting it to the appropriate adults. The child is rewarded with points for carrying the passport and for appropriate efforts, accomplishments, and behavior in the home, in the classroom, on the bus, in the gym, and so on. Points may be awarded at home for appropriate behavior and home-study activities. If the child forgets or refuses to carry the passport, he or she cannot earn points. At the appropriate time, the accumulated points are exchanged for tangible as well as social rewards. Most elementary school students respond enthusiastically to carrying the passport, receiving points and awards, and reading the positive comments adults have written about their behavior and achievement.

Parents are introduced to the passport concept and procedures at an individual or group conference. At this meeting, the method is explained and discussed. Parents' questions and concerns must be appropriately responded to by the teacher. At this session, instructions are given for making notations in the passport. Similar meetings or informal discussions should be held with other adults who will be using the passport, such as classroom teachers, special teachers, administrators, bus drivers, and so on.

The guidelines for writing comments in the passport are as follows:

1. Be brief. (Parents are busy, too.)
2. Be positive. (Parents know their child has problems. They do not need to be reinforced.)
3. Be honest. (Don't say a child is doing fine if he is not. However, rather than writing negative notes, write neutral ones or request a parent visit, telephone call, or e-mail)
4. Be responsive. (If a parent asks for help, respond immediately.)
5. Be informal. (You are a professional, but parents are still your equal.)
6. Be consistent. (If you use the passport, do so consistently and expect the same from parents.)
7. Avoid jargon.
8. If you are having a bad day, do not project your feelings on the child or parents.

Points are given to the child on the basis of a mutually agreed-on schedule and rate. A comment may be as simple as "Great day today!" or "Ask Raj to show you his math paper." Parents may reply as candidly as they wish, with comments ranging from "No time for breakfast today—may be hungry before lunch" or "Grandma's visiting—may be tired and distracted" or "Alice, Brianna's cat died last night. She may need time to process."

Daily Report Card

The Teacher-Parent Communication Program (TPCP), a **daily report card** system, was developed by Dickerson, Spellman, Larsen, and Tyler (1973). This cooperative parent-teacher communication system is designed to help children improve their in-school academic performance and social behavior in exchange for rewards at home. Although Dickerson and others do not view the program as a "cure-all," it was reported by teachers who used it as effective in modifying social behavior and academic performance. The TPCP centers around report cards issued by the teacher to the child periodically throughout the school day. The completed cards are taken home at the end of the school day. On the basis of the information on the cards, the parents either reward or do not reward the child's performance. The cards have a space for the teacher's evaluation of the child's academic performance and social behavior. The teacher may make notations on the back of the card if desired. Dickerson et al. recommend that the teacher's notations be neutral or positive. The cards are dated and signed by the teacher. A simplified version of the card is presented in Figure 11.2.

Although not included on the TPCP card, it may be helpful if the card provides space for the parent's signature and notations. The card could be returned to the teacher on the following school day by the child. Such a procedure would ensure that the parents received the card, that the child was rewarded, and that both parents and teacher were attending to the appropriate objectives.

The TPCP is initiated by the teacher, who solicits the parents' cooperation and participation. During an orientation conference, the teacher explains the program to the parents and requests their participation. The purpose and benefits of the TPCP for the child are discussed. The teacher outlines the duties and responsibilities of the child, parent, and teacher. After the parents and teacher agree to implement the TPCP, the teacher informs the child and makes him or her aware of the parents' participation. The child is given instructions concerning the purpose, objectives, and functioning of the system. The child is encouraged to participate in the process of determining his or her initial acceptable performance level and rewards.

The designers of the TPCP recommend that the daily report card system remain in force as long as the child needs it. However, after several weeks of acceptable performance by the child, the teacher, in cooperation with the parents, should begin to phase out the TPCP. Presumably, the rewards for a high level of academic performance and social behavior that naturally occur will maintain the behavior.

Travel Card

Carpenter (2001) discusses the use of travel cards to facilitate productive behaviors of students with disabilities in the general education setting, teacher collaboration, and home-school communication. The card strategy is implemented to help students with

Composite Academic Performance and Personal-Social Behavior Report

DAILY REPORT CHECKLIST

Child's Name _____

	Reading		Spelling		Arithmetic		Health		Social Studies		PE		Initials	
	Acad	Beh	Acad	Beh	Acad	Beh	Acad	Beh	Acad	Beh	Acad	Beh	Parent	Teacher
M														
T														
W														
Th														
F														
M														
T														
W														
Th														
F														
M														
T														
W														
Th														
F														

FIGURE 11.2 Simplified daily report card

disabilities overcome common barriers to successful and meaningful participation in the general education curriculum. Among the behaviors targeted are those of memory, attention, self-regulation, academic achievement, social behavior, motivation, discrimination, and generalization.

A **travel card** is carried by the student throughout the school day as he or she moves from class to class. Each student's card is based on his or her needs and allows the student to earn points for social, token, and activity reinforcers. The card includes the student's name, date, listing of classes or activities, and objectives. The card has a space for each teacher's initials to note the student's performance during the class or activity and a comment on the student's behavior.

The card encourages collaboration among special education teacher, general education teacher, and parents. The special educator is responsible for assessing the student's behaviors and developing the card as well as instructing everyone in the use of the card. The student is responsible for carrying the card throughout the school day and presenting it to each teacher. The student then tallies the points earned for the day and discusses the results with the special education teacher. On the final day of the school week, the student selects his or her "best" card of the previous week to be included in his or her portfolio. Other cards are sent home to the family.

Travel cards offer immediate feedback to students and provide daily communication to the parents as well. Carpenter (2001) reported generalization of appropriate behaviors through participation.

Parent Conferences

The parent **conference** has long been used to share information and to develop strategies on behalf of children with disabilities. Open, ongoing communication, such as the passports or travel cards, can prevent the information discussed during a conference from being a surprise. Planning the conference is essential and may involve contacting the parent before the conferences and asking questions such as the following:

- What school activities or classes does your child discuss the most?
- What seems to be his or her favorite part of school?
- Does your child talk about friends?
- What kind of help do you provide regarding homework?
- What is your child's greatest strength?
- What is your greatest concern about your child?

Even though conferences about behavioral issues may be stressful, Perl (1995) suggested that the teacher view these conferences as a way to improve relationships. The teacher should communicate genuine caring. Teachers should try to attend to parents' words, body language, and feelings, trying to understand their point of view. Perl urges teachers to assume that all parents have strengths and the capacity to work collaboratively to solve problems.

Potter and Bulach (2001) offer additional suggestions for parent conferences. An important point is to be honest about the child's behavior and to bring any relevant data and documentation to the conference. Any action plan should involve the parents, and parents' input on solutions should be sought. The most important concerns should be addressed, and an effort should be made to continually refocus the meeting. In conversation about their children, one story may lead to another. Bringing the parent back to the point should be a gentle cue. An important aspect of any conference is follow-up, which should be in writing. This follow-up note should both thank the parent for attending and restate the plan. Potter and Bulach also suggest initiating a phone call a week or two after the conference.

In structuring parent-teacher conferences, Epstein and Sherman (2006) argue that teachers should recognize that the basis of this communication is equity: Parents and teachers have equal voices in identifying strengths and needs of students. Equity can be communicated several ways. The teacher may present an agenda to the parent and ask him or her if he or she would like to add anything else. The teacher may take notes of the parents' comments and provide a synopsis to the parent. Epstein and Sherman urge teachers to clearly consider parents' suggestions and comments.

The setting of the conference should be carefully considered. Barton et al. (2004) contend that "place" is especially important in high-poverty areas. Parents may not be comfortable in the school due to their own experiences or their child's perceptions. The school may not be accessible to parents of students who use public or district transportation. Home visits also may be uncomfortable due to the safety of the setting or the parents' wariness about having a teacher in their home. Barton et al. suggest a community-based site that is easily accessible and comfortable for the parent. The public library near the home or a community center are "friendlier" sites.

A significant challenge to parents occurs as students reach adulthood. Lee, Palmer, Turnbull, and Wehmeyer (2006) suggest that they may need structures and supports as they work toward their child's self-determination. Parents who have been actively involved may need information about letting go and the concept of self-determination itself. Parents may struggle with allowing their child to make choices that may not be as successful as the solutions parents may choose. Parents who have been developing goals and plans for their child may need support in backing up to let the student develop plans and learn the consequences of his or her decisions.

Summary Points

- Parent involvement has been demonstrated to be related to higher grades and test scores, improved academic performance, increased teacher morale, and enhanced reputation of the school in the community.
- Families follow developmental cycles, and the challenges of parenting a child with a behavior problem or disability change with each cycle.
- Though parents of children with behavior problems or disabilities were originally thought to progress through stages of grieving, an integrated approach suggests that changes occur with the life cycle of the family, the age of the child, and the family's growing information about the disability.
- On the whole, families of children with behavior problems or disabilities move toward normalization.

- The psychosituational interview allows for the identification of antecedents and consequences that may be maintaining the behavior. Once these are identified, appropriate interventions may be developed.
- Parents are concerned that professionals are accessible and available, take responsibility beyond their "job," and have relationships that extend beyond the "job."
- Limited parent involvement may be more related to available time, distance, transportation, and child care needs than to the level of concern felt by a parent.
- Daily parent communication may be enhanced through the passport, daily report cards, or travel cards.
- Parent conferences are useful in sharing mutual information as well as assisting parents in managing their child.

Projects

1. Write the agenda for a parent conference. Identify what evidence you would share and when.
2. Develop a daily report card for your classroom or a classroom with which you are familiar. In addition, write the letter to parents that would initiate the use of the card.

Web Resources

For more information about involving parents, check out these resources:

The Beach Center for Disability
www.beachcenter.org

The Pacer Center
www.pacer.org

North Central Regional Education Laboratory (NCREL)
www.ncrel.org/sdrs/areas/issues/envrnmnt/famncomm/pa100.ht

References

Allen, D. A., & Affleck, G. (1985). Are we stereotyping parents? A postscript to Blacher. *Mental Retardation, 23,* 200–202.

Baker, A. J. L., & Soden, L. M. (2000). *The challenge of parent involvement research.* ERIC/CUE, 134.

Barton, A. C., Drake, J. G., St. Louis, K., & George, M. (2004). Ecologies of parental engagement in urban education. *Educational Researcher, 33*(4), 3–12.

Benson, F. & Martin, S. (2003). Organizing successful parent involvement in urban schools. *Child Study Journal, 33*(3), 187–193.

Bersoff, D. N., & Grieger, R. M., II (1971). An interview model for the psychosituational assessment of children's behavior. *American Journal of Orthopsychiatry, 41*(3), 483–493.

Blacher, J. (1984) Sequential stages of parental adjustment to the birth of a child with bandages: Fact or artifact? *Mental Retardation, 22*(2) 55–68.

Blackham, G. J., & Silberman, A. (1980). *Modification of child and adolescent behavior.* Belmont, CA: Wadsworth.

Bronfenbrenner, U. (1977). Toward an experimental ecology of human development. *American Psychologist, 32,* 513–531.

Carpenter, L. B. (2001). Utilizing travel cards to increase productive student behavior, teacher collaboration, and parent-school communication. *Education and Training in Mental Retardation and Developmental Disabilities, 36*(3), 318–322.

Courson, F. H., & Hay, G. H. (1996). Parents as partners. *Beyond Behavior, 7*(3), 19–23.

Darch, C., Miao, Y., & Shippen, P. (2004). A model for involving parents of children with learning and behavior problems in the schools. *Preventing School Failure, 48*(3), 24–36.

Dardig, J. C. (2005). The *McClure Monthly Magazine* and 14 more practical ways to involve parents. *Teaching Exceptional Children, 38*(2), 46–51.

Dickerson, D., Spellman, C. R., Larsen, S., & Tyler, L. (1973). Let the cards do the talking: A teacher-parent communication program. *Teaching Exceptional Children, 4*(4), 170–178.

Epstein, J. L., & Sherman, S. D. (2006). Ideas for research on school, family, and community partnerships. In C. F. Conrad & R. Serlin (Eds.), *SAGE handbook for research in education* (pp. 117–138). Thousand Oaks, CA: Sage.

Helff, C. M., & Glidden, M. L. (1998). More positive or less negative? Trends in research on adjustment of families rearing children with developmental disabilities. *Mental Retardation, 36*(6), 457–464.

Henderson, A., & Berla, W. (1994). *A new generation of evidence: The family is crucial to student achievement.* Austin, TX: Southwest Educational Development Laboratory.

Henderson, A., & Mapp, K. (2002). *A new wave of evidence: The impact of school, family, and community connection on student achievement.* Austin, TX: Southwest Educational Development Laboratory.

Hill, N. E., & Taylor, L. C. (2004). Parental school involvement and children's academic achievement: Pragmatics and issues. *Current Directions in Psychological Science, 13,* 161–164.

Hixson, J. (1996). Families and school together. *Rural Audio Journal, 3*(3).

Kroth, R. L., & Otteni, H. (1985). *Communicating with parents of exceptional children: Improving parent-teacher relationships* (2nd ed.) Denver:, CO Love.

Lambie. R. (2000). *Family systems within educational contexts.* Denver, CO: Love.

Lee, S, Palmer, S. B., Turnbull, A. P., & Wehmeyer, M. L. (2006). A model for parent-teacher collaboration to promote self-determination in young children with disabilities. *Teaching Exceptional Children, 38*(3), 36–41.

Lord Nelson, L. G., Summers, J. A., & Turnbull, A. P. (2004). Boundaries in family-professional relationships: Implications for special education. *Remedial and Special Education, 25*(3), 153–165.

Lustig, D. C., & Akey, T. (1999). Adaptation in families with adult children with mental retardation: Impact of family strengths and appraisal. *Education and Training in Mental Retardation and Development Disabilities, 34*(3), 260–270.

Matuszny, R., Banda, D. R., & Coleman, T. J. (2007). A progressive plan for building collaborative relationships with parents from diverse backgrounds. *Teaching Exceptional Children, 39*(4), 24–31.

Pelchat, D., Levert, M., & Bourgeois-Guerin, V. (2009). How do mothers and fathers who have a child with a disability describe their adaptation process? *Journal of Child Health Care, 13,* 239–259.

Perl, J. (1995). Improving relationship skills for parent conferences. *Teaching Exceptional Children, 28*(1), 29–31.

Potter, L. & Bulach, C. (2001). Do's and don'ts of parent conferences. *The Education Digest, 66*(9), 37–40.

Runge, A., Walker, J., & Shea, T. M. (1975). A passport to positive parent-teacher communications. *Teaching Exceptional Children, 7*(3), 91–92.

Schmalz, N. (1987). Home-school notebook: How to find out what your child did all day. *The Exceptional Parent, 17*(6), 18–19, 21–22.

Seitsinger, A., Felner, R., Brand, S., & Burns, B. (2008). A large scale examination of the nature and efficacy of teacher practices to engage parents. *Journal of School Psychology, 46*(4), 477–505.

Seligman, M., & Darling, L. B. (1989). *Ordinary families, special children.* New York: Guilford Press.

Shea, T. M., & Bauer, A. M. (1987). *Teaching children and youth with behavior disorders* (2nd ed.). Upper Saddle River, NJ: Merrill/Pearson.

Shea, T. M., Whiteside, W. R., Beetner, E. G., & Lindsey, D. L. (1974). *Microteaching module: Psychosituational interview.* Edwardsville: Southern Illinois University Press.

Smrekar, C., & Cohen-Vogel, L. (2001). The voices of parents: Rethinking the intersection of family and school. *Peabody Journal of Education, 76*(2), 75–100.

Taunt, H. M., & Hastings, R. P. (2002). Positive impact of children with developmental disabilities and their families: A preliminary study. *Education and Training in Mental Retardation, 37*(4), 410–420.

Thompson, J. R., Meadan, H., Fansler, K. W., Alber, S. B., & Balough, P. A. (2007). Family assessment portfolios. *Teaching Exceptional Children, 39*(6), 19–25.

Ulrich, M. E., & Bauer, A. M. (2003). Levels of awareness: A closer look at communication between parents and professionals. *Teaching Exceptional Children, 35*(6), 20–24.

U.S. Department of Education (1994). *Connecting families and schools to help our children succeed.* Press Release retrieved January 1, 2005 from ed.gov/?PressRelease/o1-1994/parent.html.

Wherry, J. H. (2003). *Selected parent involvement research.* The Parent Institute, Fairfax Station, VA.

CHAPTER OBJECTIVES

After completing this chapter, you will be able to do the following:

1. Describe the role of an integrative framework in developing proactive social behaviors and a positive classroom climate.

2. Describe recent legal issues related to managing behavior in schools.

3. Discuss the potential impact of students from diverse ethnic, cultural, and linguistic groups on behavior management.

4. Discuss the potential impact of students at risk for behavior problems.

5. Recognize strategies to limit bullying in schools.

6. Explain behavior management as prevention.

Issues and Concerns in Behavior Management

KEY TERMS

Bullying

Cyberbullying

Mr. Ledger is the teacher of 26 inner-city, streetwise 10th-grade adolescents. He is having little success teaching the subjects (consumer education and practical mathematics) outlined on the city curriculum guide for the 10th grade. In his opinion, very little, if any, formal learning takes place in his classroom. Each school day is filled with verbal and physical aggression among the students. Mr. Ledger is in constant fear for his physical safety. He is anxious throughout the day and emotionally fatigued when he arrives home in the evening.

Although he dislikes his present work assignment, he enjoys teaching. However, he has contemplated leaving the profession for employment in business. Mr. Ledger is desperate for some way to manage his classroom.

As usual on Friday after school, Mr. Ledger joins a group of other teachers for a little relaxation and libation at Archie's Place before going home. The conversation turns to behavior problems and behavior management. Several of Mr. Ledger's veteran colleagues offer a variety of interventions they apply with success.

Ms. Weeping relates, "I scream at them. I can outshout them. If all else fails, I cry."

Mr. Scrooge comments, "Why bother? You can't teach them anything anyway. I'm just sitting on the lid of the dumpster."

Ms. Dupuis suggests, "Just use the discipline code. They're out of my room and in the principal's office."

Ms. Fox states, "I don't fool with them. It's in the door—shut up—get to work—and out the door. No discussion, no questions, no group work, and no jokes—no nothing."

As Mr. Ledger sat in the subway on his way home, he reviewed his colleagues' suggestions. Which, if any, should he use with his students? How to decide?

Ms. Jan was employed as a teacher in a private facility of elementary school-age children with severe emotional/behavioral disorders. Although she enjoyed her work and believed she was an effective teacher, she was concerned about one of the interventions her supervisors ordered her to implement. Although they had discussed the intervention and Ms. Jan's professional reasons for viewing it as inappropriate and unethical, the supervisor remained adamant about its use.

The intervention was extinction—ignoring the head-slapping behavior of Tyrone. Tyrone slapped the sides of his head on an average of 61 times an hour during the school day. He slapped himself with such force that the hair on the side of his head had been pulled out and his temples were swollen and severely bruised.

Ms. Jan recognized that she must do something. But what? She needed her job, and she needed a positive recommendation from her supervisor if she was going to be considered for her annual pay raise.

Many issues have an impact on behavior management. In this chapter, we explore a few. In the first section of the chapter, the practitioner is urged to apply an integrative framework or perspective of behavior management rather than strategies based in a single theoretical perspective. Homework is used as an example of the linkages between developmental contexts and the need for collaboration. In addition, dealing with aggressive and resistant students is discussed. Issues specific to diversity and behavior management are explored. The chapter concludes with discussions of intervening on bullying and behavior management as prevention.

INTEGRATIVE FRAMEWORK AND BEHAVIOR MANAGEMENT

The integrative framework, introduced in Chapter 2, offers the teacher a way to organize existing perspectives of human behavior, its etiology, and its management for implementation in the classroom and school. The integrative perspective is an ecological model that stresses that the understanding of human development and behavior requires examination of the ecological contexts (see Figure 2.1) in which the individual is functioning and is an inseparable part.

According to Jones (1986), the use of behavior management interventions tends to be recursive. In the 1940s and 1950s, classroom management interventions from the biophysical perspective were dominant. Intervention emphasized the reduction of extraneous environmental stimuli, routine, drill, and the careful sequencing of instruction. In the 1960s, the psychoeducational perspective dominated behavior management. Emphasis was on counseling, individualized interventions, inferring the reasons for behavior, and positive and productive interpersonal relations. This period was followed by a behavior management perspective that emphasized behavioral and learning theory. During this period, emphasis was placed on precise behavioral and instructional objectives and persistent and consistent intervention in students' observable behaviors. Organization and management skills and individual and group reinforcement of appropriate behavior were emphasized.

With the application of the ecological framework, the movement is from the traditional emphasis on a single approach for the management of behavior to an integration of the biophysical, psychoeducational, and behavioral perspectives. In the ecological perspective, learning principles are applied (behavioral), with consideration of inter-personal relationships (psychoeducational) and with recognition of the impact of neu-rological and physical factors (biophysical) on children's behavior (Shea & Bauer, 1994). According to Bauer and Sapona (1991), the role of the teacher in behavior management is to facilitate the development of each student rather than simply to intervene in inap-propriate behavior.

Richardson, Shockley, Riley, Fajen, and Turvey (2008) describe theoretical princi-ples that provide addition background to the integrated way of looking at behavior:

- In analyzing behavior, you must look at the interactions between the organism and the environment—they cannot be separated.
- Your analysis must include the aspects of the environment that are relevant to and acted on by the student.
- Perceiving and acting are an ongoing process—rather than a linear process, there is a transaction between the individual and the environment, with one being con-tinuously changed by the other.
- Understanding a behavior is specific to each individual and his or her environment.
- "Knowing" something is a combination of what the individual sees and interprets.

To effectively use the ecological perspective of behavior management suggested in this text, "teachers, then, must relate to students as capable persons, able to make choices and manage their own behavior. More specifically, they must trust in their students' abilities" (Shea & Bauer, 1994, p. 45). We must trust that students are making what they see as the best choice in their behavior. In addition, rather than having a set intervention for a certain behavior, "It all depends." What works for one student may be completely ineffective for another.

EDUCATIONAL ISSUES THAT IMPACT ON BEHAVIOR MANAGEMENT

In the following section, issues that impact on behavior management are discussed. The discussion begins with emerging legal policies dedicated to secluding and re-straining students. The section continues with discussions of homework (a perennial issue for parents, students, and teachers) and working with students who are aggres-sive or resistant.

Secluding and Restraining Students

The practice of secluding and restraining students has long been controversial. In the last 10 years, however, concern over the use of these restrictive efforts have gained national attention and been addressed through both law and the courts. The Children's Health Act (2000) provided restrictions on the use of restraints and seclusion in any health care facility. Restraints or inclusion are only allowed in health facilities to (a) ensure the physical safety of the resident, staff members, or others, and (b) fulfill the written order of a physician or licensed medical practitioner, with duration and circumstances clearly delineated.

The Individuals with Disabilities Education Act (IDEA) regulations (discussed in Chapter 1) state that when a student with a disability demonstrates behavior that inter-feres with his or her learning or that of others, positive behavioral interventions and other supports to address the behavior must be in place. However, IDEA does not go so far as to put restrictions on other interventions. The U.S. Department of Education (2010) has begun to explore concerns about seclusion and restraint. States and territories have been asked (the strongest action the secretary of education may take) to develop or review and, if appropriate, revise their state policies and guidelines to ensure that every student is protected from unnecessary or inappropriate restraint or seclusion. States have been urged to communicate these guidelines so that administrators, teachers, and parents understand and consent to the few circumstances under which restraint and seclusion may be used, ensuring parent notification, and provided accountability for use of these strategies.

The General Accounting Office (GAO, 2008), in a study of current use of restraint and seclusion, found no federal laws restricting their use in public and private schools and a wide range of rules at the state level. The GAO reported hundreds of cases of abuse and death related to the use of these methods on schoolchildren over the previous 20 years. The report provides examples of a 7-year-old purportedly dying after being held face down for hours by school staff, 5-year-olds allegedly being tied to chairs with bungee cords and duct tape by their teacher and suffering broken arms and bloody noses, and a 13-year-old reportedly hanging himself in a seclusion room after prolonged confinement. The report included descriptions of 10 restraint and seclusion cases in which a criminal conviction, a finding of civil or administrative liability, or a large financial settlement resulted. The cases followed the patterns of (a) children with disabilities being restrained and secluded, often in cases where they were not physically aggressive and their parents did not give consent, (b) deadly restraints blocking air to the lungs, and (c) teachers and staff being untrained on the use of seclusions and restraints. In half of these criminal cases, the teachers or paraprofessionals continued to be employed.

In March, 2010, the Keeping All Students Safe Act(2010) was passed by the U.S. House of Representatives. This legislation directed the Secretary of Education to establish standards that:

- prohibit all school personnel from managing any student by using any mechanical or chemical restraint, physical restraint or handling that restricts breathing, or aversive behavioral intervention that may affect student health and safety;
- prohibit the use of physical restraint or seclusion, unless danger of physical injury to the student or others is imminent;
- require states to ensure that all school personnel receive state-approved crisis intervention training and certification in first aid and safe student management techniques;
- prohibit physical restraint or seclusion from being written into a student's education plan or individual education program as a planned intervention; and
- require schools to establish procedures to notify parents in a timely manner if physical restraint or seclusion is imposed on their child.

Most teachers have never used seclusion or restraint, nor have they even seen it used. In a survey of parents of students with severe disabilities, Trader (2010) received 1,300 responses in 2 weeks. The results were alarming, with 64.7% of the parents indicating that their children had been restrained, had been secluded, or had received aversive interventions. Restraints that the parents reported included strapping the child to a chair, using basket holds, using four-point holds (one adult holding each limb), twisting the arm behind the back (one case of which resulted in a broken arm), turning off a student's electric wheelchair to prevent movement, and using handcuffs and various other physical holds. The most common person involved in the procedures was a paraprofessional rather than a teacher, and most events occurred in a self-contained special education classroom. More than half of the parents said their child had been in seclusion between 30 minutes and 3 hours. Even though this is a survey and could be subject to problems of research methodology, these responses are frightening. Trader argues strict controls should be placed on the use of seclusion and restraint, and clear documentation must take place whenever used.

Homework

Sheridan (2009) suggests that at its best homework can help students develop study habits and skills, planning, and time management. At its worse, however, she admits that it can "wreak havoc" in the lives of children and families. One of the primary issues with homework, however, is that it occurs in settings beyond the control of the teacher. The process of homework is complex because it begins at school, transitions to home, involves caregivers, and then ends up back at school (Power, 2009).

Homework has historically been one of the most discussed topics in American schools (Gill & Schlossman, 2003). The most frequent discussions of homework, Gill and Schlossman report, is the amount of time to be given at different grade levels. Homework can become a problem when it is too long or difficult, communication between teachers and students is unclear, and students do not remember or record their assignments. In addition, homework can be problematic when there is a lack of collaboration between home and school, parent-student conflict occurs, homework is unsupervised, families and students are disorganized, or there is little feedback or few contingencies related to the homework (Power, 2009).

However, Hollen, Lovelace, and Callender (2001) contend that homework, when graded, amounts to the most unfair practice that can be used to assess student progress in school. There is also an unequal opportunity for students to complete work at home due to varying resources in families. Homework may also add to the stress level many families already confront. If homework is to be assigned, Feldman (2004) suggests:

- assign homework regularly so students are in the habit of doing homework;
- communicate your homework policy to students and parents;
- be flexible with scheduling homework;
- make sure homework matters—if it does not count, students will not do it;
- make homework varied, interesting, and at the appropriate level; and
- do not assign homework as punishment.

In a nationwide survey of general education teachers, Epstein et al. (1997) affirmed earlier research that teachers perceive communication problems among teachers and parents as a serious impediment to the effective use of homework with students with disabilities. The authors reported little consensus among general education teachers regarding who has primary responsibility for planning, coordinating, and communicating to parents about homework. Data analysis suggested that general education teachers thought that serious homework communication problems exist in both the frequency and the quality of communication with parents about homework, parental attitudes about homework, the role of the special education teachers, the availability of teachers to communicate with parents about homework, and general education teacher knowledge of learning disabilities and homework strategies. These problems varied with school level, teacher experience, and teacher preparation in working with parents. Axelrod, Zhe, Haugen, & Klein (2009) suggest that complex, time-intensive ways to have parents support homework completion may be met with resistance.

Homework in middle school has been examined. Nelson, Epstein, Bursuck, Jayanthi, and Sawyer (1998) studied examined preferences for various homework adaptations. Students were presented with 17 specific homework strategies in order to determine the reasons for their expressed preferences. Results of the study suggested that student preferences were not related to their learning or behavior disabilities or to their achievement. Rather, their reasons for adaptations they liked the most included their perceptions that particular adaptations would allow more time for other (e.g., extracurricular) activities or would make completion of homework easier. Students' reasons for adaptations they liked least included the belief that adaptations were unfair or would negatively affect their self-concept. Of the 17 suggested adaptations, the three most liked were the following:

- Assignments that are finished at school
- Opportunities for extra-credit assignments
- Grading assignments according to effort

The three least liked adaptations were the following:

- Giving shorter assignments to students with learning disabilities than to other students
- Grading students with learning disabilities more leniently than other students
- Giving different assignments to students with learning disabilities

In three related studies conducted collaboratively with general and special education elementary teachers, Bryan and Sullivan-Burstein (1997) structured systematic strategies to improve spelling and mathematics homework completion and weekly quiz performance. Three strategies resulted in significant increases in homework completion: (a) giving students real-life assignments (i.e., assignments that connected homework to events or activities in the home) plus reinforcements, (b) using homework planners, and (c) graphing homework completion. The strategies benefited students with learning disabilities and average-achieving students with homework problems more than average-achieving students with no homework problems.

Students identified as having attention-deficit disorders may struggle with completing their homework. Two types of problems emerge: (a) inattention and avoidance of homework and (b) poor productivity or not adhering to rules about when and where homework should be completed (Power, Werba, Watkins, Angelucci, & Eiraldi, 2006). Stormont-Spurgin (1997) offered several strategies for these students, with a particular emphasis on organization:

- organize cooperative homework teams;
- implement contracts and positive reinforcement strategies;
- develop and implement routines and checklists with regard to homework;
- use assignment folders and daily planners; and
- collaborate on homework assignments.

AGGRESSION AND RESISTANCE IN SCHOOL

During the past few years, student aggression, resistance, and antisocial behavior have increased significantly in classrooms and school (Myles & Simpson, 1998). Such behavior has come to the attention of the national media and, as a result, has become of great concern to many parents, teachers, administrators, and students. It is common to have security personnel in schools and on the school grounds. Students, their possessions, and their lockers are searched for various kinds of contraband. In this section we explore these problems as they confront the general education and special education teacher.

Aggression is learned and maintained in a manner similar to other behaviors (Fitzsimmons, 1998). Fitzsimmons suggests that there are three essential elements in the development and modification of aggression: modeling, positive reinforcement, and negative reinforcement (these concepts are presented in Chapter 6). The aggressive student may be modeling the inappropriate and unacceptable behavior of others, including peers, teachers, administrators, parents, and siblings. In addition, others may reinforce the aggressive behavior of the student in the environment, either wittingly or unwittingly. Finally, allowing the student to escape an activity or task may negatively reinforce the student's aggression.

Melloy (2000) describes four types of aggressive and violent behavior: situational violence, relationship violence, predatory violence, and psychopathological violence. Situations and relationship violence are the most frequently found in school. Melloy suggests that the manifestation of acting-out aggressive behavior follows a prescribed cycle—namely, calm, trigger, agitation, acceleration, peak, deescalation, and recovery. Interventions imposed to change these behaviors may include social skills and self-management instruction.

The characteristics of the aggressive student include deficits in social information processing, poor impulse control, low frustration tolerance, limited ability to generate alternative responses to stress, and limited insight into the feelings of self and others. Aggressive students frequently lack the skills needed to respond effectively to frustration (Fitzsimmons, 1998). Among the variables that may have a negative impact are (a) disorganized or inconsistent teachers, (b) failure, (c) boredom, (d) lack of positive reinforcement, (e) irrelevant curriculum, (f) overexposure to punishment, and (g) feelings of powerlessness (Abrams & Segal, 1998).

Aggressive behavior is frequently the consequence of frustration. The stages of frustration and the appropriate teacher responses are as follows (Abrams & Segal, 1998; Fitzsimmons, 1998; Myles & Simpson, 1998):

1. *Anxiety.* Student signs or uses other nonverbal cues to demonstrate his or her anxiety. At this stage, student behavior changes are minor and may or may not be linked to an impending aggressive or violent act. The teacher must be alert to minor changes in the student's behavior. The appropriate response by the teacher includes active listening, nonjudgmental talk, and surface behavior management strategies.
2. *Stress.* The student may exhibit a minor change in behavior. The surface management techniques of proximity control, interest boosting, and hurdle helping are recommended.
3. *Defensiveness.* At this stage, the student may complain or argue with the teacher. Inappropriate behaviors include verbally or physically lashing out or threatening the teacher or other students or withdrawing physically or emotionally. Among

the interventions the teacher may implement are (a) reminding the student of the rules and routines of the classroom, (b) applying conflict resolution strategies, (c) acknowledging the student's difficulties and encouraging him or her to request assistance, and (d) redirecting the student to another activity.

4. *Physical aggression.* The student loses control and may engage in a variety of behaviors, including hitting, biting, kicking, and throwing objects. The target of these behaviors may be other students, the teacher, or the setting. When physical aggression occurs, teachers should move other students to a safe place and physically escort the aggressive student from the classroom. If this is not possible, the teacher should call for assistance.

5. *Tension reduction and regaining self-control.* The student generally releases his or her anger by verbally venting or crying. The student will become sullen and withdrawn. At this stage, the teacher must decide whether punishment or supportive intervention is appropriate. Regardless, the student must be helped to gain insight into his or her feelings and behaviors. This final stage is an essential teaching and learning time.

The most effective response to the potential for aggressive behavior in the classroom and school is prevention. School personnel should plan and have in place primary, secondary, and tertiary preventive strategies (Walker, 1998). Primary prevention is designed to prevent the problem from occurring and includes a nurturing, caring environment and curriculum to help students learn effective problem-solving, conflict-resolution, and social skills. Secondary prevention strategies are available to respond to students who are at risk for violence and aggression and include, among other strategies, counseling and individualized behavior management planning and implementation. Tertiary prevention involves "wraparound services" that include the classroom, school, family, social agencies, and community services. Wraparound services are implemented to assist students who are at high risk for violence and aggression.

The therapeutic teacher is the best preventive measure for student aggressive and violent behavior (Abrams & Segal, 1998). Abrams and Segal suggest that the therapeutic teacher can manage the stress of working with students and create an environment that meets students' needs on several levels, reducing the frustration experiences by students in the classroom. The therapeutic teacher has good mental health and communicates respect, caring, and confidence in self and others, especially students. He or she displays enthusiasm for learning and positive expectations for students and creates a positive environment. The therapeutic teacher establishes trust and develops and maintains rapport with students. The teacher is nonthreatening and respects students' dignity. The teacher is a model of self-control. He or she is aware of and understands the stages of anxiety and frustration and is able to deescalate tension in the classroom.

Student noncompliance (i.e., refusal and resistance) is one of the most frustrating and time-consuming problems confronting teachers daily (Walker & Sylwester, 1998). Maag (2000) suggests that noncompliance is a "gateway" that leads to more serious forms of deviation. Guidelines for reducing noncompliance and consequently increasing compliance are the following:

- Create a nurturing and caring environment that is characterized by cooperation and responsiveness to the needs of students.
- Focus on initiating action (i.e., completing activities) rather than on terminating action (i.e., not completing activities).

- Disengage if there is noncompliance and the difficulty is escalating. Reengage when the situation becomes calm.
- Review your own behavior. If the student's behavior is similar to yours, you may be aggravating the problem.

DIVERSITY AND BEHAVIOR MANAGEMENT

Deschenes, Cuban, and Tyack (2001) suggest that there has always been a mismatch between the structure of schools and the cultural and social backgrounds of some students. They contend that there have always been students who fail in school, and the way educators have viewed these failures has led to various solutions. Deschenes et al. argue that students, their families, the ways in which schools function, cultural differences, and schools have been identified historically as the reasons for student failure. The various ways that students' problems in school have been reasoned away include the following:

- *Students who do poorly in school have some sort of defect or are responsible for their own performance.* This belief is grounded in the assumption that the school system is sound and the individual is somehow defective. Deschenes et al. contend that the current proposals requiring students to attend summer school or other remedial programs is consistent with framing the problem as the student's failure.
- *Families from specific cultures or ethnic groups do a poor job of preparing students for school and give them little support for achievement.* With this belief, rather than trying to "improve" parents, schools attempt to produce a counterculture to helps students overcome the programs of school. The boarding schools managed by the Bureau of Indian Affairs (BIA) are an example of "saving" students from the culture of their parents. The First Nations people have suffered great challenges to retaining their languages, cultures, and spiritual practices as a result of the BIA removing children, requiring the use of English, and prohibiting the practice of dances, songs, and ceremonies.
- *Schools do not differentiate their work to fit the needs of various students.* The result of this assumption was tracking students in specific curricular tracks.
- *The student's culture and that of the school are mismatched.* This assumption has resulted in efforts to make the curriculum more multicultural and increase the cultural knowledge and sensitivity of students.
- *All students should be held to the same high standards.* This current "standards movement" continues to challenge students who do not do well in the age-graded, narrow academic world of public schools.

Deschenes et al. (2001) and the National Research Council's (1999) report on high-stakes testing suggest that using the same test for all students has the potential to reinforce cultural inequalities. If students must be retained or attend summer school, they may deal with the requirement by dropping out. Because the standards movement is not able to support all students to succeed, it may contribute to social inequalities in inner-city communities.

One example of the mismatch between the culture of school and the culture of the community is the limited opportunities students are given to view themselves as valuable. Gallagher (1997) suggests several current practices in the education of students whose behavior varies from the expectations of school: (a) destructive labels, such as "behaviorally disordered," (b) assessment practices that accentuate weaknesses, (c) weakness-focused IEPs, (d) management programs that are punitive, (e) disparaging remarks, and (f) behavioral descriptions that emphasize what a student cannot do. She contends that these negative practices must be replaced by assessment that discovers strengths and management programs that are positive and increase problem solving. Behavioral descriptions should be fair and provide respect and support for the student. Dignity should be promoted through altruistic and caring experiences.

Harry, Kalyanpur, and Day (1999) suggest that educators engage in a process they call cultural reciprocity in order to enhance their work with families from cultural backgrounds unlike their own. The primary premise of cultural reciprocity is that the educator develops his or her own cultural self-awareness in order to recognize the effect of culture on professional practice. Each step of the process informs the subsequent step. The steps of cultural reciprocity include the following:

1. *Identify* the cultural values in your interpretation of a student's problems. For example, in your own culture, it may be important for an adolescent to move out of his or her parents' home upon graduation; thus, your goals may be designed to address moving out. In the student's culture, however, adult children may stay in the home, with an extended family unit.
2. *Investigate* whether the family members with whom you are working recognize and value your assumptions and how their views differ from yours.
3. *Give explicit respect* to any cultural differences identified, and explain the cultural basis of your assumptions.
4. *Work with the family* to determine the most effective way to adapt your professional assumptions and recommendations to the value system of the family with whom you are working.

Cultural reciprocity puts cultural differences on the table for discussion and problem solving. It helps families identify the values and beliefs held by the various professionals with whom they are working. The result is clearer communication.

Cook-Sather (2001) suggests that teachers may stereotype students, running the risk of letting cultural and individual biases work to their own disadvantage as educators and to the disadvantage of their students. Through direct dialogue, teachers may examine their assumptions and expectations about students. In her work with preservice teachers, Cook-Sather identifies three stereotypes: "The Perfect Slacker," "The Learning Disabled Student," and "The Jock." Through dialogue, a more complex image of the student may emerge. However, Cook-Sather reports that at times the stereotype may be so deeply ingrained that it may overshadow the evidence.

An emerging body of literature explores the mismatch between school, home, and community and the stressors generated by this mismatch. Alva and De Los Reyes (1999) however, argue that Hispanic students' social stress, affected by (a) stress, anxiety, and depression and (b) students' perception of their own competence, has a significant impact on the students' performance in school. In their research on Asian Americans, Asakawa and Csikszentmihalyi (2000) reported that the social connectedness of Asian American adolescents—including their preference for goal-oriented activities, to study together, and a strong academic orientation among the peer groups—supports their school achievement.

Cultural Issues, Teacher Behavior, and School Structures

In the social systems perspective, the meaning of schooling is generated through the interaction of the student, teacher, family, community, and school (McLaughlin & McLeod, 1996). When any student begins school, he or she must adjust to the school context. This adjustment is done in the context of the student's home culture. McLaughlin and McLeod remind us that the differences in culture in the ways in which children and adults converse and interact may be misunderstood by teachers and may lead to frustration on the part of both student and teacher. In their report on teachers' perspectives on family backgrounds of children at risk, Leroy and Symes (2001) report that teachers were most concerned about children when child abuse, alcoholism, or single and absent parents were characteristics of the family. However, teachers did not describe the relationship of these variables and students' behavior as a cause-and-effect relationship. Rather, teachers reported their concerns about lack of support for families in poverty and inequity for less affluent parents. Teachers were concerned that students and their families were consistently confronting complex and multiple risk factors. Teachers were respectful of the efforts families made on behalf of their students. Teachers consistently indicated, though, that the lack of parent involvement in and communication with the school contributes to the challenges confronting students.

Students from various groups may vary in their perceptions of traits that should be demonstrated by "good teachers." McIntyre and Battle (1998) reported that among students identified as having emotional and behavioral disorders, African American students perceived personality traits and respectful treatment of students as being more important than their white peers. Girls perceived personality traits, respectful treatment of students, behavior management practices, and instructional skills as more important than their male peers. This variation in perceptions was also identified by Lago-Delello (1998). In her study, the classroom dynamics of teacher attitude and perceptions, academic engagement and student perceptions of teacher's expectations, accommodations, and classroom interactions were perceived differently by students identified as having emotional-behavioral disorders and those who were not identified as such.

Epstein and Jansorn (2004) suggest that a program of partnerships—not a series of activities—is needed to engage members of the community with the school. They suggest forming an "Action Team for Partnerships" (ATP) comprised of parents, teachers, the principal, and community partners. This team is responsible for preparing an annual action plan for engagement. This annual plan includes a schedule of activities for family and community involvement, linked to four goals for school improvement, including two academic goals, one non-academic goal such as improving attendance, and a fourth goal to assist educators in creating a welcoming partnership climate for students, their families, faculty members, and staff members.

An example of adjusting school practices through engaging the community, Epstein and Sheldon (2002) explored the relationship of community partnerships and reducing student absenteeism and truancy. In their longitudinal study, specific partnership practices were implemented to increase student attendance. All of the school, family, and community partnerships they explored were at least "a little helpful" in improving attendance. Specifically, the activities that improved daily attendance included the following:

- Awarding students for attendance, including parties, gift certificates, and recognition at assemblies
- Increased communication with families (Epstein and Sheldon reported that the degree to which schools were successful in communicating effectively with diverse groups of families was related to gains in student attendance.)
- Providing a school contact person with whom the families can discuss attendance or other issues
- Workshop for parents on attendance and related student issues
- After-school programs, which seemed to motivate students to attend school

Epstein and Sheldon concluded that attendance improved when schools took a comprehensive approach to family and community involvement. In addition, positive activities that increased home-school connections were found to increase attendance.

Learning Styles and Diversity

Reid (1995) describes learning styles as internally based characteristics that individuals use for taking in or understanding new information. Learning styles have been described according to the preferred modes for receiving information: auditory, visual, or kinesthetic. Learning styles have been further described as multidimensional variations that include preferences for environmental, emotional, physical, sociological, and psychological variations (Kinsella, 1996). In a more practical vein, Anderson (2001) describes learning styles as the preferred manner in which an individual or a group of individuals assimilates, organizes, and uses information to make sense of the classroom. He suggests that these preferences may vary by:

- the type of information we prefer (sensory vs. intuitive);
- how we perceive information (visual vs. verbal);
- how we organize that information (inductively vs. deductively);
- how we process information (reflectively vs. actively); and
- how we understand the information (sequentially vs. globally).

Anderson (2001) argues that learning styles are not bipolar—that is, you are not either visual or verbal. Rather, learning styles fall along a continuum. These continua include reflection to impulsive, emotional to unemotional, elaborative to rote, scanning to focusing, and participant to observer.

The pervasive belief with students who vary from their peers is that after identifying students' learning strengths, the teacher should provide opportunities to learn through those strengths (Kang, 1999). Though there is much discussion about learning styles, controversy surrounds the issue of cultural reasons for differences in learning needs and styles. For example, in terms of Hispanic students, diversity is great among students who may be identified as Hispanic. The limited research conducted on learning styles of Hispanic students has focused on Mexican American students. The inconsistency of the findings of this research demonstrates the challenges in making assumptions related to culture and learning styles. Sims (1988) reported that Mexican American students did not conform to their peers. Yong and Ewing (1992) found that middle school students who were Mexican American did conform a great deal.

Differences in these findings may be attributed to the urban/rural differences of the students observed. Griggs and Dunn (1996), after completing a review of the literature on Hispanic American children, concluded that teachers should expect many Hispanic students to prefer (a) an environment in which they can conform, (b) peer-oriented learning, (c) movement, (d) a high degree of structure, and (e) variety rather than repetition.

Frisby (1993) was key in challenging the assumptions of culturally specific learning styles. He argues that the "culturally specific learning styles" arguments are grounded in flawed assumptions. He contends that each of these assumptions is easily challenged. The first assumption, that African American culture and the white school culture are fundamentally incompatible, assumes a uniformity of culture that simply does not exist. In addition, when contrasting African American and European American culture, there are many shared values, and "stylistic" differences may be superficial. The second assumption, that African American culture determines learning style, he argues, is faulty in that learning styles are multiply determined and vary from person to person, rather than from culture to culture. There is also insufficient evidence, Frisby contends, to reliably measure learning style and then match instruction to those styles. Frisby concludes by suggesting that the argument that relevant educational content and methods will help African American children's learning is flawed in that relevant content and methods help most children learn. Rather, Frisby argues that assumptions related to cultural learning styles lead to stereotyping and making excuses.

This argument is supported by Conchas's (2001) work with Latino high school students, reporting that there is no such thing as a "Latino experience" in high school, and that racial stereotypes may be key in limiting the opportunities for Latino students. Ferguson (1998) also reports that race appears to change teachers' beliefs about academic potential, and that stating that African American children learn in certain ways feeds the belief that race and performance are linked. These arguments are further supported by Berry's (2003) study of the mathematics instruction provided to African American students. He contends that African American students do not typically receive mathematics instruction consistent with mathematics education reform, and, if they did receive these practices, their achievement in mathematics may be bolstered.

BULLYING

Bullying is defined as "systematically and chronically inflicting physical hurt or psychological distress on one or more students" (National Association of State Boards of Education [NASBE], 2003, p. 1). As many as 30% of school-age children either bully or are bullied (Nansel et al., 2001). Students report, however, that teachers are typically unaware of who is being bullied by whom (Bauman & Del Rio, 2005).

Bullying has a long-lasting impact on the academic, social, emotional, psychological, and physical health of those who are bullied and their victims (Mishna, 2009). In her review of research findings on generally accepted anti-bullying prevention and intervention programs, Mishna reports that the whole-school efforts—which include various levels of positive social interaction including schoolwide policies and consequences, curriculum content, conflict resolution activities, and individual counseling—were more effective than any single intervention. Curriculum activities alone did not decrease the amount of bullying in schools. Peer-led interventions were found to have positive outcomes, but they worked in schools that already had established values of sharing, trust, and cooperation. Mishna also reports that "restorative justice" programs, in which there is support for the students to engage in forgiveness and reconciliation, reduce bullying and give students a way to increase their self-management. Mishna (2009) suggests that these strategies may also apply to cyberbullying. **Cyberbullying** is described as deliberate and ongoing harm to an individual inflicted through the electronic media (Hinduja & Patchin, 2006). Cyberbullies have many options, including sending photos, text messages, e-mail, and instant messages as well as video through cell phones and personal computers. Cyberbullying has been reported to be experienced by 20% to 35% of school-age samples (Beran & Li, 2005; Hinduja & Patchin, 2008; i-Safe National Assessment Center, 2006). Most frequently, victims are excluded or disrespected through chat rooms, instant messaging, and e-mail (Hinduja & Patchin, 2006). Girls are apparently more involved in cyberbullying than boys (Health Resources and Services Administration, 2010).

Hinduja and Patchin (2007) have identified warning signs for both cyberbully victims and perpetrators. Teachers need to know how to identify both parties because more than half of children and adolescents do not report incidences of cyberbullying to their parents or other adults (i-Safe National Assessment Center, 2006). Victims may (a) suddenly stop using the computer, (b) appear anxious when an instant message or e-mail appears on the computer screen, (c) become angry or depressed following use of the computer, (d) try to avoid going to school or outside in general, (e) avoid talking about what he or she is doing on the computer, and (f) become unusually withdrawn from friends and family members. Cyberbully warning signs include (a) quickly closing programs or switching screens when someone walks by, (b) using the computer at all hours of the night, (c) becoming abnormally upset if he or she cannot use the computer, (d) laughing excessively while using the computer, (e) avoiding talking about what he or she is doing on the computer, and (f) and using multiple online accounts or an account that is not his or her own.

Schools need to be prepared to deal with incidences of cyberbullying just as they would traditional bullying. A team may need to be appointed to address reports of cyberbullying. Schools should have established procedures when cyberbullying is reported. Willard (2007) has identified school intervention that include the following:

- Save the evidence, which is particularly important if a legal response is needed.
- Determine if the report raises concerns about disruption, violence, or suicide, and contact law enforcement if the situation appears to be dangerous or if there are any threats of violence.
- Determine appropriate responses.
- Identify the perpetrator through the assistance of technical services (the perpetrator may be disguising himself/herself as someone else).
- Support the victim by ensuring the student and parents that the school will provide assistance and support, and offer counseling and technical assistance if needed, including legal assistance or law enforcement.
- Provide guidance on how to remove or stop the cyberbullying, such as contacting the Internet service provider (ISP), forwarding messages to the ISP, and requesting that the account be terminated; contacting the mobile phone service if cyberbullying occurs with cell phone use and having the number traced; using filtering or blocking functions for e-mails, instant messaging and cell phones; and changing the e-mail address and phone numbers.

- Seek informal resolution strategies, such as contacting the parents of the perpetrator, offering counseling or mediation in the school, and seeking to determine the underlying cause.

Teachers play a key role in fighting all forms of bullying. Kochenderfer-Ladd and Pelletier (2008) however, found that teachers' beliefs about bullying had an impact on their actions. They suggest that teachers who believe that children who assert themselves will not be bullied should encourage students to stand up for themselves. They found that teachers may not involve themselves at all if they have little or no sympathy for the bullied student or if they think that bullying is typical and going to happen in schools. The third belief system of teachers reported by Kochenderfer-Ladd and Pelletier was that of those who felt students should avoid aggressive or "mean" students. These teachers tend to be actively involved with the students, helping them stay out of the way of bullies.

The Health Resources and Services Administration (2010) provides several practical strategies that are "best practice" in all types of bullying prevention and intervention:

- The social environment of the school—involving everyone—must not tolerate bullying.
- Try to determine just how often bullying is occurring.
- Get everyone on board, including parents, so that bullying prevention is everyone's job.
- Develop a coordinating group that meets regularly to identify the progress of efforts against bullying.
- Train everyone in the nature of bullying and its effects, how to respond, and how to prevent bullying.
- Enforce clear rules that do not tolerate bullying.
- Increase adult presence in sports where bullying may occur (e.g., locker rooms, secluded hallways).
- Intervene consistently when an incident occurs. All school staff must intervene, never ignoring bullying.

BEHAVIOR MANAGEMENT AS PREVENTION

Most of the behavior management literature is concerned with the remediation of academic and behavior problems in the home, school, institution, and clinic. Generally efforts have been directed toward the increase of acceptable behaviors and the decrease of unacceptable behaviors. Very few research reports and position statements have focused on the maintenance of the acceptable behaviors of normally functioning children.

Many opportunities arise in the classroom to prevent the development of inappropriate behavior by systematically maintaining the existing acceptable behavior. If teachers understand and apply the principles of behavior management (presented in Chapter 3) as part of their normal teaching methodology, many potential problems and conflicts can be avoided.

Concerned teachers monitor and evaluate their personal teaching behaviors and the learning behaviors of the students in their classrooms. They do this by systematically evaluating the teaching-learning process. They recognize that children need positive reinforcement (rewards) and that only the child being rewarded can indicate with certitude what is rewarding.

Experienced practitioners understand that they can and do reinforce inappropriate behavior on occasion. Consequently, they attempt to reward only appropriate behaviors. They realize that the younger, less experienced child needs to be immediately reinforced for exhibiting appropriate behavior. They also recognize that delayed rewards are more desirable, from a societal point of view, than immediate rewards, and that social rewards are more desirable than tangible rewards. They always give the child social reinforcement in conjunction with tangible rewards.

Prevention-minded practitioners recognize that new behaviors must be rewarded more frequently and more consistently than established behaviors and that, although continuous reinforcement is necessary when a new behavior is being established, intermittent reinforcement is ultimately desired and will effectively promote maintenance of established behaviors. Prevention-conscious practitioners systematically use high-frequency behaviors to facilitate the development of low-frequency behaviors.

By using the principles of behavior management as a standard part of the teaching-learning process, practitioners need not anxiously wait for problems to arise in the classroom but can prevent them and use the time saved to teach children what they must know to live productively in society.

Summary Points

- The integrative framework assumes that the understanding of human development requires examination of the ecological contexts in which the individual is functioning.
- Homework is a shared activity of students, parents, and teachers. Strategies that have been related to increase homework completion have included real-life assignments, homework planners, and graphing homework completion.
- Aggression is typically learned through modeling, positive reinforcement, and negative reinforcement. A cycle of calm, trigger, agitation, acceleration, peak, deescalation, and recovery is typically seen in aggressive behavior.
- Teachers and schools must actively engage in strategies to combat bullying in all forms.
- Prevention is the most effective response to the potential for aggressive behavior in the classroom and school.
- Educators and schools are obligated to address the needs of all children in their programs and must move toward pluralism.
- Behavior management can be used to prevent the development of inappropriate behavior by systematically maintaining acceptable behavior.

Projects

1. Request the bullying response plan from several schools. How are these plans the same? How do they differ?

2. Identify your state's requirements regarding seclusion and restraint. Prepare a fact sheet for parents regarding the guidelines.

Web Resources

For information about cyberbullying, visit this Web site:
www.cyberbullying.us

For information about typical bullying, see this Web site:
www.stopbullyingnow.hrsa.gov/kids

For information about school safety, see this Web site:
www.ncpc.org/topics/school-safety

References

Abrams, B. J., & Segal, A. (1998). How to prevent aggressive behavior. *Teaching Exceptional Children, 30*(4), 10–15.

Alva, S. A., & De Los Reyes, R. (1999). Psychosocial stress, internalized symptoms, and the academic achievement of Hispanic adolescents. *Journal of Adolescent Research, 14,* 343–358.

Anderson, J. (2001). Tailoring assessment to student learning styles. In L. Suskie (Ed.), *Assessment to promote deep learning.* Washington, DC: American Association for Higher Education.

Asakawa, K., & Csikszentmihalyi, M. (2000). Feelings of connectedness and internalization of values in Asian American adolescents. *Journal of Youth and Adolescence, 29,* 121–145.

Axelrod, M. I., Zhe, E. J., Haugen, K. A., & Klein, J. A. (2009). Self-management of on-task homework behavior: A promising strategy for adolescents with attention and behavior problems. *School Psychology Review, 38,* 325–333.

Bauer, A. M., & Sapona, R. H. (1991). *Managing classrooms to facilitate learning.* Upper Saddle River, NJ: Prentice Hall.

Bauman, S., & Del Rio, A. (2005). Knowledge and beliefs about bullying in schools: Comparing preservice teachers in the United States and the United Kingdom. *School Psychology International, 26*(4), 248–442.

Beran, T., & Li, Q. (2005) "Cyber-Harassment: A New Method for an Old Behavior." *Journal of Educational Computing Research, 32*(3): 265–77.

Berry III, R. Q. (2003). Mathematics standards, cultural styles, and learning preferences. *Clearing House, 76*(5), 244–249.

Bryan, T., & Sullivan-Burstein, K. (1997). Homework how-to's. *Teaching Exceptional Children, 29,* 32–37.

Children's Health Act of 2000 P.L. 106-310, 42 U.S.C. §290ii.

Conchas, G. Q. (2001). Structuring failure and success: Understanding the variability in Latino school engagement. *Harvard Educational Review, 71,* 475–502.

Cook-Sather, A. (2001). Seeing the students behind the stereotypes: The perspectives of three preservice teachers. *The Teacher Educator, 37*(2), 91–98.

Deschenes, S., Cuban, L., & Tyack, D. (2001). Mismatch: Historical perspectives on schools and students who don't fit them. *Teachers College Record, 103*(4), 525–547.

Epstein, J. L., & Jansorn, N. R. (2004). Developing successful partnership programs. *Principal, 83*(3), 10–15.

Epstein, J. L., & Sheldon, S. B. (2002). Present and accounted for: Improving student attendance through family and community involvement. *Journal of Educational Research, 95*(5), 308–318.

Epstein, M. H., Polloway, E. A., Busk, G. H., Bursuck, W. D., Wissinger, L. M., Whitehouse, F., & Jayanthi, M. (1997). Homework-related communication problems: Perspectives of general education teachers. *Learning Disabilities Research and Practice, 12*(4), 221–227.

Feldman, S. (2004). The great homework debate. *Teaching K-8, 34*(5), 6.

Ferguson, R. F. (1998). Teachers' perceptions and expectations and the black-white test score gap. In C. Jencks & M. Phillips (Eds.), *The Black White test score gap* (pp. 273–317). Washington, DC: Brookings Institution.

Fitzsimmons, M. K. (1998). *Violence and aggression in children and youth.* ERIC/OSEP Digest E572. Reston, VA: ERIC Clearinghouse on Disabilities and Gifted Education. (ERIC Document Reproduction Service No. ED429 419)

Frisby, C. L. (1993). One giant step backward: Myths of black cultural learning styles. *School Psychology Review, 22*, 535–557.

Gallagher, P. A. (1997). Promoting dignity: Taking the destructive D's out of behavior disorders. *Focus on Exceptional Children, 29*(9), 1–19.

General Accounting Office (GAO) (2008). *Seclusion and restraints: Selected cases of abuse at public and private schools and treatment centers.* Retrieved January 10, 2011, from www.gao.gov/new.items/d09719t.pdf

Gill, B. P., & Schlossman, S. L. (2003). A nation at rest: The American way of homework. *Educational Evaluation and Policy Analysis, 25*(3), 319–337.

Griggs, S., & Dunn, R. (1996). *Hispanic-American students and learning style.* ERIC Digest. Urbana, IL: ERIC Clearinghouse on Elementary and Early Childhood Education. (ERIC Document Reproduction Service No. ED393607)

Harry, B., Kalyanpur, M., & Day, M. (1999). *Building cultural reciprocity with families.* Baltimore, MD: Brookes.

Health Resources and Service Administration (HRSA). (2010). *Stop bullying now.* Retrieved January 10, 2011, from www.stopbullyingnow. hrsa.gov/kids

Hinduja, S., and Patchin, J. (2006). *Cyberbullying Fact Sheet: Parent scripts to promote dialogue and discussion.* Retrieved January 11, 2011, from www.cyberbullying.us/cyberbullying_scripts.pdf

Hinduja, S., & Patchin, J. (2007). *Cyberbullying Fact Sheet: A brief review of relevant legal and policy issues.* Retrieved January 11, 2011, from www.cyberbullying.us/cyberbullying_legal_issues.pdf

Hinduja, S., & Patchin, J. (2008). Cyberbullying: An exploratory analysis of factors related to offending and victimization. *Deviant Behavior, 29*(2), 35–32.

Hollen, E. W., Lovelace, M., & Callender, S. (2001). Homework: A bone or boost. *Principal Leadership, 1*(8), 44–48.

i-Safe National Assessment Center. (2006). *At risk online: National assessment of youth on the Internet and the effectiveness of i-safe Internet safety education.* Retrieved January 10, 2011, 5, 2007, from www.isafe.org/imgs/pdf/NAC_summary.pdf

Jones, V. (1986). Classroom management in the United States: Trends and critical issues. In D. P. Tattum (Ed.), *Management of disruptive pupil behavior in schools* (pp. 69–90). Chichester, West Sussex, UK: Wiley.

Kang, S. (1999). Learning styles: Implications for ESL/EFL instruction. *Exchanges, 37*(4), 6–9.

Keeping All Students Safe Act. (2010). Retrieved January 9, 2011, from www.govtrack.us/congress/bill.xpd?bill=h111-4247&tab=summary

Kinsella, K. (1996). Designing group work that supports and enhances diverse classroom work styles. *TESOL Journal, 6*(1), 24–31.

Kochenderfer-Ladd, B., & Pelletier, M. E. (2008). Teachers' views and beliefs about bullying: Influences on classroom management strategies and students' coping with peer victimization. *Journal of School Psychology, 46*, 431–453.

Lago-Delello, E. (1998). Classroom dynamics and the development of serious emotional disturbance. *Exceptional Children, 65*(4), 479–492.

Leroy, C., & Symes, B. (2001). Teachers' perspectives on the family backgrounds of children at risk. *McGill Journal of Education, 36*(1), 45–60.

Maag, J. W. (2000). Managing resistance. *Intervention in School and Clinic, 35*(3), 131–140.

McIntyre, T., & Battle, J. (1998). The traits of "good teachers" as identified by African American and white students with emotional and/or behavioral disorders. *Behavioral Disorders, 23*(2), 134–142.

McLaughlin, B., & McLeod, B. (1996). *Educating all our students: Improving education for children from culturally and linguistically diverse backgrounds.* Santa Cruz, CA: National Center for Research on Cultural Diversity and Second Language Learning.

Melloy, K. (2000). Development of aggression replacement behaviors in adolescents with emotional disorders. *Beyond Behavior, 10*(2), 8–13.

Mishna, F. (2009). An overview of the evidence on bullying prevention and intervention programs. *Brief Treatment and Crisis Intervention, 8*, 327–341.

Myles, B. S., & Simpson, R. L. (1998). Aggression and violence by school-aged children and youth: Understanding the aggression cycle and prevention/intervention strategies. *Intervention in School and Clinic, 33*(5), 259–264.

Nansel, T. R., Overpeck, M., Pilla, R. S., Ruan, W. J., Simons-Morton, B., & Scheidt, P. (2001). Bullying behaviors among U.S. youth: Prevalence and association with psychosocial adjustment. *Journal of the American Medical Association, 285*(16), 2094–2100.

National Association of State Boards of Education (NASBE). (2003). Bullying in schools. *Policy Update, 11*(10). Retrieved January 10, 2011, from www.nsba.org/FunctionNav/AboutNSBA/NSBA-Governance/BeliefsandPolicies.aspx

National Research Council Committee on Appropriate Test Use. (1999). *High stakes: Testing for tracking, promotion, and graduations.* Washington, DC: National Academy Press.

Nelson, J. S., Epstein, M. H., Bursuck, W. D., Jayanthi, M., & Sawyer, V. (1998). The preferences of middle school students for homework adaptations made by general education teachers. *Learning Disabilities Research and Practice, 13*(2), 109–117.

Power, T. J. (2009). Contextualizing homework interventions. *School Psychology Review, 38*(3), 305–306.

Power, T. J., Werba, B. E., Watkins, M., Angelucci, J. G., & Eiraldi, R. B. (2006). Patterns of parent reported homework problems among ADHD referred and nonreferred children. *School Psychology Quarterly, 21,* 13–33.

Reid, J. (1995). *Learning styles in the ESL/EFL classroom.* Boston, MA: Heinle & Heinle.

Richardson, M. J., Shockley, K., Riley, M. R., Fajen, B. R., & Turvey, M. T. (2008). Ecological psychology: Six principles for an embodied-embedded approach to behavior. In P. Calvo & T. Gomila (Eds.), *Elsevier handbook of new directions in cognitive science* (Section I. The embodied architecture of cognition: Conceptual issues) (pp. 161–190). Amsterdam, The Netherlands: Elsevier.

Shea, T. M., & Bauer, A. M. (1994). *Learners with disabilities: A social systems perspective of special education.* Madison, WI: Brown & Benchmark.

Sheridan, S. M. (2009). Homework interventions for children with attention and learning problems: Where is the "home" in "homework." *School Psychology Review, 38*(3), 334–337.

Sims, J. E. (1988). *Learning styles of Black-American, Mexican-American, and White-American third- and fourth-grade students in traditional public schools.* Doctoral dissertation, University of Santa Barbara, Santa Barbara, CA.

Stormont-Spurgin, M. I lost my homework: Strategies for improving organization in students with AD/HD. *Intervention in School and Clinic, 32,* 270–274.

U.S. Department of Education. (2010). Summary of restraint and seclusion policies. Retrieved January 10, 2010, from www2.ed.gov/policy/seclusion/seclusion-state-summary.html

Walker, H. M. (1998). First steps to prevent antisocial behavior. *Teaching Exceptional Children, 30*(4), 16–19.

Walker, H. M., & Sylwester, R. (1998). Reducing students' refusal and resistance. *Teaching Exceptional Children, 30*(6), 52–58.

Westling, D. L., Trader, B. R., Smith, C. A., & Marshall, D. S. (2010). *APRAIS Survey Executive Summary: Restraints, seclusion, and adversive procedures.* Retrieved January 9, 2011, from www.tash.org/dev/tashcms/ewebeditpro5/upload/APRAIS_Survey_Exec__Summary_Media.pdf

Willard. N. (2007). Cyberbullying, cyberthreats, and sexting. Retrieved January 10, 2011, from www.cyberbully.org

Yong, F. E., & Ewing, N. (1992). Comparative study of the learning-style preferences among gifted African-American, Mexican-American and American-born Chinese middle-school students. *Roeper Review, 14*(3), 120–123.

GLOSSARY

Abscissa points   points on a graph on the horizontal axis representing hours, days, sessions, or observations.

Adherence   the extent to which a behavioral plan is followed as written.

Antecedent-Behavior-Consequence (ABC) chart strategy to identify the events prior to and following a behavior linked to its occurrence.

Antecedents of effective management   a broad range of factors manipulated prior to instruction to enhance the probability that learning will occur.

Antianxiety and antipsychotic drugs   medication prescribed for calming effects.

Anticonvulsants   medication prescribed for seizures.

Antihistamines   medication to counteract the effects of various allergies.

Attitudes (in psychosituational assessment interview)   the beliefs and feelings of the referring agent—that is, the parent or parents—about the child, behavior, and environment.

Aversives   noxious and sometimes painful consequences of behavior; undesirable results of behavior the individual would normally wish to avoid.

Backward chaining   breaking a task into a series of steps and beginning instruction with the final step.

Baseline data   quantitative data collected on the target behavior before a behavior change intervention is implemented.

Behavior   the expression of the dynamic relationships between the individual and the environment.

Behavior (in psychosituational assessment interview)   the actual behavior for which the child was referred, including antecedents and consequences.

Behavioral psychology   the study of psychology from the perspective of behavior.

Behavioral model   a perspective that understands the cause of behavior as existing outside the individual in the immediate setting.

Behavior influence techniques   management techniques, based in psychodynamic theory, that are designed to be immediately responsive to ongoing unacceptable behavior.

Behavior management interventions   all those actions (and conscious inactions) teachers and parents engage in to enhance the probability that children, individually and in groups, will develop effective behaviors that are personally fulfilling, productive, and socially acceptable.

Biobehavioral model   perspective that maintains that biological causes impact behavior.

Biobehavioral interventions   preventive and curative techniques to maintain or enhance the individual's well-being.

Bullying   systematically and persistently inflicting physical or emotional distress on one or more students.

Central nervous system stimulants   medication prescribed for its effect on moderating students with ADHD.

Circle of Courage   structure for establishing self-management grounded in Native American values.

Classroom conferencing   teacher and students meet, review what has occurred, develop another response, and reconvene at a later date.

Cognitive behavior management   term applied to a group of intervention strategies implemented to instruct learners in self-control.

Collaboration   working together as equal partners with shared vision, goals, and principles.

Comprehensive interventions   interventions carried on throughout the day that are aimed at rapid, lasting, and generalized behavior change and increase the student's success.

Conference   a meeting between individuals to discuss issues.

Congruence   the goodness of fit between an individual and his or her environment.

Consequences   (see Reinforcers).

Contingency contracting   the process of contracting so that the child gets to do something he or she wants to do following completion of something the parent or teacher wants the child to do.

Continuous schedule   the presentation of the reinforcer immediately after each occurrence of the target behavior.

270

Continuum of interventions the inventory of behavior management interventions, ranging from the least restrictive to the most restrictive of a child's freedom to function in comparison with the average child, available for application in a school.

Contract an agreement, written or verbal, between two or more parties, individuals, or groups that stipulates the responsibilities of the parties concerning a specific item or activity.

Counting behavior enumerating the number of times a behavior occurs in a given period of time.

Cuing the process of using symbols to communicate essential messages between individuals.

Curriculum-based measurement (CBM) direct assessment of what is being taught.

Cyberbullying systematically and persistently harming another individual using electronic media.

Daily report card a daily home-school reporting system designed to facilitate communication on child performance.

Desensitization the process of systematically lessening a specific, learned fear or phobic reaction in an individual.

Development the continual adaptation of the child and the environment to each other.

Developmental and constructivists model a model grounded in child development and the understanding that children grow and learn through completing a series of tasks.

Diet the regulation of the intake by the individual of specific food solids and liquids.

Differential reinforcement the process of reinforcing an appropriate behavior in the presence of one stimulus and not reinforcing it in the presence of another stimulus.

Discrimination learning to act one way in one situation and another way in a different situation.

Ecological model characterized by (a) an awareness of the impact of the environment on the group and individual and the monitoring and manipulation of the environment for the benefit of the individual and group and (b) an awareness of the dynamic reciprocal interrelationship that exists between the group and individual and the environment and the monitoring and manipulation of this relationship for the benefit of the individual and group.

Ecology the study of behavior in regard to an organism's adjustment or adaptation to the environment

and the interactions between the organism and the environment.

Environment the developmental context, including people, places, and community.

Environmental interventions interventions that focus attention on the manipulation of groups and the environment in which the individual or group is functioning.

Establishing operations setting events that have an impact on the way a student responds.

Ethics the rules that guide moral (right, good, or correct) behavior.

Evidence-based practice strategies that are grounded in data and research.

Expectation (in psychosituational assessment interview) the specific performance that the adult would like the child to achieve (short-term objectives); the long-range aspirations or goals the adult has for the child.

Explicit reprimand negative feedback statements that include a statement of the behavior that is to occur.

Expressive media interventions that encourage and permit individuals to express personal feelings and emotions in creative activities.

Expulsion removal of a student from school for more than 10 days.

Extinction the discontinuation or withholding of a reinforcer that has previously been reinforcing a behavior.

Fading also known as *thinning;* the systematic and gradual elimination of prompts.

Fixed interval schedule reinforcement is presented on completion of a specific number of tasks or definite periods of time.

Formalism all individuals are born with rights and needs that are superordinate to the interests of society.

Forward shaping (or chaining) breaking a task into a series of steps, and beginning instruction with the first step.

Functional behavioral assessment (FBA) the identification of antecedent and consequent events, temporarily contiguous to the behavior, that occasion and maintain the behavior.

Generalization a learned process whereby behavior reinforced in the presence of one stimulus will be exhibited in the presence of another (also known as the transfer of learning).

Graphing (charting) behavior   preparing a visual display of enumerated behavior.

Individualized Education Program (IEP)   a team-designed document, reviewed at least annually that describes the individualized educational and related services, programming, and benchmarks for students with identified disabilities.

Individualized Transition Plan (ITP)   plan for the transition to work and the community, required when the student reaches 16.

IFSP   individualized family service plan.

Inclusion   the philosophy that all students, regardless of disability, are a vital and integral part of the general education system.

Individuals with Disabilities Education Improvement Act of 2004   (see IDEA 2004).

In-school suspension   removal of a student from regular or special education class but not from the school.

Instructional objectives   the specific learning tasks the learner must master to meet his or her long-term goals.

Integrative framework   an ecological model that stresses that the understanding of human development and behavior requires examination of the ecological contexts in which the individual is functioning and is an inseparable part.

Interobserver reliability   mathematical formula designed to determine the reliability of the behavior modifier's observations during the behavior change intervention.

Keystone behaviors   behaviors that have the potential to make the greatest positive effect on a child's behavior.

Loss of privileges   the taking away of an individual's present or future reinforcers (also known as response cost and deprivation of privileges).

Maintenance   strategies to continue the occurrence of a behavior.

Measurability   the capacity of observed behavior to be measured.

Modeling   the provision of an individual or group behavior to be imitated or not imitated by the individual.

Naturalistic interventions   strategies grounded in the typical expectations and agents in a setting.

Negative reinforcement   the strengthening of a behavior as a consequence of the removal of an already operating aversive stimulus.

Observability   the capacity of behavior to be observed in the environment—that is, seen, heard, and so forth.

Ordinate points   points on a graph on the vertical axis representing frequency, duration, and percent of occurrence.

Passport   a home-school notebook for daily parent-teacher communication concerning the child's performance.

Phasing out   systematic reduction in the presentation of reinforcers during the behavior change process.

Planning framework   a specific protocol for implementing response to intervention on behalf of students.

Positive behavioral supports   strategies to increase appropriate behavior through recognizing functions of behavior.

Positive reinforcement   presentation of a desirable reinforcer after the behavior has been exhibited; process of reinforcing a target behavior in order to increase the probability that the behavior will recur.

Principle of fairness   fundamental fairness—due process of law—that requires that in decision making affecting one's life, liberty, or vital interests, the elements of due process will be observed, including the right to notice, to a fair hearing, to representation by counsel, to present evidence, and to appeal an adverse decision.

Principle of normalization   to let the person with a disability obtain an existence as close to the normal as is possible.

Principle of respect   the right to be treated as a human being and not as an animal or a statistic.

Principles of management   generally accepted behavior management practices grounded in learning theory.

Progress monitoring   ongoing assessment of student learning and behavior in response to instructional goals and objectives.

Prompting   the process of providing verbal, visual, aural, or manual assistance to a student during the behavior change process to facilitate the completion of a task.

Prosocial classroom management management grounded in respectful, mutual teacher-student relationships.

Psychosituational assessment interview an information-gathering interview technique used to obtain from the parents (or others) descriptive data about the child's behavior and the circumstances surrounding it.

Public Law 103–382 Improving American Schools Act, often referred to as Title II.

Public Law 107–110 No Child Left Behind Act, an effort to close achievement gaps.

Punishment the addition of an aversive stimulus or the subtraction of a pleasurable stimulus as a consequence of behavior.

Quality Schools William Glasser's model for positive school climate.

Ratio schedule the presentation of the reinforcer on completion of specific tasks.

Reinforcers the consequences of a behavior (may be tangible or social, positive or negative).

Response cost strategy for reducing a behavior by attaching a penalty to its occurrence.

Response to intervention any of a variety of models of providing multi-tiered services ranging from support in the general classroom and becoming more intense depending on the student's response.

Responsive Classroom a school structure in which social development and academic development have equal emphasis.

Rule the specification of a relation between two events (may take the form of instruction, direction, or principle).

Schedule a list of activities or events in a program.

Schedule of reinforcement the pattern with which the reinforcer is presented in response to the exhibition of the behavior.

Seclusion removing an individual from contact with others.

Section 504 section of the Rehabilitation Act of 1973 designed to deter discrimination against individuals with disabilities.

Self-discipline the process of attaining control over one's personal behavior in a variety of circumstances in association with many individuals and groups.

Self-management the process of structuring one's own behavior.

Setting events those events that occur outside the educational setting and have an impact on the student's behavior.

Shaping the systematic, immediate reinforcement of successive approximations of a target behavior until the behavior is established.

SMART goals goals that are specific, measurable, attainable, realistic, and timely.

Student support team a group of professionals in the schools, including the student's teacher, who work together to design and assessment interventions.

Suspension removal of a student from school for fewer than 10 days.

Target behavior the specific behavior to be changed as a result of intervention.

Teacher-parent communication program (TPCP) a daily report card system.

Tiers of scientific, research-based, interventions levels of intensity of services provided to student in the response to intervention model.

Time-out from reinforcement the removal of an individual from an apparently reinforcing setting to a presumably nonreinforcing setting for a specific and limited period of time.

Time sampling selecting periods of time that can be devoted to observing a target behavior; assumes that selected times are representative of the total time the behavior could be observed.

Token economy a system of exchange in which the individual earns tokens, as reinforcers, and exchanges them for tangible and social reinforcers.

Transition plan a plan written for learners with disabilities who are 16 years of age (or younger when appropriate) that includes interagency responsibilities or linkage (see also Transition services).

Transition services the movement from one activity or event to another.

Transitions the interval between activities.

Travel card based on the student's needs and carried from class to class, allows the student to earn points for social, token, and activity reinforcers.

Universal Design for Learning (UDL) providing several flexible options for presenting what is to be learned, learning tasks, and engagement, so that additional accommodations for students are minimized.

Utilitarianism   the interests of society precede the interests of the individual; rights are given by society and individuals are valued for their actual, or potential, contributions to (or the degree of burden placed on) the society.

Variable interval schedule   presentation of the reinforcer is based on a behavioral response mean or average time between responses.

Variable ratio schedule   reinforcement is presented around the response mean or average of the number of times the behavior is exhibited.

Waking day interview   a strategy to identify events, situations, and occurrences in a student's daily life that have an impact on behavior.

NAME INDEX

Abrams, B., 219
Abrams, B.J., 181, 257–258
Adderholdt-Elliot, M., 186
Adelinis, J. D., 155
Affleck, G., 234
Akey, T., 234
Alber, S. B., 239
Alberto, P.A., 52, 95, 130–131
Albin, R. W., 83
Alexander, K., 219
Allen, D., 234
Allen, J.I., 185
Allen, R.C., 10, 12–13
Alva, S. A., 260
American Academy of Child and
    Adolescent Psychiatry (AACAP),
    220
Anderson, C., 141
Anderson, E., 185
Anderson, J., 262
Anderson, N., 204–205
Anderson, T., 40–41
Angelucci, J.G., 256
Antil, J.R., 31
Argyris, C., 30
Aron, A.R., 33
Arrowood, L., 222
Asakawa, K., 260
Aubert, R. E., 220
Ault, M.J., 116
Axelrod, M. I., 256
Axelrod, S., 58
Ayllon, T., 139

Bacharier, L. B., 222
Bacon, E.H., 190, 192, 214, 217
Baker A. J. L., 236
Baker, R.W., 219
Balius, F. A., Jr.; 187
Balough, P. A., 239
Bambara, L.M., 139
Banda, D.R., 241
Bandura, A., 36, 146
Barnes, M.A., 70
Barnett, D.W., 201
Barrish, H.H., 126
Bartalo, P., 72
Bartlett, L., 214
Barton, A. C., 247
Barton, L.E., 157
Bateman, B., 219
Battle, J., 261

Bauer, A. L., 223
Bauer, A.M., 6, 11, 30, 37–39, 56, 109,
    112, 127, 185, 214, 234–235, 253
Bauer, M. S., 187
Bauman, S., 263
Beare, P., 139
Beebe-Frankenberger, M. E., 71
Beetner, E. G., 190, 237
Behrens, T.E., 33
Beilinson, J.S., 132
Belsky, J., 38
Bender, W.N., 139
Benito, N., 87
Bennet, G., 73
Benson, F., 241–242
Beran, T., 264
Berdondini, L., 203
Bergerson, J., 208
Berla, W., 236
Berry III, R. Q, 263
Bersoff, D.N., 237
Bevans, K., 88
Blacher, J., 234
Blackham, G.J. 237
Bloom, S.E., 84
Boelter, E.R., 54
Bone, A., 222
Bonic, J., 185
Bourgeois-Guerin, V., 236
Bowman, L. G., 155
Bradley, R., 68, 73
Bradshaw, C., 88
Brady, K., 212
Brady, M. P., 138, 188
Brand, S., 236
Brantner, J.P., 165
Brendtro, L., 180–181
Briesch, A., 69, 154–156
Brokenleg, M., 180
Bronfenbrenner, U., 38, 235
Broome, S. A., 189
Brown, D.E., 208
Brown, L., 88
Brown, W. H., 201
Brownell, M.T., 208
Brulle, A.R, 157
Bryan, T., 256
Bryant, J.D., 70
Buck, G.H., 101–102
Buie, J. D., 166
Bulach, L.C., 246
Bulsara, M., 220

Burden, P.R., 213
Burgstahler, S., 179
Burniske, R.W., 186
Burns, B., 236
Burns, L. 223
Burns, S., 220
Bursuck, W. D., 255–256
Burton, C., 188
Busch, T., 222
Busk, G. H., 255

Callaghan, T., 212
Callahan, K., 211
Callahan, T., 187
Callender, S., 255
Calver, J., 220
Camp, E.M., 84
Cangelosi, J.S., 213
Caputo, R.A., 183
Carey, K.T., 201
Carlsen, K. H., 222
Caron, M. G., 221
Carpenter, L.B., 244, 246
Carr, E.G., 40, 201–202
Carta, J. J., 33, 35
Cartledge, G., 7–8
Castle, L., 220
Center, D.B., 214–216
Chalmers, L., 187–188
Chan, E., 219
Chase, P. N 211
Chiu, Y. I., 182
Cianciolo, P.J., 187
Cipani, E.O., 55–56
Citron, L. J., 219
Clark, J., 142
Clees, T.J., 213
Clements, B. S., 209
Cobine, G., 186
Cohen, C., 135
Cohen-Vogel, C.L., 241
Colavecchia, B., 155
Coleman, M., 206
Coleman, T.J., 241
Comarata, A., 188
Compton, D.L., 70, 73
Conchas, G.Q., 263
Cone, J.D., 109
Conroy, M. A., 201
Conroy, M., 33, 35
Contrucci, S. A., 155
Cook, P.S., 219

SUBJECT INDEX